COOKBOOK and SHOPPING GUIDE

Your supermarket guide to better buying
for practical cooking

BARBARA SULLIVAN

National Director of Consumer Affairs
The Great Atlantic & Pacific Tea Company

Simon and Schuster, New York

Published by Simon and Schuster
Rockefeller Center, 630 Fifth Avenue
New York, New York 10020

Manufactured in the United States of America

1   2   3   4   5   6   7   8   9   10

Library of Congress Cataloging in Publication Data

Sullivan, Barbara.
    A&P cookbook and shopping guide.

    Includes index.
    1. Cookery.   2. Marketing (Home economics)
I. Great Atlantic and Pacific Tea Company.   II. Title.
TX715.S9473   641.5   75–19379
ISBN 0–671–22140–X
ISBN 0–671–22141–8 pbk.

CONTENTS

Foreword: You and the A&P   7
How to Buy Better and Spend Less   9
Begin with Breakfast   22
Dairy Foods   27
Snacks and Starters   36
Great Soups   45
Meat   56
Poultry   93
Fish and Shellfish   115
Casseroles and Stretchers   128
Vegetable Versatility   137
Fruit Adds a Fresh Note   159
Salads   170
Sauces and Salad Dressings   173
Convenience Foods—Good and Easy   179
Baking   189
Bake Shop Bonuses   224
Desserts   230
Beverages   247
Entertaining   252
Health and Beauty   257
How to Save Cost and Time in Housecleaning   259
Charts
   Spice Cooking Chart   262
   Weights and Equivalent Measures of Common Foods   265
   Contents of Cans and Packages   266
   Oven Temperatures   266
   Metric System   266
   Chart of Substitutions   267
Index   269

YOU AND THE A&P

This might well be called an American People's cookbook. The story of your neighborhood A&P is the story of American growth and of the development of the world's widest range of foods and greatest choice of cooking styles. Your way is part of the variety of American cooking.

Never before has the need for better buymanship been more important. Consumers are faced with hundreds of food-buying decisions every week. This book was designed specifically to match the buying patterns of shoppers and to aid consumers in decision making. Each department of the supermarket is explored for value, economy and quality performance. And, of course, hundreds of our favorite recipes have been included, with an emphasis on high nutrition and low cost.

When you go through the door of your supermarket you walk into a fabulous pantry. This is your pantry for meats and poultry, prepared and precut for you; for produce from potatoes to persimmons in season and from artichokes to zucchini selected at local farms or brought to you from across the country or around the world. You find ready comparison of fresh products, canned and frozen for your choice, in line with economy, flavor and your given cooking purposes. There are fresh-baked breads or ready-to-bake loaves; bread crumbs for cooking, croutons for stuffing; cakes and cookies for children or gourmets. There are marrowbones and meaty beef shanks plus beans, peas, barley and herbs to season a homemade soup. You can buy a prepared dry soup mix or canned soup, condensed or ready-to-heat-and-eat soup. You can plan an economy meal, the children's lunches and a gourmet splurge all on the same shopping trip.

It takes a lot of know-how to spend your food dollars wisely. Compare the price and the yield in portions of a selection with its appeal to your family's taste before you spend your money. This book is designed to help you to shop with savings in mind, and to cook for satisfaction in eating.

The professional buyers who stock your A&P pantry need even more know-how. Their standards, skills and tips are the basis for information on how to shop advantageously for food and other items stocked at the A&P.

How and Why the A&P Came to Be

From the first store in New York City in 1859 to A&P stores in communities across the country today, the growth of the A&P has reflected changing consumer patterns, cooking styles and meal preparation techniques.

The history of the A&P is the story of quality buying for money saving. The first A&P store was set up to sell clipper-ship loads of tea at a saving; now thousands of products in each store serve varied consumer needs and wants.

Consumerism

While we in the Consumer Affairs Department work for A&P, it is our job to protect our customers . . . the way Ann Page protected them more than 40 years ago.

Yes, there really was an Ann Page. Sort of.

The only thing made up was her name, which was first used in a weekly column written by A&P home economists. The column was filled with menu ideas, recipes and all kinds of helpful advice.

We were one of the first companies to offer this kind of service to consumers. And if we say so ourselves, the idea was years ahead of its time.

But today we owe you more than advice, more than just food. To help you survive in the modern supermarket, we owe you information. That's why we developed a program called Operation Aware. It's our continuing commitment to make you a more aware shopper by reminding you of what every A&P store owes you and by informing you of ways to get the most for your money.

It's your right to be aware. It's our responsibility to do everything we can to satisfy your needs. To help you in the techniques of better buying. To back up our goods with our money-back guarantee. To aim for product freshness and consumer-minded practices such as our Butchers' Pledge to always pack the *better* side of every cut down.

Consumer Commitment

Concern with consumer values, quality and service, traditional at A&P, is re-emphasized in line with growing consumer awareness. As director of consumer affairs, I bring a consumer voice to our management.

Beginning with internal education, because the store manager is the on-the-spot director of consumer affairs, and moving to consumer education in better buying, A&P steps out to inform the consumer of ways to buy better. We can put procedures into effect, but consumers need to know for themselves how to benefit from nutrition labeling, open dating, unit pricing, the rain-check policy by which special-price merchandise is assured, and A&P's total guarantee of every product it sells.

Consumer Management

The effectiveness of this program, the true value of the products at the A&P, the contributions they make to your family life, are measured in every bag you bring home from the supermarket.

This book is designed to help all of us find and use the best possible values in shopping. Whatever your choices, learn to balance nutritional values in the meals you plan.

We have all learned much in preparing this A&P consumer guide to shopping and cooking through discussions with the buyers who know so much about meats, produce, coffee, dairy products, health and beauty aids, and other items on your shopping list. We have tested each recipe and worked with researchers and home economists, in cooperation with Sylvia Schur and all those at Creative Food Service. Most of all, we are grateful for the thousands of consumer letters we have received indicating your interests.

This book was designed specifically to answer the most frequently asked questions and, of course, to share our favorite "tried and true" recipes. It is arranged in line with your shopping interests, rather than by traditional menu patterns. Meats and poultry precede fish, for example. Economy cuts come before roasts; similar preparations are grouped for ready reference. Detailed recipes as well as quick versions are given for soups, casseroles, vegetables and other dishes.

We hope you will send along your reactions to help us provide the most meaningful consumer values for you at the A&P, in your own kitchen, and in later editions of this book.

BARBARA SULLIVAN
National Director of Consumer Affairs

HOW TO BUY BETTER AND SPEND LESS

You can eat better, feel better and save money every time you shop if you come to the supermarket with awareness. Be aware of the range of values available, of the current good buys, of products particularly worth buying because they are in good supply, seasonal or on special. By checking prices constantly you can avoid products that are unusually high, even if this means changing your usual meal pattern.

Supermarket shopping, unlike utilities and taxes, is an area where *you* can exercise your best discretion in spending. Since food and household supplies take one of the biggest single chunks out of your total budget, the decisions you make in the supermarket can add up to a sizable savings.

Your Purchasing Agent

Our buyers are the shoppers for America's pantry. To stock the supermarket, they search the country, from farms to processing plants. Some of the new products are excellent buys; some are chosen because they satisfy optional wants rather than nutritional needs or economy. Our buyers also search out the best values in basic, high-nutrition foods, from milk (or buttermilk, or cottage cheese) through cereals, meats, even soy extenders. Some of our best sources of nutrition are among the least expensive foods you buy.

Sometimes you want extra service built into the preparation of a product. You pay a little more if you choose the easy way, yet it still costs less to have this home meal than it would to eat out. Sometimes you want the luxury of a special treat from the market, a worthwhile expenditure if you plan for it. The big difference in your budget comes from the week-in, week-out techniques you practice in shopping for your regular food and household supplies.

Processing Costs More— Sometimes Saves Money

In general, the less a food product has been processed, the lower its cost to you. Hot cereals that you prepare at home are least expensive in the old-fashioned long-cooking versions, cost more in quick-cooking versions, still more when they are ready-to-eat, and most when they are presweetened and sometimes flavored.

There is often negative value in further preparation of foods before they reach you, in the loss of nutrients and the build-up of non-contributing ingredients. You must weigh your own time, your inclination for cooking and your family's tastes, as well as cost and nutritional factors, in making choices. The most careful buying and the best nutritional values do no good if foods remain uneaten, or if you do not have time for preparation.

The recipes in this book are generally arranged as you would find the departments of the supermarket. In each section, there are buying tips to help you save money. These include guides to having larger cuts of meat further cut for more than one meal; cutting up poultry for savings; moneysaving methods for soups and casseroles; economy choices in the dairy department; even how to save money and make better coffee, too.

If your time budget is tight, prepared foods are available for you in each department— they may even cost less than home-cooked

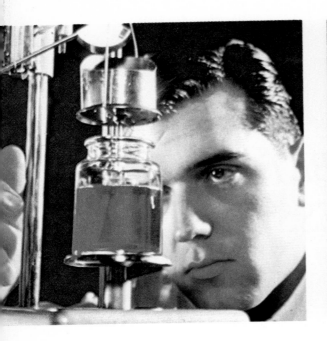

Careful selection of the products you use in recipes begins with quality control, in the field and at the plant and laboratory, for every item selected for sale in A&P stores.

versions made from scratch. On the other hand, you get homemade quality and taste, and generally can save money, in homemade versions. Make your choices to meet your changing needs.

Saving with the A&P's Private Brands

Because we buy with you in mind, special attention is given to the selection of A&P brands designed to offer you money savings, while meeting special quality standards. Compare prices and you will find you can generally save considerably by buying A&P's own compared to similar marketed brands. A&P's volume of purchases and direct sales to you make these savings possible.

These savings generally prevail, but you should compare the unit prices and nutritional values of *everything* you buy and take advantage of the best the market has to offer. For example, a specialty baker may sometimes offer his product at a price equal to the A&P's; or a canned food under a national label may be offered at an advantageous price. Or special prices on a better-quality meat cut, poultry parts, or A&P's Box O' Chicken may make these a better buy than the usual economy recommendations.

Exactly What Is a Private Brand?

A private brand is a product or line of products sold by a store under its own brand name or names. By spending less on advertising and sales promotion and by matching existing products rather than by pursuing the more expensive path of new-product development, cost savings are achieved and passed along to the consumer.

Most supermarkets have private brands, and for many, price is the prime consideration. To A&P buyers, quality comes first. Value—the best quality for the least money—is the standard by which A&P private brands are selected.

Less Money Buys More

Despite these high quality standards, our own brands are priced lower than comparable national brands. We estimate that if a customer were to buy our fine products in place of national brands, she could save as much as 20 percent on her total food bill.

In selecting A&P brands keep these points in mind:

Take advantage of sales—build up a modest reserve supply, especially of items you use regularly as staples.

Select the appropriate size for your needs.

Choose the quality you need. While Grade A is the highest quality, and provides the most uniform, best-quality product, you don't always need or want this top quality. For example, canned A&P Grade A tomatoes are whole, firm tomatoes in their own natural bright juice. At the time of this writing, they cost 10 percent less for a 16-ounce can than the national brand next to them on the shelf in a northeastern A&P supermarket. However, you don't always require Grade A tomatoes. If you are going to break them up for use in a casserole or stew, it is a needless expense to buy whole, firm fruit. We therefore offer less expensive packs, at a saving, to give you greater economy for such uses.

Choose the most economical form—A&P Instant Non-Fat Dry Milk can be an economical substitute for skim milk to save you calories as well as one-third the cost of fresh whole milk. Use it in cooking, on cereal, mixed with whole milk . . . as a substitute for "empty-calorie" (low in nutrient value) non-dairy creamers. When it comes to finding uses for A&P brands, let your imagination run wild!

Read the label—check weight, net contents and ingredients listed in order of predominance.

Compare to Save

Whatever your choice, comparisons in price and real value judgments are easier to make when you take advantage of all the information provided. If this information is missing, ask the manager to supply it.

Unit Pricing: Look for the unit-price label on the package and/or on the shelf front beneath the item it describes. It will give you the actual cost of a given weight or count and will make it possible for you to compare the cost of different sizes or different brands. The unit-price measure is given per ounce, per pound or per quart for most grocery items and frozen foods, or by count for products like napkins or paper towels, or by square inches or feet for items like foil and waxed paper. Compare unit prices with those of different sizes or different brands of similar items. Remember to compare only like items; don't compare raspberry jam with apple jelly for example. Unit prices will quickly tell you which brand of paper

From the time of the first A&P brands, A&P's own coffees have represented quality values. You can buy coffees to your taste—Bokar, Red Circle or Eight O'Clock. Each of these can be ground fresh to your specification, to meet your own coffee-brewing standards. Or, you may choose a preground or A&P instant or decaffeinated type.

towels offers 100 sheets for the least money, or whether a large jar of grape jelly is a better buy than the small jar, but remember to compare quality as well as weight or count.

Nutrition Labeling: Voluntary for many products, nutrition labeling is required for food products that make special dietary claims. Nutrition labels show the amount of each nutrient as a percentage of the U.S. Recommended Daily Allowances (U.S. RDA) in each serving. The package specifies the size of each serving and the number of servings contained in each package so that you can figure your nutrient intake more accurately.

Nutrients that must be listed on the label include protein, vitamin A, vitamin C, thiamin, riboflavin, niacin, calcium and iron. Protein, carbohydrates and fat are listed in grams per serving; and the calories per serving must also be included. This information makes meal planning for good nutrition, as well as brand comparison shopping, easier.

However, you should note that the label need not declare all nutrients, and that some products are naturally better sources for certain nutrients than others. For example, some sweetened breakfast cereals are fortified with vitamins and minerals. You may be better off to look for vitamins such as A and C in fruits and vegetables where they naturally occur, and to look to cereals for B vitamins and some proteins for which they are a natural and economical source.

Alternate Choices

When some foods are unusually high in price, use alternates of equal nutritional value to keep your budget in line. For example, check the prices of comparable portions of protein food values from the sources in the chart below. Protein needs: Note that 15–19 grams of protein meet about one-third of the day's needs for most adolescents and adults.

PROTEIN CHOICES

Food	Usual Cooked Serving	Grams Protein
Chicken	3 ounces	20
Peanut Butter	4 tablespoons	16
Lima Beans (dried)	1 cup	14
American Cheese	2 ounces	14
Eggs	2 large	12
Cottage Cheese	½ cup	16
Beef Liver	3 ounces	22
Pork and Beans	1 cup	16
Tuna Fish	3 ounces	24
Fish Sticks	3 ounces	15
Hamburger	3 ounces	21
Milk	8 ounces	9
Chili Con Carne	1 cup	19
Whole Ham	1 slice (4 ounces)	15
Ocean Perch Fillet (frozen)	3 ounces	16
Frankfurters (all meat)	2 (4 ounces)	14
Beef Chuck Steak	3 ounces	22
Bacon	4 slices	10
Pizza	2 sections	14
Sirloin Steak	8 ounces (raw)	32
Bologna	2 ounces	6
Rib Roast	8 ounces (raw)	24

Open Dating: A&P uses open dating on virtually all processed meat and poultry items,

A new kind of shelf tag lets you make accurate price comparisons at a glance!

The larger size— 2 lb. jar is the best buy.

UNIT PRICE	YOU PAY
65.3¢ PER LB 00	49¢ ANN PAGE GRAPE JELLY 12 OZ 21670 -24

UNIT PRICE	YOU PAY
42.5¢ PER LB 00	85¢ ANN PAGE GRAPE JELLY 2 LB 21690 -12

A successful shopping trip is the start of good meals. Check your shopping list and organize any coupons before you go to the check-out counter. For more efficient checking-out at the cash register, arrange your purchases with the prices visible. Put duplicate items together. Put heavy packages in front, so they may be readily packed in the bottom of the bags, with more fragile purchases on top.

Your four basic food groups are available in a range of prices and convenience to suit your family's needs: Fruits and vegetables—*use fresh produce first, store frozen and canned foods for later use.* Dairy products—*include fresh fluid, non-fat dry and canned milks for economy.* Meat, poultry, fish, eggs—*use economical beans, peanut butter and cheeses for alternate meals.* Cereals and grains—*stock a good variety in this budget-balancing group.*

As you unpack your market order, put all perishables into refrigerator promptly, moving older supplies forward, to be used first. If necessary, rewrap foods for the freezer.

What is UPC?

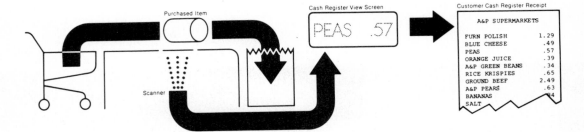

If you've started to notice those symbols and numbers that are appearing on packages in your A&P—it's the new UNIVERSAL PRODUCT CODE. The UPC code is made up of a series of bars called the symbol. The numbers printed under the symbol identify the manufacturer and the item.

The thickness of the bars of the symbol are "read" as the package is passed over the electronic scanner which will be built into the checkout stand in the supermarkets of the future.

The electronic scanner will translate, through the use of a pre-programmed computer, the UNIVERSAL PRODUCT CODE symbol into an item description and price which will appear on the cash register view screen.

The checker will be required only to handle the groceries and serve as your cashier.

CONSUMER BENEFITS:
We anticipate this new system will benefit you by providing . . .

Detailed Cash Register Receipt—a welcomed asset in planning a food budget, and will be an accurate record of items purchased and price.

Faster Checkout—cashier will merely pass each coded item over the scanner and bag it almost simultaneously.

Accuracy at Checkout—virtually eliminates errors caused by over-rings and under-rings, automatic identification of taxable items, automatic coupon handling, and correct pricing on advertised specials.

Less Out-of-Stock Items—improvements in inventory efficiency will result in fewer items being out of stock. The computer will keep track of merchandise sold and can reorder those items.

This won't happen overnight! We are gradually converting all our private labels for this purpose and so are our suppliers. But, right now, we are testing equipment so that we may bring you a proven system that will serve your needs and ours.

Now you know why we call it WEO Matic!

bakery, dairy and grocery products, where freshness is essential to quality. This makes it easy for you to see clearly that the items you purchase are fresh. The dates you find on these products are "pull dates" denoting the last day the product may be sold as fresh. This does not mean the product should be considered "bad" or "stale" after this date. You will still have reasonable time to store and use the product at home.

Our bakery products are dated as follows: "Fresh Sale Thru Aug. 2." (We will continue to offer customers extra savings on "day-old" bakery products.) Products with a shelf life of a month or less are dated with the month and day, such as "Nov. 10." Products with longer shelf life will be dated with the month, day and year, "May 1, 75."

Universal Product Code: The bars and numbers that appear on labels of products are the UPC check-out code: a series of bars (called the symbol) plus numbers (printed under the symbol) to identify the item and its manufacturer. The symbol is read at the cash register by an electronic scanner that will be built into the check-out stand in the supermarkets of the future. Through the use of a preprogrammed computer, the electronic scanner will translate the UPC symbol into an item description and price. This information will appear on the cash register view screen and at the same time

will be printed on the cash register receipt. We anticipate that this new system will benefit you by providing detailed cash register receipts and faster check-out. It will virtually eliminate cashier's errors and will permit automatic identification of taxable items, automatic handling of coupons, and correct pricing of advertised specials. It will also improve inventory control. And UPC will save you money by increasing the all-round efficiency of your supermarket.

Techniques for Saving: You spend your food budget money most wisely when you begin by shopping for nutritionally balanced meals, and buy the extras after the essentials are in your market basket. You save on each purchase when you compare prices in terms of cost per serving, rather than just cost per pound and nutritional contributions. You can save still more when you plan meals that take advantage of the good buys at the market, and when you invest a little extra thought and effort in meal preparation.

For example, one cook may spend relatively little money but more time on an inexpensive cassoulet of poultry and beans, a stew or an exotic couscous of meat, vegetables and beans served over golden grain. Another cook may spend far more money and far less time on a well-marbled steak. Each saves in a way appropriate to his or her life-style.

Fourteen Basic Steps to Saving When You Shop

1. Plan regular shopping trips. You can shop better, and save time and effort, as well as fuel and money, if you plan on major shopping trips at regular intervals and buy the most economical sizes of products you use often.

2. Make shopping a family experience. Let all members participate in comparing prices, determining real needs and evaluating quality. It is conventional to advise that the shopper leave children at home, to avoid distraction. We recommend the investment in teaching children "store manners" and in educating them in the principles of wise shopping.

3. Study the store ads before you shop. The newspaper, television and radio will advise you of specials for the week. You can save appreciably when you buy featured foods.

4. Check your home supplies and basic staples. Be sure you have the makings of special dishes you plan to cook and of frequently served favorites you might add to the menu.

5. Make a flexible shopping list. Then you can revise it as you discover unadvertised specials and items of appealing quality. Arrange this list in sections as your market is set up so that you can select various items in step-saving logical sequence.

6. Get to know the layout of your market. Shop the departments to compare different forms of the same foods. The markers above each aisle show the categories of foods in that section. Shop for packaged goods and staples first, then for perishable foods, frozen foods last.

7. Check the displays in the store to take advantage of special prices. It pays to stock up on the items you can buy for less. This is your own "stock-market investment." However, buy only what you need and can really use.

8. Buy foods in season—or when they are plentiful. This is particularly true of fresh fruits and vegetables but this advice applies to meats and poultry, too. Buy several chickens, for example, when they are at special prices. Use some fresh; wrap and freeze the rest as soon as you get home. Your freezer adds up to better economy when it is filled with good buys. You save on energy cost per pound of food stored when your freezer is full. Rotate freezer stocks for best economy and quality.

9. If you use glasses, wear them when you shop!

10. Read the package label. Check the weight and measure, as well as the ingredients, of the products you buy. Ingredients are listed on the label in the order of their weight in the product. Learn to read the labels in each department.

11. Read the unit-price label, then consider the cost of a given item in relation to its function in your family's life-style. If you are concerned with nutrition and calories, less expensive cottage cheese may be worth more to you than a high-fat natural cheese, delicious though the latter may be. If you are planning a party, a specialty cheese may be a valid choice, even though it costs more per pound than a cheese spread. The unit price guides you only to cost per unit. The individual evaluation of that cost is up to you. In items of equal basic quality, reading the unit price can save you money, and help you get exactly what you want for your money.

12. Buy the most economical size for your use. In most cases, the larger sizes offer greater economy. They cost less per unit because the cost of packaging and marketing is about the same for large or small containers. However, if you can't use a larger-sized product before it spoils, or have no space to store it efficiently, its lower price is of no use to you.

In some instances, a special offer or volume sales may make a smaller size more economical. Use unit pricing to determine the best value in your own situation.

13. Watch for store specials, coupon offers and special premiums that offer savings. Cash them in if you normally use these products or want to try them—otherwise the "special offer" will not represent a real saving for you.

14. Buy the quality that's best for your use. Most manufacturers establish a niche as either top-quality or economy packers and concentrate on products that fit in one price bracket. In both national brands and private labels, A&P aims to give you freedom of selection for the wisest use. We have indicated this in different brand names for canned vegetables and for eggs, for example. No matter what your income, it is wasteful to spend money for whole, perfect canned fruits or vegetables or solid canned tuna if you are going to break them up for salad or for cooking. You pay more for canned peas that are all the same size than for a random-size pack. Is the uniformity worth the difference to you? On the other hand, some lower cost packs include less solids and a higher proportion of liquid or other filler ingredients. Is it better to train your children to enjoy a glass of real fruit juice from time to time, and to drink water when they are

thirsty, rather than to enjoy larger amounts of fruit-flavored drinks? This is where your own value judgment comes in.

SHOPPER AWARENESS
HELPS EVERYONE

Even with the best of care, canned food sometimes spoils. If you spot a swollen can or a leaky container on the store shelves, don't buy it. Call it to someone's attention. If you find one in your home pantry, return it to the manager for replacement or a refund. NEVER USE SUCH PRODUCTS. To help prevent losses at home, store canned goods in a cool, dry place. Rotate your pantry stock. When you bring new items home from the supermarket, move current "stock" up front so you'll use it first. Place container labels forward, so you can scan them easily.

How Does Your Food Budget Compare?

There are no hard-and-fast rules about food budgets, and expenditures vary greatly, depending on family choice, style of meals and importance given to food quality. On the national average, a low-income family of four with two schoolchildren may spend almost 50 percent of its income after taxes on food. A moderate-income family may spend about 25 percent of its income on food, higher-income families proportionately less. Smart consumer families take pride in achieving low-cost meals that are high in nutrition and appetite appeal. If your food expenditures are getting out of line, examine your shopping cart. How many of the foods in it contribute to your nutritional well-being? Can you afford all the built-in service extras you are buying? Are you calculating non-food purchases as part of your food budget?

How to Save in Filling Major Food Needs

The basic foods you need every day can be bought at various prices, and at various calorie levels as well. In general, the most expensive grades of meats and dairy products are higher in fats. Many snack foods are high in carbohydrates and fats, without balanced nutrients. This makes them expensive in terms of nutri-

tional values. Sometimes you pay more for less on purpose—as when you buy a diet food product designed to be low in calories, and sometimes devoid of any nutrients, at a fairly expensive price.

The guide to the basic foods you need every day on page 20 is coupled with shopping hints to help you save as you buy foods you need.

Choose Your Meal Style

The traditional American meal pattern has evolved through the years from hearty farm breakfast, hot home lunch or dinner and light supper to one in which many families snack together more often than they sit down to complete meals.

You may plan on a satisfying breakfast, or a light meal followed by a snack. Lunch may be carried to work or to school, or may be eaten in a cafeteria; dinner may be the large meal of a weekday. Weekends, the pattern may be reversed. The style in which you eat, or your mealtime pattern, has less to do with your well-being than the actual content of the foods you choose.

Pantry Glossary

Before you leave home for the supermarket, check staples:

Refrigerator
    Milk, cream, butter, cheese, eggs
    Meats, poultry

Vegetable Bin or Refrigerator
    Potatoes, onions, carrots, turnips
    Salad greens, other fresh vegetables

Cupboard Shelves
    Cereals and grains, pasta, rice, beans
    Salt, sugar, seasonings, condiments, syrups
    Oils, fats, vinegar
    Flour, leavening, yeast, mixes, baking
        supplies, cookies

Bread Box and Freezer
    Breads, rolls

Canned Food Supplies
    Fruits, juices, vegetables, meats, fish
    Beverages—coffee, tea, cocoa

Lunch Makings

Dessert Makings

Snacks and Refreshment Additions
    Favorite foods for individual family
        members

Non-Food Items
    Household cleaning supplies
    Laundry supplies
    Health and beauty aids
    Paper supplies
    General merchandise

Note that the above list includes foods from the four basic groups. Follow a similar pattern in making a basic guideline for shopping. Check store ads to find the items being featured, or check the store windows and displays when you arrive at the supermarket, to stock up on the specifics that meet your general needs, including items for your freezer.

If you shop once a week, plan to include:

Meats, fish, poultry or substitutes for seven dinners (unless you plan to draw from your freezer or to eat out)

Cheese, prepared meats if you do not plan on dinner leftovers, canned fish, peanut butter, other lunch makings

Citrus fruits or juices or other fruits for seven breakfasts

Vegetables, green and yellow for seven dinners and for lunches; snack vegetables, such as carrots and celery, for lunch packing and for home use

Compare fresh, canned and frozen supplies

Potatoes, rice, macaroni, other grains or carbohydrates to round out seven lunches and dinners

Salad fixings, including varied greens, raw vegetables, fruits, cottage cheese

Milk—fresh, non-fat dry, evaporated or condensed, yogurt, buttermilk. Buy in the largest units to meet family needs

Eggs—plan on three or four per person per week, Grade A for table use, smaller size when economical, particularly for children and cholesterol watchers

Uncooked cereal for home preparation, dry cereal for fast meals

Breads, whole grain, enriched; breakfast rolls

Cookies and cake; or baking supplies. and/or mixes

Dessert makings and/or ice cream

Butter or margarine, oils, shortening if needed

Other food and non-food staples as needed from first list

If you make a list, remember to check it before you leave the market. Compare alternate choices as you make your selections, for best investment of your shopping dollars and best satisfaction when you get home. Save your supermarket receipts to check your monthly budget.

The Payoff

If you put all this know-how to work, will it really count at the showdown—the check-out counter? Actual tallies of customers who shop the A&P for identical quantities of similar foods indicate that if you shop carefully for the products you need, take advantage of private brands and specials, buy economical sizes and packages, and make careful selections among meats, poultry, produce, dairy items and alternative foods, you can come up with sizable savings.

GUIDE TO NUTRIENT NEEDS AND MONEY-SAVING TIPS
Based on USDA Daily Food Guide

Food Recommended

Amounts to Buy

How to Save in Buying

MEAT, POULTRY, FISH GROUP
2 or more servings
You may want to use: eggs, dried beans or peas, nuts or peanut butter, vegetable or grain combinations, alone or in combination with meats or dairy products.
Vegetables and grains are economical protein alternates, but check that you are making a fully balanced protein selection, adding dairy products or small amounts of meat, poultry or fish to complete proteins, if indicated.

Allow 2 to 3 ounces of lean cooked meat or poultry for an average portion. One egg, ½ cup cooked dried beans, 2 tablespoons peanut butter may replace 1 portion. One cup of bean and grain combination may make a portion. Small amounts used in snacks during the day can add up to a serving.

The more thinly meats or poultry or fish are sliced, or the more fully prepared for the pan, the more they are likely to cost. Save by buying larger units when you can. Cut further for meal portions.
Use all the parts, for soups, stews, pâtés, or to feed pets, as appropriate. Meats used in combination with extenders, from cereal to soy, help you utilize the incomplete proteins more effectively. Sandwiches, stews, macaroni and meat sauces, rice and beans are economical and nutritional good buys.

DAIRY GROUP
Child under 9, 2–3 servings
Child, 9 to 12, 3 or more servings
Teen-ager, 4 or more servings
Adult, 2 or more servings
Pregnant Woman, 3 or more servings
Nursing Woman, 4 or more servings

For each serving, 1 8-ounce cup of fluid milk—whole, skim or buttermilk—or evaporated, or dry milk, reconstituted. As alternates, 1-inch cube of Cheddar-type cheese or ¾ cup cottage cheese, ice milk or ice cream may replace ½ cup fluid milk.
Milk used in snacks, puddings and desserts counts as part of the daily total.

You can save on your milk bill—as much as one-third—by using reconstituted dry milk half-and-half with fluid milk; or save by using evaporated milk for cooking or for beverages. If buttermilk is a favorite at your house, you can extend 1 cup with 3 cups of reconstituted non-fat dry milk, warm and let stand several hours, then chill. Yogurt is a delicious, but expensive, form of milk. To extend yogurt, heat ¼ cup yogurt with 1 quart skim milk, hold warm several hours until clabbered, then chill.

VEGETABLE-FRUIT GROUP
4 or more portions, including:

1 good or 2 fair sources of vitamin C (Your body cannot store this, and needs to replenish daily.)

For each serving, ½ cup of vegetable or fruit, or a unit such as 1 medium apple, potato, orange, or half a medium melon or grapefruit.

Good sources: Grapefruit or grapefruit juice, orange or orange juice, cantaloupe, guava, mango, papaya, raw strawberries, broccoli, Brussels sprouts, green pepper, sweet red pepper.

Fair sources: Honeydew melon, lemon, tangerine or tangerine juice, watermelon, asparagus, cabbage, cauliflower, collards, kale, kohlrabi, mustard greens, potatoes and sweet potatoes cooked in jacket, rutabagas, spinach, tomatoes or tomato juice, turnip greens.

Appreciate the seasons and vary mealtime colors, textures and flavors with vegetables and fruits. Or reverse roles and use these as the main portion of the meal, setting off with some meat or cheese or fish if desired.
Alertness pays in shopping for fresh fruits and vegetables, and for frozen and canned products, which often cost less per pound because of quantity processing at point of production.
Count on vegetables and fruits for snacks and desserts. Remember your vitamin C by having it at breakfast, in juice or whole fruit where possible.

Food Recommended

1 good source of vitamin A

Amounts to Buy

Good sources: Dark-green and deep-yellow vegetables and a few fruits, namely: apricots, broccoli, cantaloupe, carrots, chard, collards, cress, kale, mango, persimmon, pumpkin, spinach, sweet potatoes, turnip greens and other dark-green leaves, winter squash.

How to Save in Buying

BREAD-CEREAL GROUP
4 or more portions of whole-grain or enriched products (More if these are going to be counted as part of the protein contribution.)

Make sure you select enriched or whole-grain products, allowing 1 slice of bread or similar portion, and counting only those made with whole grain or enriched flour:
1 ounce ready-to-eat cereal, ½ to ¾ cup cooked cereal, corn meal, grits, spaghetti, macaroni, noodles, rice, barley, groats or other grain.

Foods in this group can help balance the budget, and offer nutritional balance, too. The more natural the form in which you buy grain products, the more you save in cost and nutritional values.
A portion of cereal can range in price from about 5¢ for a bowl of hot oatmeal with milk to about 14¢ for an individual package of sweetened cereal with milk. Generally, larger units cost less, and this applies to breads and rolls as well as cereal packs.

OTHER FOODS AS NEEDED
To round out meals and meet energy requirements.

Select according to your budget and your needs: gelatins for dessert, non-enriched starches for cooking, sugars; butter or margarine, preserves and other spreads, other fats and sweets. Plan to include some vegetable oil (for polyunsaturated fats).

Here, too, the more fully prepared your snacks, the more you pay for them, and smaller, more fanciful packages generally cost more. Look to some old-fashioned favorites for special value; popping corn, for example, in an inexpensive cellophane bag or in a can, takes minutes to pop, adds to family fun, and costs only a few pennies a bowl.

See individual chapters for additional moneysaving shopping tips and recipes.

BEGIN WITH BREAKFAST

Breakfast starts a day off right! And breakfast can make any day more productive because it enables you to react more efficiently to what the day brings. Tests in schools and factories have indicated that skipping breakfast contributes to a midmorning slump.

From an economic point of view, breakfast is the most practical food investment of the day. Breakfast ingredients can be low cost and preparation time is brief. Since 12 to 14 hours have elapsed since the last meal, the physical need for breakfast is real, and calories eaten at breakfast are more likely to be used up in activities than those eaten late in the evening.

For efficiency in preparing breakfast, set the table the night before—even if breakfast is eaten at the kitchen counter. Decide on the morning fruit, and set out the plates and glasses you will use. Things will move more readily in the morning as a result of these few steps taken the night before.

Hot Cereals

The most economical cereals are the dry grains, such as oatmeal, many of which are available in instant as well as longer-cooking form. Cook according to package directions and add butter, raisins, brown sugar or syrup to taste. Or combine two cereals, a flake such as oatmeal and a crunchy wheat type, for example, for interesting new flavors and textures.

To cook any cereal below, place water in a heavy saucepan or in the top of a double boiler, add salt and bring to boil. Sprinkle the cereal gradually into the water, stirring constantly to prevent lumping. When cereal reaches a full rolling boil, reduce heat and cover. Cook over low heat or over boiling water for the time indicated, without stirring, until the cereal absorbs the water and becomes quite thick. Stirring during cooking tends to

CEREAL COOKING CHART

Type	Amounts for 3 to 4 Servings			Cooking Time
	CEREAL	WATER	SALT	
Coarsely ground: cracked or whole grain, such as cut oatmeal, hominy grits, cracked wheat	⅔ cup	3⅓ cups	¾ teaspoon	Check package directions—vary from 20 minutes to 1 hour or longer
Finely ground: Farina, Cream of Wheat, Ralston, Wheatena, Maltex, corn meal, grits	1 cup	4 cups	1 teaspoon	Quick-cooking, 3 to 10 minutes; non-processed, ½ to ¾ hour
Flaked: rolled oats, flaked wheat	1⅓ cups	3 cups	¾ teaspoon	Quick-cooking, 3 to 10 minutes; non-processed, ½ to ¾ hour

make cereal gummy. Cereals that require long cooking may be cooked over direct heat for 5 minutes, then over hot water until done.

For variety, add raisins or cut-up dried fruits to cereal a few minutes before it finishes cooking; or sprinkle with shredded cheese or cinnamon sugar just before serving.

Cereal Bonus: Pour leftover cooked cereal into a shallow container or loaf pan; chill. The next morning, cut into blocks, dip in crumbs, and brown in butter or margarine or bacon drippings.

Cold Cereals

Buy ready-to-eat cereals in the larger packages for economy; keep the package tightly closed to maintain freshness.

Mix-match dry cereals for new taste effects. Sprinkle with wheat germ for a nutritional plus. For variety, serve with fruits in season, or with applesauce or canned fruit, or with yogurt or ice cream for a breakfast "party."

Breakfast in Hand

Combine a mixture of whole-grain dry cereal, dried fruit, nuts, raisins and cubes of cheese in a plastic bag for breakfast en route.

GRANOLA

1 pound rolled oats
1 cup wheat germ
1 cup hulled sunflower seeds
1 cup chopped nuts
½ cup honey
½ cup vegetable oil
½ cup brown sugar
2 teaspoons vanilla
1½ cups raisins

Combine oats, wheat germ, sunflower seeds and chopped nuts in a large bowl. Combine honey, oil, brown sugar and vanilla in a small saucepan and heat without boiling. Add to the oats mixture and stir until well blended. Spread evenly in two oiled large, shallow baking pans. Bake in moderately slow oven (325°F) 20 to 25 minutes, stirring occasionally. Remove from oven; stir in raisins. Cool. Store in tightly closed container or in plastic bags. Makes about 3 pounds.

Breakfast Breads

Bread—whether slices from a loaf or in the form of muffins or other baked goods—is the perfect complement to almost all other breakfast foods. It offers good nutritional value as well as appetite appeal to complement other breakfast foods.

CINNAMON TOAST

Sprinkle hot buttered toast with a mixture of 3 tablespoons sugar and ½ teaspoon cinnamon.

HONEY TOAST

Cream together equal portions of butter or margarine and honey. Spread on hot toast. Or spread toast with prepared honey butter.

FRENCH TOAST

2 eggs
½ cup milk
½ teaspoon salt
6 slices day-old bread

Break eggs into shallow soup bowl, add milk and salt and beat with fork until light and foamy. Cut each slice of bread in half, dip in egg-milk mixture. For very soft toast, pierce bread with fork. Brown on both sides in butter or margarine or bacon drippings. Drain on absorbent paper. Serve hot with jam, jelly, syrup or honey.

QUICK MUFFINS

2 cups sifted enriched flour
2¼ teaspoons baking powder
1 teaspoon salt
¼ cup sugar
1 egg, beaten
1 cup milk
2 tablespoons vegetable oil

Lightly oil muffin pans. Sift dry ingredients together. Combine egg, milk and oil. Stir quickly into flour mixture until dry ingredients are just dampened and batter looks lumpy. Fill muffin pans two-thirds full. Bake in a hot oven (400°F) 20 minutes. Serve hot. Makes a dozen 2-inch muffins.

Bran Muffins: Substitute bran for half the flour.

Wheat-Germ Muffins: Substitute ½ cup wheat germ for ½ cup flour.

Oatmeal Muffins: Substitute 2 cups quick oats, whirled to a powder in an electric blender, for the flour.

POPOVERS

1 cup all-purpose flour
½ teaspoon salt
2 eggs
1 cup milk
**1 tablespoon melted butter or margarine or
      shortening**

Grease 6 to 8 narrow-bottomed popover cups, preheat in a hot oven (425°F). Toss flour with salt. Beat eggs with a rotary beater until thick, add milk. Add flour, beat 30 seconds, add melted butter and beat until batter is smooth. Fill hot cups a little less than half full. Bake in a hot oven (425°F) about 45 minutes until popovers are puffed and very brown. Serve at once. Makes 6 to 8 popovers.

Your Own Pancakes

Pancake mixes are so handy, we tend to forget how easy it is to mix up a batch of batter—and save money, too. If you use a mix, the bulk pack is less expensive than the shaker type, but then you do have to measure and have more utensils to wash.

PLAIN JANE PANCAKES

1 egg
1½ cups milk
**3 tablespoons melted butter or margarine or
      vegetable oil**
1½ cups enriched flour
2 teaspoons baking powder
½ teaspoon salt

Beat egg and milk, add butter. Toss remaining ingredients to mix, stir quickly into liquid just until flour is moistened. Preheat griddle very hot (a heavy iron griddle browns best) and brush with oil. Pour about ¼ cup batter onto griddle for each pancake. Brown until bubbles appear on surface; turn and brown the other side. Makes about 12 pancakes.

Fruited Pancakes: Prepare pancake batter. Lightly stir in 1 cup blueberries, chopped apple or drained crushed pineapple. Cook as directed. Serve with sugar, cinnamon and lemon wedge.

Nutty Pancakes: Add ½ cup chopped nuts to basic batter.

Hearty Pancakes: Add ½ cup slivered cooked ham, tuna or cheese to basic batter.

BRUNCH WAFFLES

2 cups enriched flour
2 teaspoons baking powder
2 tablespoons sugar
½ teaspoon salt
2 eggs, separated
2 cups milk
¼ cup melted butter or margarine

Toss dry ingredients to mix. Beat egg whites stiff. Beat egg yolks with milk, add melted butter. Add dry ingredients, stir to moisten. Fold in beaten egg whites. Bake in preheated waffle iron. Serve with syrup or sauce. Makes 6 waffles.

Cheese Waffles: Add 1 cup grated Cheddar cheese to dry ingredients and proceed as above.

Bacon Waffles: Sprinkle batter in waffle iron with diced, partly cooked bacon, then bake as above.

Apple Waffles: Before folding in egg whites, add 1 cup chopped apples, a pinch of cinnamon and 1 tablespoon sugar.

Breakfast Eggs

Top-quality Sunnybrook eggs are worth buying for breakfast; check value in terms of price for size (see page 28). The yolks of Grade A eggs are centered in the whites; they hold their shape well and will not flatten in cooking.

POACHED EGGS

Fill a skillet or shallow pan with water to depth of about 1 inch, no more than two-thirds full. Add ½ teaspoon salt for each 2 cups water. Bring to boiling point, reduce heat. Break egg into water; if more than one is being poached, crack each egg into a cup first. The water should almost cover the eggs if you want the yolks to remain yellow; cover the eggs with water if you want the yolks veiled. Cook only as many eggs at a time as the pan will hold without having them run together. Cook to desired degree of firmness, keeping the water simmering, not boiling. For soft-poached eggs, cook 3 to 5 minutes; the whites will be thoroughly set, the yolks still soft inside. For firmer yolks, cook longer. Lift eggs from water with a slotted spoon. Serve immediately on hot buttered toast or English muffins, or keep warm in a pan of warm water.

Eggs Poached in Milk: For delicate flavor and texture, substitute milk for the water in poaching eggs. Pour the milk over each serving of egg and toast—a nutritional bonus!

EGGS BENEDICT

2 English muffins, split
4 slices ham or Canadian bacon
4 poached eggs
  Hollandaise Sauce (page 173)

Toast English muffins. Cover each muffin half with a slice of broiled or pan-browned ham or bacon and a poached egg. Top with Hollandaise Sauce. Makes 2 servings.

FRIED EGGS

Heat butter, margarine, oil or bacon drippings to cover bottom of skillet. Break eggs into skillet, season with salt and pepper or hot pepper sauce to taste. Cook over moderate heat until white is set. For "basted" eggs, use a little more fat, baste as eggs begin to set, then cover skillet, cook to desired doneness.

GRITS AND EGGS

Cook grits as directed (page 22). Fry eggs as above. Spoon grits into shallow bowls. Center an egg on top, cover with fat from pan.

For eggs cooked in the shell, omelets, scrambled eggs and other egg dishes, see pages 28–30.

BRUNCH PUFF

  8 slices bacon
  2 onions, sliced
  12 slices white bread, quartered
  ½ pound Swiss cheese, shredded
  8 eggs
  4 cups milk
1½ teaspoons salt
  ¼ teaspoon pepper

Cook bacon until crisp; remove from pan. Cook onion in bacon drippings until soft. Spread half of the bread in the bottom of a greased 9-by-13-inch pan. Sprinkle with half the bacon (crumbled), onions and cheese. Repeat layers. Combine eggs, milk, salt and pepper; pour egg mixture over top layer in pan. The casserole can be prepared to this stage in advance and stored in the refrigerator until 1 hour before serving time. Bake in moderate oven (350°F) 45 to 50 minutes, until set and puffed. Makes 8 servings. For 4 servings, reduce all amounts by half, bake in an 8-inch-square pan. See photo, page 33.

Meat in the Morning

Many meats lend themselves to breakfast menus and are important sources of protein.

BACON

Whether you choose regular-sliced bacon, thin-sliced bacon for extra crispness, or thick-sliced bacon for chewiness, all are cooked the same way. Place slices in a cold skillet, fry over low heat. As fat accumulates, pour it into a container to reserve for other uses. Drain bacon on absorbent paper. Or broil or bake bacon on a rack, over a pan to catch the fat.

SCRAPPLE

  3 cups broth or water
  ¾ cup corn meal
1½ cups cooked pork, finely ground
  1 tablespoon grated onion
    Salt, pepper
  ¼ teaspoon powdered sage
  1 egg
  1 tablespoon water
    Dry bread crumbs
    Bacon drippings

Bring broth or water to a boil in the top of a double boiler over direct heat, stir in corn meal and cook, stirring constantly, until mixture boils. Reduce heat, cook 5 minutes, stirring occasionally. Add pork and onion, season well with salt, pepper and sage. Put pan over boiling water, cover, cook 45 minutes. Pack mixture into a loaf pan rinsed with cold water; chill until firm. To serve, cut into ½-inch slices. Dip slices into egg beaten with water, then coat with bread crumbs. Brown on both sides in hot bacon drippings. Serve plain, or with fried tomatoes and green peppers, tomato sauce or spinach. Makes 6 to 8 servings.

CREAMED CHIPPED BEEF

¼ pound (1 jar) dried beef, shredded
4 tablespoons butter or margarine
4 tablespoons flour
2 cups milk
4 to 6 slices toast

Cook the dried beef with the butter in a heavy skillet for 5 minutes or until the edges curl. Sprinkle flour over the beef and blend well. Remove from heat, slowly stir in the milk. Return to low heat and cook, stirring until sauce is smooth and thick. Serve on hot toast. Makes 4 to 6 servings.

> ### VERMONT BREAKFAST
>
> *The story is told by an A&P veteran that in the South, a New Englander is a man who lives north of the Mason-Dixon line. In the North, a New Englander is a man who lives in Boston. In Boston, a New Englander is a man who comes from Vermont. In Vermont, a New Englander is a man who eats apple pie for breakfast. See Vermont Apple Pie (page 210). Add a slice of Cheddar cheese for better protein balance.*

Breakfast Variety

Pie is far from the end of breakfast choices. Choose hamburger on a roll, cold fish, a hearty soup, cottage cheese sprinkled with wheat germ, yogurt and cold cereal, spaghetti and meatballs. Name your own dish, but allow time for breakfast and assure yourself the right start for the day.

DAIRY FOODS

In the dairy cases you will find milk, cream, eggs, butter and margarine and a variety of cheeses for main dishes, desserts, sauces and spreads. Ready-to-bake refrigerator biscuits and rolls are there, too, along with deli-type salads and snack specialties.

How to Buy Milk

The A&P offers four different styles of fresh milk, plus non-fat dry milk, evaporated milk and sweetened condensed milk, selling at different prices. All are excellent sources of essential calcium, proteins and riboflavin. Choose the fresh milk with the butterfat content that suits your needs and take advantage of possible savings. Take advantage also of the economies of dry and canned milk for total balance of your food budget.

Whole Milk: Fortified with vitamin D, whole milk contains approximately 3.25% butterfat. Choose this for growing children or others who need extra fat, for its rich taste as a beverage and in cooking. Contains 150 calories per 8-ounce glass.

Skim Milk: Skim milk contains all the nutrients of whole milk, except that fat is reduced to a maximum of .5%. It is fortified with vitamins A and D and is enriched with non-fat dry milk. Choose this for dieters, as a beverage and in cooking. An 8-ounce glass contains 90 calories.

Look-Fit Milk: This product contains 1% butterfat. It is fortified with vitamins A and D and is enriched with dry-milk solids. Choose this when your household includes active teenagers, hard-working adults or active athletes. An 8-ounce glass contains 110 calories.

2% Milk: Made with whole and skim milk, 2% milk is fortified with vitamins A and D and is usually enriched with non-fat dry milk. Like Look-Fit, this is a good choice for active youngsters and adults. An 8-ounce glass contains 130 calories.

Non-fat Dry Milk: This is the least expensive milk product you can buy, and the best buy. It contains all the proteins and minerals and most of the vitamins of fluid skim milk, and is fortified with vitamins A and D. It can be stored on the pantry shelf. The butterfat content is .1%. An 8-ounce glass contains 80 calories. Reconstitute and combine with fresh fluid milk for optimum flavor.

Evaporated Milk: Canned milk, with water removed, has double the food value of whole milk. This is practical to store in the pantry, economical for cooking and table use, in whole and skim forms.

Sweetened Condensed Milk: Presweetened, double-rich whole milk, this is useful for many cooking purposes, particularly for desserts, candies and other treats.

Buttermilk

Buttermilk used to be the liquid that remained in the butter churn after the butter had been formed and removed. The buttermilk you find in the dairy case today is made by adding to skim milk a bacterial culture and salt to enhance the aromatic factor in acid flavor.

Yogurt

Yogurt may be made from whole or low-fat milk—the label will give this information. A bacterial culture is added to the milk and controlled heating causes the milk to solidify.

Flavored Yogurts: Yogurt may be sweetened and flavored with vanilla; or fruit or fruit preserves may be mixed with the yogurt or added to the carton. Read the labels for a description of the contents, which can differ widely.

How to Buy Cream

Using real cream where it should be used can be a luxury without being an extravagance. The trick is to buy the right cream for the purpose.

Heavy Whipping Cream: This type of cream, which is 36% butterfat, is the highest-priced cream in the dairy case. Heavy cream can be whipped. So can the less expensive medium whipping cream, with 30% butterfat, which is available in many areas of the country.

Light Cream: Also called table cream or coffee cream, light cream contains 18% butterfat. It does not whip as well as heavy cream but is satisfyingly rich in flavor when used in beverages, or with cereals or desserts, and, of course, in cooking.

Half-and-Half: As its name implies, this product is half milk, half cream; it contains about 10.5% butterfat and is a satisfactory substitute for light cream.

Sour Cream: Sour cream is made by adding a bacterial culture to light cream, and so contains about 18% butterfat. Sour cream is used as a topping for soups, vegetables and desserts, in baking, and as an ingredient in various recipes for meat, poultry and fish.

How to Buy Eggs

Choose eggs of the quality and size you need for specific purposes. A&P Sunnybrook eggs are the finest eggs commercially available. A&P Wildmere eggs are also Grade A and of top quality. Both are suitable for any purpose and economical for cooking.

The color of the egg shell does not affect the quality of the egg in any way. If there is a price difference between brown and white eggs, it reflects the law of supply and demand.

How to Cook an Egg

Below are the standard ways to cook eggs. Eggs in these forms are often the basis of other egg recipes.

Soft-cooked Eggs: Cover eggs with water, bring rapidly just to a boil, then cook over low heat 2 to 3 minutes. Better yet, turn off heat, cover pan, let eggs stand 2 to 4 minutes. After 4 minutes, both whites and yolks will be set but still soft. At 2 minutes, the yolks will be runny.

Hard-cooked Eggs: Let eggs stand, covered, as above, 25 minutes. Cool in cold water before shelling. *Or* put eggs into cold water, bring water to a boil, simmer 10 minutes.

Fried Eggs: See page 25.

Shirred Eggs: Slip eggs onto greased individual baking dishs. Bake in a moderately slow oven (325°F) about 12 to 15 minutes, until whites are set and yolks are the way you like them.

Poached Eggs: See page 24.

Scrambled Eggs: Beat 2 eggs with 1 tablespoon milk, salt and pepper to taste. Melt butter or margarine in skillet, add eggs, reduce heat to moderate. Cook eggs quickly, pulling the solid edges into the center with a fork so that the uncooked portion flows onto the pan. Cook until eggs are no longer liquid, but still shiny and moist, 2 minutes or less for a single serving of 2 eggs.

Omelet: Beat 2 eggs with 1 tablespoon water or milk, salt and pepper to taste. Melt butter or margarine in skillet, add eggs, reduce heat to moderate. Lift cooked edges with a knife so that uncooked portion flows onto the pan. When mixture is set, but still creamy, let stand a moment to brown bottom, fold, turn onto serving dish.

Egg Dishes

Eggs are as versatile an item as you will find in your supermarket. They can be the main ingredient in any meal of the day, from dressed-up breakfast ideas to tangy omelets to main dishes to rich dessert soufflés.

POTATO SCRAMBLE

½ cup diced cooked potato
3 tablespoons butter or margarine
2 eggs
1 tablespoon milk
Salt, pepper

Brown diced potato in butter. Beat eggs with milk, salt and pepper, add to pan. Cook like plain scrambled eggs. Makes 1 serving.

Ham Scramble: Substitute ½ cup diced cooked ham for potato.

Cheese Scramble: Substitute 2 tablespoons cottage cheese, or grated Cheddar or Swiss cheese, for potato. Stir cheese into eggs in the pan and cook as above.

Bacon Scramble: Substitute 2 strips bacon, finely sliced, for potato. Omit butter.

OMELET WITH CAVIAR AND SOUR CREAM

Make omelet (page 28). Just before folding, spoon on 2 tablespoons sour cream and 1 teaspoon red caviar.

CREOLE OMELET

Make omelet (page 28). Just before folding, top with 4 tablespoons hot Creole Sauce (page 175).

QUICK SPANISH OMELET

Boil 1 can (1 pound) stewed tomatoes until thick; adjust seasoning with Worcestershire sauce and cayenne pepper. Make omelet (page 28). Just before folding, spoon on 4 tablespoons hot tomatoes.

OMELET SOUFFLÉ

4 eggs
¼ cup sour cream
   Salt, pepper
2 tablespoons snipped chives
1 tablespoon butter or margarine

Beat eggs with sour cream, add seasonings and chives, beat until light. Preheat broiling oven. Melt butter in a 7-inch skillet with a flameproof handle. Add eggs and cook over medium-high heat, pulling the edges back as they set, until the mixture is set, but still moist and creamy. Put the skillet under the broiler, 4 inches from the heat, until the top puffs and browns lightly. Makes 2 servings.

ITALIAN OMELET (FRITTATA)

2 eggs, separated
2 tablespoons chopped green pepper
2 tablespoons grated onion
2 tablespoons grated Parmesan cheese
   Salt, pepper
   Vegetable oil or butter
   Prepared spaghetti sauce

Beat egg whites until stiff. With same beater, beat yolks until light, add green pepper, onion, cheese, and salt and pepper to taste. Fold in whites. Cook like an omelet, in hot oil or butter; turn with a spatula to brown both sides. Serve hot, with prepared spaghetti sauce. Makes 1 serving.

WESTERN OMELET

6 eggs
¼ cup milk
1½ cups diced cooked ham
¼ cup chopped onion
¼ cup chopped celery
⅓ cup chopped green pepper
   Salt, pepper
¼ cup butter or margarine

Beat eggs with milk, ham and vegetables. Add seasonings to taste. Melt butter in large skillet, add eggs. Cook over moderate heat, lifting the edges with a knife as they cook to allow the uncooked portion to run onto the pan. When mixture is set, but still moist and creamy, cut into wedges. Makes 4 servings.

CHINESE OMELETS (EGGS FOO YONG)

2 tablespoons vegetable oil
½ cup chopped onion
½ cup finely chopped celery
1 tablespoon chopped green pepper
1 can (1 pound) bean sprouts, rinsed and drained
4 eggs
1 teaspoon salt
1 teaspoon soy sauce
   Oil for frying

Heat 2 tablespoons oil, add onion, celery, green pepper. Simmer, covered, about 5 minutes. Cool. Add bean sprouts. Beat eggs with salt and soy sauce, add to vegetable mixture. Heat ½ inch oil in a large skillet. Spoon mixture by tablespoons into hot oil and brown crisply on both sides, turning once. Serve with sauce (below). Makes 2 servings.

Variation: Diced shrimp or other seafood, or diced cooked chicken or pork, may be cooked with the vegetables.

FOO YONG SAUCE

1 cup chicken broth
2 teaspoons cornstarch
1 teaspoon soy sauce
¼ teaspoon sugar
   Salt, pepper

Combine chicken broth with cornstarch, soy sauce and sugar. Cook, stirring, until smooth and thick. Add salt, pepper, and more sugar to taste. Serve with Eggs Foo Yong (above).

POACHED EGGS FLORENTINE

1 package (10 ounces) frozen chopped spinach
2 tablespoons butter or margarine
** Salt, pepper**
8 eggs
1 cup Cheese Sauce (page 175)
2 tablespoons grated Parmesan cheese

Cook spinach according to package directions, drain thoroughly. Add butter and seasonings to taste. Divide into 4 flameproof individual baking dishes. Poach 8 eggs (page 24) and arrange 2 eggs in each dish. Cover with Cheese Sauce, sprinkle with grated Parmesan cheese, brown quickly under the broiler. Makes 4 servings.

EGGS GOLDENROD

** 6 eggs, hard-cooked**
** 3 tablespoons butter or margarine**
** 1 teaspoon grated onion**
** 3 tablespoons flour**
1½ cups milk
**   Salt, pepper, paprika**
** 4 slices toast**

Separate egg whites from yolks, chop whites, force yolks through a sieve. Melt butter with onion. Stir in flour, cook for a minute. Gradually add milk and cook, stirring, until sauce is smooth and thickened. Add chopped egg whites and seasonings to taste. Pour over hot toast, sprinkle with sieved egg yolks. Makes 4 servings.

CHEESE SOUFFLÉ

** 3 tablespoons butter or margarine**
** 3 tablespoons flour**
** 1 cup milk**
** 1 cup (4 ounces) grated Cheddar or Swiss**
**   cheese**
¼ teaspoon salt
**   Dash cayenne pepper**
**   Pinch powdered mustard**
** 4 eggs, separated**

Melt butter, stir in flour. Add milk gradually. Cook over low heat, stirring constantly, until sauce is thick and smooth. Remove from heat. Add cheese, stir until cheese melts. Add seasonings to taste. Beat egg yolks, stir into batter. Cool. Beat egg whites until stiff. Fold one-third of egg whites very thoroughly into batter. Fold in remaining egg whites gently. The mixture need not be perfectly blended. Bake in an ungreased straight-sided 6-cup soufflé dish in a moderate oven (350°F) about 45 minutes, until the soufflé is well puffed and richly browned. Serve at once. Makes 4 servings.

Variations: Make part of the grated cheese either Parmesan or Romano, for extra flavor. Or instead of cheese, use 1 cup finely chopped leftover meat, poultry, fish or vegetables; taste and adjust seasoning.

SHORTCUT MAIN-DISH SOUFFLÉ

1 can (10½ ounces) condensed cream of
**   mushroom soup**
1 cup (4 ounces) Cheddar cheese
6 eggs, separated

Heat soup, add cheese, stir until cheese melts. Beat egg yolks, stir into soup off the heat. Cool. Beat egg whites until stiff, fold one-third thoroughly into soup mixture. Fold in remaining egg whites gently. Bake in an ungreased straight-sided 2-quart soufflé dish in a hot oven (400°F) for 30 minutes, until soufflé is well puffed and richly browned. Serve at once. Makes 6 servings.

Variation: One cup finely chopped meat, poultry, fish or cooked vegetable may be substituted for the cheese. Add with egg yolks; adjust seasoning.

CHOCOLATE SOUFFLÉ

** 2 squares (1 ounce each) baking chocolate**
** 1 cup milk**
** 3 tablespoons butter or margarine**
** 3 tablespoons flour**
½ cup sugar
** 1 teaspoon vanilla**
** 4 eggs, separated**

Melt chocolate in milk. Melt butter, stir in flour, add chocolate milk gradually. Cook over low heat, stirring constantly, until sauce is thick and smooth. Add sugar and vanilla. Beat egg yolks well, stir into batter. Cool. Beat egg whites until stiff. Fold one-third of egg whites very thoroughly into batter. Fold in remaining egg whites gently. The mixture need not be perfectly blended. Butter a straight-sided 6-cup soufflé dish and sprinkle with sugar; add soufflé mixture. Bake in a moderate oven (350°F) for about 45 minutes, until the soufflé is well puffed and richly browned.

Or bake in a very hot oven (450°F) for about 20 minutes. This method, favored by French chefs, produces a soufflé that puffs and browns while the center is still runny—in effect, it makes its own sauce. Serve at once, with cream or whipped cream, if desired. Makes 6 servings.

Mocha Soufflé: Dissolve 2 teaspoons instant coffee in the milk with the chocolate.

Orange Soufflé: Omit chocolate, add ¼ cup orange juice, grated rind of 1 orange.

Surprise Soufflé: Layer any soufflé mixture with ladyfingers soaked in liqueur—Grand Marnier and Cointreau are favorites.

SHORTCUT DESSERT SOUFFLÉ

1 package (about 4 ounces) pudding and pie filling mix
1 cup milk
3 eggs, separated

Use chocolate, vanilla or butterscotch pudding for this quick soufflé. Add milk and cook, stirring, until sauce is thick and smooth. Beat egg yolks until light, add pudding gradually, stirring constantly. Cool about 5 minutes, stirring once or twice. Beat egg whites until stiff, fold one-third very thoroughly into pudding mixture. Fold in remaining egg whites gently. Bake in a buttered, sugar-sprinkled 6-cup soufflé dish with straight sides. Bake in a moderate oven (350°F) for 45 minutes, until well puffed and browned. Makes 6 servings.

Cheese

Read the labels in the cheese sections of the dairy cases and know what you're buying.

Natural Cheeses: A natural cheese—Cheddar or Swiss, for instance—is produced by curdling milk solids with a bacterial culture. The first cheese was probably made by accident by a bacterial culture that happened to be in the milk container, or in the air.

There are about 18 different types of natural cheeses, but hundreds of variations of these types. The differences between them depend on the butterfat content of the milk used, the method used to curdle the milk, the type of bacterial culture used, the cooking of the curd, the ripening method, the time allotted and the temperature. Different seasonings may be added to natural cheeses.

Process Cheeses: Pasteurized process cheeses are blends of natural cheeses that are heated with added gums for smoothness and salts to enhance the ripened flavor. Seasonings and ingredients such as pimientos, chives or other vegetables may be added to process cheeses.

Cheese food is pasteurized like process cheese, but it contains non-fat dry-milk solids, or whey solids and water, which make it milder in flavor and softer in texture. Cheese food melts more easily than other cheese.

Cheese spreads have a higher moisture content than either process cheeses or cheese foods, and usually include a stabilizer to keep the mixture smooth.

The Cheese Board

The dairy cases offer a wide and ever-changing selection of imported and specialty cheeses, soft and firm fresh cheeses, and process cheeses. Some of these you will use in cooked dishes—recipes using cheese range from appetizers through soups and main courses to desserts. Others should be enjoyed with thin-sliced whole-grain breads, or crackers, or crusty French or Italian bread. Offer a cheese board with an assortment of your favorite varieties before dinner, with the salad course at dinner, or with fruit as dessert after dinner. The selections below are merely a sampling of possible choices that you will want to adapt to your own taste.

Appetizer Cheese Board: Bel Paese, Muenster, Cheddar, Limburger, Roquefort.

Salad Cheese Board: Gouda, Swiss, Blue, Gorgonzola, Provolone.

Dessert Cheese Board: Brie, Camembert, Port du Salut, Edam.

Cottage Cheese

All cottage cheese is made from skim milk. The basic curds are then modified to make the various types of cottage cheese you will find in the dairy cases.

Cottage Cheese: The cottage-cheese curd is mixed with sweet- or sour-cream dressing to make a product with 4% fat content. The curd may be large, regular or tiny but the flavor remains the same. Choose the large curd for salads and other dishes where you want to retain the identity of the cheese; use the tiny curd in dips and spreads.

Pot Cheese: Usually the large curd, pot cheese is packed without added cream, which makes it lower in calories, tangier in flavor. It has a .5% butterfat content.

Low-fat Cottage Cheese: This product has a .5 to 2% butterfat content. It is designed for dieters.

Flavored Cottage Cheese: You can choose cottage cheese already mixed with vegetables or with fruits or fruit preserves. The labels will provide details about such additions.

Cheese Recipes

The many varieties of cheeses and the endless ways they can be used in cooking make cheeses ideal budget stretchers, high in protein.

SWISS FONDUE

1 clove garlic, cut
1 cup dry white wine
1 pound Swiss cheese, grated
1 tablespoon flour
1 teaspoon dry mustard
2 tablespoons Kirsch (optional)
    Cubes of French bread, each with crust

Rub heavy pottery casserole or fondue pot with garlic, set over a table cooker. Add wine and bring to boil. Toss cheese with flour and mustard. Add cheese to bubbling wine a little at a time, stirring over low heat until the cheese is melted and the mixture is creamy and smooth. Add Kirsch. Guests each spear a cube of bread on a long-handled fork and dip it into fondue. Makes 8 or more appetizer servings, 4 to 6 main-course servings.

WELSH RABBIT

2 teaspoons Worcestershire sauce
½ teaspoon dry mustard
    Dash of cayenne
    Dash of paprika
½ cup beer
1 pound Cheddar cheese, grated
4 to 6 slices toast or toasted English
    muffin halves

Mix Worcestershire, mustard, cayenne and paprika in a saucepan. Add the beer and heat. Add the cheese and cook, stirring, until it melts and the mixture is thick and smooth. Serve on toast or English muffins. Makes 4 to 6 servings.

BLUSHING BUNNY

2 eggs
1 can (10½ ounces) condensed tomato soup
½ cup light cream
½ pound Cheddar cheese, shredded
    Salt, pepper
    Nutmeg to taste
4 slices toast

In a small, heavy saucepan beat eggs well with soup and cream. Cook over low heat, stirring constantly, until mixture bubbles. Add cheese, a little at a time, stirring until cheese is melted. Season. Serve on hot toast. Makes 4 servings.

QUICHE LORRAINE

Pastry-lined 9-inch pie plate
4 thin slices cooked ham, slivered
2 tablespoons snipped chives
¼ pound Swiss cheese, shredded
1 ounce grated Parmesan or
    Romano cheese
3 eggs
1½ cups half-and-half or milk
    Salt, pepper, cayenne

Sprinkle pastry-lined pie plate with ham, chives and cheeses. Beat eggs lightly with half-and-half, season to taste with salt, pepper and cayenne. Pour into pie plate. Bake in a moderately hot oven (375°F) 45 minutes, until crust is browned and filling is set. Serve warm. Makes 8 appetizer servings, 6 main-course servings.

ONION QUICHE

In Quiche Lorraine (above), omit ham and chives. Cook 1 cup sliced onions in 2 tablespoons butter or margarine until transparent; spread on pie crust. Proceed as directed. If desired, add 3 slices bacon, cooked crisp and crumbled.

MANICOTTI

Homemade pasta (below)
1½ pounds ricotta or cottage cheese
½ pound mozzarella cheese, grated
2 eggs
2 tablespoons chopped parsley
1 teaspoon mixed dried Italian herbs
    Salt, pepper
1 jar (1 pound) spaghetti sauce
¼ cup grated Parmesan cheese

Cut homemade pasta into uniform rectangles, about 5 by 4 inches. Cook in boiling water until just tender, about 12 minutes. Blend ricotta and mozzarella cheeses with eggs; add herbs, salt and pepper to taste. Spoon filling on cooked pasta or pancakes, roll up. Arrange rolls in baking dish. Cover with spaghetti sauce and grated cheese. Bake in a hot oven (400°F) 15 minutes, until sauce is bubbling hot and topping is browned. Makes 8 servings.

Bread, milk and eggs, plus cheese, onions and bacon, transformed into a savory Brunch Puff . . . what better choice for a festive party brunch or weekend whole-family breakfast? Day-old bread does very well in this recipe. And you can prepare the casserole the night before for last-minute baking, and bring the puffy brown triumph to the table within 45 minutes. (See page 25.)

HOMEMADE PASTA

2 eggs
1½ teaspoons salt
3 cups flour
½ cup water (approximately)

Beat eggs well with salt. Beating with a fork, gradually add flour and enough water to make a firm dough that can be kneaded. Knead on a floured board until very smooth. Let stand 15 minutes. Divide in half, roll each half into a thin sheet. Cut into noodles or any desired shape, let dry 1 hour. Cook in boiling salted water until just cooked through, but not soft, 12 minutes or less.

BLINTZES

1 cup flour
1 teaspoon salt
4 eggs
1 cup milk
Butter or margarine for frying

Filling:

1½ pounds dry cottage cheese
1 egg
½ teaspoon salt
½ teaspoon grated lemon rind
Pinch nutmeg
Sugar to taste

Toss flour and salt in a mixing bowl. Beat eggs with milk, add to flour, beat until smooth. (Or combine all in blender, whirl until smooth.) Melt 1 tablespoon butter in a 6-inch skillet, pour into batter, stir. Pour 2 tablespoons batter into the buttered pan, tip pan to spread batter evenly. Cook until bottom is browned, top dry. Turn out on a towel, browned side up. Repeat, brushing the pan with more melted butter as necessary.

Blend filling ingredients, spoon onto pancakes and roll up, folding in the sides. At this point the blintzes may be stored, covered, in the refrigerator until wanted. Just before serving, brush skillet with butter, brown blintzes on both sides. Serve hot, with sour cream and preserves, or with cinnamon sugar. Makes about 6 servings.

Variations: Add fruit to cheese filling mixture, about ½ cup blueberries, sliced strawberries, crushed pineapple, raisins, dates or prunes. Or omit sugar and lemon rind from filling and serve blintzes with sour cream and smoked salmon or red caviar, as first course or main dish.

COTTAGE-CHEESE MOLD

1 quart tomato juice (or half tomato juice and half clam broth)
3 envelopes unflavored gelatin
1 cup milk
¾ cup sour cream
¼ cup mayonnaise
½ pound cottage cheese
1½ cups chopped salad vegetables—celery, cucumber, scallions, green pepper, radishes
½ teaspoon salt
Dash of pepper

Pour juice into a saucepan and sprinkle with 2 envelopes gelatin. Let stand 5 minutes. Cook over low heat, stirring, until gelatin is dissolved. Pour into shallow 2-quart mold and chill until almost firm. Meanwhile, soften remaining envelope of gelatin in ½ cup milk in a saucepan. Heat, stirring, until gelatin dissolves. Add remaining milk. Combine with sour cream and mayonnaise in a mixing bowl. Stir in cottage cheese, chopped vegetables, salt and pepper. Spoon over jellied tomato layer. Chill until firm. Unmold on a bed of greens. Makes 8 to 10 servings.

CREAM-CHEESE PIE

1 cup flour
¼ teaspoon salt
¼ cup sugar
½ cup butter or margarine

Filling:

1 pound cream cheese
2 eggs
½ cup sugar
1 tablespoon grated orange rind
1 tablespoon orange liqueur (optional)
Cinnamon sugar

Toss flour with salt and sugar. Blend in butter with a fork to make a soft dough. Pat dough against bottom and sides of a 9-inch pie plate. Mash cream cheese, beat in eggs and sugar. Add orange rind, and liqueur, if desired. Fill prepared pie shell. Bake in a moderate oven (350°F) about ½ hour, until crust is brown and filling is firm. Sprinkle with cinnamon sugar.

Cherry-Cheese Pie: Top chilled Cream-Cheese Pie with a can of cherry pie filling.

ALMOND ICED CREAM CHEESE

½ pound cream cheese
⅔ cup sugar

2 cups half-and-half
1 teaspoon almond extract (or more)
½ cup slivered almonds

Soften cream cheese at room temperature; add sugar, beat well. Add half-and-half and almond extract to taste, beat again until sugar crystals are dissolved. Freeze in refrigerator tray, at coldest possible temperature, until mixture hardens at edges. Remove to a mixing bowl, beat until smooth. Add nuts. Return to tray, freeze solid. Remove from freezer 10 minutes before serving with chocolate sauce, or fruit. Makes 6 servings.

See also Ice Cream and other desserts, pages 230–246.

Quick Refrigerator Biscuits

The refrigerator biscuits sold in tubes in A&P's dairy cases inspire a variety of imaginative uses. Serve hot for best flavor.

Wafflers: Flatten biscuits slightly, bake in waffle iron. Use instead of toast for creamed chicken, etc.

Sticky Biscuits: Grease muffin pans, add 1 teaspoon brown sugar, 1 teaspoon butter or margarine, then the biscuits. Bake as directed. Cool a minute, invert.

Apple Folds: Pat biscuits flat. On one half put a spoonful of grated apple, cinnamon and sugar to taste. Fold over, pinch edges to seal. Bake as directed.

Cocktail Folds: Fill folds (above) with cooked sausage, chopped ham and pickle, liver pâté, a cube of Cheddar.

Pigs in Blankets: Pat biscuits flat, roll around a frankfurter. Bake, seam side down, as directed.

Biscuit Ring: Arrange biscuits, overlapping, around edge of 9-inch round baking pan. Sprinkle thickly with crumbled blue cheese or other cheese, or with cinnamon, sugar and nuts. Bake as directed.

SNACK BISCUITS

Cut refrigerator biscuits in half, flatten, brush with butter or margarine, sprinkle with sesame or poppy seeds, grated cheese. Prick with fork, bake in very hot oven (475°F) about 5 minutes. Serve with cheese or cocktail spreads, or use as base for grilled snacks.

ONION BISCUITS

1 large onion, chopped
1 tablespoon butter or margarine
10 refrigerator biscuits
1 teaspoon caraway seeds
½ teaspoon salt

Fry the chopped onion in butter and top refrigerator biscuits. Sprinkle with caraway seeds and salt. Bake biscuits as directed on package or in foil on grill.

Tip: Substitute crescent rolls for refrigerator biscuits, roll up, bake as directed.

PRUNE-WALNUT BISCUITS

1 tube (8 ounces) refrigerator biscuits
2 tablespoons melted butter or margarine
10 prunes, pitted and cooked
¼ cup chopped walnuts
1 tablespoon sugar
¼ teaspoon cinnamon

Place biscuits in buttered 8-inch layer-cake pan. Brush with half the melted butter. Press a prune in center of each. Sprinkle with walnuts, sugar and cinnamon. Drizzle with remaining butter. Bake in hot oven (425°F) 15 to 20 minutes. Serve warm.

PRUNES IN BLANKETS

1 tube (8 ounces) refrigerator biscuits
20 prunes, pitted
1 tablespoon melted butter or margarine
   Cinnamon sugar

Cut each biscuit in half; flatten. Roll a prune in each half; pinch tops together and leave ends open. Bake on ungreased baking sheet in very hot oven (450°F) for about 8 minutes. Brush while hot with melted butter and sprinkle with cinnamon sugar.

SNACKS AND STARTERS

The word "snack," meaning a quick meal or light bite, goes back to Middle English, and originally meant "snatch." The emergence of the snack as a style of eating that replaces more formal meals for many people is a mid-twentieth-century happening. Whether this is good or unfortunate depends entirely on what snacks you choose.

Some nutritionists think five or six small meals each day are better for you than three very large meals. If you choose snacks carefully so that they include the basic foods you need every day, snacks can be a fine way to eat. If you replace meats with snack foods prepared only for novelty of flavor, high in fats and salts or sugars, you are making a poor investment—with low nutritional returns, and at high cost.

Snacks originally intended to whet the appetite may be piquant and tantalizing preludes to a meal. If you serve snacks instead of a meal, be sure that they have the proteins, vitamins, minerals and calories you need.

The traditional role of hors d'oeuvre as a meal prelude is well filled by many of the snacks that follow. Serve them at an evening party or cocktail hour, too.

Your choice of snack foods is as wide as the stock of the supermarket. From anchovies to zucchini, mix and match foods in small portions to make snack meals high in interest as well as economical.

It pays to keep the makings of practical, quick and nutritious snack meals on the shelf —in the cupboard and in the refrigerator. This is an investment in satisfying eating.

Choice Snacks and Starters

The following recipes explore the wide range of foods and various ways—both hot and cold—to prepare them to provide tasty snack foods.

CURRIED NUTS

2 tablespoons oil
2 cups walnuts (or other nuts)
1 teaspoon salt
½ teaspoon curry powder (or more)
   Pinch sugar

Heat oil in a skillet. Add nuts and cook slowly, stirring constantly, until the nuts are golden and crisp, about 7 minutes. Turn onto paper towels. Combine salt, curry powder and sugar, sprinkle over nuts and toss to blend. Cool. Store in an airtight jar. Makes 2 cups.

GARLIC OLIVES

1 jar (7 to 8 ounces) pitted ripe olives
3 cloves garlic
3 tablespoons olive oil

Drain olives, reserving liquid. Purée or mash garlic with olive oil. Return olives to jar with garlic and oil; add enough reserved liquid to fill. Let stand 3 days before serving.

SPICY CEREAL NIBBLES

½ cup butter or margarine
1 tablespoon Worcestershire sauce
1 teaspoon chili powder
½ teaspoon garlic salt
½ teaspoon salt

1 cup nutmeats
2 cups bite-sized shredded rice
2 cups bite-sized shredded wheat
2 cups ready-to-eat oat cereal
2 cups corn puffs

Melt butter in a large pan. Stir in Worcestershire sauce, chili powder, garlic salt and salt. Add nuts and cereals. Stir well. Bake 1 hour in a slow oven (300°F), stirring every 15 minutes. Store in tightly covered container. Makes about 2 quarts.

POPCORN

1 to 2 tablespoons oil or fat
½ cup popcorn
Salt
Melted butter or margarine

Heat oil in heavy pan or corn popper. Add popcorn, cover tightly, and cook over high heat, shaking constantly, until corn stops popping. Remove from heat and add salt and melted butter to taste.

Variations: Vary popcorn by adding to the melted butter one or more of these to taste: garlic salt, curry powder, chili powder, or grated cheese.

HOMEMADE POTATO CHIPS

Use a very sharp knife or a floating-knife vegetable peeler. Slice peeled baking potatoes as thinly as possible. Soak in cold water for 2 hours. Drain, dry thoroughly. Heat deep fat to 380°F. (A 1-inch cube of bread will brown in 1 minute when the fat reaches frying temperature.) Separate slices, put a single layer into a frying basket; cook until golden, shaking the basket frequently to keep the chips separated. Drain, turn out onto absorbent toweling or brown paper.

CUMIN DIP

½ pound cottage cheese
¼ cup sour cream
2 tablespoons grated cucumber
1 teaspoon cumin seed
1 teaspoon minced onion
¼ teaspoon salt
⅛ teaspoon chili powder

Combine all ingredients, mixing well. Serve with thinly sliced black bread, corn chips or vegetables. Makes about 1¼ cups.

CLAM DIP

8 ounces cottage cheese
3 or 4 ounces cream cheese

1 envelope (1⅛ ounces) onion soup mix
2 teaspoons Worcestershire sauce (to taste)
½ cup sour cream
1 can (8 ounces) minced clams, drained

Beat cottage cheese, cream cheese, onion soup mix, Worcestershire sauce and sour cream in small bowl to blend. Stir in clams, adding a little of their liquid if necessary to moisten. Chill. Makes about 2 cups. Serve with potato chips, corn chips or celery sticks for dipping.

BACON-FLAVORED ONION DIP

1 envelope (1⅛ ounces) bacon-flavored onion party dip mix
2 cups sour cream

Combine dip mix with sour cream and chill well. Makes 2 cups.

Bacon-Cheddar Dip: Add ¼ cup grated sharp Cheddar cheese to prepared dip.

Bacon-Egg Dip: Add 2 chopped hard-cooked eggs to prepared dip.

Bacon-Tomato Dip: Add 1 can (1 pound) tomatoes, drained and chopped, to prepared dip.

GREEN-ONION PARTY DIP

1 envelope (1⅛ ounces) green-onion party dip mix
1 cup sour cream
1 package (8 ounces) softened cream cheese

Combine dip mix with sour cream and cream cheese. Chill well. Makes 2 cups.

Green-Onion Blue-Cheese Dip: Add ¼ cup crumbled blue cheese to prepared dip.

Green-Onion Shrimp Dip: Add ½ cup chopped cooked shrimp and ¼ teaspoon dill to prepared dip.

Green-Onion Egg Dip: Add 2 chopped hard-cooked eggs to prepared dip.

GUACAMOLE

2 ripe avocados
1 clove garlic, crushed
Pinch red pepper
1 teaspoon salt
4 tablespoons lemon juice

Mash the avocados with remaining ingredients. Serve with crackers or corn chips. Makes 2 cups.

Antipasto, the traditional first course of an Italian meal, can be a light meal in itself. This tray includes artichoke hearts, pepperoni, mushrooms, stuffed olives, tuna fish, anchovies rolled around capers, black olives, sardines, provolone cheese, red and green pickled peppers and salami—no empty calories here. For more possibilities, see page 39.

CRUSTY CHEESE BALLS

1 cup grated cheese
¼ cup dry bread crumbs
1 egg, separated
¼ teaspoon dry mustard
¼ teaspoon paprika
¼ teaspoon salt
Fine bread crumbs
Fat for deep frying

Combine cheese, dry bread crumbs, egg yolk and seasonings. Fold in stiffly beaten egg white. Shape into balls about ¾ inch in diameter. Roll in fine bread crumbs. Fry in hot deep fat (375°F) until browned. Makes about 24 balls.

PEPPER-MILL CHEESE BALL

½ cup butter or margarine, softened
1 package (8 ounces) cream cheese, softened
1 cup (4 ounces) Cheddar cheese, grated
1 teaspoon grated onion
1 tablespoon coarsely ground black pepper

Combine butter and cream cheese. Add Cheddar cheese and onion, blend well. Form mixture into a ball and roll in pepper. Wrap ball in plastic wrap or foil and chill for several hours. Serve as an appetizer with crackers or toast. Makes about 1½ cups.

STUFFED PRUNES

1 container (8 ounces) cottage cheese
2 teaspoons caraway seeds
1 teaspoon anchovy paste
1 package (12 ounces) pitted prunes

Combine cottage cheese, caraway seeds and anchovy paste in a small bowl. Mix well. Make indentation in prunes with your thumb and fill with the cottage-cheese mixture. Chill.

Variations: Use this cheese filling to stuff celery, mushroom caps and cherry tomatoes.

AVOCADO AND FILLINGS

Split a ripe avocado in half lengthwise and remove seed. Sprinkle cavities and cut edges with lemon juice to prevent darkening. Fill with grapefruit sections or seafood salad or cottage cheese. Serve with French dressing seasoned with a dash of hot pepper sauce.

MELON AND PROSCIUTTO

Cut chilled honeydew melon or cantaloupe into thin wedges. Cover with very thinly sliced prosciutto. Serve with salt, pepper, and lemon or lime wedges.

Variations: Thinly sliced salami, pastrami, dried beef and similar meats may be substituted for the prosciutto. Or use ordinary ham and sprinkle it thickly with coarsely ground pepper.

ANTIPASTO

An antipasto assortment of savory foods can precede a meal, or serve as a light meal, depending on what you put into it and how much of it you eat. A colorful antipasto might begin with artichoke hearts, pepperoni, mushrooms, stuffed olives, tuna fish, anchovies rolled around capers, black olives, sardines, provolone cheese, red and green pickled peppers, and salami. (See photo, page 38.) For more variety choose from celery sticks, radishes, lettuce, scallions, hard-cooked eggs, pickled vegetables, eggplant caponata and chickpeas. Pass the vinegar and oil cruets and the pepper mill to set off your antipasto flavorfully. Your pantry shelf can hold the makings of an antipasto for use when you want it; a delicious and flexible snack meal in reserve.

DILLED CARROT STICKS

2 pounds carrots
¼ cup Worcestershire sauce
½ teaspoon peppercorns
½ teaspoon dill seed
2 bay leaves
1 quart water
2 tablespoons salt
¼ cup vinegar

Peel carrots and cut into sticks. Pack in jars or refrigerator containers. Combine and bring remaining ingredients to a boil, pour over carrots. Let stand 2 days before using. Will keep about 2 weeks. Makes about 2 quarts.

MARINATED ARTICHOKE HEARTS

1 can (1 pound) artichoke hearts
⅓ cup vegetable oil
2 tablespoons lemon juice
2 tablespoons capers, drained
½ teaspoon salt
¼ teaspoon black pepper
½ teaspoon snipped parsley

Drain artichoke hearts, cut into bite-sized pieces. Combine remaining ingredients, simmer 2 minutes. Pour over artichokes, let stand 30 minutes. Serve warm or chilled. Makes 8 hors d'oeuvre servings.

Tip: Use 1 package (10 ounces) frozen artichoke hearts in this recipe. Cook in marinade

Pizzas for a snack or a meal can have more than appetite appeal. They can make a good nutritional package including portions of each of these four basic food groups: bread, vegetable, cheese and meat. Try Pizza with varied toppings, Deep-Dish Pizza, Pizza Loaf.

until just tender. Makes 5 or 6 hors d'oeuvre servings.

BAKED STUFFED MUSHROOMS

20 large mushrooms, caps and stems
4 tablespoons butter or margarine
1 small onion, minced
1 cup coarse bread crumbs
  Salt, pepper, pinch oregano
½ cup grated cheese (Cheddar, Swiss or your choice)
3 tablespoons cooking sherry

Wipe mushroom caps with damp paper towel; wash and chop stems. Melt butter in skillet. Coat the mushroom caps with butter and arrange in shallow baking pan. Add onion and chopped mushroom stems to butter remaining in skillet, cook until golden. Add crumbs, seasonings and cheese. Toss to mix. Stir in sherry. Fill mushroom caps and bake 10 minutes in a hot oven (400°F). Serve immediately. Makes 20 stuffed mushrooms.

QUICK SMORGASBORD

An assortment of herrings in jars and canned sardines, with thin-sliced brown bread and sweet butter, makes a quick smorgasbord.

DEVILED MEATBALLS

1 pound ground beef round
1 teaspoon salt
  Cayenne pepper, nutmeg
¼ cup juice drained from sweet pickle relish
  Oil, butter or margarine for frying
½ beef bouillon cube
½ cup hot water
½ cup sweet pickle relish
¼ cup chili sauce

Blend beef, salt, pinches of cayenne and nutmeg, and pickle juice. Shape into bite-sized balls, brown on all sides in a little oil. Dissolve bouillon cube in hot water, add relish and chili sauce. Add to meatballs in pan, simmer 10 minutes. Makes about 4 dozen meatballs. Serve with picks.

GLAZED HAM SQUARES

Cut leftover ham, or canned ham, into small squares. Dip into bottled Chinese Duck Sauce, arrange on foil-lined baking sheet, heat in moderate oven (350°F). Serve hot, with picks.

FONDUE BOURGUIGNONNE

1½ pounds tender beef
1 cup butter or margarine
⅔ cup vegetable oil
  Assorted steak sauces for dipping

Trim beef and cut it into very thin 1-inch strips. Heat butter and oil in the top pan of a chafing dish over direct heat or in a fondue pot on a table burner. Each guest spears a strip of meat on a long-handled fork, cooks it to taste in the hot fat, and dips in into a choice of sauces placed in small bowls around the fondue pot. Sauces may include any hot or cold steak sauce, bottled or homemade; sour cream mixed with horseradish; mayonnaise flavored with curry or mustard. Small dishes of chopped parsley and chopped onions are also welcome. Makes 8 to 10 appetizer servings.

CUMBERLAND FRANKS

1 pound cocktail franks
½ cup currant jelly
½ teaspoon mustard
1 slice of lemon with peel, finely minced
1 slice onion, finely minced

Steam or pan-brown the franks. Combine remaining ingredients and heat gently. Serve franks with sauce for dipping.

SAUSAGE WHEEL SNACKS

1 pound finely ground pork sausage meat
  Pastry for a 1-crust pie

Roll sausage meat into 3 ropes about 1 inch thick and 10 inches long. Wrap each in thinly rolled pastry. Cut into ½-inch slices. Bake, cut side down, in a hot oven (400°F) about 20 minutes, until the pastry is brown and the sausage is cooked through. Makes about 60 snacks.

FRENCH-TOASTED SAUSAGES

8 slices white bread
8 sausage links, cooked
2 eggs
2 tablespoons milk
  Salt, pepper
  Butter or margarine for browning

Trim crusts from bread, roll a sausage link in each and secure with a toothpick. Beat eggs with milk and salt and pepper to taste. Dip rolls in egg; brown on all sides in a generous amount of butter. Serve with peach halves sprinkled with sugar and cinnamon and broiled.

APPETIZER PUFFS

Make Cream Puff Paste (page 217). Shape walnut-sized balls with a teaspoon on a greased cookie sheet. Bake in a hot oven (400°F) about 20 to 25 minutes, until the puffs are brown and dry. Carefully slice the top from puff, fill with one of the mixtures below, and replace the top. Makes 36 small puffs.

CHOPPED-LIVER FILLING

Moisten 1 cup Chopped Chicken Livers (page 110) to taste with 1 to 2 tablespoons sour cream. Fill 18 small Appetizer Puffs.

SEAFOOD FILLING

Pick over 1 can (about 7 ounces) crab meat (or use tuna or shrimp), chop finely, moisten with 2 tablespoons mayonnaise. Add 2 table-spoons each finely minced celery and parsley and a few drops onion juice. Fill 18 small Appetizer Puffs.

RED-CAVIAR FILLING

Mix 1 jar (3 ounces) red caviar with 1 cup sour cream and 1 teaspoon chopped chives or green-onion tops. Fill 18 Appetizer Puffs, top each with a little more red caviar (a 3- or 4-ounce jar). Tilt top to cover partially.

CHEESE PUFFS

Make paste for Appetizer Puffs (above), but add with the salt pinches of cayenne pepper, black pepper and dry mustard, to taste. After eggs are added, beat in ¾ cup grated cheese (Swiss, Cheddar or other). Bake as directed. Serve warm or reheated. Makes 36 puffs.

PIZZA

Packaged pizza, with dough and topping ingredients ready to use, makes pizza quick and easy. Or you can make your own crust and topping, with endless variations for the latter. (See photo, page 40.)

> 1 envelope active dry yeast
> 1⅓ cups very warm water
> 4 cups flour
> 1½ teaspoons salt
> 2 tablespoons oil
> 1 can (1 pound) pizza sauce
> ½ pound mozzarella cheese, slivered
>   Grated Parmesan or Romano cheese

Dissolve yeast in water, add flour, salt and oil, mix well to make a firm dough. Knead on a floured board until dough is smooth and elastic, and not at all sticky. Let rise, covered, until doubled, 2 hours. Punch down. Divide dough in half. Pat and stretch each half to fit an oiled 12-inch pizza pan. Press dough firmly in pans, making it slightly thicker at the edges and covering the edges of the pan. Spread with prepared pizza sauce, sprinkle with mozzarella and Parmesan cheeses. Bake in a hot oven (425°F) until crust is crisp and brown and cheese is melted, about 25 minutes. Slice and serve hot in pie-shaped wedges.

TUNA-AND-MUSHROOM PIZZA

Make Pizza (above), but cover tomato sauce with 1 can (about 7 ounces) tuna, drained and flaked, and 1 can (4 ounces) sliced mush-rooms, drained. Add cheeses, bake as directed.

PEPPERONI PIZZA

> Pizza dough (above)
> 1 can (6 ounces) tomato paste
> 1 tablespoon oil
> 1 clove garlic, crushed
> 1 teaspoon mixed Italian herbs
> ½ pound pepperoni, sliced thin
> 1 can (4 ounces) sliced mushrooms
> 1 green pepper, slivered
> ½ pound mozzarella cheese, slivered
> ¼ cup grated Parmesan cheese

Line a pair of 12-inch pizza pans with dough, covering edges of pan completely. Mix tomato paste, oil, garlic and herbs, spoon onto center of pizzas, leaving a ½-inch edge uncovered. Arrange pepperoni slices, mushrooms and green pepper in rings on tomato sauce. Sprinkle all with mozzarella and Parmesan cheeses. Bake in a hot oven (425°F) about 25 minutes, until crust is browned and filling is bubbling hot.

PIZZA LOAF

> ½ pound Italian-style sweet sausage
> 1 package (10 ounces) frozen chopped spinach
> 1 egg, beaten
>   Salt
> 8 ounces liverwurst, skinned
> 2 tablespoons milk
> 1 jar (7 ounces) pimientos
> 10 stuffed olives
> 1 package (about 1 pound) complete cheese pizza mix

Slice sausage, brown in a small skillet. Thaw and drain the spinach, mix with egg and salt to taste. Mash the liverwurst and mix it with the milk. Drain and sliver the pimientos. Slice the olives. Prepare pizza dough as directed on the package and set it in a warm place for 5 minutes. Grease a 7½-inch-by-3½-inch loaf pan. Roll out three-quarters of the dough and use it to line the loaf pan. Fill pan with layers of cheese from the pizza package, sausage, ½ cup pizza sauce from the package, spinach, pimientos, liverwurst and olives. Roll out remaining dough, cover filling, crimp edges to seal. Slash top crust to allow steam to escape. Bake in a hot oven (400°F) about 50 minutes, until crust is well browned. Makes 6 servings. (See photo, page 40.)

DEEP-DISH PIZZA

   1 envelope active dry yeast
1¼ cups very warm water
   4 cups flour
   1 egg, beaten
1½ teaspoons salt
   2 tablespoons oil
   2 cans (1 pound each) peeled whole
      tomatoes
   1 can (6 ounces) tomato paste
   2 green peppers, cut in rings
¼ pound mushrooms, sliced
   8 ounces mozzarella cheese, shredded

Dissolve yeast in water; add 2 cups flour, egg, salt and oil. Mix well; work in remaining flour to make a firm dough. Knead on a floured board until dough is smooth and elastic. Let rise, covered, until doubled, about 2 hours. Punch down. Pat and stretch dough to fit an oiled 10-inch-by-15-inch jelly-roll pan. Press dough firmly into pan, making rim slightly thicker and covering the edges of the pan. Drain tomatoes, reserving ½ cup liquid. Mix liquid with tomato paste and spread on dough. Arrange tomatoes, peppers and mushrooms over sauce; sprinkle with cheese. Bake in a hot oven (425°F) about 35 minutes, until crust is brown and cheese is melted. Makes 8 servings. (See photo, page 41.)

CLAM RAFTS

   1 can (8 ounces) minced clams, drained
¾ cup cottage cheese
   6 tablespoons sour cream
   1 teaspoon salt
¼ teaspoon pepper
   Dash cayenne
   6 crisp rye wafers
   Small onion rings
   Chili sauce

Combine clams, cottage cheese, sour cream and seasonings. Spread on crisp rye wafers. Put an onion ring on each wafer, fill ring with chili sauce. Broil 5 to 6 minutes. Makes 6 clam rafts.

ANCHOVIES ON CHEESE TOAST

Cover slices of Italian bread with mozzarella cheese. Top with crossed anchovies, drizzle with a little oil from the anchovies. Toast in oven or under grill for a few minutes, until cheese melts.

BURGER TOASTS

Season ground beef with salt and pepper, add ¼ cup ketchup per pound of beef. Spread meat generously on slices of bread, spreading to the very edge to cover bread completely. Place on buttered pan, broil about 4 inches from heat, about 5 minutes, until meat is browned. Cut each slice in half, serve immediately.

SKILLET-GRILLED SANDWICHES

2 slices bread
1 slice American cheese
2 slices tomato
   Salt, pepper, mustard, mayonnaise
   Butter or margarine or vegetable oil

Make a sandwich with bread, cheese and tomato slices. Add seasoning to taste. Brown on both sides in hot butter in a skillet.

Variations: Spread bread with deviled ham, then add tomatoes and cheese. Or add tuna fish, or slices of cooked ham, salami, chicken, bacon or other meats. Or instead of tomatoes, use cooked asparagus or green beans, or raw sliced radishes, onions or scallions.

SARDINE GRILL

Top a slice of your favorite bread (rye, pumpernickel, French, wheat, toasted English muffin) with cheese. Cover with sardines, season with lemon juice and Worcestershire sauce. Grill under the broiler until cheese melts and sardines are hot.

GRILLED GARDEN SPECIAL

Cut open a frankfurter roll, spread with cream cheese. Top with cucumber slices, diced sweet onion and sliced tomato. Dot with butter, season with salt and pepper. Grill as an open sandwich under the broiler. Or close roll and toast on both sides over hot coals.

MAC HOMEBURGERS

4 sesame-seed hamburger buns, heated
¼ cup mayonnaise
¼ cup chili sauce
1 pound ground beef
8 slices American cheese
   Lettuce
   Pickle slices
   Chopped onions

Split each hamburger bun into thirds, crosswise. Combine mayonnaise and chili sauce. Shape ground beef into 8 thin patties, broil or pan-broil (page 83). Top each patty with slice of cheese, heat to melt. Place patty on bottom third of hamburger bun, top with mayonnaise and chili sauce mixture, lettuce, pickle and chopped onion; repeat layers and cover with top third of bun. Makes 4.

GREAT SOUPS

Soup plays many roles in meal planning. It can be chock-full of meat, vegetables, and pasta or grains, so that it is a meal in itself. Or it can be a lightly garnished consommé, a clear broth to serve as a prelude to a full-course dinner. Most important, soup can be the budget watcher's best friend. A generous serving of soup satisfies appetites and nutritional requirements sufficiently so that you can cut back on the more expensive portions of the meal.

Make the most of soups, whether you prepare your own or rely on the canned and dry-mix varieties. Or enjoy the best of the whole soup world by using all of these alternately or in interesting new combinations.

Soup Stocks

Many recipes in this book call for the use of a cup or two of stock, broth or bouillon for everything from soups to sauces and stews. You can keep stock on your staple shelf in convenient forms: bouillon cubes, dehydrated broth, condensed beef or chicken broth. Or you can make your own very special stock, the natural way, at minimum expense, with bones, scraps of meat, chicken wings, necks, back and gizzards, and odds and ends of vegetables you might otherwise discard. Smart cooks now do both. Use the recipes that follow as helpful guides, not as hard-and-fast rules; vary the ingredients according to what you have on hand.

Tip: If you have a pressure cooker, you can reduce stock-cooking time by as much as two-thirds—and reduce fuel consumption too. Check the manufacturer's instructions for your particular pressure cooker and adjust pressure, cooking time and amounts accordingly.

BEEF STOCK

3 pounds beef and veal bones, cut up
   Meat scraps, as available
3 quarts water
1 teaspoon salt
½ teaspoon peppercorns
3 carrots, sliced
2 celery stalks with leafy tops, cut up
2 bay leaves and 6 sprigs parsley,
   tied together

Put bones and meat scraps into a kettle. Cover with water, add salt, peppercorns, carrots and celery. Bring slowly to a boil, skimming as necessary. Simmer, covered, very slowly, 2½ hours; add bay and parsley, simmer ½ hour longer. Strain stock; chill. Remove fat that rises to the top just before using the stock for soups and sauces; it acts as a protective seal. Makes about 2 quarts beef stock, also called beef broth or bouillon.

Brown Stock: To make beef stock with a dark-brown color, brown the bones in a hot oven (400°F) for about 30 minutes, or in a pan over direct heat, then cover with water and cook as directed.

CHICKEN STOCK

4 pounds chicken trimmings (wings, necks, gizzards)
1 pound veal or beef bones, cut up
3 quarts cold water
1 teaspoon salt

½ teaspoon peppercorns
1 onion, studded with 3 cloves
2 carrots, peeled and sliced
1 herb bouquet (celery tops, parsley, fresh
    dill and a bay leaf, tied together)

Cover chicken parts and bones with water, add salt and peppercorns. Bring to a boil, simmer 30 minutes. Skim. Add onion and carrots, cover, simmer about 1½ hours. Add herb bouquet, simmer 30 minutes longer. Strain stock; chill. Remove surface fat. Makes about 2 quarts chicken stock, also called chicken broth or bouillon.

FISH STOCK

3 pounds fish trimmings or inexpensive
    whole fish
1 onion, sliced
1 bay leaf
1 sprig thyme
10 sprigs parsley
1 carrot
1 teaspoon peppercorns
2 whole cloves
1 teaspoon salt
2 quarts cold water

Put fish and remaining ingredients into water, bring to a boil. Simmer about 1 hour over low heat. Strain stock through a fine sieve. If necessary, boil the liquid rapidly to reduce it to 6 cups. Fish stock is used as a base for fish soups, stews and sauces and to cook fish and seafood.

VEGETABLE STOCK

3 celery stalks, with leaves
3 medium onions
1 cup shredded cabbage
1 turnip
¼ medium head lettuce, shredded
1 large garlic clove
3 cloves
1 teaspoon salt
½ teaspoon peppercorns
1 bay leaf
10 sprigs parsley
2 sprigs thyme
1½ quarts water
1 can (2½ cups) tomato juice or
    3 tomatoes, cut up

Combine all ingredients in a kettle, bring to a boil, lower heat, cover, simmer 1½ hours. Adjust seasonings with salt and pepper. About ¼ to ½ teaspoon monosodium glutamate is an optional addition. Strain stock through a fine sieve. Makes about 1 quart richly flavored base for soups.

Consommés

Clear soups—call them consommé, broth or bouillon—are a perfect first course for a festive meal. Unlike thick soups and richer first courses, they spur the appetite rather than satisfy it.

BEEF CONSOMMÉ

To make consommé from homemade Beef Stock (page 45), chill stock until fat rises to the top and can easily be removed. Add the cracked shells of 2 eggs with the white that clings to them to the stock and bring slowly to a boil, stirring gently. Boil hard for 1 minute, still stirring, then simmer very slowly for 20 minutes. Skim the stock and strain it through a fine-meshed sieve. The particles will adhere to the egg white and the consommé will be perfectly clear.

CHICKEN CONSOMMÉ OR BROTH

Substitute Chicken Stock (page 45) for beef stock in recipe above, clarify as directed.

POT-AU-FEU

Make Beef Stock (page 45), adding to the ingredients a 3-pound piece of beef chuck or round. Clarify the stock as for Beef Consommé (above). Serve clarified soup first, the sliced meat and vegetables as a separate course. More vegetables may be added to the stock for the last hour of cooking.

PETITE MARMITE

Serve the soup from a Pot-au-Feu (above) in individual flameproof casseroles. Top each serving with a toasted slice of French bread, sprinkle with grated Parmesan cheese, brown under the broiler.

CONSOMMÉ BELLEVUE

2½ cups canned clam broth
1 can (10½ ounces) condensed consommé

Heat clam broth with consommé; serve piping hot in bouillon cups. Makes 5 servings.

CONSOMMÉ STRACCIATELLA

5 cups chicken broth
2 eggs
¼ cup grated Parmesan cheese
Lemon slices
Snipped parsley

Heat broth to the simmering point. Beat eggs with cheese, drop into the broth by teaspoons, allowing mixture to set in clumps. Serve garnished with lemon slices and snipped parsley. Makes 6 servings.

FRENCH ONION SOUP

 4 onions
 ¼ cup butter
 1 tablespoon flour
 4 cups hot beef stock
 ¾ teaspoon salt
   Dash pepper
 4 slices French bread, toasted
 4 ounces Parmesan cheese, grated

Slice onions thinly. Melt butter in large saucepan. Cook onions until soft and transparent, stirring often. Stir in flour and cook, stirring, 2 minutes. Add beef stock. Simmer gently 20 minutes. Add salt, pepper. Ladle into flameproof serving bowls. Top each serving with a slice of toasted French bread, sprinkle with grated cheese. Brown cheese under broiler. Serve piping hot. Makes 4 servings.

CHINESE EGG-DROP SOUP

4 cups chicken broth
1 tablespoon cornstarch
2 eggs
  Salt, pepper, soy sauce

Stir a little of the broth with the cornstarch, combine with remaining broth in 2-quart saucepan. Bring to a boil, stirring constantly. Beat eggs lightly and add to broth in a thin stream, stirring the broth constantly with a fork. Add seasonings to taste. Makes 6 servings.

CONSOMMÉ MADRILÈNE

1 envelope unflavored gelatin
1 cup cold water
2 chicken bouillon cubes
1 can (16 ounces) tomato juice
  Dash hot pepper sauce
  Salt, pepper to taste
  Lemon wedges

Sprinkle gelatin on cold water, let stand 5 minutes, stir over low heat until water comes to a boil and gelatin dissolves. Add bouillon cubes and dissolve. Add tomato juice, hot pepper sauce, salt and pepper. Chill until set. Stir with a fork, serve with lemon wedges. Makes 4 servings.

CONSOMMÉ GARNISHES

Serve clear beef or chicken consommé with a garnish of:

Cooked vermicelli or alphabet noodles
Slivered raw celery or carrot
Cooked or raw green peas
Slivered toasted almonds
Popcorn
Croutons
Lemon slices
Chopped parsley, cress, chives
Grated cheese

SPAETZLE

 3 cups flour
 ½ teaspoon baking powder
 1 teaspoon salt
 ¼ teaspoon black pepper
 ¼ teaspoon nutmeg (optional)
 4 eggs
 1 cup water

Toss together flour, baking powder and seasonings in a bowl. Beat eggs with water, add to flour mixture. Blend until batter is smooth. Pour into a colander with large holes held over a pot of boiling salted water or simmering soup. Stir to prevent the tiny dumplings from sticking together. When they rise to the surface, they are cooked. Or drizzle batter off the end of a spoon for less uniform but equally delicious spaetzle. Use as soup garnish or as side dish.

MATZOH BALLS FOR SOUP

 3 eggs, separated
 2 tablespoons chicken fat
 1 teaspoon salt
 ¼ cup water
 ¾ cup matzoh meal

Beat egg yolks until light. Add fat, salt, water, and matzoh meal. Beat egg whites until stiff, fold in. Cover, chill 1 hour. Moisten hands and shape mixture into balls about 1 inch in diameter. Drop into 2 quarts boiling salted water or boiling soup. Cook, covered, about 20 minutes, until balls puff to twice their original size. Makes about 12.

Hearty-Eating Soups

These are soups that make a meal. Add crusty bread and butter, a salad, and a dessert and you have a hearty dinner for the family. Or let the soup make a success of your next party—easy to serve to a crowd, inexpensive, a welcome change from formula party menus.

BLACK-BEAN SOUP

1½ pounds dried black beans
¼ cup butter or margarine
2 carrots, chopped
1 large onion, chopped
¼ cup Worcestershire sauce
2½ quarts water
2 bay leaves
4 chicken bouillon cubes
2 hard-cooked eggs, finely chopped
Thin slices of lemon

Soak the beans overnight, drain. Melt butter in a saucepan, brown carrots and onion. Add beans, Worcestershire sauce, water, bay leaves and bouillon cubes. Bring to a boil and simmer for about 2½ hours or until beans are tender. Discard the bay leaves. Garnish with hard-cooked eggs and a lemon slice. Serves 10.

SENATE BEAN SOUP

This soup is made in the style of the famous Senate Dining Room specialty. Now you can enjoy its rich and satisfying flavor, guaranteed to win votes at home.

1 pound dried white beans (marrow beans or Great Northern)
4 quarts water
Ham bone, with meat
2 medium onions, chopped
¼ cup butter or margarine
Salt, pepper

Cover beans with water in a soup kettle; let stand overnight. Add the ham bone and simmer in the same water, covered, until the beans are very soft, 3 to 4 hours. Skim excess fat. Cook onions in butter until golden, add to soup. Adjust seasoning with salt and pepper. Makes 10 or more servings.

CHICKEN GUMBO

1 chicken, about 4 pounds, cut up
Seasoned flour
¼ cup vegetable oil or fat
1 quart hot water
1 teaspoon salt
1 can (1 pound) tomatoes
2 quarts cold water
1 package (9 ounces) frozen okra
4 tablespoons rice
1 small onion, diced

Dredge chicken in flour seasoned with salt and pepper. Brown on all sides in hot oil in a soup pot. Cover with hot water, add salt, bring to a boil. Simmer, covered, until the chicken is very tender. The time needed will depend on the tenderness of the chicken. Cut up chicken meat, reserve meat and stock. Meanwhile, combine tomatoes and remaining ingredients in a saucepan, bring to a boil, simmer until rice and vegetables are cooked. Add chicken meat and stock, heat. Adjust seasoning with salt, pepper and paprika. Makes 10 or more servings.

MINESTRONE

2 slices bacon, diced
1 garlic clove, minced
1 onion, chopped
2 quarts beef broth
1 cup small pasta shapes (alphabets, Ditalini or Orzo)
1 potato, diced
2 carrots, diced
½ cup shredded cabbage
¼ cup diced celery
1 can (8 ounces) tomato sauce
1 can (1 pound 4 ounces) kidney beans
1 teaspoon salt
⅛ teaspoon pepper
1 tablespoon chopped parsley
½ cup grated Parmesan cheese

Cook bacon in soup pot, add garlic and onion and cook until tender. Add broth, pasta, potato, carrots, cabbage, celery and tomato sauce. Bring to boil and simmer 15 minutes, or until vegetables are just cooked. Add kidney beans, seasonings and parsley. Cook 5 minutes longer. Add cheese. Serve at once. Makes 10 servings.

SCOTCH BROTH

2 pounds lamb bones and trimmings
2 quarts water
1 tablespoon salt
8 peppercorns
1 onion stuck with 4 cloves
½ bay leaf
2 tablespoons butter or margarine
¼ cup each finely cut carrots, celery and turnip
½ teaspoon marjoram
¼ cup barley

Place meaty lamb bones in deep pot. Add cold water to cover meat by 1 inch. Add salt, peppercorns, onion and bay leaf. Bring quickly to boil. Skim. Cover and simmer 1½ hours. Cool. Skim and discard fat. (Or drop ice cubes into hot soup and the fat will collect around them.) Remove bones and dice meat. Strain broth, discard onion and pepper-

Try a new kind of bean dish. Beans represent good value as a practical protein source, especially in combination dishes. Regional favorites such as Hoppin' John, combining black-eyed peas and rice, grow in popularity across the country. (See page 129.)

corns. Heat butter in saucepan, add chopped vegetables and cook, stirring, 5 or 6 minutes. Add marjoram, broth, diced meat and barley. Simmer about 45 minutes, or until vegetables and barley are very tender and soup has thickened. Makes 6 servings. (See photo, page 151.)

Creamed Vegetable Soups

Milk and cream play an important part in these vegetable soups, as a final touch rather than as part of the basic preparation. You will want to serve creamed vegetable soups as the first course at luncheon or another light meal.

CREAM OF GREEN PEA SOUP (POTAGE ST. GERMAIN)

**2 packages (9 ounces each) frozen
    green peas
3 cups chicken broth
1 onion
1 carrot
3 lettuce leaves
¼ cup butter or margarine
1 cup light cream or milk
    Salt, pepper**

Simmer green peas in chicken broth with onion, carrot and lettuce leaves until peas are very soft. Press through a food mill or fine sieve, or purée in an electric blender. Add butter and cream, stir over low heat until hot. If desired, add more chicken broth to thin soup slightly. Adjust seasoning with salt and pepper. Makes 6 servings.

CREAM OF LEEK AND POTATO SOUP

**3 tablespoons butter or margarine
6 leeks or 12 green onions, washed and
    coarsely cut
6 potatoes, peeled and diced
2 onions
1 quart water
1 teaspoon salt
2 cups light cream or milk**

Melt butter in saucepan, add leeks and cook until lightly browned. Add potatoes, onions, water, salt and cream. Bring to a boil, simmer 45 minutes. Press soup through a sieve, or whirl in a blender to make a smooth purée. Heat, serve in cups with a pat of butter floating in each. Makes 6 servings.

FRESH CREAM OF TOMATO SOUP

**5 tablespoons butter or margarine
1 onion, chopped
3 stalks celery, slivered
2 cups fresh tomatoes, peeled, seeded, finely
    chopped
1 teaspoon sugar
3 tablespoons flour
3 cups milk scalded with a bay leaf
    Salt, pepper**

Melt 2 tablespoons butter, cook onion and celery until soft. Add tomatoes, simmer over low heat about 10 minutes. Add sugar. In another pan, melt 3 tablespoons butter, stir in flour, and cook, stirring, until blended. Gradually stir in milk, discarding the bay leaf. Cook, stirring, until sauce is smooth and thickened. Stir in hot tomato mixture (it may be strained, if desired) and add salt and pepper to taste. Makes 5 servings.

NEW ENGLAND PUMPKIN SOUP

**1 cup cooked, mashed pumpkin
2½ cups chicken broth
2 egg yolks
½ cup heavy cream
    Salt, pepper, nutmeg
    Chopped parsley or chives for garnish
    Paprika**

Force pumpkin through a sieve, or whirl in blender. Combine with broth and heat to boiling. Beat egg yolks with cream, combine with hot soup. Heat without boiling. Add salt, pepper and nutmeg to taste. Serve garnished with herbs and a dash of paprika. Makes 5 to 6 servings.

PEANUT SOUP

**½ cup butter or margarine
2 tablespoons flour
½ cup peanut butter
1 quart chicken broth
½ cup light cream
    Salt**

Melt butter in large saucepan, add flour, and cook, stirring, until blended. Stir in peanut butter and blend well. Add chicken broth and simmer 30 minutes. Add cream and salt to taste. Makes 4 to 6 servings.

SPINACH VELVET SOUP

**2 tablespoons butter or margarine
1 small onion, minced
1 tablespoon flour**

In Boston, Clam Chowder is creamy white; in Manhattan it is ruddy with tomatoes. Scotch Broth is a hearty soup or main course that makes thrifty use of lamb bones and trimmings. Enjoy soup, homemade or quickly heated, at any meal. (See Great Soups, pages 45–55.)

2½ cups milk
  1 chicken bouillon cube
  1 cup cooked spinach, puréed
    Salt, pepper

Heat butter in a saucepan. Add onion and cook a few minutes. Stir in flour and allow onion and flour to brown lightly. Add milk and cook, stirring, until thickened. Add bouillon cube and spinach. Simmer 2 to 3 minutes. Season with salt and pepper. Makes 4 servings.

CHEDDAR-CHEESE SOUP

  2 tablespoons butter or margarine
  2 tablespoons flour
  1 teaspoon salt
    Pinch of cayenne
  ½ teaspoon mustard
  2 cups milk
  ½ cup water
  1 vegetable bouillon cube
2½ cups grated Cheddar cheese
  4 slices French bread, toasted

Melt the butter in a pan over low heat. Stir in flour and seasonings. Add milk, blend. Cook, stirring constantly, until mixture comes to a boil. Simmer 2 minutes. Add water, bouillon cube and cheese, heat until cheese melts. Serve in deep bowls with a slice of toast floating on each portion. Makes 4 servings.

Hearty Fish Soups

Fish chowders and stews have a double function: in small portions they make a pleasant first course, particularly when a fish main course follows; in larger portions, they can become the main dish.

NEW ENGLAND CLAM CHOWDER

  2 cubes salt pork or 2 strips bacon, diced
  ⅓ cup chopped onion
  ¼ cup diced celery
  2 potatoes, diced
  1 cup boiling water
  1 teaspoon salt
    White pepper
  1 can (8 ounces) minced clams
1½ cups milk

Brown salt pork or bacon lightly in a saucepan. Add onion, cook in pork fat until lightly golden. Add celery, potatoes, water and seasonings. Bring to a boil and cook 15 minutes, until potatoes are tender. Add liquid from

clams and milk. Heat slowly, but do not boil. Add clams and heat. Makes 5 servings. (See photo, page 51.)

MANHATTAN CLAM CHOWDER

2 tablespoons butter or margarine
1 onion, chopped
1 green pepper, diced
2 stalks celery, diced
2 potatoes, diced
1 can (1 pound) tomatoes
1 can (8 ounces) minced clams
  Thyme, salt, pepper

Melt butter in saucepan, add onion, green pepper and celery, cook until onion is transparent. Meanwhile, cook potatoes in water to cover for 5 minutes. Measure potato water and add boiling water to make 2 cups. Add potatoes and water to pan. Add tomatoes and liquid from clams, bring to a boil, simmer 5 minutes. Season to taste with thyme, salt and pepper. Add clams, heat. Makes 4 servings. (See photo, page 51.)

SALMON CHOWDER

  1 can (1 pound) salmon
  ¼ cup butter or margarine
  1 onion, chopped
  3 tablespoons flour
  1 cup water
  1 can (1 pound) tomatoes
  3 cups milk
    Salt, pepper

Drain salmon and flake, discarding bones and skin. Melt butter, cook onion until golden, stir in flour, cook 2 minutes. Add water and tomatoes and cook, stirring, until thickened. Add milk, heat. Add salmon, heat through. Adjust seasoning with salt and pepper. Makes 6 servings.

BOUILLABAISSE AMERICAN STYLE

4 pounds assorted fish and shellfish
4 tablespoons vegetable oil
2 onions, diced
2 cloves garlic, crushed
1 can (1 pound) stewed tomatoes
2 tablespoons chopped parsley
  Salt, pepper, thyme, paprika, saffron
6 to 8 slices French bread, toasted

An American bouillabaisse may include equal amounts of several varieties of fish and shellfish: choose shrimp, rock lobster, clams, mussels, haddock, cod, turbot, sea bass, whiting or others. Use fish fillets and shelled seafood for easier eating. Heat oil, cook onions and garlic lightly. Add tomatoes, parsley and seasonings. Bring to a boil, simmer 5 minutes. Adjust seasoning. Lay fish in the pan, add cold water barely to cover. Cover the pan and simmer until fish is cooked, about 15 minutes. Serve in soup plates, over toasted slices of French bread. Makes 6 to 8 servings.

Note: If shrimp, clams or oysters are used, add them for the final 5 minutes of cooking.

LOBSTER STEW

  1 pound cooked lobster meat
¼ cup butter or margarine
4 cups milk
2 cups light cream
  Salt, pepper, paprika

Dice lobster meat and heat gently in melted butter. Heat milk and cream together, add. Heat gently, stirring constantly. Adjust seasoning. Makes 6 servings.

OYSTER STEW

1 quart oysters
  Oyster liquid plus milk to make 4 cups
2 cups light cream
  Salt, pepper, paprika

Follow procedure for Lobster Stew (above). Makes 6 servings.

Fish Bisques

Like creamed vegetable soups, creamed fish and seafood soups should precede a light main course rather than a rich roast.

CLAM BISQUE

  2 cans (8 ounces each) minced clams
3 potatoes, chopped
1 onion, chopped
1 quart scalded milk
1 bay leaf
1 clove
  Salt, pepper, nutmeg
½ cup heavy cream, heated
  2 tablespoons butter or margarine

Drain liquid from clams. Cook chopped potatoes and onion in clam liquid until tender. Add milk, bay leaf and clove, bring quickly to a boil. Discard bay leaf and clove and rub bisque through a fine sieve, or purée

it in an electric blender. Add minced clams, heat. Season with salt, pepper and nutmeg to taste. Add cream slowly, stirring constantly over low heat. Just before serving, stir in butter. Makes 5 servings.

Oyster Bisque: Substitute 1 pint of oysters for the clams. Add water to oyster liquor to make 1 cup liquid to substitute for clam liquid.

Summer Soups

Cold soups may be served in the wintertime, of course, but they taste their refreshing best when the temperature is high. They range in flavor from the Gazpacho, which is in effect a salad soup, to the creamy richness of Vichyssoise.

CURRIED CREAM OF CHICKEN SOUP

4 cups chicken broth
½ teaspoon curry powder (or more to taste)
4 egg yolks
1 cup half-and-half or milk
  Chopped chives

Season broth with curry powder. Beat egg yolks, add milk. Stir into broth and cook, stirring constantly, until slightly thickened. Do not boil. Serve very cold, sprinkled with chopped chives. Makes 6 servings.

GAZPACHO

2¼ cups chicken broth
  2 tablespoons lemon juice
  2 tablespoons vegetable oil
  1 sweet red onion, cut
  1 green pepper, seeded, cut
  1 clove garlic
  1 cucumber, peeled, cut
  3 tomatoes, cut and seeded
  2 cups tomato juice
    Salt, black pepper, hot pepper sauce

Combine chicken broth in blender jar with all ingredients except tomatoes, tomato juice and seasonings. Whirl until very smooth. Add tomatoes, whirl just until finely chopped. Add tomato juice and seasonings to taste; shake or stir. Chill thoroughly before serving, over ice cubes, if desired, or with croutons. Makes 6 to 8 servings.

Note: If you have no blender, the vegetables may be very finely chopped with a knife.

BORSCHT

2 bunches large beets (about 10)
1 large onion, chopped
3 quarts water
2 tablespoons vinegar
1 tablespoon sugar
  Salt, pepper
3 eggs, beaten
  Sour cream

Peel the beets and cut them in thick slices. Add beets and onion to water, bring to a boil, simmer for 45 minutes. Add vinegar, sugar, salt and pepper; taste and add more of each, if necessary, until the mixture has a sweet-sour taste that suits your palate. Simmer gently for 30 minutes, until the beets are very tender. Add a little of the hot soup to the beaten eggs and beat them into the borscht. Serve cold, with a spoonful of sour cream in each plate. Makes 12 servings. Borscht keeps well in the refrigerator for as long as 2 weeks.

VICHYSSOISE

¼ cup butter or margarine
 2 cups chopped onions
¼ cup chopped scallions
 4 medium potatoes, sliced
 4 cups chicken broth
 1 teaspoon salt
⅛ teaspoon pepper
 1 cup light cream
  Snipped chives or scallion greens

Melt butter, add onions and scallions and cook until tender, but not brown. Add remaining ingredients except cream and garnish, cook until potatoes are tender, about 15 minutes. Force the soup through a fine-meshed sieve or a food mill, or whirl in an electric blender. Cool, add cream. Chill. Serve sprinkled with snipped chives or scallion greens. Makes 6 servings.

Easy Souping

Condensed canned soups and dehydrated soup mixes are the answer to the harried housewife's prayer. The combinations that follow will suggest many more variations that you can adapt to foods on hand.

BUTTERMILK SOUP

  1 can (10½ ounces) condensed tomato soup
  2 cups chilled buttermilk
½ bunch watercress, finely chopped

Combine soup and buttermilk, whisking to blend. Add watercress, chill. Makes 4 servings.

QUICK MANHATTAN CLAM CHOWDER

1 can (10¾ ounces) condensed vegetable
  soup
1 can (about 8 ounces) minced clams

Put vegetable soup into saucepan; drain liquid from clams into soup can, fill with water, add to saucepan. Bring to a boil over low heat, stirring occasionally. Add clams, heat without boiling. Makes 2 or 3 servings.

TOMATO-CHICKEN NOODLE SOUP

1 envelope (4 ounces) noodle soup mix
2 cups tomato juice
2 cups boiling water
  Chopped parsley

Combine soup mix, tomato juice and water in a large saucepan and bring to a boil. Simmer 7 minutes over low heat. Sprinkle with chopped parsley. Makes 5 servings.

QUICK ONION SOUP

1 envelope (2¾ ounces) onion soup mix
4 cups boiling water
5 thick slices toasted French bread
5 tablespoons grated cheese

Add onion soup mix to boiling water. Simmer 8 to 10 minutes over low heat. Pour into 5 flameproof soup bowls, top each with toasted French bread and sprinkle with cheese. Place under broiler 1 minute or until cheese melts. Makes 5 servings.

MULLIGATAWNY SOUP

1 tablespoon butter or margarine
1 teaspoon curry powder
2 cans (10½ ounces each) condensed
  chicken-rice soup
1 soup can milk or cream

Melt butter, add curry powder and cook for a minute, stirring, until odor is very strong. Add soup, heat to boiling. Add milk, heat gently without boiling. Makes 4 servings.

SOUP POT SUPREME

1 can (10½ ounces) condensed chicken-
  noodle soup
1 cup cooked vegetables, drained
1 soup can water

Empty soup into saucepan. Add vegetables

and water. Heat, stirring occasionally, until bubbling hot. Makes 3 to 4 servings.

OLD-FASHIONED CHICKEN-VEGETABLE SOUP

1 envelope (4 ounces) noodle soup mix
1 can (5½ ounces) chicken, cut up
1 can (8 ounces) stewed tomatoes
1 cup cooked mixed vegetables
3 cups water

Combine all ingredients in a saucepan and bring to a boil. Simmer 5 to 7 minutes over low heat. Makes 6 servings.

BAYOU CHICKEN BOWL

2 thin slices cooked ham
1 can (10¾ ounces) condensed chicken-vegetable soup
1 soup can water
½ cup cooked rice
1 tablespoon chopped parsley

Dice ham; combine in saucepan with soup, water, rice and parsley. Bring to boil, stirring once or twice. Makes 3 servings.

CHICKEN-VEGETABLE SOUP ITALIANO

2 tablespoons salad oil
1 small onion, chopped
1 can (10¾ ounces) condensed chicken-vegetable soup
1 can (8 ounces) tomatoes
1 cup water
⅛ teaspoon basil
Grated Parmesan cheese

Heat oil in soup pan; cook onion until soft. Add soup, tomatoes, water and basil. Heat, stirring occasionally, until bubbling. Serve sprinkled with cheese. Makes 4 servings.

CHICKEN-MUSHROOM CHOWDER

2 tablespoons butter or margarine
¼ cup finely chopped onion

1 can (10½ ounces) condensed cream of mushroom soup
1 can (10¾ ounces) condensed chicken-vegetable soup
1 soup can milk
1 soup can water

Heat butter in saucepan, cook onion until soft. Add cream of mushroom soup, stir smooth. Stir in chicken-vegetable soup, milk and water. Heat, stirring occasionally, until bubbling. Makes 6 servings.

TOMATO CHOWDER

1 can (10½ ounces) condensed tomato soup
1 cup cooked or canned mixed vegetables
½ soup can milk
½ soup can water (or vegetable liquid)

Empty soup into saucepan. Add vegetables, milk and water. Heat, stirring occasionally, until bubbling hot. Makes 4 servings.

FRANKS 'N TOMATO SOUP

1 can (10½ ounces) condensed tomato soup
1 soup can water
2 frankfurters, sliced
3 tablespoons grated American cheese

Empty soup into saucepan. Add water and frankfurter slices. Heat, stirring occasionally, until bubbling hot. Top each serving with grated cheese. Makes 3 servings.

PURÉE MONGOL

1 can (11¼ ounces) condensed green pea soup
1 can (10½ ounces) condensed tomato soup
2 soup cans water
Slivered ham or celery or croutons for garnish

Blend soups and water, stir over low heat until bubbling hot. Garnish to taste. Makes 6 servings.

MEAT

Meat is an important feature in the diet of most American families, and, therefore, it is vital to know how to get the most for your meat dollar. While economy does not preclude the family's favorite steaks and roasts, it is also important to know how to turn the less expensive cuts into appetizing meals. The intent of this chapter is to help you on both counts.

More for Your Meat Dollar

You can buy more for your meat dollar in numbers of servings, in nutrition and in eating pleasure, too, if you take full advantage of what's offered in the meat cases. Since meat is often the most expensive item on the shopping list, economies in this department pay off in significant savings. Check weekly meat specials and supplies before you plan your meat meals. With careful shopping, you can save up to 30% on meat purchases.

In order to realize these savings, shop all the meat cases, choosing not just beef, and not just the most popular 25% of the beef cuts—that is, tender roasts and steaks. With know-how, you can prepare other cuts of beef, including less expensive chuck and round, in oven, broiler or skillet. And you can use sale-priced pork, lamb, poultry and fish as alternates to beef.

The more tender cuts of beef come from the less exercised parts, particularly the loin and rib sections. All meat from younger animals, such as pork and lamb, is tender.

The recipes in this chapter are divided according to the method of cooking. Roasts are grouped together, as are casseroles, skillet dishes, pot roasts, ground-meat dishes, steaks, barbecues, leftovers. Each of these can be prepared with your moneysaving choice of meat.

The best buy in a meat cut is generally the largest you can use within a few days, or freeze in meal portions. Your meat department will divide a large roast for you. Or practice your own cutting techniques on the uncooked meat at home to separate larger pieces of meat into practical meal units, at practical price savings. The recipes in this book are designed to show you how to make the most of complete cuts as you buy them. Make the most of all your purchases by using all the meat you buy. Bones, leftovers, even drippings, are a bonus. You can save still more by taking advantage of *all* the variety of cuts available, and of *all* the parts—including tongue, liver and heart.

"Specials" on Super Right meats offer economy for any cut, but the savings are most dramatic when more expensive cuts go on sale. Watch particularly for sales of such family-pleasing treats as rib roast and porterhouse steaks.

Plan the week's menus and make out your shopping list *after* you have checked the weekly advertisements.

To a gourmet, oxtail ragout is a great treat; to a thrifty shopper, oxtail stew is an inexpensive, tasty meal. However, bear in mind that the cost of meat on the fork may be higher than it seems when there is a high proportion of bone and fat.

Compare the cost of varied cuts of meat by considering the price of each portion rather than the price per pound. In planning your shopping list, use the following guide, modified according to your own family's tastes and appetites.

Purchase	Yield
1 pound boneless low-fat meat, such as lean meat cubes or roast	3–4 portions
1 pound boneless fatty meat	2–4 portions
1 pound small-bone meat, such as blade roast or chops	2 portions
¾–1 pound bony meat, such as spareribs	1 portion

Sensible cooking practices can make meat go further. Even bony meat extends to 3 servings per pound if it is cooked with vegetables, rice or pasta in a stew or a skillet dish. In such preparations the vegetable proteins extend the meat protein values.

To judge yield per pound of ground meat, be guided by the amount of fat it contains. Ground round is about 10% leaner than ground meat mixture or chuck, and will shrink proportionally less in cooking.

Soy protein reduces shrinkage and helps make more portions from each pound of chopped meat you buy. In addition, when the soy protein is combined with meat protein, it acts as a complete protein. The soy protein portion is lower in calories and lower in saturated fats than is the meat portion.

What Price Meat Servings

The table* on pages 58–61 enables you to compare the costs of various cuts of beef, pork, lamb, veal, poultry and fish. It shows the approximate cost of 3-ounce servings of cooked lean meat from selected cuts of meat at various prices per pound.

To use this table, locate the kind and cut you plan to buy, and follow the line on which it appears to the column headed by the price most like the current price at your market. The figure at this point is the approximate cost of a 3-ounce serving of cooked, boneless, lean meat.

"Super Right" Quality

The most exacting meat standards are used in selecting the carcasses that become the cuts in the A&P meat cases. Meat that bears the

* Source: U.S. Department of Agriculture, *The 1974 Yearbook of Agriculture.*

Super Right label is guaranteed to offer satisfaction. The conformation of the meat and its degree of finish (the amount, color and distribution of fat) must measure up to A&P specifications. The result—full value, attractive prices and fine eating quality. And remember our Butchers' Pledge: to pack the better side of every cut down. The side you can't see looks even better than the side you can see!

MEAT AND POULTRY STORAGE PERIOD
(To maintain quality)

	REFRIGERATOR 35° to 40°F	FREEZER 0°F
Fresh Meats	Days	Months
Roasts (Beef and Lamb)	3 to 5	8 to 12
Roasts (Pork and Veal)	3 to 5	4 to 8
Steaks (Beef)	3 to 5	8 to 12
Chops (Lamb and Pork)	3 to 5	3 to 4
Ground and Stew Meats	1 to 2	2 to 3
Variety Meats	1 to 2	3 to 4
Sausage (Pork)	1 to 2	1 to 2
Processed Meats		
Bacon	7	1
Frankfurters	7	½
Ham (Whole)	7	1 to 2
Ham (Half)	3 to 5	1 to 2
Ham (Slices)	3	1 to 2
Luncheon Meats	3 to 5	Freezing not recommended
Sausage (Smoked)	7	
Sausage (Dry and Semi-Dry)	14 to 21	
Cooked Meats		
Cooked Meats and Meat Dishes	1 to 2	2 to 3
Gravy and Meat Broth	1 to 2	2 to 3
Fresh Poultry		
Chicken and Turkey (Whole)	1 to 2	12
Chicken and Turkey (Pieces)	1 to 2	6
Duck and Goose (Whole)	1 to 2	6
Giblets	1 to 2	3
Cooked Poultry		
Pieces (Covered with Broth)	1 to 2	6
Pieces (Not Covered)	1 to 2	1
Cooked Poultry Dishes	1 to 2	6
Fried Chicken	1 to 2	4

Cost of 3 ounces of cooked lean from selected kinds and cuts of meat, poultry and fish at specified retail prices

KIND OF CUT	PRICE PER POUND[1] (DOLLARS)																
	.30	.40	.50	.60	.70	.80	.90	1.00	1.10	1.20	1.30	1.40	1.50	1.60	1.70	1.80	1.90

Cost of 3 ounces (dollars)

KIND OF CUT	.30	.40	.50	.60	.70	.80	.90	1.00	1.10	1.20	1.30	1.40	1.50	1.60	1.70	1.80	1.90
Beef: Brisket, bone out	.12	.16	.20	.24	.28	.33	.37	.41	.45	.49	.53	.57	.61	.65	.69	.73	.78
Chuck, bone in	.13	.18	.22	.27	.31	.36	.40	.45	.49	.54	.58	.62	.67	.71	.76	.80	.85
Chuck, bone out	.10	.14	.17	.21	.24	.28	.31	.35	.38	.42	.45	.48	.52	.56	.59	.62	.66
Ground lean	.08	.10	.13	.16	.18	.21	.23	.26	.29	.31	.34	.36	.39	.42	.44	.47	.49
Porterhouse steak, bone in	.16	.21	.26	.31	.36	.42	.47	.52	.57	.62	.68	.73	.78	.83	.88	.94	.99
Rib roast, bone in	.13	.18	.22	.27	.31	.36	.40	.45	.49	.54	.58	.62	.67	.71	.76	.80	.85
Round, bone in	.10	.13	.17	.20	.23	.27	.30	.34	.37	.40	.44	.47	.50	.54	.57	.60	.64
Round, bone out	.09	.12	.16	.19	.22	.25	.28	.31	.34	.37	.40	.44	.47	.50	.53	.56	.59
Rump roast, bone out	.10	.14	.17	.20	.24	.27	.31	.34	.38	.41	.44	.48	.51	.54	.58	.61	.65
Short ribs	.18	.23	.29	.35	.41	.47	.53	.59	.64	.70	.76	.82	.88	.94	1.00	1.05	1.11
Sirloin steak, bone in	.13	.17	.21	.26	.30	.34	.38	.43	.47	.51	.55	.60	.64	.68	.72	.77	.81
Sirloin steak, bone out	.12	.16	.20	.23	.27	.31	.35	.39	.43	.47	.51	.55	.59	.62	.66	.70	.74
T-bone steak, bone in	.17	.22	.28	.33	.38	.44	.50	.55	.61	.66	.72	.77	.83	.88	.94	.99	1.05
Fish: Fillets, fresh or frozen	.09	.12	.15	.18	.20	.23	.26	.29	.32	.35	.38	.41	.44	.47	.50	.53	.56
Steaks, fresh or frozen, backbone in	.10	.13	.16	.19	.23	.26	.29	.32	.36	.39	.42	.45	.48	.52	.55	.58	.61
Tuna, canned[1]	.08	.11	.14	.16	.19	.22	.24	.27	.30	.33	.35	.38	.41	.44	.46	.49	.52
Lamb: Leg roast, bone in	.13	.17	.21	.25	.29	.33	.38	.42	.46	.50	.54	.58	.62	.67	.71	.75	.79
Loin chop, bone in	.14	.18	.23	.27	.32	.36	.41	.46	.50	.55	.59	.64	.68	.73	.78	.82	.87
Rib chop, bone in	.17	.22	.28	.33	.38	.44	.50	.55	.61	.66	.72	.77	.83	.88	.94	.99	1.05
Shoulder roast, bone in	.14	.18	.23	.27	.32	.36	.41	.46	.50	.55	.59	.64	.68	.73	.78	.82	.87
Liver: Beef	.08	.11	.14	.16	.19	.22	.24	.27	.30	.33	.35	.38	.41	.44	.46	.49	.52
Chicken	.09	.12	.14	.17	.20	.23	.26	.29	.32	.34	.37	.40	.43	.46	.49	.52	.55
Pork: Butt, cured, bone in	.11	.14	.18	.22	.25	.29	.32	.36	.40	.43	.47	.50	.54	.58	.61	.65	.68
Ham, cured: whole, bone in	.10	.14	.17	.21	.24	.28	.31	.35	.38	.42	.45	.48	.52	.56	.59	.62	.66
whole, bone out	.08	.10	.13	.16	.18	.21	.23	.26	.29	.31	.34	.36	.39	.42	.44	.47	.49
slices	.09	.12	.16	.19	.22	.25	.28	.31	.34	.37	.40	.44	.47	.50	.53	.56	.59
canned	.08	.10	.12	.15	.18	.20	.22	.25	.28	.30	.32	.35	.38	.40	.42	.45	.48
Loin, fresh: chops, bone in	.13	.18	.22	.27	.31	.36	.40	.45	.49	.54	.58	.62	.67	.71	.76	.80	.85
roast, bone in	.15	.20	.25	.30	.35	.40	.46	.51	.56	.61	.66	.71	.76	.81	.86	.91	.96
roast, bone out	.10	.14	.17	.21	.24	.28	.31	.35	.38	.42	.45	.48	.52	.56	.59	.62	.66
Picnics: cured, bone in	.14	.18	.23	.27	.32	.36	.41	.46	.50	.55	.59	.64	.68	.73	.78	.82	.87
cured, bone out	.11	.14	.18	.21	.25	.28	.32	.35	.39	.42	.46	.50	.53	.57	.60	.64	.67
fresh, bone in	.16	.21	.27	.32	.38	.43	.48	.54	.59	.64	.70	.75	.80	.86	.91	.96	1.02
Rib chops, fresh, bone in	.15	.20	.25	.30	.35	.40	.46	.51	.56	.61	.66	.71	.76	.81	.86	.91	.96

Cost of 3 ounces of cooked lean from selected kinds and cuts of meat, poultry and fish at specified retail prices

KIND OF CUT	PRICE PER POUND[1] (DOLLARS)												
	2.00	2.10	2.20	2.30	2.40	2.50	2.60	2.70	2.80	2.90	3.00	3.10	3.20
Cost of 3 ounces (dollars)													
Beef: Brisket,													
bone out	.82	.86	.90	.94	.98	1.02	1.06	1.10	1.14	1.18	1.22	1.26	1.31
Chuck, bone in	.89	.94	.98	1.02	1.07	1.12	1.16	1.20	1.25	1.29	1.34	1.38	1.43
Chuck, bone out	.69	.73	.76	.80	.83	.87	.90	.94	.97	1.01	1.04	1.08	1.11
Ground lean	.52	.55	.57	.60	.62	.65	.68	.70	.73	.75	.78	.81	.83
Porterhouse steak,													
bone in	1.04	1.09	1.15	1.20	1.25	1.30	1.35	1.41	1.46	1.51	1.56	1.62	1.67
Rib roast, bone in	.89	.94	.98	1.02	1.07	1.12	1.16	1.20	1.25	1.29	1.34	1.38	1.43
Round, bone in	.67	.70	.74	.77	.80	.84	.87	.90	.94	.97	1.00	1.04	1.07
Round, bone out	.62	.66	.69	.72	.75	.78	.81	.84	.87	.90	.94	.97	1.00
Rump roast,													
bone out	.68	.72	.75	.78	.82	.85	.89	.92	.95	.99	1.02	1.06	1.09
Short ribs	1.17	1.23	1.29	1.35	1.41	1.46	1.52	1.58	1.64	1.70	1.76	1.82	1.88
Sirloin steak,													
bone in	.85	.89	.94	.98	1.02	1.06	1.11	1.15	1.19	1.24	1.28	1.32	1.36
Sirloin steak,													
bone out	.78	.82	.86	.90	.94	.98	1.02	1.06	1.09	1.13	1.17	1.21	1.25
T-bone steak,													
bone in	1.10	1.16	1.21	1.27	1.32	1.38	1.43	1.49	1.54	1.60	1.65	1.71	1.76
Fish: Fillets, fresh													
or frozen	.59	.62	.64	.67	.70	.73	.76	.79	.82	.85	.88	.91	.94
Steaks, fresh													
or frozen,													
backbone in	.65	.68	.71	.74	.78	.81	.84	.87	.90	.94	.97	1.00	1.03
Tuna, canned[1]	.55	.57	.60	.63	.66	.68	.71	.74	.76	.79	.82	.85	.87
Lamb: Leg roast,													
bone in	.83	.88	.92	.96	1.00	1.04	1.08	1.12	1.17	1.21	1.25	1.29	1.33
Loin chop,													
bone in	.91	.96	1.00	1.05	1.10	1.14	1.19	1.23	1.28	1.32	1.37	1.42	1.46
Rib chop, bone in	1.10	1.16	1.21	1.27	1.32	1.38	1.43	1.49	1.54	1.60	1.65	1.71	1.76
Shoulder roast,													
bone in	.91	.96	1.00	1.05	1.10	1.14	1.19	1.23	1.28	1.32	1.37	1.42	1.46
Liver: Beef	.54	.57	.60	.62	.65	.68	.71	.73	.76	.79	.82	.84	.87
Chicken	.58	.60	.63	.66	.69	.72	.75	.78	.81	.84	.86	.89	.92
Pork: Butt, cured,													
bone in	.72	.76	.79	.83	.87	.90	.94	.97	1.01	1.05	1.08	1.12	1.16
Ham, cured:													
whole, bone in	.69	.73	.76	.80	.83	.87	.90	.94	.97	1.01	1.04	1.08	1.11
whole, bone out	.52	.55	.57	.60	.62	.65	.68	.70	.73	.75	.78	.81	.83
slices	.62	.66	.69	.72	.75	.78	.81	.84	.87	.90	.94	.97	1.00
canned	.50	.52	.55	.58	.60	.62	.65	.68	.70	.72	.75	.78	.80
Loin, fresh:													
chops, bone in	.89	.94	.98	1.02	1.07	1.12	1.16	1.20	1.25	1.29	1.34	1.38	1.43
roast, bone in	1.01	1.06	1.12	1.17	1.22	1.27	1.32	1.37	1.42	1.47	1.52	1.57	1.62
roast, bone out	.69	.73	.76	.80	.83	.87	.90	.94	.97	1.01	1.04	1.08	1.11
Picnics:													
cured, bone in	.91	.96	1.00	1.05	1.10	1.14	1.19	1.23	1.28	1.32	1.37	1.42	1.46
cured, bone out	.71	.74	.78	.81	.85	.88	.92	.96	.99	1.03	1.06	1.10	1.13
fresh, bone in	1.07	1.12	1.18	1.23	1.29	1.34	1.39	1.45	1.50	1.55	1.61	1.66	1.72
Rib chops, fresh,													
bone in	1.01	1.06	1.12	1.17	1.22	1.27	1.32	1.37	1.42	1.47	1.52	1.57	1.62

KIND OF CUT	PRICE PER POUND[1] (DOLLARS)																
	.30	.40	.50	.60	.70	.80	.90	1.00	1.10	1.20	1.30	1.40	1.50	1.60	1.70	1.80	1.90

Cost of 3 ounces (dollars)

KIND OF CUT	.30	.40	.50	.60	.70	.80	.90	1.00	1.10	1.20	1.30	1.40	1.50	1.60	1.70	1.80	1.90
Poultry: Chicken, whole, ready-to-cook	.14	.19	.23	.28	.32	.37	.42	.46	.51	.56	.60	.65	.70	.74	.79	.84	.88
Turkey, whole, ready-to-cook	.14	.19	.23	.28	.33	.38	.42	.47	.52	.56	.61	.66	.70	.75	.80	.84	.89
Veal: Chuck roast, bone in	.14	.19	.23	.28	.33	.38	.42	.47	.52	.56	.61	.66	.70	.75	.80	.84	.89
Leg roast, bone in	.16	.21	.26	.31	.36	.42	.47	.52	.57	.62	.68	.73	.78	.83	.88	.94	.99
Loin chop, bone in	.12	.16	.20	.24	.28	.32	.36	.40	.44	.48	.52	.56	.60	.64	.68	.72	.76
Rib chop, bone in	.15	.20	.25	.30	.34	.39	.44	.49	.54	.59	.64	.69	.74	.79	.84	.89	.94

1 For tuna fish, use price for 13-ounce can.

ROASTING TIMETABLE
Oven Temperature Moderately Slow (325°F)

Cut	MINUTES PER POUND		
	Rare	*Medium*	*Well Done*
Beef Roasts with bone (Standing Rib, Blade Roast, etc.)	18 to 20 (140°F Int. Temp.)	22 to 26 (160°F Int. Temp.)	28 to 30 (170°F Int. Temp.)
Boneless Beef Roasts (Rolled Rib, Tenderized Rolled Chuck, Round or Eye Round Roasts)	30 to 33 (140°F Int. Temp.)	34 to 37 (160°F Int. Temp.)	38 to 42 (170°F Int. Temp.)
Pork Loin or Shoulder Roasts			35 to 40 (185°F Int. Temp.)
Fresh Ham			30 to 35 (185°F Int. Temp.)
Pork Spareribs			40 to 45 (185°F Int. Temp.)
Boned Pork Shoulder Boned Tenderloin			40 to 45 (185°F Int. Temp.)
Ready-to-Cook or Parboiled Regular Ham			12 to 15 (165°F Int. Temp.)
Ready-to-Eat Ham			8 to 10 (155°F Int. Temp.)
Leg of Lamb or Shoulder Square-Cut	25 to 27 (155°–160°F Int. Temp.)	28 to 31 (165°–170°F Int. Temp.)	32 to 34 (175°–180°F Int. Temp.)
Boned Leg, Cushion Roast or Rolled Breast of Lamb	25 to 29 (155°–160°F Int. Temp.)	30 to 34 (165°–170°F Int. Temp.)	35 to 42 (175°–180°F Int. Temp.)
Leg of Veal, Standing Rump, Veal Shoulder, Breast			30 to 35 (170°F Int. Temp.)
Boneless Veal Roasts			35 to 40 (170°F Int. Temp.)
Meat Loaf		About 1 hour	
Crown Roast of Pork			35 to 40 (185°F Int. Temp.)
Crown Roast of Lamb		About 1 hour	

KIND OF CUT	PRICE PER POUND[1] (DOLLARS)												
	2.00	2.10	2.20	2.30	2.40	2.50	2.60	2.70	2.80	2.90	3.00	3.10	3.20
	Cost of 3 ounces (dollars)												
Poultry: Chicken, whole, ready-to-cook	.93	.98	1.02	1.07	1.12	1.16	1.21	1.26	1.30	1.35	1.40	1.44	1.49
Turkey, whole, ready-to-cook	.94	.98	1.03	1.08	1.12	1.17	1.22	1.27	1.31	1.36	1.41	1.45	1.50
Veal: Chuck roast, bone in	.94	.98	1.03	1.08	1.12	1.17	1.22	1.27	1.31	1.36	1.41	1.45	1.50
Leg roast, bone in	1.04	1.09	1.15	1.20	1.25	1.30	1.35	1.41	1.46	1.51	1.56	1.62	1.67
Loin chop, bone in	.80	.84	.88	.92	.96	1.00	1.04	1.08	1.12	1.16	1.20	1.24	1.28
Rib chop, bone in	.99	1.04	1.08	1.13	1.18	1.23	1.28	1.33	1.38	1.43	1.48	1.53	1.58

The Economy of Quality

The best meat you can afford is often your best buy. If you buy a pound of short ribs at about 98¢ a pound, you can serve a scant 2 portions at 49¢ each. If you buy a boneless round at about $1.49, you can serve 4 portions at 38¢ each. However, if all you have is about $1.00 for the meat portion of a meal, you can stretch the least expensive cut by cooking it with extenders—vegetable, bean or cereal.

The Freezer Bank

Meat you buy at lower-than-usual prices is an investment that pays off when you use some and rewrap and store the rest in your home freezer for future use.

To make the most of this opportunity to save:

1. Wrap meats in single-meal or single-portion quantities.

2. Put two sheets of paper between pairs of shaped patties or steaks so that they can easily be separated while still frozen.

3. Wrap the meat tightly in moisture/vapor-proof paper. Lay the meat in the center of the wrap, bring the long edges together, fold the paper over and over, butchers' style, flat against the meat. Fold the ends of the wrap the same way, to make a tight seal. Tie firmly, or seal with freezer tape.

4. Label each package with contents and date of storage. Be sure to use the meat before the recommended storage time is up.

5. Meat purchased frozen with its original freezer wrapping intact can be stored in your home freezer without rewrapping. Other meat purchases should be rewrapped for freezing.

6. Store-wrapped packages can be safely stored in the refrigerator for the times shown on the chart on page 57.

Beef Chuck Roast—Three Meals

Buy a blade chuck roast, about 5 to 6 pounds. With a sharp-pointed knife, cut away the bone and cartilage at the base of the meat, following the contour of the bone. Set bone aside for soup.

Cut out the tender, well-marbled sections of meat, outside the blade bone. Trim fat and slice meat into thin steaks, about ⅜ inch thick. Prepare as Steaks Diane (page 62) or wrap and freeze for later use.

Remove center bone and cartilage and add to soup bones.

Cut out the center roast, a small, fairly uniform roast. In removing this section, follow the contour of the blade bone and the membranes.

Trim away fat, cut remaining pieces of meat into cubes for stew. Add scraps to soup bones.

Cut in this way, a 5-pound chuck will make three meals for a family of three to four, plus a hearty soup. For large families, buy a larger chuck roast or a pair when they are on special, and proceed as above. (See photo, page 72.)

MARINATED CHUCK ROAST

2-pound boneless chuck roast
¼ cup olive oil
1 tablespoon vinegar
1 clove garlic, mashed
1 onion, sliced
2 bay leaves
¼ teaspoon each dry mustard, marjoram,
   pepper
½ teaspoon salt

The center portion of an arm or blade chuck roast may be marinated and used as an oven roast. Blend oil, vinegar and remaining ingredients. Turn meat in marinade to coat all sides. Let stand 1 hour at room temperature, longer in the refrigerator, turning occasionally to season the meat evenly. Roast, uncovered, in a moderately slow oven (325°F) to the rare or medium-rare stage for maximum tenderness. (See chart, page 60.) Baste occasionally with remaining marinade. Makes 8 servings.

TENDERIZED CHUCK ROAST

Sprinkle both sides of blade or arm chuck roast with commercial tenderizer, using ½ teaspoon per pound. Do not use salt. Pierce meat with fork to allow tenderizer to penetrate. Roast meat as above.

OVEN ONION POT ROAST

Place boned chuck roast (about 2 pounds) on a square of heavy-duty aluminum foil. Sprinkle with 2 tablespoons dry onion soup mix. Turn, sprinkle second side with 2 tablespoons onion soup mix. Seal package with a butchers' fold to make it airtight. Arrange package on a shallow baking pan. Roast in a moderate oven (350°F) about 2½ hours, or until the meat is tender. Open foil to test meat with a fork. Makes 4 servings.

For more pot roasts, see pages 70–73.

STEAKS DIANE

1 pound thin-sliced beef
3 tablespoons butter or margarine
1 tablespoon chopped parsley
1 tablespoon chopped chives
2 teaspoons Worcestershire sauce
2 teaspoons prepared steak sauce
   Salt, pepper

Steaks for Steaks Diane may be sliced from cuts ranging from fillet and sirloin to round and chuck. If necessary, tenderize the steaks with commercial tenderizer. Brown meat quickly on both sides in butter; the steaks should be pink in the middle. Remove to a warm serving dish. Add remaining ingredients to pan, stir over heat until blended. Pour quickly over steaks, serve at once. Makes 4 servings.

OLD-FASHIONED BEEF STEW

1 pound chuck, cut into 1½-inch cubes
   Flour, salt, pepper
2 tablespoons fat
1 onion, sliced
2 or 3 potatoes, halved
4 or 5 carrots
4 or 5 onions

Shake chuck cubes in a paper bag with flour, salt and pepper. Heat fat and sliced onion in a heavy pan fitted with a lid. Brown meat cubes well on all sides. Add enough boiling water barely to cover the meat. Cover the pan and simmer for about 1½ hours. Add the vegetables, along with more water, if necessary. Cover and cook about ½ hour longer, until meat and vegetables are tender. Serve with rice, noodles or dumplings (page 72). Makes 4 servings.

Pork Loin—Three Meals

When your market offers specials on pork loins, buy a full half, or a whole loin if you have room in your freezer, and enjoy extra savings. Use part of the loin to make a delicious small roast. Slice double-thick chops for stuffing, or extra-thin chops for quick cooking in skillet or broiler. Use the rest of the loin, cut into chunks, for a sauerkraut casserole. (See photo, page 75.)

Or ask the butcher to slice off the ribs with an inch-thick layer of meat on them for country-style ribs.

PORK LOIN ROAST, CURRANT GLAZE

4-pound pork loin
2 cloves garlic
1 teaspoon sage
½ teaspoon nutmeg
2 teaspoons salt
½ teaspoon pepper
2 onions, diced
1 carrot, diced
   Whole cloves

Glaze:

¼ **cup currant jelly**
1 **teaspoon dry mustard**

Rub meat with garlic mashed with seasonings. Spread vegetables in shallow roasting pan. Arrange meat on vegetables, bones down. Add 1 cup water. Roast in a moderately slow oven (325°F) for 1½ hours. Slash fat in crisscross pattern. Stud with cloves. Blend jelly with mustard, spread on fat. Roast about 1 hour longer, until thermometer registers 180°F and pork is thoroughly cooked. Carve between ribs. Makes 6 to 8 servings.

STUFFED PORK CHOPS

4 **double pork chops**
4 **slices bread**
¼ **cup raisins**
1 **teaspoon brown sugar**
¼ **teaspoon curry powder**
⅛ **teaspoon cinnamon**
2 **tablespoons minced onion**
1 **teaspoon salt**
½ **cup syrup from any canned fruit**
1 **tablespoon lemon juice**

Slit chops to make pockets. Trim crusts from bread, cube. Combine with raisins, sugar, curry, cinnamon and onion. Stuff chops. Sprinkle chops with salt, arrange on shallow pan. Bake in a moderate oven (350°F). When chops begin to brown, mix syrup and lemon juice, pour over chops. Bake about 1 hour, until chops are cooked through, basting occasionally. Remove chops to serving platter. Skim fat from pan juices, add ½ cup water to pan, and cook and stir for a minute or two, scraping the pan. Strain sauce over the chops. Makes 4 servings.

CHOUCROUTE GARNI

2 **pounds pork chunks from loin**
  Salt, pepper
2 **onions, chopped**
2 **cloves garlic, minced**
1 **can (28 ounces) sauerkraut, drained**
2 **beef bouillon cubes**
2 **cups water**
1 **tablespoon caraway seeds**
1 **bay leaf**
2 **apples, peeled, sliced**

Ask the butcher to cut the bony end of the pork loin into chunks. Trim fat. Season meat with salt and pepper. Render a little of the fat in a skillet, brown pork chunks on all sides, transfer to a flameproof casserole. Add onions, garlic and sauerkraut. Dissolve bouillon cubes in water (or use 1 cup water, 1 cup wine) and add to casserole. Add caraway seeds and bay leaf. Cover, simmer about 1½ hours, until meat is tender. Taste, adjust seasonings. Add apples, simmer 5 minutes longer, until fruit is cooked through. Discard bay leaf. Makes 6 servings.

Fresh Pork Shoulder—Three Meals

Fresh pork shoulder picnic is often on sale at very attractive prices. This is a meaty cut with many possibilities, almost like a small ham. Roast simply or have the butt boned, leaving a pocket for stuffing. Remove a 1-pound slice of the roast to make cubes for cassoulet. Save the bones for cabbage soup.

STUFFED PORK SHOULDER PICNIC

4-**pound fresh pork shoulder, boned, with**
  pocket
4 **tart apples, peeled, chopped**
4 **prunes, pitted, chopped**
⅛ **teaspoon cinnamon**
1 **tablespoon sugar**
¼ **teaspoon salt**
  Salt, pepper to taste

Fill the pocket in the pork shoulder with a mixture of the fruit, cinnamon, sugar and salt. Close opening with skewers. Season meat with salt and pepper. Roast on rack in shallow roasting pan in a moderately slow oven (325°F) about 4 hours (see chart, page 60). Meat may be basted, if desired, with sherry or with syrup saved from canned fruit. Makes 8 servings.

CASSOULET

1 **pound dried white beans**
1 **medium onion, sliced**
1 **teaspoon salt**
½ **pound smoked Polish sausage, sliced**
1 **pound fresh pork, cubed**
2 **cloves garlic, minced**
½ **bay leaf, crushed**
1 **teaspoon minced parsley**
1½ **cups canned tomatoes**
½ **cup white wine or sherry or apple juice**
  Salt, black pepper

Soak beans overnight in water to cover, Drain. Add onion, salt and fresh water to cover. Simmer, covered, 2 hours. In a heavy skillet, brown sausage. Remove, brown pork cubes in fat. Discard fat. Add remaining ingredients, cover, simmer 15 minutes. Drain beans, combine with meat in casserole. Adjust seasoning with salt and freshly ground black pepper. Bake in a moderate oven (350°F) 1½ hours. Makes 8 servings.

PORK CABBAGE SOUP

    Bones from fresh pork shoulder
    2 quarts water
    2 teaspoons salt
    1 bay leaf
    1 onion, stuck with 5 cloves
    2 large onions, minced
    3 tablespoons butter or margarine
    1 teaspoon caraway seeds
    2 medium potatoes, peeled and quartered
    1½ pounds green cabbage, chopped

Cover bones with water. Add salt, bay leaf and onion stuck with cloves. Bring to a boil, simmer 1 hour. Cook the minced onions in butter until golden. Add strained hot stock, caraway seeds and potatoes. Cook 15 minutes. Add cabbage, simmer about 10 minutes, until vegetables are tender. Makes 8 servings.

Veal Shoulder—Three Meals

A veal shoulder, weighing about 3 to 5 pounds, can offer three luxury meals at a reasonable price, if you cut it right! A pound of scaloppine, thin slices of boneless meat, will make a meal for four. The center section can be roasted as is, or boned and rolled for an easy-to-carve meal. Use the rest of the meat to make a veal stew.

VEAL SCALOPPINE NEAPOLITAN

    1 pound thin-sliced veal
    Flour
    ¼ teaspoon oregano
    Salt, pepper
    ¼ cup oil
    1 small onion, minced
    1 garlic clove, crushed
    1 can (8 ounces) tomato sauce

Dust scaloppine with flour, season with oregano, salt and pepper, pound to flatten. Heat oil in skillet, brown scaloppine on one side, turn. Add onion and garlic to pan, cook until second side of meat is browned. Add tomato sauce, cover, simmer until tender. Makes 4 servings.

ROASTED ROLLED VEAL MARINARA

    Center portion of veal rump or shoulder,
        about 3 pounds
    2 cloves garlic, slivered
    Salt, pepper, oregano
    4 bacon strips
    1 cup chicken bouillon
    1 cup prepared marinara spaghetti sauce

Have center portion of large veal rump or shoulder boned, rolled and tied. Poke slits in the meat with a sharp-pointed knife, insert garlic slivers. Sprinkle with seasonings. Arrange meat on rack in roasting pan; lay bacon strips on top, pour bouillon over all. Roast in a moderately slow oven (325°F) about 40 minutes per pound. (See chart, page 60.) To serve, carve in thin slices, arrange on heated serving platter. Skim excess fat from pan. Add marinara sauce to pan and cook, scraping in brown bits. Pour over meat. Makes about 8 servings.

FRENCH VEAL STEW (BLANQUETTE DE VEAU)

    2 pounds boneless veal, cut from shoulder
        or breast
    1 onion, studded with 4 cloves
    1 carrot, scraped
    1 bay leaf
    ½ teaspoon thyme
    2 teaspoons salt
    ¼ cup butter or margarine
    1 can (1 pound) small white onions, drained
    1 can (6 ounces) mushrooms, drained
    ¼ cup flour
    1 tablespoon lemon juice
    Salt, white pepper
    2 egg yolks
    ½ cup milk or cream
    Chopped parsley

Combine veal, onion, carrot, bay leaf, thyme and salt in a pot, cover with boiling water. Bring to a boil, cover the pot, simmer 1 hour, until veal is tender. Remove veal to a serving platter, keep warm; reserve the veal stock. Melt butter in a skillet, sauté onions and mushrooms until very lightly golden. With a slotted spoon, remove vegetables and arrange around veal on platter. Add flour to butter remaining in the skillet, stir over low heat. Strain veal stock and boil rapidly if necessary to reduce to 3 cups. Stir into flour mixture and cook, stirring, until sauce is smooth and thick. Add lemon juice and salt and white pepper to taste. Beat egg yolks with milk, warm with a little hot sauce, combine. Pour sauce over veal and vegetables on platter. Sprinkle with parsley. Makes 8 servings.

Leg of Lamb—Three Meals

Leg of lamb becomes an economical choice when you cut it—or have the meatman cut it—to make three different meals.

Slice four steaks from the sirloin end of the leg, to broil to taste.

Cut thin slices of the meat from the underside of the remaining portion of the leg. These make scaloppine so tender and flavorful that you can use them in favorite recipes in place of veal, at a substantial saving.

The rest of the leg makes a family roast, to glaze or not, as you prefer.

Roast leg of lamb, served with mint jelly, or with a tangy fresh mint sauce, is a favorite choice for parties as well as for family meals.

ROAST LEG OF LAMB

Rub leg of lamb with salt and pepper. Arrange on rack in open roasting pan, fat side up. Roast in a moderately slow oven (325°F) about 28 minutes per pound for medium. Insert a meat thermometer so that its tip is in the center of the roast, not touching bone or fat. At the medium-done stage it will read 165°F. Serve roast with mint jelly or fresh Mint Sauce (below). A whole leg will make 8 to 10 servings. If desired, the lamb may be glazed during the final hour of cooking with undiluted frozen fruit juice, jellied cranberry sauce or one of the following glazes.

MINT GLAZE

Mix 1 onion, chopped, ½ cup mint jelly, ¼ cup chopped fresh parsley. Discard excess fat in roasting pan, add 1 cup beef bouillon. Spoon mint glaze over meat. Finish roasting, basting occasionally with pan juices.

HONEY-MUSTARD GLAZE

Blend ½ cup prepared mustard with ½ cup honey, 1 teaspoon salt, ¼ teaspoon pepper. Spread on lamb for last hour of roasting.

FRESH MINT SAUCE FOR LAMB

Combine ¼ cup finely chopped mint leaves, firmly packed, with 2 tablespoons brown sugar and 1 cup vinegar. Let stand about 2 hours. Stir occasionally to dissolve the sugar. Serve cold, with hot roast lamb.

LAMB SCALOPPINE

1 pound scaloppine cut from lamb leg
  Flour, salt, pepper
1 egg
1 tablespoon water
  Seasoned bread crumbs
  Oil for frying
1 cup shredded Swiss cheese (optional)

Pound scaloppine to flatten. Dust both sides with seasoned flour. Dip into egg beaten with water, then into bread crumbs. Brown on both sides in 1 inch hot oil. Makes 4 servings. If desired, sprinkle the scaloppine with cheese and cook, covered, until cheese begins to melt.

BROILED LAMB STEAK

4 lamb steaks from leg
1 clove garlic
1 teaspoon salt
½ teaspoon oregano
½ teaspoon paprika
¼ teaspoon pepper
¼ cup wine vinegar
¼ cup oil

Have steaks cut about ¾ inch thick. Combine remaining ingredients in shallow platter to make marinade. Coat steaks on both sides, let stand at room temperature 30 minutes to 1 hour, turning occasionally to season evenly. Broil indoors or out, 6 minutes each side for rare, 7 minutes for medium. Makes 4 servings.

Favorite Economy Oven Roasts

The most-wanted beef roasts in the market today are those cut from high-quality sirloin tip, top or bottom round, rump or chuck. These are compact, boneless or semi-boneless, and a very good buy. They are easy to carve and have little waste.

Boneless Roasts: Top-quality round roasts, eye of round, rump, sirloin tip, and cross-rib chuck roast can be simply seasoned and roasted as they are. While these are not the most tender cuts of beef, they make very good eating at a comparatively low cost per serving. A marinade adds extra flavor to the meat, makes it more tender, and will serve as gravy. Round roasts are lower in fat than chuck cuts. See chart, page 60, for suggested roasting temperatures and times.

Other beef cuts may be tenderized with commercial tenderizer, following package directions, and roasted to enjoy rare. Rolled roasts of pork, lamb and veal are naturally tender.

MARINATED ROLLED BEEF ROAST

Rolled beef rump roast, about 5 pounds
¼ cup oil
½ cup red wine
2 tablespoons vinegar
¼ cup ketchup
1 tablespoon Worcestershire sauce
1 onion, minced
2 cloves garlic, crushed
1 teaspoon grated horseradish

Cover meat with marinade made by mixing oil, wine and remaining ingredients. Let stand 1 hour at room temperature, longer in the refrigerator. Roast on rack in open pan in a moderately slow oven (325°F) to the rare or medium-rare stage for maximum tenderness, best flavor. (See chart, page 60.) Baste occasionally with marinade. Makes 10 or more servings.

BONED PORK SHOULDER ROAST

1 fresh pork shoulder picnic, about 4 pounds
1 pound sausage meat
½ cup chopped onion
¼ cup chopped celery tops
¼ cup chopped parsley
2 cups soft bread crumbs
½ teaspoon sage
½ teaspoon thyme
Salt, pepper, cayenne, nutmeg
¼ cup water

Have meatman bone the fresh shoulder picnic and make a pocket for stuffing. Brown sausage with onion, celery and parsley, stirring with a fork. Add crumbs, seasonings and water, stir over low heat to combine. Stuff pocket with this mixture, sew or skewer opening. Arrange meat on rack in roasting pan. Roast in a moderately slow oven (325°F) until thoroughly cooked. (See chart, page 60.) Insert thermometer in thickest part of meat, not in stuffing; it should read 185°F. Slice through meat and stuffing to serve. Makes 8 or more servings.

ROLLED LAMB SHOULDER

1 lamb shoulder, boned and trimmed, about 4 pounds
1 cup Italian-style salad dressing

Coat lamb shoulder with dressing, let stand 2 hours at room temperature. Roll up, tie. Arrange on rack in roasting pan, roast in a moderately slow oven (325°F) to rare or medium-rare stage. (See chart, page 60.) Makes about 8 servings.

The Great Roasts

For many roast beef fans, the classic luxury is the rib roast. Newport or Delmonico roasts are from the large end of ribs, cut short, with top muscle removed. If the price is right, buy the 10-inch rib roast. Have the short ribs cut off and barbecue them for another meal. (See photo, page 71.)

RIB ROAST OF BEEF, BROWNED POTATOES

Place roast in shallow open pan, rib bones down. Season with pepper. Do not add water. Roast according to timetable on page 60. Peel small whole potatoes (quarter large potatoes); soak in cold water. Drain potatoes and add to pan for last hour of cooking. Turn potatoes in drippings to coat all sides. Season with salt and pepper. Let roast stand 15 to 20 minutes before carving, so that juices set. If desired, make gravy with pan drippings. Spoon off all but 3 tablespoons fat. Add 2 to 3 tablespoons flour to the fat and drippings in the roasting pan. Cook for a minute or two over low heat, blending well. Slowly add 2 cups water, stirring and scraping the bottom of the pan. Simmer over medium heat, stirring often, until gravy is smooth and thickened. Season to taste; strain into sauceboat. A 3-rib roast will serve 6 or more.

BARBECUED BEEF SHORT RIBS

2–3 pounds beef short ribs
1 cup pineapple juice
2 tablespoons honey
1 tablespoon vinegar
1 tablespoon brown sugar
¼ cup soy sauce
1 teaspoon ground ginger

Place meat in large bowl. Blend juice and remaining ingredients, spoon over ribs to coat. Let stand 1 hour at room temperature or overnight in the refrigerator. Drain meat, place on rack in roasting pan and roast in a moderate oven (350°F) 40 to 50 minutes, until well browned, brushing occasionally with marinade. Or ribs may be barbecued over charcoal grill, 4 inches from heat, until well browned on both sides. Makes about 4 servings.

Fillet of Beef

The ultimate of beef luxury, fillets are some-times sold whole and untrimmed, at a price that allows you to cut yourself one or even two regal beef dinners, plus one or two meals made with the pieces left from the shaping of uniform fillets for roasting. Enjoy fillet cubes for kebabs, small fillet steaks or thin fillet slices for Oriental dishes.

ROAST FILLET OF BEEF

Rub trimmed fillet of beef with butter or margarine, sprinkle with salt and pepper. Roast in a very hot oven (450°F) about 30 to 45 minutes, depending on size and thick-ness of the meat, basting occasionally with the pan juices. Use a meat thermometer; remove meat promptly when it reaches 140°F, the rare stage. A 5-pound fillet makes 12 or more servings.

BEEF WELLINGTON

Prepare roasted fillet of beef, as above, but remove meat from oven after 25 minutes and let it cool. Prepare pastry for 2-crust pie, roll into rectangle. Lay cooled fillet on pastry, spread top with 1 cup Chicken-Liver Pâté (page 110) mixed with ¼ cup sliced black olives or chopped mushrooms. Wrap fillet completely in pastry, moisten flaps, seal. Arrange seam side down on baking sheet. Cut decorative slashes in top, insert meat ther-mometer. Bake in a hot oven (425°F) about 25 minutes, until pastry is browned and ther-mometer reads 140°F.

MOCK BEEF WELLINGTON

Use a long, slender eye round roast, tenderized or marinated (see page 65), instead of fillet.

Extendible Roasts

The following roasts have a good deal of bone in them, but both are complemented with stuffing, which extends the meat and helps provide a hearty meal.

STUFFED BREAST OF VEAL

    1 veal breast (about 4 pounds)
     Salt
 ⅓ cup butter or margarine
 ½ cup chopped celery
    1 onion, chopped
    6 cups bread cubes

 ¾ teaspoon each salt, paprika, basil leaves
    4 strips bacon
    1 can (8 ounces) tomato sauce

Ask the butcher to cut the breast bone from the veal and make a pocket between ribs and meat. (Breast of veal prepared for stuffing may often be found in the meat case.) Salt the meat inside and out. To make the stuffing, melt butter, add vegetables, cook until glazed. Add bread cubes and seasonings. Stir over moderate heat until the mixture is well blended and lightly toasted. Stuff the veal breast, fasten with skewers. Arrange on bak-ing pan, top with bacon strips. Roast in a moderately slow oven (325°F) about 30 minutes per pound. The meat thermometer, inserted in the thickest part of the meat, not in the stuffing, will read 180°F. Half an hour before the cooking time is up, pour tomato sauce over bacon and meat. Makes 4 to 6 servings.

CROWN ROAST OF LAMB WITH CRANBERRY STUFFING

    2 lamb racks (14–16 ribs) and ground trim-mings
     Salt and pepper
    1 package (8 ounces) dry stuffing mix
    1 cup fresh cranberry sauce or 1 can (8 ounces) whole cranberry sauce
 ¾ cup boiling water
 ¼ pound butter or margarine
    1 tablespoon finely chopped fresh parsley
    1 teaspoon dried mint
     Fresh cranberries (optional)

Have butcher shape lamb racks into a crown and grind the trimmings. Season crown with salt and pepper. Combine stuffing mix, cran-berry sauce, water, butter, parsley, mint and ground lamb. Pile stuffing mixture into center of crown. Bake in a shallow pan in a moder-ately slow oven (325°F) about 1 hour, until delicately brown. If tops of bones begin to scorch, cover with foil. Arrange fresh cran-berries in a garland around outer edge of crown, if desired. Carve between bones to serve. Makes 7 or 8 servings.

Crown Roast of Veal or Pork: Prepare as above. Increase cooking time to about 1½ hours.

Ham

Buy a whole ham and have it cut in half. Have steaks removed if you like. Or roast the ham whole and use the leftovers in a series of new meal creations, from a handsome broiled ham steak to split pea soup cooked with the ham bone. (See photo, page 69.)

BAKED GLAZED HAM

Check the label to ascertain whether your ham is fully cooked and ready to eat, or whether it requires cooking before eating. Remove the wrapping, arrange ham in baking pan. Bake in a moderately slow oven (325°F) for designated time. "Fully Cooked Hams" require 10 to 12 minutes per pound to reach 125°F on the meat thermometer. "Cook Before Eating Hams" take 18 minutes per pound, if whole, 25 minutes per pound in small portions, to reach 155°–165°F on the meat thermometer. Half an hour before the ham is done, brush with one of the glazes below, finish baking.

ANN PAGE MARMALADE GLAZE

Mix ¼ cup each orange marmalade and prepared mustard, ½ teaspoon powdered cloves. Spread on ham for last half hour of baking time.

BROWN-SUGAR GLAZE

Stud ham with whole cloves, cover with a layer of brown sugar moistened with prepared mustard. Bake as usual, basting occasionally with apple juice or cider.

MADEIRA GLAZE AND SAUCE

Baste ham during final half hour of baking with mixture of 1 cup Madeira wine and 1 can (10¾ ounces) beef gravy; serve remainder as sauce.

CUMBERLAND GLAZE AND SAUCE

Combine grated rind of 1 orange and 1 lemon, 1 cup currant jelly, 1 cup red wine. Bring to a boil in saucepan. Stir 2 tablespoons cornstarch to a paste with 2 tablespoons water, add to pan, stir over heat 1 minute. Add juice of orange and lemon. Use to baste ham during final half hour of baking; serve remainder as sauce.

APRICOT GLAZE AND SAUCE

Blend 1 can (12 ounces) apricot nectar with 2 tablespoons lemon juice, ½ cup brown sugar, 2 tablespoons soy sauce. Simmer 5 minutes. Baste ham during final half hour of baking; serve remainder as sauce.

PEACH GLAZE

Blend 1 cup peach jam, ¼ cup vinegar, ½ teaspoon cinnamon, 1 tablespoon brown sugar. Spread on clove-studded ham half an hour before removing from oven.

BROILED HAM STEAK WITH PEACHES

   Ham steak, 1 inch thick
 1 can (17 ounces) peach halves
¼ teaspoon ground ginger
 2 teaspoons vinegar or lemon juice

Trim rind from the ham steak and slash the edges to prevent curling. Preheat broiler. Drain the peaches, reserve ½ cup syrup. Mix peach syrup with ginger and vinegar or lemon juice. Arrange ham on broiler pan 4 inches from heat and broil for 10 minutes each side. Baste the ham with syrup mixture as it broils. During the last 10 minutes, arrange peach halves at side of ham slice, baste with pan drippings. Makes 4 servings.

HAM STEAK WITH ORANGE SLICES

Pan-brown a ham steak in a skillet in butter or margarine; add thick slices of orange when ham is nearly done, brown lightly. Cover, simmer 5 minutes. Remove ham to serving dish, garnish with orange slices. Add ¼ cup water or dry white wine to pan, stir and scrape over medium heat until sauce is well blended. Strain sauce over ham. Makes 2 to 4 servings.

PEA SOUP WITH HAM

   Meaty ham bone
 1 pound split peas, soaked
 2 carrots, diced
 1 onion, chopped
⅛ teaspoon thyme
 1 bay leaf
 2 teaspoons salt
   Dash pepper

Bring 2 quarts of water to a boil in a large kettle. Add peas, soaked according to package directions, and remaining ingredients. Bring to a boil, cover, simmer 2 hours, stirring occasionally. Discard bay leaf. Remove bone, dice meat, add to soup. Makes 12 servings.

Country Ham

Old-fashioned country hams, with their rich, deep-smoked flavor, are sometimes on sale at

A marmalade-glazed baked ham makes delectable fare for any Easter gathering, from brunch to late-night dinner. On any day of the year, it can star in two acts and three curtain calls, including Ham with Cumberland Sauce (page 68), Scalloped Potatoes with ham and Pea Soup with Ham.

the market, particularly during the New Year and other holiday seasons. Or you can order them specially.

To Prepare: Your ham may be crusted with mold; use a firm-bristled brush to remove the mold thoroughly. Soak the scrubbed ham in cold water for at least 12 hours, and preferably up to 24 hours. Drain, cover with fresh cold water, and simmer for 4 to 5 hours, until tender. A meat thermometer should register 150°F. Cool the ham, remove the rind, and score the fat. Stud with cloves and glaze with brown sugar seasoned with mustard, or with fruit jam; or spread the fat with maple syrup or honey.

To Bake: Bake in a hot oven (400°F) about 30 minutes, until the crust is glazed and the meat thermometer registers 165°F. Serve in thin slices.

Pot Roasts

Long, slow simmering in moist heat, on top of the range or in the oven, can transform inexpensive cuts of beef and other meats into meals you will be proud to serve.

BASIC POT ROAST

3-pound pot roast—top or bottom round or
    rump
¼ cup flour
1 tablespoon salt
⅛ teaspoon pepper
1 teaspoon mixed herbs
2 tablespoons fat
1 cup sliced onion
1 cup water
½ cup beef bouillon, wine, or tomato sauce
6 potatoes, quartered
6 carrots, in chunks

Dust pot roast with flour mixed with salt, pepper and herbs. Heat fat in heavy pot, brown meat on all sides. Add onion, brown lightly. Add liquids. Cover pan, simmer 2 hours. Add vegetables and more liquid, as needed. Simmer, covered, 30 minutes, or until meat is tender. Meat slices more easily when cold, improves with reheating in the pan gravy. Makes 10 to 12 servings.

POT ROAST FRENCH STYLE (BOEUF À LA MODE)

4- to 5-pound round roast of beef
2 cups dry red wine
2 tablespoons sherry (optional)
1 onion, stuck with 4 cloves

1 bay leaf
2 sprigs parsley
    Pinch thyme, nutmeg
    Black pepper
2 teaspoons salt
    Cracked veal knuckle (optional)
6 carrots, peeled
12 small white onions, peeled

Brown meat on all sides in a heavy pot, fat side first. Add wine and sherry, onion, bay leaf, parsley and seasonings. If desired, add cracked veal knuckle for extra richness. Cover pot, cook slowly about 2½ hours, until meat is almost tender. Add vegetables, continue to cook until meat and vegetables are tender. Check occasionally, add more wine or a little water as needed. Remove meat to platter, slice. Add vegetables. Strain the sauce, pour some over meat, pass rest separately. Makes 10 to 12 servings.

JELLIED POT ROAST

Slice Pot Roast French Style (above) and arrange slices on a platter. Pour the cooled gravy over it, chill until jelled. Serve cold.

YANKEE POT ROAST

3- to 4-pound bottom round, rump, brisket or
    chuck
1 can (10½ ounces) condensed tomato soup
    Pinch thyme or other herb

Brown meat well on all sides in heavy kettle; add soup and seasoning. Cover, cook over low heat about 2½ to 3 hours, until meat is tender. Remove meat to platter, slice, cover with sauce. Makes 8 to 10 servings. (If desired, add carrots, potatoes or mixed vegetables after meat has been cooking for 2 hours. Season. Cover; cook until vegetables are done and meat is tender.)

SAUERBRATEN

Marinade:

2 cups vinegar
2 cups water
10 whole cloves
4 bay leaves
6 peppercorns
2 tablespoons salt
2 tablespoons sugar

4 pounds beef rump or sirloin tip
2 onions, peeled and sliced
1 lemon, sliced

Grace your holiday table with the king of roasts—standing prime ribs, carved by cutting down to the bone, then releasing along the bone. Stretch this rich flavor into a second meal of delectable hash and a third of Deviled Beef Bones. See pages 66 and 73 for recipes and cooking chart, page 60 for temperature and time for roast beef to your taste.

You can save money by buying a large chuck roast and cutting it yourself to make three meals: Chuck Roast, Steaks Diane and Old-fashioned Beef Stew. (See page 62.)

½ cup flour
2 tablespoons fat
3 cups strained marinade
6 gingersnaps

Combine all marinade ingredients. Bring to a boil, pour over meat, onions and lemon in a deep bowl. Let stand at least 2 days, turning the meat 2 or 3 times during this period to season it evenly.

Remove meat from marinade, rub with 2 tablespoons flour. Brown meat on all sides in hot fat in a heavy pan or Dutch oven. Add the strained marinade, cover, cook slowly over low heat for 3 hours, until meat is fork tender. Remove meat to platter. Crumble gingersnaps, blend with remaining flour. Add to pan gravy and cook, stirring constantly, until thickened and smooth. Correct seasoning. Pour part of the sauce over the meat and serve the rest separately. Makes 10 servings.

PORK SHOULDER POT ROAST

5- or 6-pound fresh pork shoulder
1 clove garlic, sliced
1 tablespoon flour
1 teaspoon salt
⅛ teaspoon nutmeg
1 cup red wine
1 teaspoon minced parsley

Trim excess fat from pork. Slit meat next to the bone, insert slices of garlic. Combine flour, salt and nutmeg, rub into the meat. Melt some of the trimmed fat in a heavy skillet. Brown meat on all sides. Transfer to oven casserole, add red wine and parsley. Cover, bake in a moderately slow oven (325°F) for 2½ hours. Uncover, bake ½ hour longer. Makes 10 to 12 servings.

BRAISED LAMB SHANKS

4 lamb shanks
2 tablespoons oil
2 carrots, sliced
2 stalks celery, sliced
1 onion, sliced
1 teaspoon salt
  Pepper to taste
2 tablespoons flour
1 beef bouillon cube
1 cup water
½ cup red wine (optional)
  Bay leaf
¼ teaspoon thyme
1 can (6 ounces) sliced mushrooms, with
    liquid
1 can (1 pound) boiled white onions, drained

Brown lamb shanks on all sides in oil in a heavy pot or Dutch oven. Remove. To fat in pot, add carrots, celery and onion, cook until glazed. Add salt and pepper. Sprinkle with flour and cook for a moment, stirring, until flour takes on color. Add bouillon cube, water and wine (or use all water). Cook, stirring, until blended. Return shanks to pot, add spices, cover and simmer about 1¼ hours, until meat is tender. Discard bay leaf. Add mushrooms and onions, heat. Makes 4 servings.

The Rest of the Roast

Sometimes it saves both time and money to buy a larger roast than you need for a single meal and to plan on using the leftovers. Many easy-to-make dishes begin with "planned-over" roast beef, lamb, pork or veal . . . a delicious variety of casseroles and hashes that have become classic family favorites.

DEVILED BEEF BONES

Cut the leftover ribs of a rib roast into serving portions, trim excess fat. Sprinkle with vinegar, spread with mustard. Dip into melted butter or margarine and into fine dry bread crumbs. Broil slowly, turning often, until the crumbs are golden. Serve with leftover gravy, highly seasoned with mustard, Worcestershire sauce and hot pepper sauce, to taste. (See photo, page 71.)

WONDERFUL ROAST-BEEF HASH

2 cups diced cold roast beef
2 cups diced cooked potatoes
¼ cup minced onion
⅔ cup milk
4 tablespoons Worcestershire sauce
½ cup chopped parsley
  Salt, pepper
2 tablespoons fat beef drippings

Combine all ingredients except the drippings and blend well. Heat the drippings in a heavy skillet, add hash mixture and press down evenly. Cook over medium heat until hash is very crisp and brown on bottom. With spatula, fold in half like an omelet, cook over low heat about 5 minutes. Makes 4 servings.

Tip: Top each serving with a poached egg.

PORK-FRIED RICE

2 cloves garlic, minced or crushed
2 medium onions, chopped
2 tablespoons oil

½ green pepper, cut in strips
1 cup finely diced cooked pork
2 cups cold cooked rice
3 eggs, well beaten
3 tablespoons soy sauce

Cook garlic and onions in oil until soft, about 2 minutes; add the pepper, cook 2 minutes longer. Add pork and rice; heat, stirring constantly. Quickly stir in the beaten eggs and soy sauce and cook, stirring, until eggs are set. Makes 4 to 6 servings.

ENGLISH PORK PIE

2 cups diced cooked pork
1 can (6 ounces) mushrooms, drained
1 stalk celery, finely diced
2 tablespoons butter or margarine
⅛ teaspoon powdered sage
2 tablespoons minced parsley
1 tablespoon flour
½ cup water
1 cup gravy, leftover or canned
½ cup cream or milk
  Salt and pepper
  Pastry for 1-crust pie

Trim fat from pork before dicing. Brown mushrooms and celery in butter; add sage and parsley. Sprinkle with flour, stir 1 minute. Slowly add water. Simmer, stirring, until smooth. Add gravy and cream, adjust seasoning with salt and pepper. Add pork, pour into 1½-quart casserole. Top with pastry crust. If pork filling is hot, bake at 450°F until crust is golden, about 15 minutes. If pie has been made ahead, bake at 350°F for 30 minutes. Makes 4 servings.

LAMB CURRY

6 tablespoons oil
½ to 1 tablespoon curry powder
½ cup chopped onion
½ green pepper, finely diced
1 clove garlic, crushed
1 tart green apple, diced
½ teaspoon salt
¼ cup chopped celery
2 cups diced cooked lamb
1½ cups water

Heat oil in large skillet, add curry powder to taste, and cook, stirring, until odor becomes strong. Add onion, green pepper and garlic, and cook until soft. Add apple, salt and celery, cook until apple softens and thickens the sauce. Add lamb and water and simmer 20 to 25 minutes. Makes 4 servings. Serve with rice, chutney and bowls of salted pea- nuts, minced cucumber, grated coconut, rai- sins.

TURKISH LAMB-AND-EGGPLANT CASSEROLE

1 small eggplant, unpeeled
4 tablespoons oil
2 tablespoons butter or margarine
3 medium onions, chopped
1 clove garlic, finely chopped
2 cups diced cooked lamb
3 large ripe or 1 can (16 ounces) tomatoes
1 teaspoon salt
¼ teaspoon pepper

Cut eggplant into small cubes. Heat half the oil and butter in a flameproof casserole, cook cubes. In a skillet cook onions and garlic in remaining oil and butter. Add lamb to onions, cook 1 minute, add tomatoes and cook 3 or 4 minutes longer. Combine with eggplant in casserole, season with salt and pepper. Bake in a moderate oven (350°F) for ¾ hour, until bubbling hot. Makes 4 servings.

Easy Stewing

Stews are easy to make, easy to eat. Buy stew meat already trimmed and cubed at the market, or you may want to concoct a stew with bits trimmed from a large roast. All stews are slowly simmered in liquid until the meat is tender and the sauce is flavored with whatever herbs, spices and liquids are used in the recipe. You can cook a stew top-range over low heat in a tightly covered pot or you can let it simmer in the oven in a covered casserole. The latter method takes longer but requires less attention. Top-range stews may need the addition of more liquid as they cook.

FRENCH-STYLE BEEF STEW (BOEUF BOURGUIGNONNE)

2½ pounds chuck beef, cut into large cubes
½ cup flour
2 teaspoons salt
¼ teaspoon pepper
4 slices bacon, cut into small squares
2 cloves garlic, chopped
1 carrot, chopped
2 onions, chopped
1 bay leaf
½ teaspoon thyme
2 cups dry red wine
2 pounds whole young carrots
2 pounds small white onions

Buy a pork loin half and cut it up before cooking for an economical way to get extra-thick pork chops, a small roast and/or Choucroute Garni, a tasty dish of pork pieces cooked with sauerkraut, flavored with apples and caraway seeds. (See pages 62–64.)

The Great American Meat Loaf is varied in its ways, always economical and infinitely good. This family favorite is ketchup-topped and is made with a combination pack of ground beef, pork and veal—or all beef, to your taste. (See page 84.)

Butter or margarine
1 teaspoon sugar
½ pound mushroom caps
Chopped parsley

Coat beef cubes with a mixture of flour, salt and pepper. Brown together meat, bacon, garlic and chopped carrot and onions. Add bay leaf, thyme, wine and enough water to cover meat. Simmer over low heat or in a moderate oven (350°F), covered, for 2 hours, until tender. Discard bay leaf. Cook young carrots and small white onions separately in boiling salted water. Drain. Brown in a little butter, sprinkle with sugar, and cook until sugar melts and glazes vegetables. Cook mushroom caps in butter. Add all vegetables to stew and sprinkle with chopped parsley. Makes 8 or more servings.

HUNGARIAN GOULASH

1 pound boneless beef
1 pound boneless veal
1 tablespoon paprika
3 tablespoons oil
2 medium onions, sliced
1 can (16 ounces) tomato purée
½ cup water
1 teaspoon salt
  Dash pepper
½ teaspoon caraway seeds (optional)

Cut beef and veal into uniform 1-inch cubes. Sprinkle with paprika. Heat oil in a heavy pan, brown meat on all sides. Add onions, tomato purée, water and seasonings. Cover, simmer slowly until meat is tender, about 1½ hours. Serve with buttered noodles. Makes 8 servings.

OXTAIL RAGOUT

3 pounds oxtails
¼ cup flour
1 teaspoon salt
3 tablespoons fat
½ cup chopped onion
½ cup chopped celery
1 clove garlic, chopped
1 bay leaf
¼ teaspoon thyme
1 can (1 pound) tomatoes
1 cup red wine
2 carrots, cubed
12 small white onions
  Minced parsley and chives for garnish

Soak the oxtails in hot water 15 to 20 minutes. Rinse, dry, and dredge with flour blended with salt. Brown in fat over high heat, push to one side of the pot. Add chopped vegetables, brown lightly. Add herbs, tomatoes and wine. Cover, bring to boil, simmer gently for 2 to 3 hours. During last half hour, discard bay leaf, add carrots and white onions. Serve sprinkled with minced parsley and chives. The flavor of this dish improves with keeping, so make the dish a day ahead if possible, and remove hardened fat before reheating. Makes 4 to 6 servings.

HUNGARIAN PORK AND SAUERKRAUT (SZEKELYS GULYAS)

2 pounds lean pork cubes
1 tablespoon fat
1 tablespoon paprika
¼ cup minced onion
2 cloves garlic, minced
1½ teaspoons salt
1½ pounds sauerkraut, rinsed and drained
1 cup canned tomatoes
½ teaspoon caraway seeds
½ cup sour cream

Brown pork lightly in hot fat in heavy pot. Pour off excess fat. Add paprika, onion and garlic, cook until onion is soft. Add salt, sauerkraut, tomatoes and caraway seeds. Cover. Simmer gently until meat is tender, about 3 hours. Add sour cream just before serving. Makes 8 servings.

IRISH LAMB STEW

2 pounds boneless lamb cubes
1 quart boiling water
1 bay leaf
2 onions, quartered
2 teaspoons salt
4 potatoes, quartered
3 carrots, cubed
2 turnips, diced
1 stalk celery, diced
1 package (10 ounces) frozen peas
3 tablespoons flour
¼ cup cold water
  Salt and pepper
  Chopped parsley for garnish

Cover lamb cubes with boiling water, add bay leaf, onions and salt. Bring to boil, cover, reduce heat and simmer gently until meat is almost tender, about 1½ hours. Discard bay leaf. Add potatoes, carrots, turnips and celery and cook 30 minutes longer. Add peas for last 5 minutes. Remove meat and vegetables to a serving dish. Mix flour with cold water, add to the gravy. Bring to a boil, cook, stirring, until gravy is thickened and smooth. Season to taste with salt and pepper. Pour gravy over lamb and vegetables and garnish with parsley. Makes 8 servings.

RUSSIAN LAMB STEW

   2 pounds lamb, trimmed
   ⅓ cup flour
   1½ teaspoons salt
   ¼ teaspoon pepper
   2 tablespoons butter or margarine
   2 cups beef bouillon
   1 teaspoon dried mint flakes
   8 small carrots
   2 onions, sliced
   1 cup diced celery
   ¾ cup diced rutabaga or turnip
   12 large mushrooms
   ¾ cup dry red wine

Cut lamb into uniform cubes; dredge with flour mixed with salt and pepper. Melt butter, brown lamb cubes on all sides. Add remaining ingredients. Simmer, covered, 2 hours, until meat is fork tender. Makes 8 servings.

Skillet Stews

Not all stews require long cooking. Tender chops make skillet stews in half an hour or less, and some other cuts will produce a stew in an hour or less.

BEEF STROGANOFF

   1 pound top round steak or sirloin tip
   2 tablespoons butter or margarine
   ½ cup chopped onion
   1 teaspoon salt
   ¼ teaspoon pepper
   ½ cup tomato juice
   1 can (4 ounces) mushrooms
   1 cup beef bouillon
   2 tablespoons flour
   ½ cup sour cream

Cut steak into thin strips. Brown strips quickly in butter, add chopped onion, salt and pepper; cook until onion is soft. Add tomato juice, mushrooms with their liquid and bouillon. Cover, cook over low heat until meat is very tender, about 30 minutes. Blend flour with a little water, add to pan and cook, stirring, until sauce is smooth. Add sour cream to pan off the heat, stir to blend well. Makes 4 servings.

SKILLET SWISS STEAK

   1 to 1½ pounds arm chuck steak, 1 inch thick
   ¼ cup flour
   Salt, pepper
   2 tablespoons oil
   ½ onion, sliced
   1 cup tomato juice

Dredge the steak with a mixture of flour, salt and pepper. Pound meat with the edge of a plate or with a mallet. Heat oil in a heavy skillet, brown meat on both sides. Add onion and tomato juice. Bring the liquid to the boiling point, cover the skillet and simmer over low heat about 1 hour, until meat is tender. Turn occasionally and add a little water, if necessary. Makes 4 servings.

PORK CHOPS CHARCUTIÈRE

   6 pork chops, 1 inch thick
   ¾ teaspoon salt
   ½ cup finely chopped onion
   1 clove garlic, minced
   4 tablespoons tomato paste
   ½ cup pitted green or black olives
   1½ tablespoons capers
   1 cup water

Trim excess fat from chops. Heat a heavy skillet, rub with fat cut from the chops, sprinkle with salt. Arrange chops in skillet, brown lightly on both sides; remove. Cook onion and garlic in skillet until soft; add remaining ingredients, simmer 5 minutes. Return chops to skillet, cover and simmer 25 minutes. Makes 6 servings.

VEAL CHOPS PAPRIKA

   3 tablespoons butter or margarine
   1 teaspoon paprika
   4 loin veal chops
   1 tablespoon ketchup or tomato sauce
   ½ cup water
   ½ cup sour cream

Heat butter and paprika to the sizzling point in a heavy skillet. Brown veal chops quickly on both sides. Add ketchup and water and simmer over low heat, covered, until the chops are tender, about 25 minutes. Remove chops to a serving platter. Add the sour cream to the skillet and heat, scraping in the brown bits that cling to the skillet. Spoon sauce over the chops. Makes 4 servings.

LAMB SHOULDER CHOPS IN WINE

   4 shoulder lamb chops
   ½ teaspoon salt

¼ teaspoon pepper
½ teaspoon crushed rosemary
2 tablespoons fat
½ cup dry red wine
1 tablespoon instant minced onion

Rub lamb chops with salt, pepper and rosemary. Brown quickly on both sides in hot fat in a skillet. Add wine, cover, simmer over low heat until meat is tender, about 25 minutes. During last 10 minutes add minced onion. Remove chops to serving platter, boil sauce to reduce slightly, pour over the chops. The sauce should be thin. Makes 4 servings.

Scaloppine

Scaloppine, the delicately thin slices of meat originally cut from the veal leg, can also be cut from the veal rump or shoulder—at less cost. What's more, recipes traditional for veal scaloppine can be made with scaloppine cut from lamb, pork, even turkey. For more scaloppine recipes, see pages 64 and 65.

SCALOPPINE

1 pound thin-sliced veal (or pork, lamb
 or turkey)
 Flour
 Salt, pepper
¼ cup butter or margarine
 Lemon wedges (optional)
½ cup wine, chicken bouillon or
 tomato sauce (optional)

Dust scaloppine with flour, sprinkle with salt and pepper. Pound with a mallet or the edge of a plate to flatten. Melt butter (or use half butter, half oil) in a skillet, brown slices on both sides. Serve with lemon wedges. Or, add liquid, cover, simmer until tender, about 15 to 20 minutes. Makes 4 servings.

SCALOPPINE ALLA MARSALA

Prepare scaloppine as above; add ½ cup Marsala wine and 1 can (6 ounces) mushrooms.

All Broiled Dinners Are Special

Whatever meat you are broiling, whether it's a tender beefsteak or a succulent rib lamb chop or a simple hamburger patty, remember that broiling is dry heat—the driest of all—and it can toughen even a choice porterhouse steak.

Rare meat is more tender than well-done

meat; turn just once and do not overcook. If there is any doubt about the tenderness or quality of the cut, marinate it before broiling, or use commercial tenderizer.

Preheat the broiling oven and the pan, and rub the pan with fat so the meat will not stick to it. Slash the fat around the edges to prevent curling. Don't salt the meat before broiling. Standard broiling pans permit the melting fat to drip down, away from the heating unit and the danger of catching fire.

Basting the meat during broiling will help to keep it moist. If a marinade has been used to tenderize the meat, baste with this during the cooking. A commercial barbecue sauce, fruit juice or one of many easy homemade barbecue sauces may be used. Some quick and easy barbecue sauces follow.

Note: Use the broiling charts in this section as rough guides only, not as exact indications of time required for broiling various cuts to desired degree of doneness. Broilers of various kinds—electric, gas, charcoal—differ greatly in the amount of heat they give off and retain. Other factors, such as wind and atmospheric temperature, also affect results. To be sure that your steak is cooked the way you like it, make a small slit with a sharp-pointed knife near a center bone.

BARBECUE SAUCES

Sherry Sauce: Combine 2 tablespoons sherry, ¼ cup tomato juice, 1 tablespoon soy sauce, ¾ teaspoon salt, dash of freshly ground black pepper. Use with beef, lamb.

Chinese Glaze: Combine 2 tablespoons honey, ¼ cup soy sauce, 1 teaspoon garlic powder, ½ teaspoon salt. Wonderful with pork.

Anchovy Sauce: Mash 2 cloves garlic, combine with 2 tablespoons anchovy paste, ¼ cup oil, dash cayenne pepper, 1 beef bouillon cube, ½ cup water; heat to boiling. Excellent with steak.

Vinaigrette Sauce: Combine ¼ cup olive oil, 2 tablespoons vinegar, ¾ teaspoon salt, ¼ teaspoon black pepper. Use with lamb or beef.

Salsa Borracho: Combine ¼ cup red wine, ¼ cup oil, dash cayenne pepper, 2 tablespoons ketchup, 1 tablespoon grated onion, ¾ teaspoon salt. Hamburger special.

Tarragon Marinade: Blend ½ teaspoon crushed dried tarragon or 1 tablespoon minced fresh tarragon with 2 tablespoons ketchup, 2 tablespoons oil, ½ teaspoon salt, 1 teaspoon vinegar. Fine for beef.

BEEF BROILING CHART

Cut	Thickness	How Far from Heat	Broiling Time Each Side (Minutes)		
			Rare	Medium	Well Done
Chuck Steak (Tenderized)	1 inch	3 inches	6	8	10
Round Steak (Tenderized)	¾ inch	2 inches	4		
Flank Steak	¾ inch	2 inches	4		
Rump Steak (Tenderized)	1 inch	3 inches	8		
Sirloin	1 inch	3 inches	8	10	12
	1½ inches	4 inches	12	15	18
Porterhouse (T-bone) or Rib	1 inch	3 inches	5	7	8
	1½ inches	4 inches	9	10	13
	2 inches	4 to 6 inches	18	20	22
Filet Mignon	1 inch	3 inches	5	7	

GARLIC STEAK

Rub steak (porterhouse, sirloin, chuck or tenderized round) with cut clove of garlic. Brush with oil. Wait an hour before broiling as usual.

PEPPERCORN STEAK

Pound ¼ cup peppercorns in paper bag to crush. Press firmly into both sides of steak. Broil and serve as usual.

STEAK FLAMBÉ

Broil a 4-pound steak to taste, slice for serving. Melt ½ cup butter or margarine, add 2 jiggers gin or whiskey. Warm, ignite, and pour, flaming, over sliced steak. Makes 4 to 6 servings.

FLANK STEAK

Flank steak, about 1½ pounds
3 tablespoons oil
1 tablespoon vinegar
1 teaspoon pepper
¼ teaspoon basil
1 clove garlic, mashed

Pierce meat with a fork. Mix remaining ingredients in a shallow platter, turn steak to coat. Let stand 30 minutes, turning occasionally. Broil about 5 minutes each side, basting often with the marinade. Carve into very thin diagonal slices. Pass salt shaker. Makes 5 to 6 servings.

LONDON BROIL

Thick cuts of round, sirloin or rump can be marinated and broiled as in the recipe above.

FILET MIGNON

Place 4 filets, cut 1 inch thick, 3 inches from heat. Broil 5 minutes each side for rare. Serve as is, with salt and freshly ground pepper; or with Maître d'Hôtel Butter or Anchovy Butter; or with bottled steak sauce.

Maître d'Hôtel Butter: Combine ½ cup soft butter or margarine, ½ teaspoon parsley, juice of ½ lemon, salt and pepper.

Anchovy Butter: Combine ½ cup soft butter or margarine, ½ teaspoon lemon juice, half of 2-ounce can of anchovy fillets, diced:

LAMB BROILING CHART

(For Chops and Steaks, 4 inches from Heat)

Thickness	Broiling Time Each Side (Minutes)		
	Rare	Medium	Well Done
1 inch	5	6	7
1½ inches	7	9	11
2 inches	9	11	15

MINTED LOIN LAMB CHOPS

Sprinkle 4 inch-thick loin lamb chops with salt and pepper. Cook on rack in preheated broiler, 4 inches from heat, for 5 to 6 minutes each side, turning once. Remove from oven, pour off all fat. Add water to broiler pan, scrape in brown bits, heat to boiling point. Add ¼ cup mint jelly, stir until jelly is melted. Strain sauce over hot chops. Makes 4 servings.

LAMBURGERS

1½ pounds ground lamb
¼ cup chopped onion
¼ cup dry red wine
1 egg, beaten
1 teaspoon salt
⅛ teaspoon pepper
¼ teaspoon rosemary
¼ teaspoon thyme

Combine ingredients, blend well. Shape into 6 patties. Broil, 3 to 4 inches from heat, 5 to 6 minutes on each side. Makes 6 servings.

BROILED PORK CHOPS WITH ORANGE GLAZE

4 loin pork chops, trimmed
 Salt, pepper
1 can (6 ounces) frozen orange juice concentrate
2 tablespoons honey
½ teaspoon cinnamon
1 teaspoon salt

Slash the edges of the chops to prevent curling. Season with salt and pepper. Broil, 4 inches from heat, brushing often with mixture of juice and remaining ingredients, about 15 minutes. Turn, broil, basting often, until thoroughly cooked and well browned. Makes 4 servings.

Pan-Broiled Meats

Pan-broiled meats are cooked in a heavy skillet with barely enough fat to prevent the meat from sticking when it is first put into the pan. Or the fat may be omitted and the pan heavily sprinkled with salt, which will also prevent sticking. Pan-broiling has all the flavor advantages of broiling—plus the convenience of one-pan cooking over direct heat. Enjoy pan-broiled beef and lamb on the rare side for maximum tenderness.

PAN-BROILED MINUTE STEAKS

Brush a heavy skillet with fat, heat. Add 4 minute steaks (or tenderloin steaks, or slices from lamb roast), cook about 2 minutes each side for rare. Remove. In same skillet melt ¼ cup butter or margarine, add ¼ cup sherry, heat, pour over steaks. Remind guests to add salt and pepper to taste.

FRENCH PEPPER STEAK

Have 1½ pounds top round steak cut 1 inch thick. Sprinkle both sides with unseasoned meat tenderizer, pierce with fork. Crack 2 to 3 tablespoons peppercorns, press into both sides of steak with the edge of a plate. Heat a large skillet, brush with 1 teaspoon oil, brown steak quickly on both sides. Reduce heat and cook about 5 minutes. Add to pan drippings 1 tablespoon Worcestershire sauce and 1 tablespoon lemon juice; swirl in pan, pour over steak. Makes 4 to 6 servings.

Great on the Grill

Steaks: First choice for the grill is steak—thick and tender, slightly crusty on the outside, pink and juicy within. Whether you use less expensive cuts such as chuck and round steaks for grilling, or splurge with porterhouse, sirloin, rib steaks, or even filet mignon, there is something special about steaks seasoned with the flavor of an outdoor fire.

Don't add salt until serving time. Check the broiling timetable on page 80 for times. To test for doneness, make a narrow slit in the center.

Be sure that the charcoal is hot and coated with gray ash before you begin to cook. Arrange meats on grill close to the coals. Use a hinged wire broiler for easy turning—or turn the steak with tongs rather than a fork, because piercing the meat will release the juices.

ORIENTAL STEAK

1 large clove garlic, crushed
1 teaspoon minced fresh ginger root or
 ⅛ teaspoon powdered ginger
1 tablespoon sugar
1 tablespoon cider vinegar
¼ cup soy sauce
4 tablespoons dry white wine
2 pounds round steak, 1 inch thick

Mash garlic and ginger root with mortar and pestle until pastelike (or mash crushed garlic and ginger powder with back of spoon). Dissolve sugar in vinegar, combine with soy sauce, wine and garlic-ginger paste. Marinate steak in mixture for several hours, turning occasionally. Grill to desired degree of doneness, slice on diagonal. Makes 6 to 8 servings.

SALT-MINE STEAK

This is the exception to the rule that steaks should not be salted before cooking. Coat both sides of steak with a half-inch layer of wet, coarse salt, pressing firmly. Broil in a hinged broiler, 15 minutes on each side. Crack off salt (it serves as a seal, and will not flavor the meat). Slice and serve with butter or margarine and salt and pepper.

SIRLOIN-TIP GRILL

3½ pounds sirloin tip
2 tablespoons wine vinegar
2 cloves garlic, crushed
½ teaspoon freshly ground black pepper
⅛ teaspoon powdered cloves
½ cup olive oil

Select well-marbled beef. Mix vinegar, garlic, pepper and cloves in a bowl. Turn meat to coat, add oil, cover bowl. Let stand 2 hours or more, turning often. Grill, 5 inches from coals, turning often to cook evenly on all sides, 45 minutes to 1 hour for rare to medium meat. Slice thin. Makes 6 to 8 servings.

GREAT RIBS ON THE GRILL

Allow 1 pound pork spareribs per main-dish serving or ½ pound per appetizer serving. Or use meatier country-style ribs, about ¾ pound per serving, or 1 pound lamb ribs. (To shorten roasting time for pork, bring ribs to a boil in water to cover. Simmer 5 minutes, drain.) Weave on rotisserie spit or lay flat on oiled grill. Sprinkle with salt and pepper. Cook slowly, 6 to 8 inches from coals, 1 to 1½ hours, until well done. There may be fat flare-ups—be prepared to quench the flames with water. After the first half hour of cooking, brush ribs often with any barbecue sauce.

MARMALADE SPARERIBS

6 pounds spareribs
4 large cloves garlic, crushed
1 tablespoon salt
1 cup chicken consommé
1 cup orange marmalade
¼ cup vinegar
¼ cup ketchup

Cover ribs with mixture of remaining ingredients, let stand several hours, or overnight in refrigerator. Weave on spit or lay on oiled grill, roast slowly 1½ hours, turning and brushing often with marinade, until thoroughly cooked. Makes 6 servings.

BUTTERFLIED LAMB LEG, GRILLED

1 lamb leg, boned
1 tablespoon oil
2 cloves garlic, crushed
1 teaspoon salt
¼ teaspoon pepper

Ask the A&P butcher to bone a leg of lamb, butterfly style. Skewer any loose pieces of meat compactly. Rub both sides of lamb with oil combined with garlic and seasonings, place on oiled grill. Broil, 4 inches from heat, about 15 minutes per side. Makes 8 servings.

CURRIED LAMB RIB BARBECUE

2 lamb breasts, 2 pounds each
2 cloves garlic, crushed
½ cup soy sauce
½ cup pineapple juice
2 teaspoons curry powder

Trim excess fat from breasts. Combine remaining ingredients, pour over meat, marinate overnight. Weave on barbecue spit, cook 8 inches from coals until tender, about 1½ hours. Or lay on oiled grill, turn often while cooking. Makes 4 servings.

BARBECUED HAM STEAK

Have center ham steak cut ½ inch thick. Slit fat around edge at intervals. Arrange ham in center of square of heavy-duty foil, spread with favorite barbecue sauce. Wrap foil over ham, sealing edges well. Lay on grill over hot coals, cook 15 minutes; turn, grill 15 minutes longer. Makes 4 to 6 servings.

Kebabs Are Great on the Grill

The first shish kebab was probably pieces of lamb, *kebab,* speared on a *shish,* or sword, and cooked over an open fire. The kebab has now become the most varied of all barbecue specialties. Cubes of any meat or fish can be combined with fruits and vegetables for grilling. Favorite vegetables include eggplant, zucchini and other squash, tomatoes, mushrooms, onions, green and red peppers. Pineapple is probably the fruit most often found on a skewer, but apricots, peaches and oranges are also popular.

Cubes from less tender cuts of beef and other meats tenderize in the marinade.

ORIENTAL PORK KEBABS

1½ pounds lean pork in 1-inch cubes
1 cup soy sauce
1 tablespoon honey
1 clove garlic, crushed
1 tablespoon brown sugar
1 tablespoon sherry
6 whole cherry tomatoes
12 thick slices onion
12 large mushroom caps

Marinate pork cubes for several hours in mixture of soy sauce, honey, garlic, sugar and sherry. Thread on skewers alternately with vegetables. Broil, 4 or 5 inches from heat, turning and brushing often with sauce, until pork is golden brown and thoroughly cooked. Makes 6 servings.

TURKISH KEBABS

1½ pounds boneless lamb or beef cubes
½ cup dry white wine

¼ teaspoon nutmeg
¼ teaspoon rosemary
1 teaspoon fresh dill, minced; or
    ¼ teaspoon crushed dill seed
1 large onion, minced
2 tablespoons minced parsley
Salt

Place cubes of meat in large bowl. Combine remaining ingredients, except salt, and pour over meat. Cover, let stand in refrigerator 12 to 24 hours. Lift from marinade, thread on skewers. Grill until done to taste, brushing often with marinade. Season with salt. Makes 6 servings.

SHISH KEBAB

1½ pounds 1½-inch cubes of lamb, cut
    from leg or shoulder
½ cup oil
¼ cup red wine vinegar
2 cloves garlic, mashed
Any combination of eggplant cubes,
    zucchini cubes, whole cherry tomatoes,
    mushroom caps, slices of onion, slices
    of green and red pepper
Salt

Cover meat with mixture of oil, vinegar and garlic, let stand 1 hour at room temperature or overnight in the refrigerator. Thread meat and choice of vegetables alternately on skewers. Grill over charcoal or in the broiler until the meat is browned to taste and the vegetables are tender but still crisp. Baste often with the marinade. Season with salt. Makes 6 servings.

HAM KEBABS

12 cubes (1½ inch) cooked ham
1 can (1 pound) apricot halves
¼ cup oil
¼ cup vinegar
1 tablespoon horseradish
¼ teaspoon garlic powder
1 tablespoon honey
1 tablespoon soy sauce

Place cubes of ham in deep bowl. Drain syrup from fruit, combine ¼ cup with remaining ingredients, pour over ham. Marinate 1 hour. Spear ham cubes on skewers alternately with the apricot halves. Cook over charcoal, 4 to 5 inches from heat, turning and brushing frequently with sauce, until ham is golden on all sides, about 15 minutes. If desired, squares of green pepper and onion slices may be added to the skewers. Makes 4 servings.

Great Burgers

You can, and will, cook hamburgers indoors, in the broiler or the skillet. But they're especially great on the grill! Try these recipes both ways.

Burgers on the Grill: A hinged wire broiler is useful for grilling hamburgers. Turn often to check the progress of the browning—charcoal-grilled meats should be richly browned but not burned. Basting with a sauce (page 79) helps to keep the meat moist. Any of these may be broiled indoors, as well.

Burger Breads: Instead of using toasted hamburger buns, still the first choice of many, serve grilled burgers on onion rolls or poppy-seed rolls; or on toasted English muffins, French bread, or rye or pumpernickel. For a change, brush bread with garlic-seasoned melted butter.

Burger Garnishes: Ketchup or chili sauce is a basic burger garnish; a slice of tomato, sweet onion or pickle is a pleasant option.

BASIC BURGERS

To each pound of ground sirloin, round or chuck, add 1 teaspoon salt, ¼ teaspoon pepper, 1 tablespoon water, if desired. Shape into 4 patties, slightly larger in diameter than hamburger rolls. Broil, 3 inches from heat, over charcoal or in a preheated broiler, 2 minutes each side for rare, slightly longer for medium. Or pan-broil: Brush heavy skillet lightly with fat, brown burgers on both sides, 4 minutes or a little longer in all. Makes 4 servings. (See photo, page 97.)

EXTRA-MOIST BURGERS

To each pound ground beef, add 2 tablespoons ketchup, 1 slice of bread softened in 2 tablespoons milk, ¼ teaspoon pepper, ½ teaspoon any dried herb and 1 teaspoon salt. Blend thoroughly, shape into 4 patties. Brush with softened butter, broil. Makes 4 servings.

HAMBURGERS PROVENÇALE

Make Extra-Moist Burgers (above), broil. Grill seasoned tomato slices in broiler alongside burgers. Spread crusty rolls with 2 tablespoons melted butter or margarine blended with crushed clove of garlic; toast rolls. Serve burgers on toasted buns with grilled tomatoes as topping.

PIZZABURGERS

After broiling burgers lightly, cover each with a slice of mozzarella or other cheese, continue to broil until cheese melts. Arrange on a toasted English muffin half, top with spaghetti sauce, sprinkle with a bit of oregano.

WINEBURGER STEAKS

To each pound of ground beef, add ¼ cup red wine, 1 tablespoon grated onion, ½ teaspoon salt. Shape 3 oval patties and broil in broiler or over grill, basting with following sauce: ¼ cup butter or margarine melted with 2 tablespoons red wine, a split garlic clove, salt, pepper and cayenne to taste. Pour remaining sauce over meat to serve. Makes 3 servings.

CHEESE-FILLED BURGERS

To each pound ground beef, add 1 teaspoon salt, 1 teaspoon Worcestershire sauce, 2 tablespoons ice-cold water. Form into 8 very thin patties. Place slice of cheese between each 2 patties, pressing edges of meat together to seal. Pan-broil in lightly greased hot skillet. Makes 4 servings.

BLUE-CHEESE BURGERS

Prepare thin patties, as above, sandwich patties with a mixture of ¼ pound blue cheese, crumbled, and 2 tablespoons mayonnaise. Press edges together to seal, broil as above. Makes 4 servings.

TOMATO-STUFFED BURGERS

Form 8 thin patties, as above. Sandwich with thin slices of tomato and a little finely chopped or grated onion. Pinch edges of meat together to seal. Broil. Makes 4 servings.

ORIENTAL HAMBURGERS

Shape 1 pound meat into 4 patties. Marinate 5 minutes in mixture of ½ cup soy sauce, 2 tablespoons brown sugar, ¼ teaspoon ginger. Remove from marinade, pan-broil in heavy skillet in which a small amount of fat has been melted. Makes 4 servings.

SPINACH SAUCE FOR HAMBURGERS

Coarsely chop ½ pound raw spinach and 1 green pepper. Put in electric blender, a handful at a time, with blender at low speed. Add 2 tablespoons chopped onion, then slowly add 4 tablespoons olive or salad oil, ¼ teaspoon salt and 1 teaspoon vinegar. Serve as relish with hot hamburgers on buns.

Chopped Meat

A pound of ground beef, simply seasoned and shaped into hamburgers, will serve four. Add stretchers like bread or crackers or cereal, and moisteners like milk, ketchup or tomato sauce, and you increase the number of servings as well as the nutritional content of the burger.

Ground chuck combines economy with flavor, has a good proportion of fat, and is therefore especially juicy. Many cooks prefer it for these reasons. Ground round is the leanest of chopped meats, and is therefore lower in calories. Chopped sirloin, the most expensive ground meat, is first choice for the luxury of superb flavor and tenderness. Serve burgers or "steaks" of chopped sirloin without the addition of any seasoning except salt and pepper.

Meat-loaf mixture consists of equal parts of beef, pork and veal. Since it contains pork, it can be used only in loaves, meatballs and other long-cooking preparations. Choose ground meat to suit your menu: chuck for family favorites such as chili con carne, round for a meat loaf and chopped sirloin for special occasions. Ground meat is perishable; plan to use it—or freeze it—within 24 hours of the time it was ground.

THE GREAT AMERICAN MEAT LOAF

2 pounds meat-loaf mixture (mixed ground beef, pork and veal)
1 slice bread, crumbled
½ cup milk
2 eggs
1½ teaspoons salt
¼ teaspoon pepper
¼ cup chopped onion
2 tablespoons chopped parsley
½ cup ketchup

Use meat-loaf mixture or all beef, as you prefer. Soak bread in milk. Add eggs, beat well. Blend with meat and remaining ingredients except ketchup. Shape into a loaf, arrange in buttered baking pan. Pour ketchup over loaf. Bake in a moderately slow oven (325°F) 1½ hours, basting occasionally with the pan sauces. Makes 8 servings.

Variations:
1. Add ¼ cup chopped green pepper.
2. Add 2 tablespoons pimiento-stuffed olives.
3. Substitute crushed unsweetened crackers for the bread.
4. Omit the milk and add the ketchup to the meat mixture.
5. Omit the bread and add 1 cup wheat germ.

6. Layer meat with 1 can (4 ounces) drained mushroom slices.
7. Garnish meat loaf with 4 strips crisp-cooked bacon.

(See photo, page 76.)

MEAT LOAF VIENNESE

1½ pounds meat-loaf mixture (mixed ground beef, pork and veal)
1 teaspoon salt
¼ teaspoon pepper
1 slice bread, crumbled
½ cup water
1 egg
¼ cup minced parsley
1 small onion
1 beef bouillon cube
½ cup hot water
¼ cup chili sauce
1 teaspoon paprika
1 tablespoon flour
½ cup water
1 cup sour cream

Combine meat, salt, pepper, bread soaked in water, egg, parsley, and onion. Dissolve bouillon cube in hot water, add to mixture, blend well. Fill a greased 9-inch loaf pan, spread with chili sauce. Bake in a moderate oven (350°F) one hour. Remove meat loaf from pan. Scrape drippings into a skillet, add paprika and flour, stir over low heat for a minute. Slowly stir in ½ cup water and cook, stirring, until sauce is thick and smooth. Add sour cream, heat. Serve over slices of meat loaf. Makes 6 servings.

SKILLET MEAT-LOAF DINNER

1 pound ground beef
1 slice bread, crumbled
¼ cup water
1 egg
1 teaspoon salt
⅛ teaspoon pepper
1 tablespoon vegetable oil
4 new potatoes, peeled and halved
4 medium carrots, peeled and quartered
1 can (8 ounces) tomato sauce
¼ teaspoon basil
¼ cup ketchup
1 pound zucchini, peeled and diced
½ teaspoon salt

Combine beef, bread, water, egg, 1 teaspoon salt and pepper. Shape into oval meat loaf. Heat oil in large skillet, brown meat loaf on both sides. Add potatoes, carrots, tomato sauce, basil. Cover top of loaf with ketchup. Reduce heat, cover pan, simmer ½ hour. Add zucchini, sprinkle vegetables with ½ teaspoon salt. Cover pan, cook 15 minutes longer, or until vegetables are tender. Makes 4 servings.

FRIKADELLEN

1½ pounds meat-loaf mixture (mixed beef, pork and veal), finely ground
2 onions, grated
2 cups soft bread crumbs
1½ cups milk
2 eggs
1½ teaspoons salt
¼ teaspoon pepper
3 to 4 tablespoons bacon drippings
2 tablespoons flour
1½ cups beef bouillon

Ask the meatman to grind the meat mixture again. Mix with onions. Soak bread crumbs in milk with beaten eggs, salt and pepper. Combine with meat, blend thoroughly. Heat 3 tablespoons bacon drippings in a heavy skillet. Shape small meatballs with a teaspoon, brown on all sides in the hot fat, adding more fat as needed. Remove meatballs. Add flour to pan juices and cook, stirring, for a minute; gradually add bouillon. Cook, stirring, until sauce is thickened and smooth. Adjust seasoning. Return meatballs to pan, heat through. Makes 6 servings.

MAGNIFICENT MEATBALLS

2 pounds ground beef
1 can (1 pound) tomatoes
1 cup fine soft bread crumbs
1 egg
1¼ teaspoons salt
2 teaspoons grated onion
8 slices bacon, cut in half
½ cup sour cream

Combine beef, tomatoes, bread crumbs, egg, salt and onion. Form into 16 balls. Wrap each in a half slice of bacon, place in a baking dish seam side down. Bake in a moderate oven (350°F) 45 minutes to 1 hour. Spoon off excess fat. Stir sour cream into pan juices. Makes 8 servings.

SWEDISH MEATBALLS

1 pound ground veal
1½ pounds ground beef
1 onion, grated
½ cup bread crumbs

1 cup milk
2 eggs
2 teaspoons salt
½ teaspoon pepper
  Dash nutmeg
3 tablespoons butter or margarine
1 tablespoon flour
1 cup sour cream

Mix veal and beef with onion. Soak bread crumbs in milk, add to meat with eggs. Season with salt, pepper and nutmeg to taste. Shape small balls, brown in hot butter in an oven-proof skillet, shaking pan to brown all sides and keep meatballs round. Remove meatballs to a serving dish. Add flour to pan juices, stir to blend, cook for a few minutes. Gradually add sour cream and cook, stirring, until sauce is thick and smooth. Do not boil. Pour over meatballs. Makes 8 to 10 servings.

LILLIE'S CHILI

1 pound ground beef
1 onion, chopped
1 green pepper, chopped
1 clove garlic, chopped
1 can (6 ounces) green chili peppers, chopped
  Salt, pepper
1 tablespoon chili powder
1 can (1 pound) tomatoes
1 can (6 ounces) tomato paste
1 can (1 pound) red kidney beans

Cook meat in a large skillet, stirring continuously with a fork, until it loses its red color. Drain off excess fat. Add onion, pepper, garlic, chili peppers and seasonings, cook onions until soft. Add tomatoes and paste, simmer about 1 hour. Add beans, heat. Makes 4 or more servings.

CHILI PIE

Prepare Lillie's Chili (above). Pour into greased 2-quart casserole. Top with cornbread mix, made according to package directions. Bake in a hot oven (400°F) about 25 minutes, until crust is golden.

MOUSSAKA

1 pound ground lamb
1 small eggplant
½ cup oil
2 tablespoons butter or margarine
4 medium onions, sliced
3 cloves garlic, minced
1 teaspoon salt
½ teaspoon thyme
½ teaspoon oregano

½ cup canned tomatoes
½ cup dry white wine
½ cup fine bread crumbs

Topping:

2 tablespoons butter or margarine
2 tablespoons flour
1½ cups milk
½ teaspoon salt
⅛ teaspoon nutmeg
2 eggs, separated

In a heavy skillet, cook lamb over medium heat, stirring, until brown. Drain fat; set meat aside. Slice eggplant without peeling, brown on both sides in oil in same skillet, remove. Add butter to skillet, cook onions and garlic, stirring, until soft. Add meat, salt, herbs, tomatoes and wine. Cover, simmer 30 minutes. Cool, stir in half the crumbs. Fill a 2-quart baking dish with alternate layers of eggplant and meat.

Topping:

In a saucepan melt the butter, add flour. Stir over low heat for 5 minutes, until the roux is golden. Gradually stir in the milk. Cook, stirring, until the sauce is smooth and thick. Season with salt and nutmeg. Beat egg yolks, warm with a little sauce, combine with sauce in pan over heat. Cool slightly. Beat egg whites until stiff, fold in. Pour sauce over meat, sprinkle with remaining crumbs. Bake in moderate oven (350°F) for 1 hour, until top is golden. Makes 8 servings.

International Specialties

Surprise the family with these samplings of international cuisine.

From the Orient

CHINESE PORK AND PEPPERS

1 pound lean pork
2 tablespoons oil
½ cup sliced onions
½ cup green pepper, cut in strips
1 can (4 ounces) mushroom stems and pieces
1 teaspoon cornstarch
½ cup water
1 tablespoon brown sugar
½ tablespoon vinegar
1 tablespoon soy sauce

Cut pork into small pieces, using sharp knife or kitchen shears. Brown lightly in hot oil. Add onions, green pepper strips and drained mushrooms. (Reserve mushroom liquid.)

Cook about 3 minutes; remove meat and vegetables. Stir cornstarch into fat in pan. Slowly add liquid drained from mushrooms and water. Stir over low heat until sauce is slightly thickened and smooth; add brown sugar, vinegar and soy sauce. Simmer 1 minute. Taste and add salt, if needed. Return pork and vegetables to pan, heat. Serve with hot boiled rice. Makes 4 servings.

SWEET-AND-PUNGENT PORK

1 pound lean pork, cut into small cubes
1 egg
3 tablespoons water
½ cup flour
½ teaspoon salt
   Oil for frying
1 cup canned pineapple cubes
1 green pepper, cut in strips
½ cup vinegar
¼ cup brown sugar
1 tablespoon molasses
1 teaspoon soy sauce
1¼ cups water
1 medium tomato, diced
2 tablespoons cornstarch

Pork cubes should be of uniform size, for even cooking. Beat egg with 3 tablespoons water, add flour and salt to make smooth batter. Dip pork cubes into batter. Heat oil to 360°F, fry pork cubes, a few at a time, until golden. Drain on absorbent paper, keep warm in a slow oven. In a saucepan, combine pineapple, green pepper, vinegar, sugar, molasses, soy sauce and 1 cup water. Cook, stirring, until mixture comes to a boil. Add tomato. Blend cornstarch with ¼ cup cold water, stir in. Cook, stirring, until sauce is thickened. Pour over pork in serving dish. Makes 4 servings.

SUKIYAKI

2 pounds beef sirloin
1 large Bermuda onion
½ pound mushrooms
3 stalks celery
12 scallions
¼ pound spinach
1 can (7 ounces) water chestnuts
2-inch square suet
¾ cup bouillon
½ cup soy sauce
¼ cup sherry
1 tablespoon sugar

Cut beef sirloin into paper-thin strips, across the grain. Slice onion thinly, cut mushrooms into vertical slices, slice celery into diagonal pieces. Cut scallions into 3-inch lengths, tear spinach leaves in half, drain liquid from water chestnuts. Arrange foods in attractive pattern on large serving platter. At the table, heat suet to grease skillet, remove. Add meat slices, brown lightly. Push to side of pan, add onion, scallions, mushrooms, celery. Combine bouillon, soy sauce, sherry and sugar. Add to pan. Add water chestnuts. Stir gently. Cover, cook 5 minutes. Add spinach, cover, cook 3 minutes. Serve with hot boiled rice. Makes 6 servings.

From Germany

BEEF BIRDS (LINDEN ROULADEN)

2 pounds round steak, ¼ inch thick
1 clove garlic, cut
½ pound pork sausage meat
2 tablespoons chopped onion
2 tablespoons chopped celery
1½ cups soft bread crumbs
¼ teaspoon salt
⅛ teaspoon pepper
⅛ teaspoon thyme
8 to 10 bacon strips
1 cup red wine

Cut the round steak into 8 to 10 pieces about 4 by 5 inches in size. Rub with cut clove of garlic. In a heavy skillet, brown the pork sausage, drain all but 1 tablespoon of the drippings from the pan. Add onion and celery, cook until soft. Add bread crumbs, brown lightly; add seasonings. Divide stuffing on the steaks, roll up, wrap each with a bacon strip, secure with a toothpick. Brown rolls in a skillet. Drain fat, add wine to skillet. Reduce heat, cover, simmer 45 minutes to 1 hour, until meat is tender. Makes 8 to 10 servings.

From Italy

VEAL CACCIATORE

2 pounds veal shoulder
2 tablespoons butter or margarine
½ cup sliced onion
2 cloves garlic, minced
1 can (1 pound 13 ounces) tomatoes
½ pound fresh mushrooms; or 1 can
   (6 ounces) button mushrooms, drained
½ teaspoon oregano
½ cup dry red wine
   Salt and pepper

Have butcher cut veal shoulder into cubes. Brown cubes lightly in butter. Add onion, garlic, tomatoes, mushrooms (if canned mushrooms are used, add later, with wine) and oregano. Cover, simmer over low heat 30 minutes. Add wine, cook 15 minutes longer. Add salt and pepper to taste. Makes 4 to 6 servings.

Sausage Sensations

You can find many different kinds of sausages from all over the world at your A&P, with variations according to season and location. Favorites include:

1. Fresh sausages—made of ground fresh pork, well seasoned with spices and herbs. These come in links (some of them partially cooked, ready to brown and serve) and in bulk packages from which patties may be sliced.

2. Cooked smoked sausages—a category that includes frankfurters, knockwurst and bologna. These are already cooked and need only heating.

3. Uncooked smoked sausages—the most popular of these are the Italian sausages, both hot and "sweet," the garlicky Polish sausage and mettwurst. These keep well but must be cooked before eating.

4. Cooked sausages, not cured—a type that includes liverwurst, blood sausage and Braunschweiger. These can be used cold or hot.

5. Dry sausages—can in fact be very pleasantly juicy, are eaten as is. They must be kept under refrigeration. The list includes salami, cervelat and pepperoni.

TOAD IN THE HOLE

1 pound small pork sausage links
2 eggs
1½ cups milk
1 cup flour
½ teaspoon salt
Pinches nutmeg and thyme

Pierce sausages with a fork, place on a 13-inch-by-9-inch baking pan, bake in a very hot oven (450°F) 15 minutes, until brown, shaking the pan occasionally to brown the links evenly. Meanwhile, beat eggs with milk, flour, salt and spices to make a light batter. Remove sausages from baking pan. Drain off all but 4 tablespoons fat. Pour the batter into the hot pan, quickly arrange sausages in the batter, return at once to the oven to bake about 25 minutes, until crust is well puffed and richly browned. Serve hot. Makes 6 servings.

SAUSAGE DUMPLINGS

1 cup biscuit mix
1 egg, well beaten
½ cup milk
½ cup finely chopped cervelat, salami or pepperoni

Combine biscuit mix, egg and milk, add finely chopped sausage. Roll to ½-inch thickness on floured board, cut into small shapes, drop into boiling soup. Cover, simmer 12 to 15 minutes, until puffy and light. Makes dumplings for 4 servings.

SAUSAGE-STUFFED PEPPERS

1 cup finely diced salami
1 package (8 ounces) seasoned bread stuffing
1 tablespoon minced onion
½ cup hot water
6 green peppers
Salt and pepper
1 tablespoon oil
1 can (1 pound) prepared spaghetti sauce

Bologna or pepperoni may be used in this recipe instead of salami. Combine bread stuffing, onion and salami, mixing lightly with a fork. Moisten with hot water. Cut off tops of peppers, scoop out seeds and pith. Blanch peppers in boiling salted water 5 minutes, drain. Sprinkle inside with salt and pepper, fill with sausage mixture. Set peppers upright in lightly oiled baking dish, pour spaghetti sauce around them. Bake in a moderately hot oven (375°F) 20 to 25 minutes, until peppers are tender. Makes 6 servings.

Quick Tricks with Franks

While frankfurters belong to the sausage family, the All-American Hot Dog has assumed such an important role in our lives that it deserves a section to itself. Frankfurters are already cooked and can even be eaten cold.

Freeze frankfurters, wrapped in plastic wrap or foil, in meal-size portions. They can be cooked while still frozen almost as quickly as if thawed.

STUFFED DOGS

Slit franks to make a pocket. Fill with a sliver of Swiss or Cheddar cheese to fit, brush with mustard, wrap with strip of bacon and secure with wooden picks. Grill in broiler oven or in hinged steak holder over barbecue grill. Turn once, cook until bacon is crisp. Other stuffings: strip of pickle, spoonful of baked beans.

FRANKS SIMMERED IN BARBECUE SAUCE

6 to 8 frankfurters
2 tablespoons oil
½ cup prepared barbecue sauce
1 teaspoon instant minced onion
½ cup tomato juice

Slice frankfurters diagonally, brown lightly in oil, add barbecue sauce, onion and tomato juice. Simmer, uncovered, until sauce has reduced and thickened. Serve hot with rice. Makes 3 to 4 servings.

FRANKFURTERS MEXICAN

Melt 2 tablespoons shortening in skillet, add 4 to 6 cubed frankfurters, brown lightly. Add 1 can (1 pound) meatless chili, 1 teaspoon instant minced onion and 1 can (1 pound) tomatoes. Simmer, uncovered, about 15 minutes. Add additional chili powder, if desired. Makes 4 servings.

SAUERKRAUT RELISH FOR FRANKS

Rinse and drain 1 can (3 cups) sauerkraut, add ¾ teaspoon caraway seeds, ⅛ teaspoon celery seeds, ⅔ cup sour cream. Stir over moderate heat until heated through. Keep warm. Serve with hot dogs in buns.

SPEARED DOGS

Cut frankfurters in thirds, spear on skewers alternately with bread-and-butter pickles, cubes of cheese and canned drained onions. While grilling, brush with melted butter or margarine blended with prepared mustard. Serve in hero-size buns.

CHILI DOGS

1 pound ground beef
2 cups canned tomatoes
1 clove garlic, crushed
Salt, pepper
1 to 2 teaspoons chili powder
1 cup chopped onion

Brown meat, stirring with a fork. Add tomatoes and garlic, bring to boil, cover, simmer 20 minutes. Add salt, pepper and chili powder to taste. Makes about 4 cups. Spoon sauce over hot grilled franks on rolls, top with chopped onion.

FRANKS IN WRAPS

Roll refrigerator biscuits into long ropes. Wrap each in spiral around a frank and skewer, securing ends. Grill until golden, 5 inches from coals, about 10 minutes.

Variety Meats for Variety

Not least of the meat bargains to be found in the market are the "innards"—livers, brains, kidneys, hearts, sweetbreads.

Livers come in a variety of distinctive textures and flavors, from the mild and tender chicken liver to the robust and firm-textured beef liver.

Lamb and veal kidneys are naturally tender and can be broiled or pan-browned quickly. Beef kidneys have excellent flavor, but require about 1½ hours of moist cooking for tenderness.

Hearts of beef, lamb, veal and pork all require long cooking for tenderness, but they're worth the effort.

PAN-BROWNED LIVER

Trim slices of beef liver (or calf's or lamb's or pork liver), dust with flour seasoned with salt, pepper and crushed oregano. Brown quickly on both sides in butter, margarine or oil. Serve with crisp bacon strips, if desired. Liver should be slightly pink in the middle for best flavor and maximum tenderness, except for pork liver, which must be well done.

BROILED LIVER

Trim slices of beef liver (or calf's or lamb's liver), brush with butter or margarine or with prepared French dressing. Arrange on broiling pan, with strips of bacon alongside, if desired. Broil 3 inches from heat, turn to brown both sides. Season with salt and pepper. Do not overcook.

LIVER AND ONIONS

1 pound sliced beef or calf's liver
3 tablespoons flour
¾ teaspoon salt
¼ teaspoon pepper
3 tablespoons bacon fat
½ cup sliced onions

Cut the liver into serving portions, discarding skin and veins. Wash and dry. Combine flour, salt and pepper, dredge liver pieces. Heat fat in skillet, brown liver on both sides, remove from pan. Add sliced onions to the pan and cook, covered, until soft. Return liver to pan, heat. Makes 4 servings.

HEART PIE

1 pound veal or pork hearts
4 tablespoons butter or margarine
1 onion, sliced
1 teaspoon salt
⅛ teaspoon thyme
½ cup chopped onion
2 raw potatoes, chopped
1 package (¾ ounce) beef gravy mix
1 teaspoon minced parsley
   Pastry for 1-crust pie

Trim hearts, cut into cubes. Melt half the butter in a saucepan, brown cubes lightly. Add sliced onion, salt, thyme and water to cover. Simmer, covered, until meat is tender, about 40 minutes. Drain, reserve stock. Melt remaining butter, add chopped onion and potatoes, cook until golden. Add cooked heart. Prepare beef gravy mix as directed on package, using 1¼ cups of the reserved heart stock instead of water. Combine gravy with meat and vegetables. Add parsley. Taste and adjust seasoning. Pour into a shallow baking dish, cover with pastry, slash crust. Bake in a hot oven (400°F) about 20 minutes, until crust is golden. Makes 4 servings.

BEEFSTEAK-AND-KIDNEY PIE

1 pound beef kidneys
1 pound boneless beef
¼ cup flour
½ teaspoon salt
⅛ teaspoon pepper
3 tablespoons vegetable oil or shortening
2 cups water
2 beef bouillon cubes
¼ teaspoon marjoram
1 teaspoon Worcestershire sauce
2 medium potatoes, cut in ½-inch cubes
12 small white onions
   Pastry for 1-crust pie

Remove outer membrane from kidneys; split in half, trim away white veins and fat. Wash and dry; cut into pieces. Cut beef into cubes. Combine flour, salt and pepper; coat kidneys and beef. In heavy skillet or Dutch oven, heat oil over medium heat. Brown kidneys and beef. Add water, bouillon cubes, marjoram and Worcestershire sauce. Cover, simmer 30 to 45 minutes, until nearly tender. Add potatoes and onions, cook 30 minutes longer. Turn into shallow 1½-quart casserole. Roll out pastry, cover pie. Bake in hot oven (425°F) about 30 minutes. Makes 6 to 8 servings.

LAMB KIDNEYS IN WINE SAUCE

4 lamb kidneys
2 tablespoons butter or margarine
1 teaspoon prepared mustard
¾ teaspoon salt
⅓ cup dry red wine
½ cup sour cream (optional)

Remove membrane from kidneys, trim away tubes. Slice kidneys crosswise, soak briefly in hot water, rinse and dry well. Melt butter in skillet or chafing dish, brown kidneys quickly on all sides. Lower heat, stir in mustard and salt. Add wine and simmer, covered, 4 or 5 minutes—no longer. Blend in the sour cream, heat through. Makes 4 servings.

TONGUE WITH RAISIN SAUCE

1 beef tongue, smoked or corned
2 carrots
3 stalks celery, with leaves
1 large onion, stuck with 4 cloves
1 teaspoon peppercorns
1 tablespoon mixed pickling spices
   (optional)

If the tongue seems excessively salty, soak it in cold water for several hours. Wash the tongue well, cover it with fresh cold water, and add remaining ingredients. Simmer, covered, about 3 hours, or 45 minutes per pound, until the thickest portion of the tongue is tender. Test with a fork. Cool in the broth. Reserve broth to make sauce. Remove skin from tongue, trim and discard bone and gristle from thick end. Cut meat into thin diagonal slices. Serve hot with Raisin Sauce (below).

RAISIN SAUCE FOR TONGUE

2 tablespoons fat
2 tablespoons flour
2 cups strained tongue broth
½ cup raisins
1 lemon, grated rind and juice
¼ cup brown sugar
   Salt, cinnamon, cloves

Melt fat, add flour, stir over low heat until blended. Add broth, cook until thickened and smooth. Add raisins, lemon rind, sugar; simmer a few minutes, stir in lemon juice. Season to taste with salt, cinnamon and cloves. Pour over hot sliced tongue.

PIG KNUCKLES AND GREENS

4 cured pig knuckles or 2 jowls
2 onions

1 teaspoon sugar
½ teaspoon peppercorns
½ teaspoon crushed dried hot peppers
1 bay leaf
1 stalk celery with green top
4 pounds collard or turnip greens, well
   washed

Split knuckles or jowls in half. Cover with water, add onions, seasonings and celery. Bring to a boil and simmer, covered, for about 2 hours. Discard bay leaf. Add greens, simmer about 1 hour longer, until meat is tender. Makes 4 servings.

Barbecued Pig Feet: Allow 4 fresh pig feet, split in half, to serve 4. Cook as above, adding ¼ cup vinegar and a little salt to the water. When the feet are tender, transfer them to a baking dish, cover with favorite barbecue sauce, brown in a moderate oven (350°F) until crisp, basting often.

Ham Hocks with Black-eyed Peas: Soak 2 cups black-eyed peas in cold water overnight. Drain. Simmer ham hocks in water and spices, as for Pig Knuckles and Greens. After 2 hours, add peas, simmer until meat and peas are tender, about 45 minutes. Makes 6 servings.

CHITTERLINGS (CHITLINS)

5 pounds chitterlings (pig intestines), ready
   to cook
2 cloves garlic
1 onion
3 sprigs parsley
1 teaspoon peppercorns
1 teaspoon dried crushed red pepper
1 cup vinegar
   Salt

Cover chitterlings with boiling water, add remaining ingredients. Simmer about 3 hours, until tender. Cut into bite-sized pieces. Cooked chitterlings may be pan-fried, or simmered in favorite tomato sauces. Makes 6 servings.

TRIPE CREOLE

1 pound tripe
1 tablespoon salt
2 tablespoons oil, or butter or margarine
1 onion, sliced
1 clove garlic, minced
1 can (1 pound) stewed tomatoes
   Salt and pepper to taste

Cover tripe with water, add 1 tablespoon salt, bring to a boil. Simmer about 1½ hours, until tripe is tender. Drain, cut into bite-sized strips. Heat oil, cook tripe, onion and garlic 10 minutes, stirring occasionally. Add tomatoes, heat. Adjust seasoning with salt and pepper. Makes 4 servings.

CALF BRAINS WITH BROWNED BUTTER

1 pound calf brains
1 teaspoon salt
2 tablespoons vinegar
1 egg, beaten with salt and pepper
   Bread crumbs
¼ cup butter or margarine
1 tablespoon lemon juice
2 teaspoons drained capers (optional)

Soak the brains in cold salted water for 15 minutes, rinse, remove white membranes and thin outer covering with blood vessels. Cover with cold water, add salt and vinegar, simmer 20 minutes. Cool in broth; or drop into cold water to cool quickly. If desired, cut into slices. Dip into well-seasoned beaten egg and bread crumbs to coat. Melt butter in skillet, brown brains on both sides. Transfer brains to serving dish. Continue to cook butter in pan until it is brown. Add lemon juice and capers, heat, pour over brains. Makes 2 servings.

Can-Opener Economy

Canned meats, tender, perfectly cooked and wastefree, are a real boon. They make fine shelf or refrigerator staples. Canned hams become the center of a handsome buffet display. Other canned meats you will want to try include Canadian bacon, picnic hams, luncheon meat, tongue and Vienna sausages.

CANNED HAM

Since canned hams are already cooked, they may be sliced and served cold, just as they come from the can. Or they may be glazed, cold or hot.

COLD GLAZED HAM

1 canned ham, 3 pounds
1 cup water
½ teaspoon whole peppercorns
2 bay leaves
1 package lemon gelatin dessert
½ teaspoon salt
1 tablespoon vinegar
½ cup mayonnaise
1 envelope unflavored gelatin

½ cup cold water

1 cup hot water

Radishes, cucumber, green pepper, carrots, cut into shapes

Arrange ham on a rack set over a tray. Simmer water with peppercorns and bay leaves for 10 minutes. Strain. Add lemon gelatin and salt to liquid, stir to dissolve. Add vinegar. Cool until syrupy. Blend in mayonnaise. Cool until slightly thickened, spoon a layer over ham, chill until set. Add another layer of glaze, chill. Repeat until ham is thickly covered with the creamy glaze. Meanwhile, soften unflavored gelatin in cold water, add hot water to dissolve, cool until syrupy. Dip cut vegetables into clear glaze, arrange on ham. Chill. Coat with glaze. Chill until set.

Corned Beef

Corned-beef brisket in vacuum-sealed plastic bags is always available at the A&P.

CORNED BEEF AND CABBAGE

Cover corned beef with cold water in large kettle, add 1 onion pierced with 8 whole cloves, 1 bay leaf. Simmer, covered, 35 to 45 minutes per pound, or until meat is fork tender. About 15 minutes before cooking time is up, skim off excess fat. Discard onion and bay leaf. Add 1 head cabbage, cut in wedges, cook until tender. Serve with plain boiled potatoes, cooked separately. A 4-pound piece of corned-beef brisket makes 8 or more servings.

POULTRY

When you consider poultry in your meal planning, you know that you can purchase anything from a package of chicken wings to an enormous turkey—anything from a snack on the run to the main course for a large gathering.

Chicken

Chicken is one of the best food buys in the market, thanks to modern methods of feeding and processing. It is a prime source of low-cost protein, lower in calories and in saturated fat than red meats. No wonder American families have chicken on the menu twice as often as they did a generation ago.

Enjoy it in dozens of ways: roasted or baked, fried or oven-crisped, broiled or braised. Use every scrap of chicken you buy. Freeze wing tips, necks, giblets, skin, even bones, to accumulate a stockpile for the soup pot. A single chicken liver makes a delicious spread, and the flavorful chicken fat can be rendered to serve many cooking uses.

The chicken you buy at the A&P always meets the same high quality standards for meatiness, flavor and value.

You save most when you buy a whole chicken and cut it up yourself. But watch for A&P's special "Box O' Chicken," which consists of specially priced legs and breasts—a real bargain when you need to feed a family.

When is each type of chicken the best buy? Your own taste and menu plans will affect choices, but the following guide is your clue to best value for the dollar.

Broiler-Fryers: Approximately 12 weeks old and weigh from 2 to more than 3 pounds. This is a meaty all-purpose chicken that lends itself to all cooking methods. Always a good buy, sometimes a spectacular buy.

Roasters: Weigh 3¼ pounds or more. The proportion of meat to bone is greater in larger birds, so roasters cost more per pound than broiler-fryers. You pay more, but you get more. Best in the oven or on the rotisserie, fine for stewing.

Fowl: Older than 9 months. Fowl are less tender, more flavorful, than younger birds. Choose fowl for braising and stewing and for soups.

Capons: Castrated roosters weighing 4 to 8 pounds or more. They are very meaty and tender and command a premium price . . . a special-occasion luxury to enjoy roasted, braised or stewed.

Chicken Parts: You can buy as many breasts or even boned breast "cutlets" as you require for a deluxe luncheon, legs and thighs for frying or for a barbecue, wings, necks and backs for soup, chicken livers and gizzards by the pound. This is a convenient way to buy, and a money-saver if you always prefer only one section of the bird. But in most cases, you will do better to buy as many whole birds as required to accumulate a given number of breasts or thighs for a specific occasion, and store the remaining parts in the freezer for future use.

Turkey

Turkey is important all year around, too. The bigger the turkey, the lower the price per

Here is the know-how for Thanksgiving turkey and all the trimmings: tasty stuffing, cranberries prepared two ways, Creamed Onions, Mashed Sweet Potatoes with a tang of grated orange rind, subtle nutmeg accent. And, ah, those leftovers!

pound, the greater the proportion of meat to bone, and the lower the price per portion. Turkey offers more meat per pound than chicken.

The leftovers of a properly roasted turkey are moist and juicy, and can be used in any recipe calling for cooked chicken.

Allow ¾ to 1 pound ready-to-cook weight (the larger figure for smaller birds) for each serving. Birds that weigh between 16 and 20 pounds are most popular, but you may choose to pay slightly more for a hen turkey weighing under 15 pounds. Hens are likely to be plumper and more tender than the big toms.

Turkey Parts: You can also buy turkey halves or quarters or parts—legs, thighs, wings, breasts. Watch for frozen turkey steaks, cutlets, ground meat and sausages, as well as boneless turkey roasts, preseasoned and ready to cook in their disposable pans.

Duckling

There is no such thing nowadays as a tough duck, and the names duck and duckling are used interchangeably. The tender young ducks you find at the A&P, usually in the freezer compartment, weigh 5 to 6 pounds and make 4 servings. Duck livers are very large and very rich, and make an excellent pâté (see page 110). Duck fat, like chicken fat, can be used for cooking.

Goose

Goose is a holiday favorite, almost always roasted, preferably with a fruit stuffing that contrasts pleasantly with the very rich, very fat meat. You can special-order goose at the A&P at any time of year. A young goose suitable for roasting weighs from 8 to 12 pounds; a 10-pound goose is just right for the average family party of 10 people.

Goose fat, like duck and chicken fat, is very useful in cooking. Remove it and render it separately, in a pan over low heat. Use goose liver as you would chicken or duck livers in a pâté (see page 110).

Rock Cornish Hens

Rock Cornish hens enjoy well-deserved popularity as a party bird, and are a favorite for small families. A whole bird, weighing an average of 1¼ pounds, makes an attractive single serving.

Any recipe for chicken can be adapted for use with Rock Cornish. Allow a little extra time per pound for cooking the Rock Cornish to tenderness.

How to Fry Chicken

Chicken can be fried in hot fat deep enough to cover it completely, or in fat deep enough to cover it halfway, in which case it must be turned to finish frying.

Hydrogenated fats, corn, peanut and soybean oils, and lard are all good choices for deep-frying chicken. The temperature of the fat should be maintained at 370°F. Use a fat thermometer or an electric pan with a thermostatic control, or the old-fashioned method of browning a 1-inch cube of day-old bread in the fat. The bread should brown in 1 minute.

Fry a single layer of chicken at a time, drain on paper towels and transfer to a baking sheet in a moderate oven to keep hot. The white meat cooks more quickly than the dark.

Test browned chicken for doneness by pressing the thickest part of the meat. It will feel tender and will spring back from the touch. If it needs more cooking, finish in a moderate oven (350°F).

FRIED CHICKEN

To prepare chicken for frying, remove and reserve the wing tips, neck, back and giblets for another use. Cut the chicken into 8 pieces: 2 legs, 2 thighs, 2 wings, 2 breast pieces. Or fry cut-up chicken or chicken parts. If the breast pieces are unusually large, they may be cut in half, either before or after frying.

Crisp Fried Chicken: Shake ½ cup flour in a bag with 1 teaspoon salt, black pepper and other seasonings as desired. Add ½ teaspoon (or more) of any of the following to lend interesting flavor: garlic powder, chili powder, paprika, nutmeg, curry powder, poultry seasoning, rosemary, thyme. Or use seasoned salt instead of ordinary salt. A little monosodium glutamate intensifies the natural chicken flavor. Shake the chicken pieces in the bag, one at a time, to coat. Fry as above.

Crusty Fried Chicken: Combine ½ cup flour with ½ cup soft, fine bread crumbs. Add 1½ teaspoons salt and seasonings to taste (above). Spread the crumbs on a dinner plate. Dip chicken into ½ cup milk or buttermilk in a flat soup plate, press crumb mixture firmly on all sides. Lay pieces side by side on a tray and refrigerate for 1 hour to dry the coating. Fry as above.

Batter-Fried Chicken: Mix ¼ cup flour with 1 teaspoon salt. Add ½ cup milk and 2 eggs. beat with rotary beater until smooth. Dip pieces of chicken into this batter, drain excess. Fry as above.

Corn-Meal Crust: Mix in a paper bag ½ cup flour, ¼ cup corn meal, 1 teaspoon salt, and 1 teaspoon paprika or other seasoning (above). Dip chicken pieces in ½ cup milk, shake in bag to coat evenly. Fry as above.

Maryland Fried Chicken: Mix in a paper bag ½ cup flour, 1 teaspoon salt and seasonings (above). Shake chicken in bag to coat with flour. Dip into egg lightly beaten with 2 tablespoons water. Drain, coat with ½ cup fine dry bread crumbs. Dry on a tray in the refrigerator for 1 hour before frying. Fry as above.

Oven-Fried Chicken

If you like the crisp crustiness of fried chicken, but don't want the trouble of frying, or the extra fat that frying adds to the chicken, you can have it your way—chicken that looks and tastes like fried chicken but is actually baked in the oven!

OVEN-FRIED CHICKEN

  1 broiler-fryer, cut up
  ½ cup sour cream (or buttermilk, or
      evaporated milk, or mayonnaise)
  1 teaspoon salt
  Pepper, cayenne pepper
1½ cups fine, soft bread crumbs or
      crumbled cornflakes

Coat chicken thoroughly with a mixture of the sour cream and seasonings. Press crumbs firmly against chicken. Arrange pieces skin up on a greased baking sheet, side by side. Bake in a moderate oven (350°F) about 50 minutes, until chicken is tender, cooked through and crusty brown. Makes 4 servings.

Oven-Fried Chili Chicken: Shake chicken one piece at a time in a paper bag with ½ cup flour mixed with 1½ teaspoons each salt and chili powder, and pepper, paprika, cayenne and turmeric to taste. Arrange chicken on a baking pan generously coated with melted chicken or bacon fat. Bake as above.

Oven-Fried Garlic-Butter Chicken: Season chicken with salt and pepper. Melt ½ cup chicken fat, butter or margarine with 2 cloves crushed garlic. Dip pieces of chicken into fat, then into fine cracker crumbs or matzoh meal seasoned to taste with salt and pepper. Arrange on an oiled baking pan and sprinkle with remaining butter. Bake as above.

Oven-Fried Herb Chicken: Dip chicken pieces into oil, then into mixture of 2 cups herb-seasoned stuffing mix (rolled into fine crumbs) and 2 ounces grated Parmesan cheese. Arrange on an oiled baking pan, drizzle lightly with oil. Bake as above.

Broiled Poultry

All poultry, split or quartered, may be broiled—indoors or out. As noted in the meat chapter, broiling produces a dry heat, but frequent basting insures juicy, succulent results. For variety, try basting with any of the sauces below, or on page 107.

BROILED CHICKEN

Split or quarter broiler-fryers, depending upon size. Remove backbones and wing tips and reserve for the soup pot. Flatten the pieces so that they will cook evenly. Brush with fat; season. Arrange the chicken on a broiling pan and broil, skin side up, about 6 inches from the heat, until the skin browns lightly. Baste with butter or margarine or one of the basting sauces below, turn, and broil until the underside is browned. Continue to cook, turning and basting often, until the chicken is done, 30 to 45 minutes in all. The white meat cooks more quickly than the dark meat.

Note: To broil chicken out of doors, lay a double thickness of foil on the grill, 6 inches from the coals, and proceed as above, cooking the chicken skin side toward the heat first. Turn up the edges of the foil to hold in the juices. Cook slowly, and *don't overcook!*

Orange Basting Sauce: Combine ¼ cup orange marmalade, ¼ cup frozen concentrated orange juice, ¼ cup melted butter or margarine, and 1 teaspoon salt. Yield: About ¾ cup, for 1 chicken.

Pineapple Basting Sauce: Drain syrup from 1 can (1 pound 13 ounces) pineapple slices, combine with ¼ cup lemon juice, ¼ cup

When summer comes, an outdoor meal creates a vacation mood in your own backyard and time off from the kitchen. Barbecue chicken and burgers, fresh corn on the cob or other seasonal specials.

melted butter or margarine and 2 tablespoons soy sauce. Broil pineapple slices and use to garnish chicken. Yield: About 1½ cups, for 2 chickens.

Tarragon Basting Sauce: Melt ½ cup butter or margarine with 2 sprigs fresh, or ½ teaspoon dried crushed, tarragon and let stand ½ hour or longer. Yield: About ½ cup for 2 chickens.

Butter Basting Sauce: Combine ¼ cup melted butter or margarine, 1 teaspoon paprika, 1 teaspoon dry mustard, 1 teaspoon curry powder and 2 teaspoons salt. Yield: About ¼ cup, for 1 chicken.

Garlic Basting Sauce: Melt ¼ cup butter or margarine with 1 clove pressed garlic. Add 1 to 2 teaspoons salt, ½ teaspoon oregano, ½ teaspoon basil; let stand in warm place for 30 minutes before using. Yield: About ¼ cup, for 1 chicken.

LEMON-BROILED CHICKEN

　1 broiler-fryer, cut for broiling
½ lemon
　　Salt, pepper
¼ cup butter or margarine, melted
　2 tablespoons sugar

Flatten the pieces of chicken and lay them side by side on a broiling pan. Rub the chicken with the cut lemon, to coat with juice. Sprinkle with salt and pepper, brush with melted butter, sprinkle with sugar. Let stand in warm place for 30 minutes. Broil as above, basting with melted butter and turning often.

MARINATED BROILERS

　1 broiler-fryer, cut for broiling
　1 teaspoon salt
¼ cup salad oil
　1 clove garlic, pressed
¼ teaspoon crushed pepper

Flatten chicken, sprinkle with salt and cover with a mixture of the remaining ingredients. Let stand in the refrigerator for 1 to 2 hours, turning occasionally. Broil as above, basting frequently with the marinade.

DEVIL-CRUSTED CHICKEN

　1 broiler-fryer, cut for broiling
　　Salt, pepper
　　Oil
　2 cups fine fresh bread crumbs
¼ cup butter or margarine

**1 teaspoon prepared mustard
　Dash Worcestershire sauce**

Flatten chicken, season with salt and pepper, brush with oil. Broil 5 minutes each side, to firm flesh slightly. Combine remaining ingredients and press firmly on chicken. Finish cooking, 30 to 35 minutes.

BROILED TURKEY

Baby turkeys, weighing from 4 to 6 pounds, may be broiled, indoors or over charcoal. Split bird in half and reserve the backbone for the soup pot. Fasten wings to body with skewer. Spread skin side with butter or margarine. Broil 5 inches from heat about 30 minutes, until skin is a rich golden brown. Turn, brush again with butter, and broil about 45 minutes longer, until turkey is tender and there is no tinge of pink in the juices. Baste frequently with melted butter and a little water or stock, or with any of the basting sauces on page 96 and above.

TO SKIN DUCKLING

The thick skin and heavy layers of fat that characterize duckling add to the richness of a roasted bird. Long roasting allows the fat to melt and the excess can be removed. But when duck is to be cooked by methods other than roasting, it is often skinned before cooking.

Using a small knife, slit the skin down the bird's backbone and down the breast, cut through the fat close to the flesh without cutting into the meat, and loosen the skin. With fingers and an occasional assist from the knife, the duck can be peeled almost like an orange.

Cut the skin into squares and render the fat (see page 110), which is excellent for cooking. The brown, crisp crackles may be crumbled into a liver pâté (see page 110), or salted and used as a cocktail nibble.

BROILED DUCK

Skin the duck (above), split it, and remove wing tips, backbone and large breast bones. Brush halves on all sides with a mixture of 2 tablespoons sherry and 2 teaspoons soy sauce. Let stand for 30 minutes. Broil, bony side toward the flame (do not use rack), for about 20 minutes, basting frequently. Turn and broil skin side for about same time. Test with a fork for tenderness, and be sure that juices show no tinge of pink. Just before removing the duck from the broiler, brush it with 2 tablespoons honey seasoned with a pinch of ginger and a little black pepper. Let duck glaze and brown quickly, watching to prevent glaze from scorching.

BROILED ROCK CORNISH HENS

  3 large Rock Cornish hens, split in half
¼ cup melted butter or margarine
  Salt, pepper, marjoram
  1 pound mushrooms (caps only)
  2 tablespoons lemon juice or cognac
  2 tablespoons chopped parsley

Brush split hens on both sides with melted butter, season with salt, pepper and marjoram. Arrange skin side down on a preheated broiling pan and broil about 3 to 4 inches from the heat for 10 minutes. Turn and broil 10 to 12 minutes longer, until skin is richly browned. Baste with more butter. If more cooking is necessary, turn birds again. Arrange on a serving platter. While hens are broiling, cook mushroom caps in the butter. Add lemon juice or cognac and chopped parsley. Pour mushroom sauce over broiled Rock Cornish hens. Makes 6 servings.

Pan-Browned Chicken

Chicken can be pan-browned, or sautéed, easily and quickly, to serve as is, or as the base for a very elegant chicken dish.

PAN-BROWNED CHICKEN

Cut the chicken into serving pieces and pound pieces with the flat of a knife; the entire surface of each should touch the bottom of the skillet. Loosen the skin at the end of the drumsticks so that the flesh at the end will not dry out. Detach wings from breasts and cut the breast meat away from the bones. Season with salt and pepper. Use a skillet large enough to cook all the pieces at once. You will need about 4 tablespoons cooking fat. For extra flavor, use butter, clarified to eliminate the easily burned milk solids. Melt the butter in a small pan and pour the clear liquid off the milky sediment that will settle at the bottom. Or use rendered chicken fat (see page 110) for its distinctive taste. Brown the chicken slowly, covered, skin side first. Cook white meat about 25 minutes in all, dark meat 35 minutes. Remove cooked chicken to

a serving dish, spoon pan juices over it. Makes 4 servings.

CHICKEN BERCY

  1 pan-browned broiler-fryer, as above
  1 tablespoon minced onion
  1 teaspoon flour
¼ cup dry white wine
¼ cup water
  2 tablespoons tomato paste
  Salt, pepper
  Chopped parsley for garnish

Remove the cooked pan-browned chicken to a serving platter. Add onion to the pan juices and cook until glazed. Add flour and stir for a minute. Add wine, water and tomato paste, stir and scrape in the brown bits that cling to the pan, and cook, stirring constantly, until the sauce is thickened and smooth. Add salt and pepper to taste. Pour the sauce over the pan-browned chicken, sprinkle with chopped parsley. Makes 4 servings.

CHICKEN WITH MUSHROOMS

  1 pan-browned broiler-fryer, as above
  1 pound mushrooms
¼ cup water
  1 tablespoon lemon juice
  2 tablespoons butter or margarine
  Salt
  1 tablespoon chopped onion
  1 clove garlic, crushed
  1 teaspoon flour

While the pan-browned chicken is cooking, wash mushrooms and simmer in water, lemon juice and butter, with a dash of salt, for 10 minutes. Remove the cooked chicken to a serving platter. Add onion and garlic to the pan juices and cook, stirring, for a minute or two. Sprinkle with flour, stir. Add mushrooms and their liquid. Cook, stirring, until the sauce is smooth. Return the chicken to the pan to heat, if desired, or simply pour the mushrooms and sauce over the chicken. Makes 4 servings.

CHICKEN À L'ORANGE

½ cup flour
  2 tablespoons grated orange zest
  2 teaspoons paprika
  1 teaspoon salt
  1 broiler-fryer, cut up
¼ cup oil
  1 tablespoon butter or margarine
  1 tablespoon flour

¾ cup orange juice
¼ cup Marsala wine
  Salt, pepper, sugar

Mix flour, orange zest and seasonings in a paper bag and shake chicken to coat evenly. Brown lightly in hot oil, turning often. Cover skillet and cook until chicken is tender, about 40 minutes in all. Remove chicken to a heated platter. Pour off oil. In same pan, melt butter, stir in flour. Add orange juice and cook, stirring in the brown bits until sauce is smooth and thick. Strain sauce into another pan, reheat, and add wine; do not boil. Adjust seasoning with salt, pepper and sugar. Pour over chicken. Makes 4 servings.

Poultry in a Skillet

You can prepare a chicken dinner in minutes, cook it in half an hour, and enjoy never-ending variations on a delicious theme. The secret? Cook your chicken in a skillet. Use a large, heavy skillet fitted with a lid to produce anything from a Quick Chicken Cacciatore to a classic Chicken in Red Wine. With a little more cooking time, you can produce skillet meals with other poultry, too.

QUICK CHICKEN CACCIATORE

  1 broiler-fryer, cut up
    Flour, salt, pepper
  4 tablespoons oil
  1 can (4 ounces) mushrooms
¾ cup ketchup or chili sauce
¼ cup water

Dredge chicken pieces with seasoned flour, brown on all sides in hot oil in skillet. Add mushrooms and their liquid, ketchup, and water. Bring to a boil, lower heat, cover the skillet, and simmer about 30 minutes, until chicken is tender. Shake pan occasionally, and baste chicken with pan sauce. Serve with rice or spaghetti. Makes 4 servings.

CHICKEN WITH RICE AND PEAS

  1 broiler-fryer, cut up
    Salt, pepper
  3 tablespoons oil
  1 onion, chopped
  1 green pepper, chopped
  1 cup rice
  1 can (1 pound) tomatoes
  1 cup water
    Small piece bay leaf

  1 can (16 ounces) peas, drained
¼ cup chopped pimiento

Season chicken with salt and pepper, brown on all sides in oil, remove. Add onion and green pepper to pan, stir over low heat until golden. Add rice, stir until golden. Add tomatoes, water and bay leaf. Bring to a boil, stir. Return chicken to pan, cover, simmer 30 minutes, until chicken is tender. Discard bay leaf. Add peas and pimiento, heat through. Makes 4 servings.

COUNTRY CAPTAIN

  1 broiler-fryer, cut up
¼ cup flour
  1 teaspoon salt
  1 teaspoon curry powder
¼ cup oil
  1 onion, chopped
  1 clove garlic, chopped
  1 green pepper, sliced
  1 can (8 ounces) tomato sauce
  2 cups water
¼ teaspoon hot pepper sauce
¼ cup raisins
  2 tablespoons toasted slivered almonds

Coat chicken with flour mixed with salt and curry powder. Heat oil in skillet, brown chicken pieces on all sides. Remove. Brown onion, garlic and green pepper lightly in skillet. Add tomato sauce, water, pepper sauce and raisins and cook, stirring, for a minute or two. Return chicken to skillet, cover, simmer about 30 minutes, until chicken is tender, shaking the pan and spooning the sauce over the chicken occasionally. Serve sprinkled with almonds. Makes 4 servings.

CRANBERRY CHICKEN

  1 broiler-fryer, cut up
⅓ cup flour
  1 teaspoon salt
    Pepper, nutmeg
¼ cup butter or margarine
  1 cup whole cranberry sauce
    Juice of 1 lemon
    Prepared horseradish, drained, to taste

Dust chicken pieces with flour combined with salt, pepper and nutmeg, brown slowly in butter. Combine cranberry sauce, lemon juice and horseradish. Spoon half mixture over chicken, cover pan, and simmer for about 20 minutes. Add remaining mixture and simmer 10 to 15 minutes longer, until chicken is tender. Makes 4 servings.

CHICKEN IN RED WINE
(COQ AU VIN)

1 broiler-fryer, cut up
1 teaspoon salt
¼ teaspoon pepper
¼ cup oil
¼ cup cognac (optional)
6 small onions
1 clove garlic, minced
1 can (4 ounces) mushrooms
1½ cups red wine
1 cup chicken bouillon
1 tablespoon tomato paste
Pinch thyme
1 tablespoon minced parsley

Season chicken with salt and pepper. Heat oil in skillet, brown chicken on all sides. Add cognac, ignite. When flame dies, cover the skillet and cook over moderate heat about 10 minutes. Add onions and garlic and stir over heat for a minute to glaze. Add remaining ingredients, except parsley. Bring the sauce to a boil, lower heat, and simmer, covered, about 30 minutes, until chicken is tender, shaking the pan and spooning the sauce over the chicken occasionally. Makes 4 servings.

CHINESE CHICKEN

1 broiler-fryer, cut in small pieces
1 teaspoon salt
¼ teaspoon pepper
2 tablespoons lemon juice
1 teaspoon sugar
3 tablespoons oil
1 green pepper, cut in strips
2 cups celery in thin diagonal slices
½ cup chicken broth
1 tablespoon cornstarch
3 tablespoons soy sauce
2 fresh tomatoes, in wedges

Season chicken with salt, pepper, lemon juice and sugar. Heat oil in skillet, brown chicken on all sides. Add green pepper, celery and chicken broth. Cover, cook 20 minutes. Dissolve cornstarch in soy sauce, add to skillet. Cook, stirring, until smooth. Add tomatoes and cook 5 minutes. Makes 4 servings.

DUCKLING IN RED WINE

1 duckling, 5 to 6 pounds
⅔ cup red wine
1 clove garlic, pressed
Pinch marjoram
1 teaspoon chopped parsley
Salt, pepper
2 tablespoons butter or margarine
1 cup sliced mushrooms
2 teaspoons cornstarch
¼ cup water

Skin duckling (see page 98) and cut it into serving pieces, reserving wing tips, backbone and large breast bones for another use. Put the duckling into a bowl and cover with wine mixed with garlic, marjoram, parsley, salt and pepper. Marinate for about 1 hour, turning the pieces from time to time. Melt the butter in a heavy skillet fitted with a lid. Brown duckling pieces on all sides. Add marinade, cover pan, and simmer about 40 minutes, until duckling is tender. Remove pieces to a serving dish. Skim excess fat from pan juices, add sliced mushrooms to pan, simmer for 5 minutes. Stir in cornstarch mixed to a paste with water, and cook, stirring, until sauce is clear and thick. Adjust seasoning with salt and pepper and pour sauce over duckling. Makes 4 servings.

ROCK CORNISH HEN SKILLET

4 Rock Cornish hens
2 tablespoons butter or margarine
¼ cup bacon fat or rendered poultry fat
4 tablespoons flour
2 cups chicken consommé
Herb bunch (parsley, celery tops, bay leaf)
3 cups green peas, fresh or frozen
Salt, pepper

Brown hens on all sides in butter in a skillet, remove. Add bacon or poultry fat and flour to skillet and cook, stirring, until the mixture is a rich golden color. Add chicken consommé and cook, stirring in the brown bits, until sauce is thickened and smooth. Return the hens to the skillet, add the herb bunch. Cover and simmer 20 minutes, add peas and simmer 10 to 20 minutes longer, until hens are very tender. Season with salt and pepper. Discard herb bunch. Arrange hens on a platter and spoon green peas and sauce around them. Makes 4 servings.

Chicken en Casserole
(Oven Method)

The words "chicken en casserole" describe chicken browned in a flameproof casserole or skillet, in butter or other fat, then covered with a flavorful sauce and cooked until tender, top-stove or in the oven. The latter method of finishing requires less attention, an important advantage for the busy cook.

PINEAPPLE CHICKEN EN CASSEROLE

1 broiler-fryer, cut up
⅓ cup flour
1 teaspoon salt
  Pinch nutmeg
  Pinch ginger
¼ cup oil
2 tablespoons sugar
¼ teaspoon salt
1 tablespoon cornstarch
¼ cup soy sauce
1 can (1 pound 13 ounces) pineapple chunks

Coat chicken with flour mixed with salt and spices, brown in oil in a skillet. Remove chicken to casserole, set skillet aside. Mix sugar, salt and cornstarch in small saucepan, stir in soy sauce and syrup drained from pineapple, and cook, stirring, until sauce is thick and clear. Pour over chicken in casserole, cover, and bake in moderate oven (350°F) about 45 minutes, until chicken is tender. Sauté pineapple chunks in the fat remaining in the skillet in which chicken was browned, arrange over chicken. Makes 4 servings.

ORANGE-GINGER CHICKEN

1 broiler-fryer, cut up
  Salt, paprika
½ cup butter or margarine
3 tablespoons flour
2 tablespoons brown sugar
1 cup water
1½ cups orange juice
½ teaspoon ginger
  Salt, pepper
  Hot pepper sauce
1 unpeeled orange, sliced paper-thin
1 can (8 ounces) sweet potatoes, or 4 to 6 small boiled sweet potatoes

Season chicken and brown on both sides in ¼ cup butter in a flameproof casserole. Remove chicken, add remaining butter, stir in flour and brown sugar. Slowly stir in liquids and scrape in brown bits that cling to pan. Cook, stirring constantly, until sauce is thick and smooth. Adjust seasoning to taste with ginger, salt, pepper and hot pepper sauce. Return chicken to sauce. Cover the casserole, bake in a moderate oven (350°F) 15 minutes. Add orange slices and potatoes, bake 20 minutes longer, until chicken is tender. Makes 4 servings.

CASSEROLE BRUNSWICK STEW

1 broiler-fryer, cut in small pieces
  Salt, pepper
2 tablespoons bacon fat
3 cups canned tomatoes
½ cup sherry
2 teaspoons Worcestershire sauce
1 cup fresh or frozen okra
1 cup canned corn kernels
2 tablespoons butter or margarine

Season chicken pieces with salt and pepper. Brown in bacon fat in flameproof casserole. Add remaining ingredients. Bake, covered, in a moderate oven (350°F) about 30 minutes, until chicken and vegetables are tender. Makes 4 servings.

Baked Chicken

Baked chicken is cooked in the oven with a little liquid. This method of cooking requires a minimum of attention and yields a maximum of tender, unshrunken meat and rich, full-flavored gravy.

BAKED CHICKEN AND MUSHROOMS

1 whole broiler-fryer
  Salt, pepper
¼ cup melted butter or margarine
¾ cup muscatel or other sweet dessert wine
1 teaspoon salt
  Paprika, curry, powdered rosemary
1 cup sour cream
½ pound sliced mushrooms, or 2 cans (4 ounces each) mushrooms and liquid

Season chicken, arrange in baking dish. Combine butter, wine and seasonings, pour over chicken. Let stand in refrigerator for 1 to 2 hours, turning occasionally. Bake, breast down, in moderate oven (350°F), 30 minutes. Brush bird with half the sour cream, turn, bake 20 minutes longer. Baste with remaining sour cream. Add mushrooms to pan liquid. Continue baking until chicken is tender, about 25 to 30 minutes. Makes 4 servings.

BAKED CHICKEN FLORENTINE

2 broiler-fryers, cut up
2 tablespoons butter or margarine
  Salt, pepper
½ cup water
2 packages frozen spinach
1 tablespoon butter or margarine
1 onion, chopped
½ clove garlic, pressed
1 cup sour cream

Lay pieces of chicken side by side in a large baking dish that can be brought to the table. Dot with 2 tablespoons butter and sprinkle with salt and pepper. Pour water into dish. Bake, uncovered, in a moderate oven (350°F) for 30 minutes, until chicken pieces brown. Meanwhile, boil and drain frozen spinach and season with salt and pepper. Shape ring of spinach around chicken. Melt 1 tablespoon butter, cook onion and garlic lightly, stir in sour cream, heat. Pour sauce over chicken and spinach. Cover dish with a lid or with foil and bake 30 to 40 minutes longer, until chicken is tender. Makes 8 servings.

BAKED CHICKEN AND BISCUITS

1 broiler-fryer, cut up
1 can (10½ ounces) condensed cream of mushroom soup
1 soup can water
1 chicken bouillon cube
¼ cup butter or margarine
Paprika
Salt, pepper
1 package refrigerator biscuits
Celery seeds

Arrange chicken in baking dish just large enough to hold the pieces side by side. Mix soup and water with crushed bouillon cube, add to baking dish. Dot chicken with butter. Sprinkle with paprika, salt and pepper. Cover, bake in moderate oven (350°F) about 40 minutes. Remove cover, arrange refrigerator biscuits on chicken. Sprinkle with celery seeds. Bake, uncovered, until biscuits are brown and chicken is tender, about 20 minutes. Makes 4 servings.

Stuffing a Bird for Roasting

Stuffing may be prepared ahead but it should not be put into the bird until just before roasting.

Packaged dry stuffing mixes make a useful base. Add an individual touch with cooked sausage, meat, chopped chestnuts, walnuts or other nuts, the cooked giblets of the bird, chopped raw oysters or cooked shrimp, or soaked and chopped dried fruit. The basic homemade bread-stuffing recipe, below, can be varied in the same way.

Spoon stuffing very lightly into the bird to allow for expansion, filling neck as well as body cavity, if desired. Sew or skewer the skin firmly into place over the openings.

If your family likes stuffing so much that

the bird won't hold enough, bake an extra pan of it. Moisten with a little pan gravy, cover, and place in oven during last 45 minutes of roasting time.

A 1-pound loaf of bread makes 8 cups large, soft crumbs. Allow 1 cup prepared stuffing for each pound of dressed weight of bird.

Leftover stuffing should be removed from the bird, refrigerated separately and used promptly.

BREAD STUFFING

1 onion, chopped
1 stalk celery, chopped
¼ cup melted butter or margarine
5 to 6 cups large, soft bread crumbs
½ tablespoon chopped parsley
¼ teaspoon poultry seasoning
1 egg, beaten
Salt, pepper

Cook chopped onion and celery in butter until they just begin to take on color. Toss with remaining ingredients and adjust seasoning. Makes enough for a large roasting chicken.

SOUTHERN CORN-BREAD-AND-SAUSAGE DRESSING

1 pound sausage meat
1 onion, chopped
5 cups crumbled corn bread (page 198)
Salt, pepper
Marjoram, sage, thyme
3 eggs, beaten

Brown sausage meat in a skillet, stirring with a fork to break into particles. Add onion, brown lightly. Add crumbled corn bread, adjust seasoning with salt, pepper and pinches of herbs, tasting as you go. Add eggs and toss lightly to combine. Makes enough to stuff a large chicken.

FRUITED-RICE DRESSING

2 cups rice
½ cup prunes, soaked
3 tart apples, peeled and chopped
½ cup melted butter or margarine
½ teaspoon paprika
¼ teaspoon poultry seasoning
Salt, pepper, cinnamon to taste

Cook rice. Combine all ingredients and toss with a fork to mix. Use to stuff a 5- to 7-pound duck.

WILD OR BROWN RICE STUFFING

1½ cups wild or brown rice
¼ cup chopped onion
¼ cup butter or margarine
½ pound mushrooms, sliced
2 tablespoons chopped parsley
½ teaspoon poultry seasoning
Salt, pepper

Cook wild or brown rice according to package directions. Brown rice costs a fraction of the price of wild rice and makes a satisfactory substitute. Cook chopped onion in butter for 5 minutes; add mushrooms and cook 5 minutes longer, stirring. Combine all ingredients and season to taste. Makes enough for 6 Rock Cornish hens. Double recipe for a 12-pound turkey.

OYSTER STUFFING

18 oysters
2 cups large, soft bread crumbs
2 tablespoons melted butter or margarine
1 tablespoon parsley
Grated rind of half a lemon, or to taste
1 tablespoon dry white wine
1 egg
Salt, pepper to taste

Drain oysters, reserve liquid. Mix oysters with remaining ingredients, add oyster liquid to moisten. Makes enough to fill a turkey breast cavity.

TO TRUSS A BIRD FOR ROASTING

Trussing, or tying the legs and wings of a bird close to the body, helps keep a roaster in shape, keeps the stuffing in and makes the bird easier to balance on a spit. Lay the bird on its back, legs toward you. Push the legs close back against the body. Lay the center of the twine across the ends of the legs and bring both ends under and up between the legs. Cross the ends, bring them around the tail, knot the twine and cut. Tie the wings and neck flap flat against the body, knot the twine again.

Roasted Poultry

Roasting—the time-honored way to prepare the Thanksgiving turkey—can be applied to all types of poultry, and at all times of the year.

TIMETABLE FOR ROASTING POULTRY
OVEN TEMPERATURE MODERATELY SLOW (325°F)

(NOTE: Since poultry varies greatly in size, conformation and fat, cooking time can only be approximate.)

Poultry	Dressed Weight (In Pounds)	Cooking Time (In Hours)
Chicken	Less than 3	1–1½
	4–5	2–2½
Capon	7–9	3½–4
Turkey	5–6	2½–3
	7–12	3½–4½
	13–18	4½–5½
	More than 18	6 or more
Duck	4–6	2–2½
Goose	10–12	3½–4½

ROAST CHICKEN

Choose a large broiler-fryer chicken, weighing about 3½ pounds, or a 5- to 7-pound roaster. Truss (see page 104), if desired. Sprinkle the bird inside and out with salt, pepper, and garlic powder, ginger, sage or paprika. Rub with butter, margarine or other fat. Arrange on a rack in a roasting pan, breast side down. Roast in a moderate oven (350°F) until the back is lightly browned. Turn, baste with ½ cup water mixed with 2 tablespoons fat. Or use orange juice, or water and lemon juice, or wine, or your favorite basting sauce (see page 96). Continue to roast until the bird is uniformly browned, allowing about 25 minutes per pound. The chicken is done when the drumstick meat feels soft, the leg joint moves easily, and a thermometer inserted between leg and body registers 185°F. If you have no thermometer, pierce the leg joint with a fork; the juices should run clear, with no pink tinge.

Roast Capon: Prepare and cook like roast chicken.

Butter-Crust Roast Chicken: Prepare a chicken for roasting in the usual way. Cream ½ cup butter or margarine and blend well with 1 cup flour to make a soft paste. Season lightly with salt, pepper and poultry seasoning. Spread the paste thickly over the chicken. Roast as usual.

Anchovy Roast Chicken: Wash, dry and mash 5 anchovy fillets to a paste. Mix with ⅓ cup softened butter or margarine. Spread on a chicken for roasting. Use no salt.

Ginger Roast Chicken: Mix together ¼ cup soy sauce, 1 pressed garlic clove, 3 tablespoons peanut oil, 1 teaspoon powdered ginger and ½ teaspoon sugar. Brush marinade on chicken prepared for roasting, cover loosely, and refrigerate for 2 hours, turning occasionally. Roast in the oven or on a spit, basting with marinade.

Glazed Roast Chicken: Half an hour before chicken is tender, spread it with ½ cup currant jelly melted over hot water.

Sherry-Basted Chicken: Prepare a chicken for roasting in the usual way. Grease a baking dish, cover bottom with 1 minced onion, and add chicken. Roast breast down in a moderate oven (350°F) about 45 minutes. Mix and heat together ½ cup sherry and ¼ cup honey. Turn chicken breast up and baste with sauce. Roast about 30 minutes longer, basting often with sherry-honey mixture, until tender.

GRAVY FOR ROAST CHICKEN

Remove roasted bird to platter, let stand in warm place to set juices. Stir 2 tablespoons flour into the pan drippings and cook for a minute or two. Add 2 cups Chicken Stock (page 45) or 2 cups hot water and 2 chicken bouillon cubes. Stir, scraping in the brown bits that adhere to the pan. Cook for 5 minutes, stirring often. Adjust seasoning. Strain gravy into a sauceboat, serve with roast chicken.

ROAST TURKEY, CHESTNUT STUFFING

1 turkey, about 12 pounds
½ cup butter, margarine or other fat

Brush turkey with butter, fill neck and breast cavities with Chestnut Stuffing (below), sew or skewer openings. Truss bird (see page 104), if desired, or tuck legs under flap, or under wire retainers that often come with frozen birds. Arrange on a rack in a roasting pan, breast side up. Cover the breast with a cloth dipped in melted fat, or with a tent shaped from aluminum foil. Roast in a moderately slow oven (325°F) about 20 minutes per pound (see chart, page 104). When the bird is cooked, a thermometer inserted between thigh and body will read 185°F, the leg meat will feel soft to pressure, and the drumstick will move easily in its socket. Let turkey stand 15 minutes before carving.

See photo (page 94).

CHESTNUT STUFFING

3 pounds chestnuts
3 cups crushed crackers

⅓ cup melted butter or margarine
¾ cup milk

Cut a cross through shell on flat side of chestnuts, cover with water, bring to a boil, simmer 5 minutes. Drain and cool the nuts. Peel shells and inner skin. Cover with fresh water, bring to a boil, simmer until tender, testing with a metal skewer after 5 minutes. Crumble nuts, mix with remaining ingredients. Makes enough for a 12-pound turkey.

TURKEY BROTH

Turkey giblets (heart and gizzard), neck, wing tips
1 carrot
1 onion
Few sprigs parsley
2 celery tops
4 cups water
1 teaspoon salt

Simmer turkey parts and vegetables in water with salt until meat is tender. In a pressure cooker, use only 3 cups water. Strain broth. Use in leftover turkey recipes, or to make gravy to serve with the roast. Makes 3 cups.

TURKEY GRAVY

Pour off all but 6 tablespoons fat from the pan in which the turkey was roasted. Add ⅓ cup flour and cook, stirring, for a minute or two. Add 3 cups Turkey Broth (above) and cook, stirring and scraping in the brown bits that cling to the pan, until the sauce is smooth and thickened. Adjust seasonings with salt and pepper, strain into a heated gravy boat. Makes 3 cups.

ROAST TURKEY PARTS

Half Turkey: Allow 1 cup stuffing for every pound dressed weight. Mound the stuffing in the shape of the body cavity on a rack covered with several thicknesses of foil or with greased heavy brown paper. Brush turkey half with butter, margarine or fat, season it, and fit it over the stuffing. Cover with a cloth dipped in melted fat, or with a tent of foil, and roast in a moderately slow oven (325°F) for about 25 minutes per pound. Spoon out the stuffing and serve it separately. Carve the bird as you would a whole turkey lying on its side.

Breast of Turkey: Proceed as above, covering the skin side with foil, but roast only about 20 minutes per pound.

Turkey Quarters: Stuffing should be baked separately during the last half hour. It may be moistened with some of the pan juices. Stretch the turkey skin to cover the meat, and sew or skewer it in place. Put the quarters on a roasting-pan rack, skin side down, and cover with fat-moistened cloth or with foil. Roast in a moderately slow oven (325°F) about 30 to 35 minutes per pound. White meat cooks more quickly than dark, and the time varies greatly according to the shape and conformation of the quarters.

Stuffed Drumstick: Remove all the tendons from the drumstick, cut out the bone and pound the meat to flatten it. Spread with stuffing and roll back into shape. Skewer the roll firmly. Spread the outside of the roll with butter or margarine and seasonings and cover it lightly with foil or with a cloth moistened with fat. Roast on a rack in an open pan for about 2 hours in a moderate oven (350°F).

ROAST DUCKLING, APPLE STUFFING

    1 duckling, 5 to 6 pounds
     Salt, pepper
 1½ cups soft bread crumbs
    2 tablespoons diced onion
 1½ cups peeled and diced green apples
    1 teaspoon poultry seasoning
    1 tablespoon minced parsley

Rub the duck inside and out with salt and pepper. Mix remaining ingredients, season to taste. Stuff duck. Roast on rack in pan, uncovered, in moderately slow oven (325°F) about 25 minutes per pound. Pour off and reserve fat as it accumulates for other cooking uses. Makes 4 servings.

DUCK À L'ORANGE

 1 duckling, 5 to 6 pounds
   Salt, pepper
 1 orange, peeled and sectioned
 1 cup white wine
 1 cup consommé
   Juice and grated rind of 1 orange
   Juice and grated rind of ½ lemon
 1 tablespoon sugar
 1 tablespoon wine vinegar
 1 tablespoon cornstarch (optional)
   Sugar, salt, pepper

Rub the bird with salt and pepper. Put the orange sections inside duck, roast in a very hot oven (450°F) for 15 minutes. Reduce heat and finish roasting in a moderately slow oven (325°F), allowing about 20 minutes per pound. Baste frequently with white wine. Remove the bird to a platter. Skim off and reserve the excess fat for other uses. Add consommé to pan, stirring and scraping in the brown bits. Add grated fruit rinds and juices, simmer for 5 minutes. Brown sugar and wine vinegar in a very small pan and add this caramel mixture to the sauce. (Thicken, if desired, with 1 tablespoon cornstarch mixed to a paste with a little water.) Simmer until sauce is clear. Adjust seasoning, adding more sugar, salt and pepper to taste. Pour some of the sauce over the duckling and serve the rest in a heated sauceboat. Garnish the platter with orange sections. Makes 4 servings.

ROAST GOOSE WITH ONION-AND-APPLE STUFFING

 1 goose, 8 to 10 pounds
   Salt, pepper, marjoram
 4 large onions, boiled
 2 apples, peeled and chopped
 4 cups bread crumbs
 1 teaspoon mustard
   Salt, pepper, sage
 ½ cup water

Season goose inside and out with salt, pepper and a little marjoram. Chop the onions and combine with apples, bread crumbs and mustard. Adjust seasoning to taste with salt, pepper and sage; stuff the goose and skewer the openings. Truss (see page 104). Lay goose on its side on a rack in a roasting pan. Pour ½ cup water into the pan. Roast bird in a hot oven (450°F) for 1 hour. Pour off fat as it accumulates and reserve for other uses. Baste the bird with the pan juices. Reduce heat to moderate (350°F) and roast bird until tender, allowing about 15 to 20 minutes per pound in all. Turn goose from side to side every half hour and occasionally add a little water to pan juices. During last 15 minutes, turn goose on its back and brown the breast. Makes 6 to 8 servings.

ROASTED ROCK CORNISH HENS

 2 cups Brown Rice Stuffing (page 104)
 4 Rock Cornish hens
   Soft butter or margarine
   Salt, pepper
 ½ cup chicken consommé
 ¼ cup dry white wine
 1 teaspoon cornstarch

Stuff hens and sew the opening. Truss hens loosely, as you would chicken (see page 104), and rub with soft butter. Season with salt and pepper. Roast in a very hot oven (450°F) for about 15 minutes, until hens begin to brown. Lower heat to moderate (350°F) and roast about 30 to 40 minutes longer, until tender. Arrange the hens on a serving platter and keep them warm. Stir liquids into the juices in the roasting pan and simmer, scraping in the brown bits, for 5 minutes. Add cornstarch, dissolved in a little water, and cook until sauce is clear. Strain sauce through a fine sieve over the birds on the platter. Makes 4 servings.

Roasting Poultry in Bags or Foil

Birds wrapped for cooking in special roasting bags or in aluminum foil require shorter cooking time for tender, juicy results. A&P's own oven bags come with a helpful recipe booklet. For best results, follow the directions exactly.

Like birds roasted in a bag, birds roasted in foil are self-basting. In addition, foil permits the use of higher temperatures, and thus shorter cooking times. Truss (see page 104) a seasoned bird carefully, so that no bones protrude to tear the foil. Lay the bird on a sheet of foil large enough to cover it completely and allow generous folds for sealing. Bring the ends of the foil together over the top of the bird and fold them down twice or more over the breast. Fold the ends in the same way.

Birds roasted in this way will brown lightly, even in the wrap, but if you want crisp skin, open the foil or the bag for the last 20 minutes of cooking time.

TIMETABLE FOR FOIL-WRAPPED ROAST TURKEY

Roast to an Internal Temperature of 185°F
OVEN TEMPERATURE HOT TO VERY HOT
(425°–450°F)

Dressed Weight (In Pounds)	Total Cooking Time (In Hours)
7–9	2¼–2½
10–13	2¾–3
14–17	3½–4
18–21	4½–5
22–24	5½–6

To roast chicken in foil, roast at 400°F for about 1¼ hours.

Rotisseried Chicken

Rotisseries come in many forms—for indoors and outdoors, electrically or manually operated. Whatever type of rotisserie you have, the results will be the same—delicious.

ROTISSERIED CHICKEN

Truss the chicken (see page 104) and balance it carefully on the spit. Brush with butter or margarine and season to taste. Roast at moderate heat (350°F) for about 25 minutes per pound, basting every 15 minutes.

BASTING SAUCES FOR ROTISSERIED CHICKEN

¼ cup melted butter or margarine, 1 tablespoon Worcestershire sauce.

¼ cup melted butter or margarine, 1 tablespoon prepared mustard, 1 tablespoon wine vinegar.

¼ cup melted butter or margarine, ¼ cup vermouth.

¼ cup melted butter or margarine, juice of 1 lime, pinch cayenne pepper.

¼ cup melted butter or margarine, small clove garlic, puréed, pinch each basil and oregano.

Poultry Parts

For these most luxurious of poultry recipes, the most luxurious part of the bird is used—the tender breasts. Use the breasts as they are or bone them. To bone, peel away the skin; separate the flesh from the bones with the point of a small, sharp knife, pulling with your fingers.

BREASTS OF CHICKEN PARMESAN

4 chicken breasts, boned and skinned
Flour
1 egg
1 tablespoon water
½ teaspoon salt
Pepper
½ cup dry bread crumbs
¼ cup grated Parmesan cheese
½ cup oil
1 package (10 ounces) frozen spinach
Salt
Lemon juice
2 tablespoons butter or margarine
1 pound mushrooms, sliced
Chopped parsley

Pound chicken breasts to flatten them. Dredge

with flour. Beat egg lightly with water, salt and pepper; dip chicken into this mixture and into bread crumbs mixed with cheese. Brown slowly in hot oil. Cook spinach, drain, and season with salt and lemon juice to taste. Pile spinach on a serving dish and top with cooked chicken breasts. Pour off oil in which chicken was cooked. To the pan, add 2 tablespoons butter. Cook sliced mushrooms for 5 minutes. Pour mushrooms and their butter over the chicken and spinach. Sprinkle with chopped parsley. Makes 4 servings.

CHINESE ALMOND CHICKEN

4 chicken breasts, boned and skinned
4 tablespoons oil
2 tablespoons flour
1 teaspoon sugar
4 tablespoons soy sauce
2 cups sliced mushrooms
    Salt
1 cup almonds

Cut chicken into 1-inch squares and brown in 2 tablespoons hot oil, stirring. Mix flour, sugar and soy sauce. Add to pan and cook, stirring constantly, 5 minutes. Add mushrooms, cover pan, and cook 20 minutes, until chicken is tender. Adjust seasoning with salt. Meanwhile, blanch almonds in boiling water, slip off skins, and split almonds in half. Brown almonds in remaining hot oil and drain on paper toweling. Fold toasted almonds into chicken mixture. Serve with hot boiled rice. Makes 4 servings.

CHICKEN AND CLAMS

    4 chicken breasts, boned and skinned
    1 can (about 8 ounces) minced clams
    1 cup bottled clam broth
1½ tablespoons butter or margarine, softened
1½ tablespoons flour
    Salt, pepper
    Nutmeg
    Chopped parsley for garnish

Lay chicken breasts side by side in a heavy skillet, add liquid from minced clams and clam broth. Cover skillet and simmer chicken for 25 minutes, until meat is cooked through and very tender. Remove chicken to a serving dish and keep it warm. Mix butter and flour to a paste and add bit by bit to the clam broth in the skillet. Cook, stirring, until sauce thickens. Add minced clams and adjust seasoning. Heat without boiling and pour over the chicken. Sprinkle with chopped parsley. Makes 4 servings.

OVEN-POACHED TURKEY BREAST

To cook a turkey breast especially for salad, or for any recipe requiring cooked meat, season the turkey, wrap it in aluminum foil, and roast it in a moderate oven (350°F) for 2½ hours or longer, until it is very tender to the pressure of a finger. Cool before slicing.

STEAMED TURKEY BREAST

Lay the turkey breast on a rack in a small pan, sprinkle it with salt, and add 3 cups water, a small onion, a stalk celery and a few sprigs parsley. Bring liquid to a boil, skim. Cover pan, simmer gently for about 3 hours or longer, until turkey is very tender to the fork. Cool the meat before slicing it to use in cooked turkey dishes.

TURKEY SCALOPPINE PARMIGIANA

1½ pounds raw turkey breast meat
    Salt, pepper
½ cup flour
1 egg, beaten
½ cup grated Parmesan cheese
¼ cup oil
1 onion, chopped
1 clove garlic
1 can (8 ounces) tomato sauce
1 can (1 pound) tomatoes
1 teaspoon salt
¼ teaspoon pepper
1 teaspoon sugar
¼ teaspoon thyme
½ pound mozzarella cheese

Cut turkey into thin slices, pound to flatten. Season with salt and pepper. Dip into flour, into beaten egg and into ¼ cup Parmesan cheese. Brown on both sides in a skillet in hot oil. Arrange in a shallow pan. To skillet add onion and garlic, cook until brown. Add tomato sauce, tomatoes and seasonings, simmer 5 minutes. Pour sauce over scaloppine. Top with sliced mozzarella, sprinkle with remaining Parmesan. Bake in a moderate oven (350°F) about 15 minutes, until cheese melts and browns. Makes 6 servings.

TURKEY VIRGINIA

    Cooked turkey breast meat
4 slices ham, ¼ inch thick
¼ cup butter or margarine
4 large mushroom caps, whole
3 tablespoons flour

2 cups Turkey Broth (page 105)
Salt, pepper, paprika
Grated Parmesan cheese, or fine dry bread crumbs mixed with melted butter or margarine

Cut 4 uniform slices from turkey breast. Cook the ham lightly in butter and remove it to a flameproof serving dish. Cover each ham slice with a slice of turkey. Brown mushrooms gently in some butter and arrange on the turkey. Add flour to butter and cook, stirring, for a few minutes without browning. Add turkey broth and cook, stirring, until sauce is thick and smooth. Adjust seasoning and pour sauce over turkey. Sprinkle with grated Parmesan cheese, or with bread crumbs mixed with melted butter, and brown topping quickly under the broiler. Makes 4 servings.

BARBECUED TURKEY

8 to 10 pounds turkey parts
Salt, pepper
½ cup water
½ cup oil
½ cup vinegar
¼ cup brown sugar
1 tablespoon gravy browning sauce
1 tablespoon soy sauce

Season turkey parts with salt and pepper and lay side by side in shallow baking pan. Brown lightly in a hot oven (400°F) about 20 minutes. Blend remaining ingredients and pour half over turkey. Cover pan, reduce temperature to moderate (350°F) and bake 2½ hours. Turn the pieces and baste with remaining sauce often. Add water as needed to prevent scorching. Makes 10 to 15 servings.

CHICKEN WINGS

Cut off and reserve bony wing tips for soup. Season meaty wings to taste, fry in deep fat. (See page 95.) Or oven-fry if you prefer. (See page 96.) Serve hot with a tomato cocktail sauce. Allow 1 wing per guest for hors d'oeuvre, 3 as a luncheon or supper serving.

DEVILED TURKEY WINGS

2 cooked turkey wings
¼ cup butter, margarine or poultry fat
Fine dry bread crumbs
2 tablespoons wine vinegar
1 clove garlic, bruised
1 teaspoon dry mustard

½ bay leaf
½ teaspoon salt
1 teaspoon paprika
Black pepper, cayenne pepper
¼ cup ketchup
1 teaspoon Worcestershire sauce
1 tablespoon butter or margarine

Brown turkey wings in hot butter, dip in bread crumbs, pressing crumbs firmly, and brown again. Remove to serving dish. Make a sauce by adding remaining ingredients to the pan. Simmer for 5 minutes, discard bay leaf and garlic, and pour sauce over the turkey wings. Makes 2 servings.

MARINATED CHICKEN DRUMSTICKS

2 pounds broiler-fryer drumsticks
Water to cover
Bay leaf, celery tops, peppercorns, salt
1 cup wine vinegar
1 tablespoon pickling spices
1 clove garlic, bruised

Cover drumsticks with water, add seasoning, cook until tender, about 30 minutes. Strain broth and boil rapidly to reduce it to 3 cups. Combine broth with vinegar, spices and garlic to make marinade. Skin the drumsticks and cover with marinade. Chill 12 hours or overnight, turning to season evenly. Serve as hors d'oeuvre, 1 for each guest.

GRILLED CHICKEN LEGS

Lay chicken legs on squares of foil. Sprinkle with onion salt and pepper and top each with 1 teaspoon butter or margarine. Wrap carefully. Grill on a rack, over a moderately hot charcoal fire, for about 40 minutes, turning packets frequently for even cooking. Test for tenderness by pressing meat between thumb and forefinger.

DEVILED CHICKEN LEGS

8 chicken legs
4 tablespoons butter or margarine
1 teaspoon ketchup
1 teaspoon Worcestershire sauce
2 teaspoons curry powder
¼ teaspoon cayenne pepper

Make a series of evenly spaced gashes on both sides of chicken legs. Cream butter with remaining ingredients. Spread mixture on legs, working it into cuts. Broil over charcoal (above) and serve hot, or for a picnic, broil at home and serve cold. Makes 4 servings.

TURKEY SOUP

The remains of a roast turkey make an excellent soup. Put bones, skin and shreds of meat into a large kettle. Add an onion, a large carrot, a celery stalk with the leaves, and a sprig or two of parsley. Add 2 quarts cold water, 1 tablespoon salt and 8 peppercorns. Bring liquid to a boil and simmer soup for 2 hours or longer. Strain broth and adjust seasoning. Serve with boiled noodles, dumplings, chow mein noodles or any desired garnish; or cook diced carrot, a few green beans, diced potato, sliced mushrooms or other vegetables in the soup.

Chicken Livers

Chicken livers may be purchased frozen or fresh, by the pound. Allow ¼ pound chicken livers per portion as a main dish. Trim livers, if necessary, wash and dry thoroughly before cooking.

CHOPPED CHICKEN LIVERS

2 chicken livers
1 onion, sliced
  Rendered Chicken Fat (below), or
    butter or margarine
2 hard-cooked eggs
  Salt, pepper

Simmer chicken livers and onion in fat, in a covered skillet over low heat, until livers are cooked through and onion is translucent. Transfer contents of skillet to a chopping bowl. Add eggs, chop all together with a chopping knife. Add salt and pepper to taste, plus more chicken fat or butter to make a moist mixture. Serve as a spread with crackers or thin-sliced whole-grain bread; or as a stuffing for cherry tomatoes.

CHICKEN-LIVER PÂTÉ

Prepare recipe above, but whirl cooked ingredients in blender to make a very smooth paste. Double the quantities and use the pâté in preparing Beef Wellington (page 67).

SPAGHETTI CARUSO

1 pound chicken livers
2 tablespoons olive oil
2 tablespoons butter or margarine
2 onions, chopped
2 cloves garlic, crushed
1 can (4 ounces) mushroom slices
  Salt

1 can (1 pound 13 ounces) Italian
    tomato purée
1 can (6 ounces) Italian tomato paste
  Salt, pepper, sugar, basil, oregano
1 pound spaghetti, cooked

Slice chicken livers. Heat oil and butter together and cook onions and garlic until both are golden. Add sliced livers. Drain mushrooms, reserve liquid. Add mushrooms to livers, salt lightly. Cook for 3 minutes. Stir in mushroom liquid, tomato purée and paste, and seasonings. Simmer, covered, 45 minutes. Taste and adjust the seasoning. Serve over spaghetti cooked al dente—until tender but still firm to the teeth. Makes 6 servings.

RISOTTO WITH CHICKEN LIVERS

½ pound chicken livers
¼ cup butter or margarine
1 small onion, chopped
½ cup sliced mushrooms
½ green or sweet red pepper, shredded
2 cups rice
4 cups hot chicken broth
  Salt, pepper
  Grated Parmesan cheese

Brown livers on both sides in melted butter with onion, mushrooms and pepper. With perforated spoon transfer livers and vegetables to flameproof casserole. Add rice to butter in pan, stir over low heat until it takes on color, transfer to casserole. Add chicken broth and simmer over low heat until rice is tender and broth is absorbed. Adjust seasoning with salt and pepper. Serve with grated cheese. Makes 4 servings.

CHCKEN LIVERS EN BROCHETTE

Sandwich slices of chicken liver dipped in soy sauce between slices of water chestnuts. Wrap in strips of bacon and fix on skewers. Broil until bacon is crisp. Serve as hors d'oeuvre.

Chicken Extras

No part of a chicken (or any other poultry) need be wasted—an economy to be remembered and practiced.

RENDERED CHICKEN FAT

Rendered chicken fat has numerous uses in recipes where rich, chickeny flavor is desirable, for frying and as a shortening. Large quantities of yellow chicken fat can be removed from the cavities and from under the skin of roasters and pullets. All giblets are coated with fat. Or you can buy chicken fat by the pound. Cut the fat into dice and cook in a heavy skillet, over low heat, until the liquid fat is rendered and the remaining cracklings are crisp and dry. Cook an onion slice or two in the fat until it is translucent. Discard onion. Strain the fat into a jar, cover, store in the refrigerator.

CHICKEN GIZZARDS AND HEARTS

Simmer gizzards and hearts in salted water to cover for 30 to 45 minutes, or cook them in a pressure cooker, until they are very tender. Grind or chop the cooked meat and add it to gravy, to the stuffing for a bird to be roasted, to spaghetti sauce, or to Spanish rice or a risotto.

DEVILED CHICKEN SPREAD

  1 cup cooked chicken gizzards, hearts and other meat
  1 teaspoon prepared mustard
¼ cup mayonnaise
  Onion salt, pepper, cayenne pepper

Grind the cooked chicken and blend well with mustard and mayonnaise. Season highly and use as a canapé spread. Makes about 1 cup.

GIBLET STEW

  2 pounds chicken gizzards, necks and wings
¼ cup chicken fat or oil
  2 onions, chopped
  1 clove garlic, pressed
  2 tablespoons flour
  Salt, pepper
  4 cups hot water
⅔ cup rice
  1 pound chopped beef
  3 tablespoons water
  1 teaspoon salt
  Chili powder

Brown gizzards and other parts in hot oil with onions and garlic. Sprinkle with flour, salt and pepper. Cook, stirring, for a few minutes. Gradually add hot water and cook, stirring, until mixture thickens slightly. Cover pan and cook for 1 hour, stirring occasionally. Add rice, stir. Mix chopped beef with water and season it with salt and a little chili powder. Form small balls the size of walnuts and add them to the stew. Simmer for 25 minutes, until rice is tender. Makes 6 servings.

Cooked Chicken and Turkey Dishes

Most "leftover" chicken dishes taste even better if they are made from freshly poached chicken. To keep leftover roasted, broiled or fried poultry moist, wrap tightly for refrigerator storage. For dishes calling for substantial amounts of cooked chicken, begin with poached chicken, or with turkey.

POACHED CHICKEN

Simmer chicken, whole or in quarters, until tender in water to cover, with a stalk of celery, an onion and a little salt. Strain the broth and reserve it to use in other recipes. Cut the chicken meat from the bones in generous slices. Any unused portion of poached chicken may be wrapped in moisture/vaporproof paper and stored in the freezer.

NEW ENGLAND OYSTER-CHICKEN PIE

  1 Poached Chicken (above)
  2 cups oysters
  2 tablespoons butter or margarine
  1 teaspoon salt
¼ teaspoon pepper
  4 tablespoons butter or margarine
  4 tablespoons flour
  2 cups milk
  Pastry for 1-crust pie

Bone the chicken and cut into chunks. Combine with oysters in a buttered casserole. Dot with 2 tablespoons butter; sprinkle with salt and pepper. Melt 4 tablespoons butter in a saucepan, stir in flour, add milk and stir over medium heat until thickened and smooth. Add salt and pepper to taste. Pour sauce over chicken and oysters. Top with crust, slit to allow escape of steam. Bake in a hot oven (400°F) for 35 minutes. Makes 8 servings.

CHICKEN PIE

  1 Poached Chicken (above)
½ green pepper, slivered
  2 tablespoons chopped parsley
  1 can (1 pound 13 ounces) boiled white onions
  2 tablespoons butter or margarine
  2 tablespoons flour
  2 cups chicken broth (from poaching)
  Salt, pepper
  1 teaspoon grated lemon zest
  Pie pastry for 1-crust pie

Bone the chicken and cut it into chunks. Fill

a buttered 2-quart baking dish with layers of chicken, slivered green pepper, parsley and onions, beginning and ending with chicken. Melt butter, stir in flour, and cook for 2 minutes, stirring constantly. Stir in chicken broth and cook, stirring, until sauce thickens. Simmer for 5 minutes. Adjust seasoning with salt and pepper and add lemon zest. Pour sauce over chicken and vegetables in baking dish. Cover with pie crust, slash to allow steam to escape, and bake in a hot oven (400°F) for about 20 minutes, until crust is browned. Makes 4 to 5 servings.

CHICKEN À LA KING

    1 Poached Chicken (above)
    4 tablespoons butter or margarine
    4 tablespoons flour
    2 cups chicken broth (from poaching)
    2 cans (3¼ ounces each) mushrooms,
        drained
    1 tablespoon chopped green pepper
    1 tablespoon chopped pimiento
    1 tablespoon chopped onion
    ¼ cup sherry
    ¼ cup heavy cream
      Salt, pepper
    4 slices toast or toasted English muffins
      Parsley for garnish

Bone the chicken and cut it into uniform pieces. Melt butter, stir in flour and cook, stirring, for a minute or two. Stir in broth and cook, stirring occasionally, until sauce is thick and smooth. Fold in chicken and vegetables and heat through. Add sherry and cream and heat without boiling; adjust seasoning with salt and pepper. Serve on toast points or toasted English muffins. Garnish with parsley sprigs. Makes 4 servings.

JELLIED CHICKEN LOAF

    1 Poached Chicken (above)
    1¾ cups hot chicken broth (from poaching)
    2 envelopes gelatin
    ¼ cup cold water
    2 cups peas, cooked or canned
    1 can (5 ounces) water chestnuts, sliced
    ¼ cup blanched almonds, chopped
    2 small sweet gherkins, chopped
    1 cup mayonnaise
      Watercress for garnish

Cut chicken into uniform dice (2 cups). Heat chicken broth. Soften gelatin in cold water and dissolve it in hot broth. Cool until syrupy. Fold in chicken and remaining ingredients, except watercress, and pour into oiled 2-quart

bread pan. Chill to set. Unmold on chilled platter and garnish with watercress. Makes 4 to 6 servings.

CHICKEN FRITTERS

    1½ cups chicken broth
    ¼ cup butter or margarine
    1 cup flour
    4 eggs
    1¼ cups cooked chicken, ground
    2 tablespoons minced onion
    4 tablespoons chopped walnuts
    1 teaspoon salt

Bring broth to a boil with butter. Remove pan from fire and add flour, all at once, stirring vigorously with a wooden spoon. Stir until mixture forms a ball and leaves the sides of pan. Beat in the eggs, one at a time. Beat in remaining ingredients. Drop mixture by tablespoons into hot (390°F) deep fat and fry to a golden brown. Makes about 2½ dozen small fritters.

Chicken Puffs: Drop mixture by large spoonfuls onto a greased baking sheet. Bake in a hot oven (400°F) 10 minutes, reduce heat to 350°F, bake 20 minutes longer, until puffs are richly browned. Makes 12.

TEXAS CHICKEN SALAD

    2 cups diced cooked chicken
    1 pink grapefruit, sectioned and free of pith
    ½ cup chopped celery
    1 cup seedless green grapes
    ½ cup simple French dressing (3 parts oil,
        1 part vinegar)
    ½ cup mayonnaise
    1 tablespoon chopped chives
    1 tablespoon chopped parsley
      Salt, pepper
      Lettuce

Toss chicken, grapefruit, celery and grapes with French dressing. Chill 1 hour in the refrigerator. Drain off excess dressing and mix salad with mayonnaise. Add chives and parsley, salt and pepper to taste. Serve in lettuce cups. Makes 4 servings.

FROZEN CREAM CHICKEN SALAD

    2 cups diced cooked chicken
    1 cup crushed pineapple, drained
    1 teaspoon lemon juice
    1 cup heavy cream, whipped
    ¼ cup chopped peanuts
      Salt, white pepper
      Watercress for garnish

Combine chicken, pineapple and lemon juice, chill 1 hour. Fold in whipped cream and chopped nuts, season with salt and white pepper to taste. Freeze in oiled mold, without stirring, 4 to 6 hours. Unmold on watercress-ringed platter. Makes 4 servings.

JELLIED TURKEY IN ASPIC

2 cups cooked turkey
1 envelope gelatin
¼ cup cold water
2 cups hot turkey broth
1 tablespoon lemon juice
   Salt, pepper
   Hot pepper sauce
   Cutouts of green pepper, pimiento,
     hard-cooked eggs, black and green
     olives
   Watercress
   Tomato wedges

Cut turkey into uniform strips or dice. Soak the gelatin in cold water and dissolve it in hot broth. Season with lemon juice, salt, pepper and a dash of hot pepper sauce. Cool until syrupy. Line a chilled 1-quart mold with a layer of aspic, tipping the mold to coat it. Chill mold until aspic is firm, repeat until the aspic is ⅓ inch thick. Before adding and chilling the final layer, decorate the mold with green pepper, pimiento, hard-cooked eggs, and black and green olives. Fill the mold with turkey strips. Add remaining aspic and chill until set. Unmold on a chilled serving plate and garnish with watercress and tomato wedges. Makes 4 servings.

TURKEY AND NOODLES

 2 cups cooked turkey
¼ cup minced onion
⅓ cup butter or margarine
⅓ cup flour
 2 cups milk
 1 cup turkey broth
   Salt, pepper, poultry seasoning
½ pound noodles, cooked just tender
½ cup grated American cheese
½ cup buttered bread crumbs

Cut turkey into uniform dice. Brown minced onion lightly in butter. Stir in flour and slowly add milk and turkey broth. Cook, stirring, until sauce is smooth and thickened. Add turkey and seasonings to taste. Fill buttered casserole with alternate layers of creamed turkey, noodles, and grated cheese, ending with cheese. Top with buttered crumbs. Bake in a moderate oven (350°F) for about 30 minutes,

until sauce bubbles and topping browns. Makes 6 servings.

TURKEY-AND-STUFFING CASSEROLE

 2 cups cooked turkey
½ cup butter or margarine
½ cup flour
 3 cups turkey broth
½ cup milk
   Salt, pepper
 2 eggs
 3 cups leftover bread stuffing
½ cup slivered almonds, toasted

Cut turkey into slices. Melt butter, stir in flour, and gradually add turkey broth and milk. Season and cook, stirring, until sauce is smooth and thick. (Or use 3½ cups leftover turkey gravy.) Beat eggs, warm them with a little hot sauce, and add to sauce. Heat for 3 minutes without allowing sauce to boil. Put turkey stuffing into a buttered casserole. Pour two-thirds of the sauce over stuffing. Put turkey on stuffing and cover with remaining sauce. Sprinkle with slivered almonds. Bake in a moderate oven (350°F) about 30 minutes, until topping browns and sauce is bubbling hot. Makes 6 servings.

TURKEY MOUSSE

2 cups cooked white turkey meat
2 envelopes gelatin
2 cups turkey broth
2 tablespoons butter or margarine
2 tablespoons flour
1 teaspoon minced onion
2 cups cream, whipped
   Watercress
   Mayonnaise
   Sour cream
   Capers

Force turkey twice through the finest blade of a food chopper, or purée in electric blender with a bit of turkey broth. Soften gelatin in 1 cup broth. Melt butter, stir in flour and cook for a minute without browning. Add 1 cup broth and cook, stirring, for 5 minutes. Add gelatin, stir to dissolve. Add onion. Cool until thick and syrupy. Fold in turkey and whipped cream. Pour into a mold that has been dipped into cold water. Let mousse chill and set thoroughly, at least 2 to 3 hours. Unmold onto a bed of watercress and serve with mayonnaise thinned with sour cream and flavored with a few capers. Makes 8 servings.

TURKEY TERRAPIN

2 cups cooked turkey
2 hard-cooked eggs
3 tablespoons flour
  Pinch dry mustard
2 tablespoons melted butter or margarine
1½ cups hot milk
1 can (5 ounces) water chestnuts, sliced
12 pimiento-stuffed olives, sliced
2 tablespoons lemon juice
  Salt, pepper, cayenne
4 slices toast or crisp corn bread

Dice turkey. Mash the hard-cooked egg yolks to a paste with flour, mustard and butter. Stir into hot milk and cook over low heat, stirring, until sauce is smooth. Chop egg whites, add with turkey, chestnuts, olives and lemon juice, adjust seasoning. Serve hot on buttered toast or crisp corn bread. Makes 4 servings.

TURKEY CHOW MEIN

2 cups cooked turkey
3 tablespoons salad oil
2 cups celery, in diagonal strips
2 onions, sliced thin
½ pound mushrooms, sliced
1 cup turkey broth
1 tablespoon cornstarch
3 tablespoons soy sauce
1 can (5 ounces) water chestnuts, sliced
1 can (1 pound) bean sprouts,
  rinsed and drained
  Chow mein noodles
  Boiled rice

Cut turkey into narrow strips. Heat oil in a large skillet and cook celery and onions over high heat until translucent. Add mushrooms and cook a minute longer. Add broth and cornstarch mixed with soy sauce. Cook until sauce is clear. Add chestnuts, bean sprouts and turkey. Heat and serve on Chinese fried noodles, with plain boiled rice as an accompaniment. Makes 4 servings.

FISH AND SHELLFISH

Fish is a best buy, nutritionally and economically. Low in calories and high in protein, fish also contains significant amounts of some vitamins and minerals. Take advantage of the wide variety of fish—fresh, canned and, most important, frozen—at your A&P.

Buy frozen fish for immediate use or for home storage in your own freezer; you will find a good selection of fresh-frozen fish, wastefree and simple to prepare, at economical prices. For many recipes it is not necessary to thaw the fish before cooking. For others, you may thaw the fish just until you can separate the fillets, or perhaps enough so that you can fold them.

In addition to this reliable, consistent supply of frozen fish, you will find fresh fish in season at your A&P, usually ready to cook; that is, with scales and entrails (and often fins and gills) removed. There may be steaks cut from large fish and boneless fish fillets. Plan to use fresh fish the day you buy it. Home-frozen fish, unlike the commercially frozen product, has a limited storage life.

If your neighborhood A&P should feature fresh whole fish "in the round," that is, just as it came from the water, the fish-service man will be glad to clean and slice or fillet it for you.

Your A&P also makes it possible for you to enjoy an excellent assortment of shellfish and bivalves, fresh-frozen, or cooked, or canned, in addition to frequent specials on scallops, raw clams, fresh shrimp in the shell, or other regional varieties.

Most of the recipes in the shellfish section can be adapted for use with other kinds of seafood.

How to Cook Fish

Fish may be baked, fried in deep fat or in minimum fat, broiled, steamed, or poached—simmered in liquid—on the range or in the oven. But not all varieties of fish should be cooked in all these ways. The "best" method for a particular fish depends largely on its fat content. See the chart below for specific recommendations. With these as a guide, make substitutions at your convenience in the recipes that follow.

FISH COOKING GUIDE

Fish Suitable for Baking

Bass	Pollack
Bluefish	Pompano
Carp	Red Snapper
Cod	Salmon
Eel	Sea Trout
Flounder	Shad
Haddock	Sole
Hake	Swordfish
Halibut	Trout
Mackerel	Tuna
Mullet	Turbot
Perch	Weakfish
Pickerel	Whitefish
Pike	Whiting

Fish Suitable for Baking Whole, Stuffed

Bass	Mackerel
Bluefish	Mullet
Cod	Pike
Haddock	Shad
Hake	Whitefish

Fish Suitable for Deep-Frying and Pan-Frying

Abalone	Perch
Bass	Pickerel
Butterfish	Pike
Catfish	Pollack
Cod	Pompano
Crappie	Porgy
Croaker	Red Snapper
Eel	Salmon
Flounder	Sea Trout
Grunt	Smelts
Haddock	Sole
Hake	Swordfish
Halibut	Trout
Mackerel	Turbot
Mullet	Whitebait

Fish Suitable for Cooking in Liquid, Steaming

Carp	Perch
Cod	Pike
Drumfish	Pollack
Eel	Salmon
Haddock	Scrod
Hake	Whiting
Halibut	

Fish Suitable for Broiling

Bass	Pompano
Bluefish	Salmon
Butterfish	Sand Dab
Cod	Scrod
Flounder	Shad
Haddock	Sole
Hake	Swordfish
Halibut	Trout
Herring	Tuna
Mackerel	Turbot
Perch	Whitefish
Pike	Whiting
Pollack	

Baked Fish

Fish baked whole, head and tail intact, stuffed or not, makes a handsome entrée. Fortunately, the benefits of baking—extra juiciness and flavor and ease of preparation—apply equally to fish steaks or even fillets.

BAKED BLUEFISH CREOLE

1 bluefish, 4 to 5 pounds
1 onion, chopped
1 green pepper, chopped
4 tablespoons butter or margarine
1 can (1 pound 4 ounces) tomatoes
    Salt, pepper, cayenne pepper, nutmeg

Have the bluefish cleaned, but leave head and tail on. Cook chopped onion and pepper in 2 tablespoons butter until golden, add tomatoes and seasonings, simmer for 5 minutes. Pour sauce into a baking dish that can be brought to the table. Add fish, sprinkle with salt and pepper. Cover with oiled aluminum foil. Bake in a moderate oven (350°F) for 30 minutes, remove the foil, dot the fish with remaining butter, and continue to bake until the fish begins to brown and is just cooked. Makes 6 servings.

BAKED WHITING CREOLE

Prepare 4 or 5 Whiting as above, reducing baking time to 20 minutes. (See photo, page 117.)

BAKED STUFFED RED SNAPPER

1 whole red snapper, 4 to 5 pounds
    Salt, pepper
1½ cups soft bread crumbs
1 egg, beaten
¼ cup melted butter or margarine
1 tablespoon chopped onion
1 tablespoon chopped parsley
1 teaspoon salt
¼ cup dry white wine

Have fish cleaned and dressed; leave head and tail intact for handsomer effect. Wipe inside and out with a wet cloth. Season with salt and pepper. Combine remaining ingredients except wine and toss with a fork to blend. Stuff body cavity lightly. Skewer the opening to close. Line a baking pan with aluminum foil, oil generously. Lay fish on foil, brush with a little melted butter and baste it with wine. Bake in a hot oven (400°F) about 60 minutes, or until the flesh flakes readily when tested with a fork and looks white and opaque. Makes 6 servings. See chart (page 115) for other fish that can be baked in the same way.

Variations: Add sliced cooked mushrooms, or celery, or water chestnuts, or oysters or crab meat to the stuffing mixture.

ROLLED STUFFED HADDOCK FILLETS

½ cup chopped onion
½ cup butter or margarine
3 cups soft bread crumbs
1 teaspoon salt
    Pepper
1 teaspoon poultry seasoning
1 cup mayonnaise
6 haddock fillets, about 2 pounds

Brown onion in butter. Toss with bread crumbs, seasonings and half the mayonnaise.

Whiting is a fish with triple virtues: modest price, delicate flavor and just one center bone—one of the best protein buys in the market. Here it swims in a sea of tomatoes flavored with onion and green pepper, a natural to serve with rice or potato slices. Try the same sauce with frozen fillets for an easy-serve meal. (See page 116.)

Spread stuffing on fillets, roll up, and fit each into a buttered custard cup. Bake in moderate oven (350°F) for 20 minutes. Spread with remaining mayonnaise and bake until topping is brown. Makes 6 servings. You may also try this recipe with flounder, sole or hake fillets.

BAKED HALIBUT STEAKS

Have fish steaks for baking cut ½ inch thick or more. Brush with butter, margarine or oil, sprinkle with seasonings. Arrange on foil-lined, greased baking pan. Bake in a hot oven (400°F) about 15 to 20 minutes, until fish loses its translucency and flakes readily with a fork. For other steaks suitable for baking, see chart on page 115.

SALMON STEAKS WITH TOMATOES AND CREAM

2 pounds salmon steaks
½ teaspoon salt
¼ teaspoon pepper
1 tablespoon butter or margarine
1 cup Italian plum tomatoes, drained
1 onion, cut in thin rings
½ cup cream

Wipe steaks with a damp cloth and lay side by side in a buttered baking dish. Sprinkle with salt and pepper. Dot with butter and cover with tomatoes and onion rings. Bake in a hot oven (425°F) for 10 minutes. Pour cream over fish and bake 10 minutes longer. Serve with buttered noodles. Make 6 servings. Try this with any fish suitable for baking (see page 115).

WHITEFISH FILLETS WITH CHEESE SAUCE

2 pounds whitefish fillets
3 tablespoons lemon juice
4 tablespoons butter or margarine
½ cup sliced mushrooms
4 tablespoons flour
2 cups milk
1 cup grated Swiss or American cheese
Salt, pepper
Paprika, Worcestershire sauce
¼ cup grated Parmesan cheese

Lay fillets side by side in a buttered baking dish, sprinkle with lemon juice. In saucepan, melt butter, cook mushrooms lightly, remove with a slotted spoon, scatter over fish. Add flour to butter in pan, cook for a minute, stirring. Gradually stir in milk and cook, stirring, until sauce is smooth and thickened. Add

grated Swiss or American cheese, stir until cheese melts. Season with salt, pepper, paprika, Worcestershire sauce to taste. Cover fish with cheese sauce, sprinkle with Parmesan cheese. Bake in a moderate oven (350°F) 25 minutes. Makes 6 servings. Any white-fleshed fish fillets may be cooked this way.

SCALLOPED SOLE

1 pound sole fillets
1 tablespoon butter or margarine
1 cup thinly sliced onion
3 potatoes, thinly sliced
1½ teaspoons salt
¼ teaspoon pepper
¼ teaspoon poultry seasoning
3 eggs
1½ cups hot milk
1½ tablespoons melted butter

Cut fish in inch-wide strips. Butter a 2-quart casserole. Layer fish, onion and potatoes in casserole, sprinkling each layer with seasonings. Beat eggs with hot milk, pour over fish. Cover casserole, bake in a moderate oven (350°F) for 45 minutes. Uncover, bake until egg mixture is set. Brush with melted butter and brown under broiler. Makes 3 to 4 servings. Any thin fillets of lean firm fish (flounder, perch, haddock) may be used instead of sole.

SPANISH MACKEREL

6 mackerel fillets
Salt, pepper, cayenne, nutmeg
1 large onion, sliced
2 tablespoons chopped pimiento
6 thin slices peeled tomato
6 anchovies
3 tablespoons chopped scallions
1 cup sliced mushrooms
¼ cup white wine
1 cup fresh soft bread crumbs
½ cup butter or margarine, melted

Sprinkle mackerel fillets with seasonings and lay them side by side in a large, shallow baking dish, generously coated with oil. Spread with onion and pimiento, and top each fillet with a tomato slice and an anchovy. Sprinkle with scallions and mushrooms. Add wine to the pan; let stand 2 hours in the refrigerator. Toss bread crumbs with melted butter, sprinkle on fish. Bake in a moderate oven (350°F) for 20 to 30 minutes, until fish is just cooked and topping is browned. Makes 6 servings.

NORWEGIAN FISH PUDDING

1½ pounds halibut fillets
2 tablespoons cornstarch
1 teaspoon salt
Dash white pepper
Dash grated nutmeg
1½ cups cream
3 egg whites
Salt

Put the halibut through the finest blade of a food chopper several times. Add cornstarch and seasonings. Beat with a wooden spoon to make a smooth mixture, adding cream slowly. (Or whirl all ingredients except egg whites in an electric blender until smooth.) Beat egg whites with a pinch of salt until stiff, fold carefully into fish mixture. Pile mixture in a buttered 6-cup baking dish. Set dish in a pan of hot water, bake in a moderate oven (350°F) for about 1 hour, until mixture is firm to the touch and a knife inserted near the center comes out clean. Turn pudding out onto a warm serving plate and serve with Shrimp Sauce (page 123). Makes 6 servings. This can be made with cod, hake or any white fillet.

"OVEN-FRIED" FILLETS

1½ pounds fish fillets
½ cup milk
1 teaspoon salt
Seasoned bread crumbs (packaged), or dry crumbs, salt, pepper
2 tablespoons butter or margarine

Dip fillets in milk mixed with salt, coat with bread crumbs. Lay side by side in buttered shallow baking pan. Dot with butter and bake in a very hot oven (500°F) for about 10 minutes, until crust is brown. Makes 4 to 5 servings.

Deep-Fried Fish

Fish suitable for deep-frying include fillets and steaks of lean-fleshed fish—cod, flounder, haddock, hake, ocean perch, sole, scrod, weakfish and whiting are among the most frequently available. Small whole fish, such as smelts, are also deep-fried, as are shellfish.

DEEP-FRIED FISH FILLETS

2 pounds fish fillets (or steaks or whole small fish)
1 egg

1 tablespoon milk
Salt, pepper
1 cup corn meal, flour, or cracker or bread crumbs

Cut fish into serving portions. Beat egg with milk, salt and pepper. Dip fillets into egg mixture, then into corn meal. Heat to 370°F on the fat thermometer enough fat to cover the fish. Cook a single layer of fish at a time, in a frying basket if possible, until portions are evenly golden brown. Allow 3 to 5 minutes in all, depending on the thickness of the fish. Lift out of fat, in the basket or with a slotted spoon, drain. Transfer to paper towels to drain thoroughly. Serve hot. Makes 6 servings.

FISH AND CHIPS (BATTER-FRIED FISH)

2 pounds lean fish fillets
1½ cups flour
¼ teaspoon salt
2 teaspoons baking powder
2 eggs
2 cups milk
Flour for dredging
Salt and pepper

Cut fish into ¾-inch strips. Toss flour in bowl with salt and baking powder. Make a hollow and put eggs and half the milk in it. Beat until smooth, gradually working in flour from sides. Stir in remaining milk. Or place batter ingredients (but only 1 cup of the milk) into electric blender, and blend until smooth; stir in remaining milk. Heat fat to 370°F, dredge fish lightly with flour seasoned with salt and pepper. Dip fish into batter, drain excess, fry until golden. Serve with French-fried potatoes and tartar sauce. Makes 4 to 6 servings.

CODFISH BALLS

½ pound salt codfish
2 quarts cold water
4 cups diced potatoes
4 tablespoons butter or margarine
2 eggs, beaten
Freshly ground black pepper

Shred codfish and soak it overnight in cold water. Pour off half the water, add fresh hot water to cover. Add potatoes, bring to a boil and simmer until potatoes are tender; drain. Mash fish and potatoes well; stir in butter, eggs and freshly ground black pepper to taste. Roll fish mixture into small balls with floured hands. Fry in deep hot fat (370°F) until golden. Serve with bacon strips and tartar sauce. Makes 6 servings.

Pan-Browned Fish

One of the simplest and most satisfactory ways of cooking fish is to brown it in a small amount of butter or other flavorful fat. Test the fish—whole, steak or fillet—with a fork for doneness. It should flake readily. Do not overcook, or you sacrifice juiciness and tenderness.

TROUT WITH BROWN BUTTER

  6 trout (fresh or frozen)
½ cup flour
½ teaspoon salt
   Dash pepper
¼ cup oil
  4 tablespoons lemon juice
  3 tablespoons chopped parsley
¼ cup butter or margarine

Thaw frozen trout just until they are limber. Wipe fish with a damp cloth, dry thoroughly. Dust with flour seasoned with salt and pepper. Heat oil in a skillet, slowly brown trout on both sides. Do not overcook. Remove fish to a serving platter and sprinkle with lemon juice and chopped parsley. Wipe out skillet with a paper towel, melt butter in it and let butter cook to a rich golden brown. Pour at once over trout and serve. Makes 6 servings.

PACIFIC SOLE HAWAIIAN

  1 package (1 pound) frozen Pacific sole
     fillets
¼ cup flour
   Salt, pepper
  1 medium onion, sliced
½ green pepper, sliced
  4 tablespoons oil
¼ cup sugar
1½ tablespoons cornstarch
½ teaspoon salt
¼ cup vinegar
  1 cup cold water
  1 tablespoon soy sauce
½ cup canned pineapple tidbits, drained

Cut fillets in serving pieces. Coat with flour seasoned with salt and pepper. Cook onion and green pepper in 2 tablespoons oil for 2 minutes, remove, keep warm. Add remaining oil to pan, brown fish on both sides. Mix remaining ingredients in a saucepan. Cook, stirring, until thick. Arrange fillets on platter, top with vegetables and hot sauce. Makes 3 to 4 servings.

SHAD ROE ON TOAST

Soak shad roe for 15 minutes in water seasoned with salt and 1 teaspoon lemon juice. Remove membrane. Sponge dry and brown lightly in a generous amount of melted butter or margarine. Serve on toast, sprinkled with chopped parsley, a few capers and more butter. One pair of shad roe makes 2 servings.

Broiled Fish

Small whole fish, larger fish split in half, fillets and fish steaks may be broiled in the oven or in a hinged broiler over a charcoal fire outdoors. Don't overcook!

BROILED SWORDFISH STEAKS

  2 pounds inch-thick swordfish steaks (or
     salmon or halibut steaks)
  6 tablespoons lime juice
  2 tablespoons soy sauce
  2 dashes bitters
¼ cup butter or margarine

Wipe fish with damp cloth. Mix lime juice, soy sauce and bitters in shallow dish, turn fish to coat, let stand 30 minutes. Arrange on preheated broiler pan lined with foil and well oiled. Dot generously with butter. Broil until browned, turn, dot with more butter, broil until second side is brown. Test with fork for doneness. Serve with lemon wedges. Makes 6 servings.

LEMON-BROILED FISH FILLETS

Let 2 packages (1 pound each) any frozen fish fillets thaw until they can be separated. Wipe dry, season with salt and pepper, sprinkle with lemon juice. Line a preheated broiling pan with foil, oil the foil generously, add fish, brush with melted butter or margarine. Broil under moderate heat until brown; test with a fork for doneness. It is not necessary to turn fillets or thin, split fish. Serve with butter and lemon or with a sauce. Makes 6 servings.

LEMON-BROILED TROUT

Have trout cleaned. Split if they are very large. Arrange, skin side up, on preheated broiling pan covered with oiled foil. Sprinkle fish with lemon juice, brush with butter or margarine. Brown, turn carefully, brush again with lemon juice and butter, brown other side. Test for doneness with a fork. Serve with butter and lemon. Allow 1 small trout for each serving.

FISH TERIYAKI

1½ pounds fillets of cod, haddock or scrod
½ cup soy sauce
2 tablespoons sherry
3 tablespoons sugar
½ teaspoon ginger
1 clove garlic, mashed

Slice fish into thin strips. Combine remaining ingredients, pour over fish, let stand ½ hour. Thread fish strips on skewers or bamboo picks. Broil quickly and serve hot. Invite guests to cook their own on a charcoal hibachi or a table broiler. Makes 3 to 4 main-dish servings, 8 or more hors d'oeuvre servings.

HADDOCK KEBABS

Cut 1 package (1 pound) partially thawed haddock fillets into strips 1 inch wide, 4 inches long. Coat with ⅓ cup bottled French dressing, let stand ½ hour. Coil strips, fix rolls on skewers, alternately with tomato wedges, onion chunks, and green pepper squares. Brush fish and vegetables with dressing. Broil under moderate heat until browned; turn carefully, brown other side, brushing again with dressing. Makes 3 servings.

Steamed Fish

Steamed fish are cooked, wrapped or unwrapped, in moist heat—the steam—over, never in, boiling water.

STEAMED FISH CHINESE STYLE

1 whole sea bass, 2 pounds
1 tablespoon slivered scallions
1 tablespoon sherry
1 tablespoon soy sauce
1 tablespoon oil

Have the fish cleaned and scaled, but leave head and tail intact. Arrange on a platter that will fit on the rack in your steamer or on a makeshift rack in an ordinary large pan fitted with a lid. Mix scallions, sherry, soy and oil. Spoon over fish on platter. Pour 2 inches water in the steamer, place the rack in the center, and bring the water to a boil. Put the platter holding the fish on the rack, cover the pot, and steam the fish steadily for about 20 minutes to ½ hour, until the flesh flakes readily. Serve on the platter; guests help themselves. Makes 2 main-dish servings, 6 servings as one of several main courses in a Chinese menu.

STEAMED SHAD AND SHAD ROE IN FOIL PACKETS

2 pounds shad fillets
1 pair shad roe
  Water, salt
1 teaspoon lemon juice
2 cloves garlic, pressed
6 scallions, minced
  Salt, pepper, cayenne

Cut shad fillets into 1-inch squares. Parboil shad roe for 15 minutes in boiling salted water to cover, seasoned with lemon juice. Plunge roe into cold water, discard membrane, mash. Mix with remaining ingredients and divide onto 6 squares of foil. Lay shad squares on roe. Fold and seal packets and steam on rack in fish kettle for 45 minutes. Serve with rice. Makes 6 servings.

Fish Cooked in Liquid

Some of the most spectacular and most famous of fish dishes are cooked in simmering, not boiling, liquid—the decorative poached salmon so often seen on elaborate buffets, for instance, and the elegant, yet simple skillet-simmered fillets of white-fleshed fish garnished with mushrooms, or with grapes, or with shrimp and mussels. Fish balls are poached in liquid, and liquid plays a major role in fish stews of various kinds (see page 116).

NEW ENGLAND POACHED SALMON

2 tablespoons butter or margarine
1 large onion, chopped
1 large carrot, diced
3 stalks celery, chopped
2 quarts water
6 whole peppercorns
2 whole cloves
1 bay leaf
2 tablespoons vinegar or lemon juice
2 sprigs parsley
4-pound piece of salmon or 6-pound
    whole fish

Melt butter in a fish poacher or large saucepan and simmer chopped vegetables until soft. Add water, seasonings, vinegar and parsley; simmer, covered, for 1 hour. Wipe salmon with a damp cloth, wrap in cheesecloth, tie lightly. Gently lower fish into simmering liquid and cook very slowly for 40 minutes. Lift the fish carefully from liquid, unwrap, and serve on a hot platter with Egg

Sauce (page 175). Add boiled potatoes and fresh green peas to make a typical New England July 4th dinner. Makes 12 servings. Any firm-fleshed fish may be cooked by this method.

Cold Salmon, Mayonnaise: Cool the poached fish in the cooking liquid. Arrange on a serving platter. Garnish with hard-cooked eggs, sliced cucumber, parsley or watercress. Serve with a well-flavored mayonnaise.

FISH FILLETS BONNE FEMME

2 pounds fish fillets (sole, flounder, hake)
Salt, pepper
1 cup sliced mushrooms
½ small onion, minced
1 cup white wine
1 tablespoon lemon juice
2 tablespoons butter or margarine
2 tablespoons flour

Season fillets with salt and pepper, lay side by side in a generously buttered skillet. Add mushrooms, onion, wine and lemon juice. Cover skillet, simmer over moderate heat about 10 minutes, until the fish is opaque and flakes readily with a fork. Transfer fish to a flameproof serving dish, keep warm. Blend butter with flour, add to pan juices, stir over heat until thickened and smooth. Spoon sauce over fish, put under broiler for a minute to brown lightly. Makes 4 to 6 servings.

SOLE WITH SEEDLESS GRAPES (SOLE VÉRONIQUE)

2 pounds fillets of sole (or other fish)
1 cup white wine
½ cup water
2 tablespoons lemon juice
1 bay leaf
½ onion, sliced
3 peppercorns
3 tablespoons butter or margarine
2 tablespoons flour
½ cup milk
Salt, pepper
1 cup seedless grapes

Arrange fillets side by side in a baking dish. Cover with wine, water and lemon juice. Add bay leaf, onion, peppercorns. Cover the dish, bake in a moderately slow oven (325°F) 15 to 20 minutes, until the fish is opaque and flakes readily. Remove fish to a serving platter and keep warm. Strain the liquid and reserve. Melt 2 tablespoons butter in a saucepan, stir in flour and 1 cup strained liquid, and cook,

stirring, until sauce is smooth and thick. Add milk and salt and pepper to taste. Melt remaining tablespoon butter in a small pan, heat grapes. Spoon sauce over fish, garnish with grapes. Makes 6 servings.

POMPANO TROPICALE

2 oranges, rind and juice
4 tablespoons butter or margarine
1 tablespoon minced onion
6 pompano fillets
¼ teaspoon salt
½ cup water
1½ tablespoons lemon juice
1 tablespoon flour
1 cup cream or milk
2 egg yolks, beaten
¼ cup sherry
Dash cayenne

Peel thin strips of orange rind with a vegetable peeler, cover with water, simmer 3 minutes. Drain, reserve rind. Melt 2 tablespoons butter in a skillet, cook onion until transparent. Arrange fish on onions, sprinkle with salt. Combine water, orange juice and lemon juice; strain over fish. Sprinkle with orange rind. Simmer, covered, 12 minutes, until fish is opaque and flakes readily. Remove fish to a serving platter, keep warm. Reduce pan juices to ⅓ cup by boiling rapidly. In small saucepan, melt 2 tablespoons butter, stir in flour, add cream, and cook over low heat, stirring, until sauce is smooth and thickened. Warm egg yolks with a little sauce, combine. Add reduced pan juices, sherry, and seasoning to taste. Spoon sauce over fish. Makes 6 servings.

FILLET OF FLOUNDER MARGUERY

2 pounds flounder fillets
3 cups strained Fish Stock (page 46)
   or clam juice
3 tablespoons butter or margarine
2 tablespoons flour
½ cup heavy cream
Salt, pepper
18 cooked shrimp
18 mushrooms, sliced and cooked in butter,
   or 1 can (8 ounces) mushrooms

Fold fillets in three. Heat fish stock in a large skillet, add the folded fillets and poach about 10 minutes. Remove to a serving platter, cover and keep warm. Boil the fish liquid to reduce it to 1 cup. Melt butter in a separate pan, stir in flour, and cook for a few minutes without browning. Add the broth; cook, stirring, until sauce boils. Simmer 2 to 3 minutes. Add cream, heat. Add salt and pepper if needed. Scatter shrimp over fish. Add mushrooms and their juices to fish sauce. Pour hot sauce over fillets. Put the dish under the broiler for a few minutes to brown sauce very lightly. Makes 6 servings. This dish is also delicious with bass, lemon sole, scrod or weakfish.

FISH IN TOMATO SAUCE

 1 package (1 pound) frozen haddock fillets
    (or other)
 3 tablespoons oil
 1 onion, chopped
 2 tablespoons chopped parsley
 1 can (8 ounces) tomato sauce
 ½ cup water
 ½ teaspoon salt
    Pepper

Thaw fillets until they can be separated. Heat oil, brown onion lightly. Add remaining ingredients except fish, cover, simmer 5 minutes. Add fish, cook 10 minutes, until fish flakes easily. Makes 3 servings.

CATFISH STEW

 1 package (1 pound) frozen ocean catfish
    fillets
 4 slices bacon, cut in small pieces
 1 onion, minced
 1 clove garlic, minced
 1 can (1 pound) stewed tomatoes
 1 cup water
 1 teaspoon salt
 ⅛ teaspoon pepper
 1 teaspoon dried parsley flakes

Cut fish into chunks. In saucepan, cook bacon, onion and garlic until onion is transparent. Add stewed tomatoes, water, seasonings and parsley. Bring to a boil. Lower heat and add catfish. Simmer, covered, about 10 minutes, until fish is done. Makes 3 to 4 servings.

Cooked Fish Dishes

Most cooked fish dishes are made not from leftovers but from fish specially cooked for the purpose or, even more often, from canned fish, such as salmon and tuna. Poaching and steaming, which leave the fish moister than other methods, make the best cooked fish for these dishes.

FISH SOUFFLÉ WITH SHRIMP SAUCE

 ⅓ cup butter or margarine
 ½ cup flour
 2 cups milk
 4 eggs, separated
    Salt, pepper
 ½ teaspoon sugar
 2 pounds hake or other fish, poached or
    broiled
 1 tablespoon butter or margarine
 2 tablespoons fine bread crumbs
    Salt

Melt ⅓ cup butter and stir in flour. Add milk and cook slowly, stirring, until sauce thickens. Beat egg yolks, beat a little of the hot sauce into them, combine with sauce. Season with salt, pepper and sugar. Flake fish and fold in. Butter a 2-quart casserole, sprinkle with bread crumbs. Beat egg whites with a pinch of salt until stiff, fold carefully into fish mixture. Heap in prepared casserole. Set casserole in a shallow pan of hot water and bake in a moderate oven (350°F) for about 40 minutes, until soufflé is well puffed and browned. Serve immediately with Shrimp or Lobster Sauce (below). Makes 6 servings. Other poached or broiled fish to use for a soufflé include haddock, cod, pike and fluke.

Shrimp or Lobster Sauce: Add 1 cup finely diced cooked shrimp or lobster meat to 1 cup White Sauce (page 174). Season with 1 to 2 tablespoons sherry.

COD KEDGEREE

 1 pound codfish fillets, poached
 2 teaspoons minced onion
 1 tablespoon butter or margarine
 1 tablespoon flour
 1 cup light cream
 4 hard-cooked eggs, chopped
 ¼ teaspoon salt
 ⅛ teaspoon black pepper
 ¼ teaspoon curry powder
    Hot boiled rice

Flake fish coarsely. Cook onion in melted butter. Blend in flour, slowly stir in cream. Bring to a boil, simmer for a few minutes and add chopped eggs, flaked fish and seasonings. Serve over hot boiled rice. Haddock, salmon, lobster or crab may be used in place of cod. Makes 4 servings.

JELLIED FISH SALAD

 1 envelope gelatin
 ¼ cup cold water

2 cups hot tomato juice
1 teaspoon minced onion
1 tablespoon horseradish
¼ cup lemon juice
   Salt, pepper
1 cup diced celery
1 pound fish, cooked and flaked (halibut,
   whiting, scrod or any white fish)
   Hard-cooked eggs
   Lettuce
   Mayonnaise

Soften gelatin in cold water and dissolve it in hot tomato juice. Add onion, horseradish, lemon juice, salt and pepper to taste. Chill until thick and on the point of setting. Gently fold in celery and fish flakes. Pour mixture into a salad mold which has been dipped into cold water. Chill for several hours, until jelly is firm. Unmold onto a chilled plate and garnish with quartered hard-cooked eggs and lettuce leaves. Serve with mayonnaise. Makes 6 servings.

Shellfish Recipes

Your A&P makes it possible for you to enjoy seafood at its best by regularly offering an excellent assortment of shellfish and bivalves, fresh-frozen, or cooked, or canned, in addition to frequent specials on scallops, raw clams, fresh shrimp in the shell and other regional varieties. Most of the recipes which follow can be adapted for use with other kinds of seafood.

Certain shellfish are almost always in the A&P's frozen-food cases: shrimp, Alaska king crab, rock lobster tails, langostina. Canned shrimp, crab and lobster are on the shelves. Cooked crab meat, ready to use, is with the fresh fish.

In a word, you can buy shellfish frozen, fresh raw or fresh cooked, or canned, according to the market supply, for use interchangeably in these recipes.

STEAMED CLAMS

Put ½ cup water in the bottom of a deep kettle. Add clams and cover. Bring to a boil, steam about 5 minutes, until the shells are open. Serve with melted butter or margarine and the broth, strained.

CLAM FRITTERS

1 can (8 ounces) chopped clams
2 eggs, beaten
½ teaspoon salt
   Pepper

1¼ cups flour
1½ teaspoons baking powder

Combine clams and their broth with beaten eggs, salt and pepper. Mix flour and baking powder, add. Fry by spoonfuls in hot (375°F) deep fat until golden. Makes 4 servings.

WINE-STEAMED MUSSELS (MOULES MARINIÈRE)

12 dozen live mussels in the shell
2 cups white wine (or half wine, half water)
6 tablespoons butter or margarine
3 tablespoons flour
½ cup chopped parsley
   Salt, pepper

Scrub mussel shells well under running water. Put the mussels in a deep kettle, add wine, bring to a boil. Cover the pot and steam for 7 minutes, or until the shells open. Arrange mussels in 6 large soup plates. Melt the butter in a saucepan, blend in the flour and add 1 cup of the mussel broth gradually, stirring constantly until the sauce thickens. Add remaining broth and parsley, bring the sauce to a boil, add salt and pepper to taste. Pour the sauce over the mussels. Serve immediately. Makes 6 to 8 servings.

DEVILED OYSTERS

4 cups shelled oysters
3 tablespoons butter or margarine
1 onion, chopped
1 tablespoon parsley, chopped
1 teaspoon Worcestershire sauce
2 eggs, beaten
¾ cup fine, fresh bread crumbs
1 tablespoon melted butter or margarine

Cut oysters in thirds. Melt 3 tablespoons butter and cook onion until just tender, but not browned. Stir in oysters, parsley and Worcestershire sauce. Remove from heat. Add eggs and ½ cup bread crumbs, toss to mix lightly. Pile in 6 oiled individual ramekins or scallop shells and sprinkle with remaining ¼ cup bread crumbs tossed with 1 tablespoon melted butter. Bake in a hot oven (425°F) until topping browns, about 15 minutes. Makes 6 servings.

DEVILS ON HORSEBACK

Wrap oysters in squares of bacon, fix on skewers. Broil until bacon is crisply browned, turning once. Allow 3 oysters to an hors d'oeuvre serving.

Variation: Marinate oysters for broiling in equal parts sherry and lemon juice.

OYSTERS CASINO

2 cups oysters
½ cup green pepper, minced
1 tablespoon lemon juice
4 strips bacon, diced

Drain oysters. Arrange on an ovenproof platter. Sprinkle with green pepper, lemon juice, bacon. Bake in a hot oven (450°F) for 10 minutes. Makes 6 servings.

SCALLOP KEBABS

Allow 6 scallops to a serving. Dip them in olive oil seasoned with salt, pepper and chopped chervil. Arrange the scallops on a skewer, separating them with whole bay leaves. Brown lightly over hot coals or under the broiler. Do not overcook. Serve with Lemon-Butter Sauce (page 174).

SCALLOPS IN CHEESE SAUCE (COQUILLES SAINT-JACQUES)

2 pounds scallops
Fish Stock (page 46)
2 cups Cheese Sauce (page 175)
Salt, pepper
1 tablespoon chopped parsley
¼ cup grated Parmesan cheese

Simmer the scallops in fish stock to cover for 8 minutes. Drain scallops, reduce the fish stock over high heat to about ½ cup. Add the reduced stock to cheese sauce and blend with scallops. Season with salt and pepper to taste, add parsley. Pile mixture into individual flameproof baking dishes or shells, sprinkle with grated Parmesan cheese, brown topping under broiler. Makes 6 servings.

Coquilles Saint-Jacques with Mushrooms: Add ¼ pound mushrooms, sliced and cooked for 5 minutes in 2 tablespoons butter or margarine with a dash of lemon juice.

Curried Coquilles Saint-Jacques: Use Cream Sauce (page 174) instead of cheese sauce, and season with curry powder to taste, beginning with 1 teaspoon.

SCALLOP CURRY

2 tablespoons butter or margarine
1 small onion, chopped
1 teaspoon curry powder (or more, to taste)
1 tablespoon flour
⅔ cup light cream
½ teaspoon salt
Dash cayenne
2 teaspoons apricot or other preserves

½ cup white wine
1½ pounds sea scallops
1 teaspoon lemon juice

Melt butter, add onion and curry powder. Cook over low heat, stirring, 5 minutes. Add flour, stir a moment. Add cream, salt, cayenne and preserves; bring to a boil, stirring. Reduce heat, simmer 5 minutes, stirring constantly. Heat wine, add scallops, simmer 8 minutes. Add curry cream sauce and lemon juice, adjust seasonings with salt and more lemon juice. Makes 4 to 6 servings.

SCALLOPS NEWBURG

2 pounds scallops
4 tablespoons butter or margarine
½ cup sherry
1½ cups cream
4 egg yolks, beaten
½ teaspoon salt
Pepper
2 dashes hot pepper sauce (optional)
⅛ teaspoon dry mustard (optional)

Brown scallops in butter. Add sherry and simmer 5 minutes. Remove from heat. Stir cream into beaten egg yolks and very slowly, stirring constantly, add to scallops and pan juices. Add seasonings, to taste. Cook slowly, stirring, until sauce thickens; do not boil. Serve immediately over toast triangles or hot boiled rice. Makes 6 servings. Shrimp, lobster or crab may be substituted for scallops.

STEAMED LOBSTER

If you find a live lobster in the fish case, you have a treat in store. The cooking couldn't be simpler. Put the lobster in a large pot with about 4 inches of cold water. Add a celery stalk and bay leaf if desired. Cover the pot, quickly bring the water to a boil and simmer 8 minutes.

To Stretch a Lobster: Split cold steamed lobster in half, remove meat from tail in one piece, fill with vegetable salad mixture, top with lobster and mayonnaise. Serve to 2.

ROCK LOBSTER THERMIDOR

6 frozen rock lobster tails
3 tablespoons butter or margarine
2 tablespoons flour
1 cup light cream
½ teaspoon poultry seasoning
¼ teaspoon dry mustard
1 teaspoon salt

⅛ teaspoon pepper
½ teaspoon paprika
2 tablespoons sherry
½ cup bread crumbs
3 tablespoons grated Parmesan cheese
1½ tablespoons butter or margarine

Boil rock lobster tails and cool. Split shells, being careful not to break them, and remove meat in large chunks. Melt 3 tablespoons butter in saucepan, blend in flour. Add cream slowly and cook, stirring, until sauce thickens. Add seasonings, sherry and lobster meat, pile into reserved shells. Sprinkle with bread crumbs mixed with grated cheese. Dot with butter and set under broiler to brown. Makes 6 servings. Shrimp, scallops or crab meat may be prepared by the same recipe and baked in individual ovenproof casseroles.

LOBSTER SALAD

2 cups cooked lobster meat, diced
¼ cup stuffed olives, chopped
2 hard-cooked eggs, diced
1 teaspoon capers
¼ cup French dressing or mayonnaise
    Lettuce leaves
    Cucumber slices, tomato wedges for
        garnish

Toss lobster meat with olives, eggs, capers, and dressing. Chill. Serve on lettuce leaves, garnish with cucumber and tomato. Makes 6 servings. Substitute shrimp, crab meat or any flaked, cooked lean fish for lobster meat, if desired.

LANGOSTINA MARINARA

1 pound frozen cooked langostina
1 can (1 pound) Marinara sauce
    Grated Parmesan cheese

Combine langostina with canned sauce and heat slowly. Serve on rice or spaghetti, sprinkle with grated Parmesan cheese. Makes 4 servings.

Shrimp Marinara: Cooked shrimp may be substituted for langostina.

DEVILED CRAB

1 pound cooked crab meat
3 tablespoons butter or margarine
3 tablespoons flour
½ teaspoon salt
    Pepper
½ teaspoon dry mustard
¼ teaspoon paprika

    Cayenne pepper
1 cup milk
1 can (3 or 4 ounces) chopped mushrooms
2 drops Worcestershire sauce
1 teaspoon lemon juice
2 drops hot pepper sauce
¾ cup buttered bread crumbs

Pick over crab meat and discard bits of shell. Melt butter and blend in flour. Add seasonings, slowly stir in milk and cook, stirring, until smooth and thickened. Add mushrooms, Worcestershire sauce, lemon juice and hot pepper sauce. Simmer 5 minutes. Fold in crab meat, heat 5 minutes. Pile mixture into individual flameproof shells or ramekins and top with buttered bread crumbs. Set under broiler until crumbs brown. Makes 4 servings.

CRAB MEAT LOUIS

3 cups cooked crab meat
1 cup mayonnaise
1 tablespoon chopped stuffed olives
⅓ cup bottled French dressing
⅓ cup ketchup
    Onion salt, pepper
    Hot pepper sauce
    Lettuce
3 hard-cooked eggs, cut in wedges
3 tomatoes, quartered
    Watercress

Pick over the crab meat and discard bits of shell. Combine mayonnaise, olives, French dressing and ketchup. Add seasonings to taste. Toss dressing with crab meat and mound on lettuce. Garnish with eggs, tomatoes and watercress. Makes 6 servings.

SHRIMP

When you find shrimp in the shell in the fish case, you have a choice of peeling and deveining them either before or after cooking. Fresh-frozen shrimp are usually already shelled and deveined.

BOILED SHRIMP

Plunge shrimp into simmering water seasoned with mixed shrimp spice, poach gently just until the shells are red. Shrimp cook completely in 6 minutes or less, depending upon their size. Cool the shrimp in the poaching water, remove shells and black intestinal veins. Boiled shrimp can be reheated as an ingredient in other recipes, but avoid overcooking them.

BROILED SHRIMP

2 pounds raw shrimp
1 cup oil
2 cloves garlic, crushed
½ teaspoon salt
⅛ teaspoon black pepper
2 tablespoons minced parsley

Shrimp are often broiled in the shell, for dramatic effect, but they may be deveined before cooking. Slit the back of the shell with a sharp knife and lift out the black intestinal vein. Combine oil with garlic and remaining ingredients, blend well. Dip shrimp in seasoned oil, arrange on broiling pan. Pour remaining oil over shrimp. Broil 3 inches from heat, turning once, about 5 minutes, or until shells are pink. Makes 4 servings.

SHRIMP CREOLE

1 pound shrimp, peeled and deveined
2 tablespoons oil
1 medium onion, chopped
1 clove garlic, minced
1 medium green pepper, chopped
½ cup chopped celery
1 can (8 ounces) tomato sauce
¾ cup water
2 cups hot cooked rice

Use fresh or uncooked frozen shrimp for this dish. Heat oil and cook onion, garlic, green pepper and celery slowly about 5 minutes. Stir in tomato sauce and water, simmer about 10 minutes. Add shrimp and cook until shrimp is pink, about 3 minutes. Serve over hot rice. Makes 4 servings.

SHRIMP-FRIED RICE

2 pounds shrimp, cleaned and deveined
Salt, pepper
¼ cup oil
1 onion, chopped
1 cup sliced mushrooms
1 cup sliced celery
6 cups cold cooked rice
3 eggs, beaten
3 tablespoons soy sauce

Sprinkle shrimp with salt and pepper. Heat oil in deep heavy pot. Add shrimp and vegetables and cook, stirring constantly, until shrimp are bright pink, 5 to 6 minutes. Add rice, cook and stir until rice is hot. Add beaten eggs, cook and stir until eggs are firm. Add soy sauce, salt and pepper to taste. Makes 6 to 8 servings.

HAWAIIAN COCONUT BUTTERFLY SHRIMP

3 pounds jumbo shrimp
Juice of 3 lemons
Salt, pepper
1 teaspoon curry powder
¼ teaspoon powdered ginger
4 cups flour
4 teaspoons baking powder
1 cup milk
½ cup water
Freshly grated coconut

Peel and devein shrimp, slit halfway through, flatten to form butterflies. Marinate 1 hour in lemon juice seasoned with salt, pepper, curry powder and ginger, turning once. Drain shrimp and dredge lightly in flour. Combine remaining flour and baking powder with milk and water, beat well, let batter stand 10 minutes. Add the marinade from shrimp, blend. Spread freshly grated coconut on a flat baking pan and toast lightly in a moderate oven (350°F). Dip shrimp into batter and coat with toasted coconut. Fry in hot fat (370°F), drain and serve with Chinese Fruit Sauce (page 174) or Japanese Soy Sauce Dip (page 175).

SHRIMP TEMPURA

1 pound shrimp
2 eggs
½ teaspoon salt
Pinch baking soda
1 cup water
1 cup flour

Dipping Sauce:

½ cup sherry
¼ cup soy sauce
1 teaspoon powdered ginger
1 teaspoon sugar

Shell and devein shrimp. Beat eggs well, add salt, baking soda and water, stir in flour to make a thin batter. Dip shrimp into batter, drain, fry in hot (370°F) deep fat until brown. Serve at once. To make dipping sauce, combine sherry and remaining ingredients in a saucepan, bring to a boil, cover, simmer 5 minutes. Makes 3 to 4 servings.

Note: Fish strips, or green beans, eggplant sticks, green onion sections, sweet potato slices or mushrooms may be dipped into the batter and fried to serve with the shrimp.

CASSEROLES AND STRETCHERS

For dishes that add substance to meals and extend or replace meats in delicious ways, count on casseroles.

Rice, beans, corn meal, and noodles or macaroni are generally good sources of incomplete proteins—that is, they lack some, but not all, of the essential amino acids present in a complete protein, such as meat. But when you combine any of these with small amounts of meat, fish, cheese, eggs or milk, they function as complete proteins.

Also, you can obtain complete proteins by combining incomplete proteins. For instance, in the Southern favorite Hoppin' John, black beans supply the amino acids that rice lacks, isoleucine and lysine; rice supplies tryptophan and the sulphur-containing amino acids in which black beans are deficient. Together, rice and beans add up to a complete protein —and to a delicious casserole, easy on the cook, easy on the budget!

Beans

You will find a wide range of dried and canned beans on your supermarket shelves, and it's a good idea to stock some in your pantry to have handy for a main-course dish or to extend meat leftovers.

NEW ENGLAND BAKED BEANS

  1 package (1 pound) pea beans
  1 medium onion, sliced
 ¼ pound lean salt pork, cut up
 ¼ teaspoon salt
 ¼ teaspoon pepper
 ½ teaspoon dry mustard
 ¼ cup molasses
  2 tablespoons brown sugar

Cook beans as package directs. Drain beans and save cooking liquid. Put onion in a 3-quart bean pot or casserole. Add beans. Bury pieces of salt pork in the beans. Combine 1 cup bean liquid with remaining ingredients; pour over beans. Cover bean pot and bake in a slow oven (300°F) 6 to 8 hours. Check occasionally and if beans seem dry, add more bean liquid or boiling water. Uncover during last hour of baking, season to taste. Makes 6 to 8 servings. (See photo, page 181.)

SOUTHWESTERN COWPOKE BEANS

  3 tablespoons bacon fat or lard
  1 large onion, chopped
  1 clove garlic, chopped
  1 can (1 pound) whole tomatoes
  2 cans (1 pound each) red kidney beans
  1 cup cubed cooked ham, pork or sausage
  2 teaspoons chili powder
   Salt and pepper
   Dash Worcestershire sauce
 ½ cup coarsely crushed corn chips

Heat fat in a large skillet; cook onion and garlic until softened. Add remaining ingredients, except corn chips, and bring to boil. Simmer over low heat about 20 minutes. Pour into serving dish and sprinkle with corn chips. Makes 6 servings. (See photo, page 181.)

BEAN LOAF

2 cans (1 pound each) kidney beans, drained
4 ounces seasoned, textured soy protein meat extender
1 cup water to moisten soy (or as directed)
1 onion, chopped
½ cup slivered celery and leaves
1 cup soft bread crumbs
2 eggs
1 tablespoon ketchup
Salt, pepper

Mash drained beans, or whirl in blender to purée. Soak soy protein in water for 5 minutes. Combine with beans and remaining ingredients. Adjust seasoning with salt and pepper. Bake in an oiled 9-inch loaf pan in a moderately hot oven (375°F) about 40 minutes, until the loaf is crusty and browned. Makes 6 servings.

CHICK-PEAS AND BACON

4 slices bacon, cut up
1 can (1 pound) chick-peas, drained
2 tablespoons finely chopped onion
Salt and pepper

Fry bacon until crisp; remove pieces from pan. Add drained chick-peas and onion to fat in pan. Heat through, stirring occasionally. Remove vegetables from pan with slotted spoon, drain excess fat. Sprinkle with salt, pepper and bacon pieces. Makes 4 servings.

HOT BEAN SALAD

3 tablespoons oil
3 scallions, sliced (including green)
1 can (1 pound) white beans, drained
1 tablespoon vinegar
1 tablespoon chopped parsley
¼ teaspoon oregano
Dash of sugar
Salt and pepper

Heat oil, add onion, cook 2 or 3 minutes. Add beans and remaining ingredients. Heat through. Makes 3 to 4 servings.

LIMA BEAN-AND-CHEESE CASSEROLE

1 package (10 ounces) frozen lima beans
4 slices bacon, diced
1 small onion, chopped
¼ cup chopped celery
1 cup shredded process American cheese
Salt and pepper
Dash Worcestershire sauce

Cook frozen lima beans as package directs, reserve liquid. Fry bacon until half cooked; remove from pan. Cook onion and celery in bacon fat until softened. Combine lima beans, ¼ cup cooking liquid, onion, celery, cheese and seasonings in a greased 1-quart casserole. Top with bacon pieces. Bake in a moderate oven (350°F) 20 to 25 minutes, until bubbling hot and browned. Makes 3 to 4 servings.

LIMA BEAN-AND-CORN CASSEROLE

Omit bacon and substitute 2 tablespoons butter or margarine for bacon fat in above recipe. Add 1 can (8 ounces) kernel corn, undrained, to casserole.

REFRIED BEANS

¼ cup lard, bacon fat or oil
1 can (1 pound) red beans, drained
Salt and pepper
¼ cup shredded Monterey Jack or Swiss cheese

Heat fat in skillet. Add beans, 1 tablespoon at a time, mashing before adding the next spoonful. When beans are all mashed and hot, season with salt and pepper and add cheese. Stir until cheese starts to melt. Makes 3 to 4 servings.

HOPPIN' JOHN

¼ pound sliced bacon, diced
1 cup rice
2 cups water
Salt and pepper
1 can (15 ounces) black-eyed peas, drained

Cook bacon until crisp; remove from pan. Drain all but 2 tablespoons fat from pan; add rice and stir until grains are coated. Add water and salt and pepper. Bring to boil, cover and reduce heat to very low. Simmer 15 minutes, uncover, add peas and bacon pieces. Cover and cook 5 minutes longer. Makes 3 to 4 servings. (See photo, page 49.)

LENTIL CASSEROLE

1 package (1 pound) lentils
5 cups water
2 tablespoons oil
1 large onion, sliced
1 clove garlic, minced
2 ribs celery, sliced
3 carrots, sliced
2 teaspoons salt

¼ teaspoon pepper
1 bay leaf
½ teaspoon marjoram

Soak lentils in water several hours. Heat oil in a large casserole and cook onion, garlic, celery and carrots for 5 minutes. Add seasonings, lentils and water. Bring to a boil, reduce heat. Simmer, covered, about 35 minutes, stirring occasionally, until lentils are tender and liquid is absorbed. Discard bay leaf. Makes 4 to 6 servings.

EASY CASSOULET

¼ pound salt pork, cubed
½ pound sweet Italian sausage, sliced
½ pound hot Italian sausage, sliced
1 broiler-fryer chicken, cut up
   Salt and pepper
1 large onion, chopped
1 clove garlic, minced
2 cans (20 ounces each) white kidney beans
1 can (10½ ounces) condensed chicken broth
¾ cup water
½ cup dry bread crumbs

In a 4-quart casserole, brown salt pork and sausages. Remove meat, drain all but 3 tablespoons fat. Season chicken pieces with salt and pepper; brown in fat. Add onion and garlic, cook until softened. Drain beans, reserve liquid. Add beans to casserole along with 1 cup reserved bean liquid, broth, water, sausage and bacon pieces. Bake, uncovered, in a moderately hot oven (375°F) 30 minutes. Sprinkle with crumbs, bake 15 minutes longer. Makes 8 servings.

Potatoes

All forms of potatoes may be used in casseroles—fresh uncooked, canned, instant and leftovers.

SHEPHERD'S PIE

2 tablespoons oil
1 small onion, chopped
2 cups cubed cooked lamb or beef
1 package (10 ounces) frozen carrots and peas, thawed enough to separate
1 cup leftover or canned gravy
¼ teaspoon marjoram
   Salt and pepper
2 cups mashed potatoes (may be made with instant potatoes)
1 egg, beaten

Heat oil in a 1½-quart casserole and cook onion until softened. Add lamb, carrots and

peas, gravy and seasonings, bring to simmer. Combine potatoes and egg; pile around edge of casserole. Bake in a hot oven (425°F) about 20 minutes, until potatoes brown. Makes 4 servings.

SAUSAGE–SWEET POTATO–APPLE CASSEROLE

1 can (1 pound 8 ounces) sweet potatoes
5 apples, peeled, cored and sliced
2 tablespoons brown sugar
½ teaspoon salt
2 tablespoons butter or margarine
6 to 8 link sausages

Slice potatoes and layer with apple slices in a greased 2-quart baking dish, sprinkling layers with sugar and salt and dotting them with butter. Arrange sausages on top. Bake in a moderately hot oven (375°F) 45 minutes, until sausages are brown and apples are tender. Makes 6 servings.

SCANDINAVIAN POTATO-AND-ANCHOVY CASSEROLE (JANSSON'S TEMPTATION)

4 to 5 medium potatoes, peeled and thinly sliced
2 medium onions, thinly sliced
1 can (about 2 ounces) flat anchovies, drained
   Pepper
1½ cups half-and-half (milk and cream)
2 tablespoons butter or margarine

Layer potatoes, onions and anchovies in a well-buttered 2-quart baking dish, sprinkling each layer lightly with pepper and ending with potatoes. Add half-and-half, dot with butter. Bake in a hot oven (400°F) 45 minutes, until potatoes are tender and most of liquid is absorbed. Makes 4 servings.

Spaghetti Sauces

A wide variety of prepared spaghetti sauces is available at the A&P, ready to use. For special occasions, or when time permits, you may want to try your hand at a homemade sauce.

TOMATO SAUCE FOR SPAGHETTI

2 tablespoons oil
1 large onion, chopped
1 small green pepper, chopped
1 small clove garlic, chopped

1 teaspoon salt
½ teaspoon sugar
⅛ teaspoon pepper
1 can (6 ounces) tomato paste
1 can (1 pound, 12 ounces) tomatoes
½ teaspoon oregano
½ teaspoon basil
¼ cup grated Parmesan cheese

Heat oil, add onion, green pepper and garlic and cook until tender. Add remaining ingredients except cheese. Simmer ½ hour, stirring occasionally. Stir in cheese before serving. Makes 6 to 8 servings.

Meat Sauce: Cook ½ pound ground beef with onion, pepper, garlic. Proceed with recipe as above.

CRAB SAUCE FOR SPAGHETTI

¼ cup oil
½ cup chopped onions
1 teaspoon chopped garlic
1 teaspoon chopped celery
1 teaspoon chopped parsley
1 cup solid-pack tomatoes
1 can (8 ounces) tomato sauce
2 teaspoons salt
1 teaspoon black pepper
½ teaspoon paprika
1½ cups water
1 pound cooked crab meat, picked over
¼ cup sherry
Grated cheese

Heat the oil in a saucepan and cook onions, garlic, celery and parsley until golden. Add tomatoes, tomato sauce and seasonings. Simmer 15 minutes. Add water, cook 1 hour. Add crab meat and sherry and simmer for 5 minutes. Serve piping-hot over cooked spaghetti. Sprinkle with grated cheese. Cooked shrimp or lobster may be substituted for crab meat. Makes 6 to 8 servings.

RED CLAM SAUCE FOR SPAGHETTI

2 tablespoons oil
1 clove garlic
1 can (about 8 ounces) minced clams, undrained
½ green pepper, chopped
1 can (1 pound) Italian-style tomatoes
½ teaspoon oregano
½ teaspoon salt
⅛ teaspoon pepper
2 tablespoons minced parsley

Heat oil in large skillet and cook garlic until golden brown. Discard garlic. Drain clams, save liquid. To oil in skillet, add pepper, tomatoes, seasonings and clam liquid. Simmer over low heat 10 minutes, stirring occasionally to break up tomatoes. Add clams and parsley, heat. Pour over cooked spaghetti. Makes 3 to 4 servings.

WHITE CLAM SAUCE FOR SPAGHETTI

¼ cup oil
1 clove garlic, halved
1 can (about 8 ounces) minced clams, undrained
¼ teaspoon salt
⅛ teaspoon pepper
2 tablespoons chopped parsley

Heat oil, add garlic, cook 5 minutes. Discard garlic. Add clam liquid, salt, pepper and parsley. Simmer for 5 minutes. Add clams, heat. Pour over cooked spaghetti. Makes 3 to 4 servings.

CARBONARA SAUCE FOR SPAGHETTI (BACON-AND-EGG SAUCE)

6 slices bacon
2 tablespoons butter or margarine
1 clove garlic
¼ cup finely chopped onion
½ pound spaghetti, cooked
2 eggs, beaten
2 tablespoons chopped parsley
2 tablespoons grated Parmesan cheese
¼ teaspoon pepper

Dice bacon and cook until almost crisp. Remove from pan and reserve. Drain all but 2 tablespoons bacon drippings from skillet, add butter, garlic and onion to pan, cook over low heat until onion is softened. Discard garlic clove. Put hot cooked spaghetti into a large bowl. Stir in eggs, parsley, cheese and pepper. Add cooked onions with pan drippings and bacon pieces, toss to mix. Makes 3 to 4 servings.

Pasta

In addition to the familiar spaghetti, noodles and macaroni, pasta comes in many sizes and shapes—all nutritious and economical.

SPAGHETTI WITH MEATBALLS

¾ pound ground beef
1 tablespoon finely chopped parsley
1 tablespoon grated Parmesan cheese
¼ cup dry bread crumbs
1 egg

1 tablespoon milk
¼ teaspoon salt
1 tablespoon vegetable oil
1 jar (16 ounces) spaghetti sauce
1 package (8 ounces) spaghetti
  Grated Parmesan cheese

Combine ground beef with parsley, cheese, crumbs, egg, milk and salt; shape into 16 balls. Heat oil in skillet and brown meatballs on all sides. Add sauce and simmer 15 minutes. Meanwhile, cook and drain spaghetti as package directs. Spoon sauce and meatballs over cooked spaghetti and sprinkle with grated cheese. Makes 3 to 4 servings.

MACARONI AND CHEESE

  1 package (8 ounces) elbow macaroni
  3 tablespoons butter or margarine
  3 tablespoons flour
  ¼ teaspoon salt
  ⅛ teaspoon pepper
1½ cups milk
1½ cups grated American cheese
  1 cup soft bread crumbs
  2 tablespoons melted butter or margarine
  ½ teaspoon paprika

Cook and drain elbow macaroni as package directs. Meanwhile, melt butter over low heat. Blend in flour and seasonings. Gradually add milk, stirring until sauce thickens. Add cheese and stir until melted. Stir in cooked macaroni. Pour into greased 1½-quart casserole. Toss bread crumbs with melted butter and paprika. Sprinkle over macaroni. Bake in a moderately hot oven (375°F) for 25 minutes or until bubbling and browned. Makes 4 servings.

LINGUINE ALFREDO

  1 package (1 pound) linguine
  ¼ pound butter or margarine
  ½ cup grated Parmesan cheese
  ¼ cup cream
    Freshly ground pepper to taste

Cook and drain linguine as package directs. Melt butter in a deep skillet. Stir in hot cooked linguine and cheese. Add cream, toss to mix. Sprinkle with pepper. Makes 6 to 8 servings.

SEA SHELLS WITH QUICK TUNA SAUCE

1 package (8 ounces) sea shells
2 tablespoons oil
1 clove garlic, sliced
1 can (7 ounces) tuna

1 jar (16 ounces) spaghetti sauce
1 tablespoon chopped parsley

Cook and drain sea shells as package directs. Meanwhile, heat oil and cook garlic until soft. Add tuna, stirring to break up. Add spaghetti sauce and parsley and heat through. Pour sauce over cooked sea shells. Makes 3 to 4 servings.

MOSTACCIOLI WITH SAUSAGE-TOMATO SAUCE

1 pound Italian sausage, sweet or hot
1 small onion, chopped
1 green pepper, chopped
1 jar (16 ounces) spaghetti sauce
1 package (8 ounces) mostaccioli
  Grated Parmesan cheese

Cut sausages into pieces and cook in a large skillet over medium heat until lightly brown. Add onion and green pepper and cook until vegetables are softened and sausages are well browned. Drain excess fat from pan. Add spaghetti sauce, bring to boil, simmer 15 minutes. Meanwhile, cook and drain mostaccioli as package directs. Spoon sauce and sausage pieces over cooked mostaccioli. Sprinkle with grated cheese. Makes 3 to 4 servings.

HUNGARIAN POPPY-SEED NOODLES

  1 package (8 ounces) extra-wide noodles
  2 tablespoons butter or margarine
  1 cup sour cream
  1 cup cottage cheese
  2 tablespoons poppy seeds
  1 to 1½ teaspoons paprika
  ½ teaspoon Worcestershire sauce
    Salt and pepper

Cook and drain noodles as package directs. Return to saucepan, toss with butter. Stir in remaining ingredients. Heat through without boiling. Makes 4 servings.

BEEF-AND-MACARONI CASSEROLE

  1 package (8 ounces) medium noodles
  ½ pound process American cheese
  1 pound ground beef
  1 small onion, chopped
  1 clove garlic, minced
  ½ teaspoon chili powder
  1 can (10½ ounces) condensed tomato soup
  1 can (1 pound) cut green beans, drained

Cook and drain noodles as package directs. Shred cheese. In a large skillet, brown beef, onion, garlic and chili powder, stirring with a fork. Add soup, all but ½ cup cheese, green beans and cooked noodles. Turn into greased 2-quart baking dish. Top with reserved cheese. Bake in moderate oven (350°F) ½ hour, until bubbling and browned. Makes 6 servings.

FRANK-MAC MEAL

1 package (8 ounces) elbow macaroni
2 tablespoons butter or margarine
1 pound frankfurters, sliced
1 small onion, chopped
½ small green pepper, chopped
1 can (10½ ounces) condensed tomato soup
½ cup milk
1 can (17 ounces) kernel corn, undrained

Cook and drain elbow macaroni as package directs. Meanwhile, heat butter in a saucepan and brown frankfurter slices. Add onion and green pepper, cook until tender. Stir in tomato soup, milk, corn and cooked macaroni. Heat through. Makes 6 servings.

EGG BOWS WITH CHICKEN LIVERS

1 package (12 ounces) egg bows
¼ cup oil
1 cup chopped onion
1 pound chicken livers, cut up
1 jar (16 ounces) spaghetti sauce
1 can (4 ounces) chopped mushrooms, undrained
¼ cup grated Parmesan cheese

Cook and drain egg bows as package directs. Meanwhile, heat oil and cook onion until transparent. Add chicken livers and cook, stirring, until lightly browned. Add spaghetti sauce and mushrooms. Simmer 10 minutes. Stir in cheese and cooked egg bows and heat through. Makes 4 servings.

PERCIATELLI AND ZUCCHINI

1 package (8 ounces) perciatelli
¼ cup oil
1 onion, chopped
1 pound zucchini squash, sliced
1 jar (16 ounces) spaghetti sauce
½ teaspoon dried basil
2 tablespoons grated Parmesan cheese

Cook and drain perciatelli as package directs. Meanwhile, heat oil in a skillet and cook onion and sliced squash until tender. Add sauce and basil, heat through. Pour over cooked perciatelli and sprinkle with Parmesan cheese. Makes 3 to 4 servings.

RIGATONI SAUSAGE BOWL

1 package (8 ounces) rigatoni
½ pound sausage meat
1 cup soft bread crumbs
¼ cup milk
1 egg
1 teaspoon salt
¼ teaspoon pepper
1 jar (16 ounces) spaghetti sauce
Grated Parmesan cheese

Cook and drain rigatoni as package directs. Meanwhile, cook sausage meat in a skillet over medium heat, stirring with a fork, about 15 minutes. Drain excess fat. Add crumbs, milk, egg and seasonings, mix well. Stir in sauce, heat. Pour over cooked rigatoni and toss to mix. Sprinkle with grated cheese. Makes 3 to 4 servings.

MEZZANI WITH CREAMY CHEESE SAUCE

1 package (8 ounces) mezzani
2 tablespoons butter or margarine
1 can (10½ ounces) condensed cream of mushroom soup
¼ cup milk
¼ teaspoon oregano
½ cup ricotta or cottage cheese
2 tablespoons grated Parmesan cheese
¼ cup sour cream

Cook and drain mezzani as package directs. Melt butter. Stir in soup and milk. Add oregano, ricotta and Parmesan. Cook over low heat, stirring occasionally, just to a simmer. Stir in sour cream and heat through. Add cooked mezzani and heat 2 minutes longer. Makes 3 to 4 servings.

SEA SHELLS FLORENTINE

1 package (8 ounces) sea shells
1 package (10 ounces) frozen chopped spinach
1 can (10½ ounces) condensed cream of mushroom soup
¼ cup milk
⅛ teaspoon nutmeg
¼ cup sour cream
2 tablespoons butter or margarine
Grated Parmesan cheese

Cook and drain sea shells as package directs. Cook and drain spinach as package directs. Stir soup, milk and nutmeg into drained spinach. Cook over low heat, stirring occasionally, just to a simmer. Stir in sour cream and heat through. Toss hot cooked sea shells with butter. Spoon spinach sauce into serving dish; top with cooked sea shells and sprinkle with grated cheese. Makes 3 to 4 servings.

ELBOW SPAGHETTI-AND-HAM SKILLET

  1 package (8 ounces) elbow spaghetti
  1 tablespoon oil
  2 tablespoons minced onion
  1 small clove garlic, minced
½ pound cooked ham, cubed
  1 jar (16 ounces) spaghetti sauce
½ cup grated Cheddar cheese
  2 tablespoons minced parsley

Cook and drain elbow spaghetti as package directs. Meanwhile, heat oil in a skillet; add onion, garlic and ham. Cook until ham is lightly browned. Add spaghetti sauce. Simmer 10 minutes over low heat. Add cheese, parsley and cooked elbow spaghetti, toss to mix. Makes 3 to 4 servings.

BAKED LASAGNE WITH MEAT SAUCE

  1 package (1 pound) lasagne
½ pound ground beef
½ pound sweet Italian sausage, sliced
  1 jar (32 ounces) spaghetti sauce
  1 pound ricotta or cottage cheese
½ pound mozzarella cheese, shredded
½ cup grated Parmesan cheese

Cook and drain lasagne as package directs. Brown ground beef and sausage slices in a skillet, stirring with a fork. Pour excess fat from pan. Add spaghetti sauce and simmer 10 minutes. Pour about 1 cup sauce into a greased 9-inch-by-13-inch baking dish. Top with half the cooked lasagne, ricotta and mozzarella; add about 1½ cups sauce. Make second layer with remaining lasagne, ricotta and mozzarella. Add rest of sauce and sprinkle with grated Parmesan cheese. Bake in a moderately hot oven (375°F) about 30 minutes, until bubbly and browned. Let stand a few minutes before serving. Makes 8 servings.

CHEESE LASAGNE

  1 package (1 pound) lasagne
  2 pounds ricotta or cottage cheese
  2 eggs
¾ cup grated Parmesan cheese
¼ cup chopped parsley
  Salt and pepper
  1 jar (32 ounces) spaghetti sauce

Cook and drain lasagne as package directs.

Meanwhile, combine ricotta cheese with eggs, ½ cup grated Parmesan cheese, parsley, and salt and pepper to taste. Pour 1 cup sauce into a greased 9-inch-by-13-inch baking pan. Top with half the cooked lasagne and half the cheese mixture; add about 1½ cups sauce. Cover with remaining lasagne and cheese mixture. Add remaining sauce, sprinkle with ¼ cup grated Parmesan cheese. Bake in a moderate oven (350°F) 30 minutes, until brown. Let stand a few minutes before serving. Makes 8 servings.

ELBOW MACARONI SUPPER SALAD

  1 package (8 ounces) elbow macaroni, cooked and drained
  1 cup cooked cut-up shrimp (or other seafood, poultry or meat)
½ cup diced celery
¼ cup sliced radishes
  2 tablespoons chopped dill pickle
  1 tablespoon chopped chives
½ cup mayonnaise
¼ cup sour cream
  2 tablespoons ketchup

Toss cooked elbow macaroni with remaining ingredients. Chill. Makes 3 to 4 servings.

Cereals

Cereals are another versatile item to keep on your pantry shelves because they can be used to extend leftover meat, poultry, fish and vegetables and to create dishes in their own right.

BAKED BARLEY WITH MUSHROOMS

  3 tablespoons butter or margarine
  1 medium onion, chopped
1½ cups barley
½ pound mushrooms, sliced
  3 cups hot chicken bouillon

Melt butter in 2-quart casserole. Add onion and cook, stirring, until golden. Add barley and stir until lightly browned. Add mushrooms, cook 3 minutes, stirring constantly. Add bouillon, stir well, cover and bake in a moderate oven (350°F) 1¼ hours, until barley is tender, but not mushy. Check during baking, and if barley seems dry, add a little boiling water. Makes 6 servings.

BUCKWHEAT GROATS

1½ cups buckwheat groats
  1 egg
  3 cups boiling-hot chicken bouillon

2 tablespoons butter or chicken fat
Salt and pepper

Mix buckwheat groats and raw egg in a saucepan. Stir over low heat until grains are separate. Add bouillon, cover pan, reduce heat and simmer 20 minutes until groats are tender and bouillon is absorbed. Add butter and seasonings. Makes 6 servings.

GROATS AND NOODLES

Prepare groats as above. Cook 2 cups broad noodles in boiling salted water until tender. Drain and stir into groats. Add butter and seasonings.

GROATS AND CORN

Prepare groats as above. Heat 1 can (8 ounces) kernel corn. Drain and stir corn into groats. Add butter and seasonings.

WHEAT PILAF

3 tablespoons butter or margarine
3 green onions or 1 medium onion, sliced
1 cup cracked wheat (bulgur)
2 cups beef bouillon

Heat butter in a saucepan; cook onion until golden. Add cracked wheat and stir until golden. Add bouillon, bring to boil and cover. Reduce heat to very low and simmer about 20 minutes, until liquid is absorbed and wheat is tender. Makes 4 to 6 servings.

GNOCCHI

3 cups milk
½ cup butter or margarine
1 teaspoon salt
¾ cup farina
¾ cup grated Parmesan cheese
2 eggs, beaten

Heat milk, ¼ cup butter, and salt just to boiling. Gradually stir in farina and cook, stirring, until thick. Beat in ½ cup of the cheese. Add eggs. Turn into a 9-inch square pan, chill until firm. Cut into small squares. Arrange overlapping squares in a greased shallow baking dish or casserole. Dot with remaining butter and sprinkle with remaining cheese. Bake in a hot oven (425°F) until golden brown, about 25 minutes. Makes about 6 servings.

CORN-MEAL MUSH

2½ cups water
½ teaspoon salt
1 cup yellow corn meal

Butter or margarine
Spaghetti sauce (optional)

Bring 2 cups water to boil with salt. Mix corn meal with ½ cup cold water, stirring until smooth. Stir this mixture into the boiling water; reduce heat to low and cook, stirring often, until corn meal is thick, about 30 minutes. Top each portion with a pat of butter, or with spaghetti sauce. Makes 4 to 6 servings.

SPOON BREAD

½ cup white corn meal
1 teaspoon salt
1½ cups milk
1 teaspoon sugar
1 tablespoon butter or margarine
2 eggs, well beaten
1 teaspoon double-acting baking powder

Mix corn meal and salt in a saucepan. Add milk and sugar and cook, stirring, until mixture is thick and smooth, about 5 minutes. Add butter, cool. Beat in eggs and baking powder. Pour batter into a buttered 1-quart casserole. Bake in a moderately hot oven (375°F) until set and browned, about 25 minutes. Spoon from casserole, top each serving with pat of butter. Makes 4 to 6 servings.

TAMALE CASSEROLE

2 tablespoons oil
1 onion, finely chopped
1 can (15 ounces) tamales in chili gravy
1 can (8 ounces) cream-style corn
½ cup sliced green pepper
½ cup ripe olives, sliced
½ cup beef bouillon
2 teaspoons chili powder
1½ teaspoons salt
Pinch cayenne
1 cup grated Cheddar cheese

Heat oil in a 1-quart casserole; cook onion until golden. Remove wrapping from tamales and put them in the casserole. Add remaining ingredients. Bake in a moderately slow oven (325°F) 30 minutes. Makes 4 servings.

RICE AND PEAS ITALIAN STYLE (RISI E BISI)

3 tablespoons butter or margarine
1 small onion, chopped
¼ pound sliced boiled ham
1 cup rice
3 cups beef bouillon
Salt and pepper

1 package (10 ounces) frozen peas
3 tablespoons Parmesan cheese

Heat butter in a saucepan, cook onion until golden. Sliver ham, add with rice, stir until rice is lightly golden. Add bouillon and seasonings. Bring to a boil, cover, simmer 10 minutes. Add peas, stir gently to separate. Cover, cook about 10 minutes, until rice and peas are tender. Adjust seasonings to taste. Top each serving with Parmesan cheese and extra butter if desired. Makes 3 to 4 servings.

SPANISH RICE

¼ cup oil
1 medium onion, chopped
¼ cup chopped celery
1 clove garlic, minced
1 can (1 pound 13 ounces) tomatoes, with liquid
1 teaspoon salt
¼ teaspoon basil
⅛ teaspoon pepper
1 cup rice

Heat oil, cook onion, celery and garlic until softened. Add tomatoes and seasonings. Bring to a boil, stirring occasionally to break up tomatoes. Simmer 5 minutes, stir in rice, cover, simmer about 20 minutes, until rice is tender and liquid is absorbed. Makes 4 to 6 servings.

RICE PILAF

¼ cup butter or margarine
2 cups rice
4 cups water
4 chicken bouillon cubes
½ cup raisins
¼ cup chopped toasted almonds

Heat butter, add rice and stir until golden. Add water and bouillon cubes, stir, bring to boil. Add raisins, cover pan, reduce heat, simmer about 20 minutes, until rice is tender and liquid is absorbed. Stir in almonds. Makes 6 to 8 servings.

CURRIED RICE

Prepare rice as in above recipe, but stir 1½ to 2 teaspoons curry powder into the butter.

VEGETABLE VERSATILITY

Colorful vegetables are a key to healthful meals. Deep-yellow and dark-green vegetables are rich sources of vitamin A, and all vegetables contain valuable amounts of other important vitamins and minerals. Serve raw vegetables often, in salads and as nibbles. Cook vegetables in minimum amounts of liquid, as briefly as possible, to preserve nutrients. Use leftover juices and vegetables, cooked or raw, in soups and casseroles for a bonus of good flavor and good nutrition.

Availability of Vegetables

Fresh Vegetables: You can buy a wide array of fresh vegetables every month of the year, particularly in large cities. Make it a point to enjoy the vegetables of each season, lower in cost because they come from local farms. The trip is short, supplies are abundant, and the crisp, fresh flavor is unbeatable.

New potatoes, slender green asparagus sprouts, crisp young beans, baby eggplants, local corn and other first vegetables of the season offer special quality and seasonal pleasure worth enjoying. French cooks call these *primeurs,* and you can gather a fine harvest through the year by watching the A&P vegetable counters for "firsts" of seasonal vegetable supplies.

Wash all vegetables carefully before serving or cooking. Pare as close to the skin as possible. A floating-knife vegetable peeler and a small sharp knife are worthwhile investments.

Quick-Frozen Vegetables: These capture and extend the season for you. They are ready to cook, or to heat in prepared sauces. Sometimes combinations of vegetables and seasonings are right in the package. Frozen vegetables cook in less time than fresh because the freezing process includes quick blanching. Put the frozen vegetables into a pan with about ¼ cup boiling water. Separate with a fork for quicker cooking. To avoid loss of nutrients, cover the pan tightly and cook quickly until vegetables are just tender-crisp.

Canned Vegetables: These offer convenience and economy, and retain more nutrients than fresh vegetables improperly cooked or held for too long. In preparing canned vegetables, cook down the liquid from the can rapidly, then add vegetables to heat briefly in the concentrated liquid.

Basic Vegetable Cooking Methods

Boiling: Cook vegetables as quickly as possible in a small amount of rapidly boiling water in a covered pan. Have the water boiling before vegetables are added, and bring it back to a boil as quickly as possible. Cook vegetables just until tender. To shorten the cooking time of large vegetables, cut them into smaller, uniform pieces before cooking. Shred cabbage or cut into wedges, separate cauliflower into flowerets, cube turnips.

Vegetables with high moisture content, such as spinach, are best cooked with just the moisture that clings to the leaves after washing.

Braising: For quickly braised, bright-colored vegetables, cook in a skillet with a small amount of oil and a few tablespoons of water. Cook covered, stirring occasionally, just until vegetables are cooked but still crisp. A few lettuce leaves added to the pan provide extra flavor and moisture, particularly for green peas and beans. Or braise fresh spinach for 2 or 3 minutes in clarified butter in a heavy skillet.

Baking and Oven-Steaming: Vegetables baked in their skins retain more nutrients than those cooked by any other method. This applies to squash and eggplant as well as to potatoes and yams.

Most vegetables may be oven-steamed. Prepare them as for boiling, place in a baking dish with a small amount of water or other liquid, sprinkle with salt and pepper, dot with butter, cover tightly and bake until tender. This takes longer than cooking over direct heat. It is practical when the rest of the meal is being roasted or the oven is in use to bake a cake or dessert.

Steaming: Prepare vegetables as for boiling and place in a perforated pan or rack over boiling water; cover and steam until tender. Steaming takes longer than boiling or braising, but there is no cooking water in which the nutrients may dissolve. Vegetables such as cabbage and onions have a stronger flavor when steamed. Green vegetables, except peas and spinach, tend to lose color.

Pressure Cooking: Pressure cookers make it possible to cook vegetables in minimum water in a fraction of the time needed for regular boiling. Follow the manufacturer's directions for the pot you own. Pressure cooking is especially convenient for large quantities of long-cooking vegetables.

Microwave Cooking: You can cook many vegetables right on the serving plate in a microwave oven in minimum time. Microwave works particularly well for small portions and for frozen vegetables. Follow directions for the equipment you own. Vegetables cooked in

VEGETABLE BUYING GUIDE

Description of Food as Purchased	Size of Market Unit	Size of Serving or Measure of Food as Used	Servings or Measures per Market Unit
Fresh:			
Vegetables served raw			
Lettuce (head or leaf), cabbage	Head	1 cup shredded or pieces	5 to 6
Carrots, celery, onions	Pound	1 cup chopped	2½
Tomatoes	Pound	½ cup sliced	5½
Vegetables served cooked			
Asparagus, beets, broccoli, cauliflower, onions, summer squash	Pound	½ cup cooked cut up	3 to 3½
Brussels sprouts, cabbage, carrots, green beans, potatoes	Pound	½ cup cooked whole or cut up	4½ to 5
Potatoes for mashing	Pound	½ cup cooked mashed	3½
Collards, kale, spinach	Pound	½ cup cooked pieces	4 to 5
Canned:			
Bean sprouts, beets, carrots, whole kernel corn, beans (green, kidney, lima), okra, peas, potatoes	15 to 16 ounces	½ cup heated, drained	3½
Asparagus, greens	14 to 15 ounces	½ cup heated, drained	2¾
Tomatoes	28 ounces	½ cup heated	6¾
Frozen:			
Asparagus, kale, okra, spinach	10 ounces	½ cup cooked, drained	2½
Broccoli, Brussels sprouts, carrots, cauliflower, whole-kernel corn, beans (green, lima), peas, summer squash	9 to 10 ounces	½ cup cooked, drained	2¾ to 3¼
French-fried potatoes	9 to 10 ounces	½ cup cooked	2¾ to 3¼

Source: U.S. Department of Agriculture, *The 1974 Yearbook of Agriculture.*

a microwave oven, covered, lose less of their natural moisture than in other methods of cooking.

Tips on Cooking Vegetables

To preserve nutrients, texture and color, cook vegetables as briefly as possible.

Root Vegetables: Potatoes, carrots, yams, turnips and other root vegetables carry nutrients and flavor right under the skin. Where possible, simply wash and boil in the skin, then plunge into cold water and strip thin outer skin. Season after cooking.

Red Vegetables: Red cabbage tends to turn blue unless the cooking water contains some acid. Add lemon juice, vinegar or a tart apple to the pot. Cook whole beets, without adding acid, in their skins, with an inch or two of stalk left on, to reduce color loss. If beets are cut before cooking, use the smallest possible amount of cooking water.

White Vegetables: Cook rapidly in covered pan to retain whiteness. If cooking water is very hard, white vegetables may turn slightly yellow. To prevent this, add a little lemon juice or vinegar to the water. Overcooking white vegetables causes them to become grayish.

Leafy Greens: While modern precepts say to cook leafy greens just until tender, in the smallest possible amount of water, old-time tradition, particularly in the South, calls for long cooking in large quantities of water. If you choose this method, follow custom and serve the flavorful "pot likker," which contains many soluble nutrients, to sip along with the meal.

Vegetable Platters

Three or more vegetables may be combined to make an attractive plate or individual vegetable dinner. Vary vegetables in size, shape, color, flavor and texture, and add cheese sauce, nuts, yogurt or an egg to round out the meal.

Vegetable Recipes

In the following pages you will find recipes for all the vegetables that are likely to grace your dining table. At the end of the chapter there is a group of mixed-vegetable recipes.

ARTICHOKES

Choose compact globes, with fresh, dark-green color, tight leaves. Wash artichokes thoroughly. Cut off the stems, discard tough bottom leaves. Snip hard tips from leaves. Place artichokes upright in a deep saucepan. Add juice of 1 lemon, a garlic clove and 2 to 4 tablespoons oil to pan. Add about 1 inch of boiling salted water. Cover and boil 20 to 30 minutes, or until artichokes are tender. Test by piercing at the base.

To eat, pull off leaves one at a time with fingers, dip into melted butter, Hollandaise Sauce (page 173), or other dip, and scrape pulp off base of leaf with your teeth. When you reach the prickly "choke," or fuzzy center, remove it with a knife and fork and discard. Under this is the heart—often considered the choicest part. Cut it into bite-size pieces.

STEAMED ASPARAGUS

Select straight, crisp, green stalks with close-clinging scales. Snap the tough ends from bottom of stalks (they will break at the tender point). Wash thoroughly, trimming large scales if stalks are sandy. Stand asparagus bunch in a straight-sided deep pot or in the bottom half of a double boiler or in a coffeepot. Add 1 cup boiling salted water. Cover pot, or invert other half of double boiler to cover, and steam until tender, about 12 minutes. Each pound of fresh asparagus makes about 4 servings. Serve with butter or margarine, lemon juice, or Hollandaise Sauce (page 173).

Tip: Use tough stalk ends of asparagus in soups.

GREEN BEANS

Select crisp pods with bright color. Very fresh green beans will snap when you bend them. (Compare price of fresh beans, even in season, with that of frozen beans.) Snap or cut the ends from the beans. Leave whole or cut into uniform lengths or diagonal strips, French style. Cook in 1 inch boiling salted water until just tender, 15 minutes or less. Season with salt or garlic salt and pepper, toss with butter or margarine.

Wax beans may be substituted in any green-bean recipe.

GREEN BEANS AMANDINE

Brown ¼ cup blanched, slivered almonds in

¼ cup butter or margarine. Sprinkle over 2 pounds cooked green beans. Makes 8 servings.

GREEN BEANS WITH MUSTARD SAUCE

Combine ¼ cup melted butter or margarine with 1 tablespoon mustard and heat through. Use to season hot green beans.

GREEN BEANS AND MUSHROOMS

1 pound fresh green beans
½ pound fresh mushrooms
2 tablespoons butter or margarine
1 teaspoon salt
¼ cup water
3 large lettuce leaves

Trim ends from beans. Cut beans into slivers lengthwise, using knife or a small bean cutter. Wipe mushrooms, trim stems. Melt butter in skillet over moderate heat. Place mushrooms in layer at bottom. Add green beans, salt and water. Cover with lettuce leaves. Cover pan and cook 8 minutes. Discard lettuce. Makes 4 servings.

MARINATED GREEN BEANS

2 cans (1 pound each) green beans; or
    2 packages (9 ounces each) frozen; or
    1¼ pounds fresh, cooked
¾ cup salad oil
6 tablespoons vinegar
2 tablespoons chopped fresh parsley
1 tablespoon finely chopped onion
1 tablespoon chopped olives
2 teaspoons salt
¼ teaspoon pepper

Drain beans. Combine remaining ingredients and mix well. Add beans and toss lightly. Chill several hours. Serve on lettuce, spooning some of the sauce over each serving. Makes 6 to 8 servings.

FRIED GREEN BEANS

Drain cooked or canned green beans, dry well with paper towels. Roll beans in flour highly seasoned with salt and pepper. Fry a few at a time in bacon fat or oil in a heavy skillet until they are well browned. Drain on paper towels.

GREEN BEANS AND BACON

¼ pound salt pork or slab bacon
1 pound fresh green beans, trimmed
1 cup water
1 small onion, chopped

Brown pork in heavy saucepan. Add green beans, water and onion. Simmer at least 40 minutes, or 2 to 3 hours for old-fashioned Southern-style beans. Makes 4 servings.

SUCCOTASH

1 pound fresh lima beans in the shell
4 ears sweet corn
2 tablespoons butter or margarine
½ cup light cream
    Salt, pepper

Shell lima beans, cover with boiling salted water and cook, uncovered, until tender, 15 to 20 minutes. Drain. Cook corn in boiling water about 5 minutes. Scrape kernels from corncobs, mix with beans. Add butter, cream, salt and pepper to taste and simmer 5 minutes. Makes 4 to 6 servings. Canned or frozen vegetables may be substituted for fresh in this recipe.

BEETS

Scrub beets well and trim tops, leaving 1 to 2 inches of stem. Cover with salted water and cook 30 minutes to an hour, until beets are tender. Drain, hold under cold running water, peel. Cut off tops and roots. Slice if desired. Reheat with a little butter or margarine, and lemon juice or vinegar to retain vivid color. Canned beets may be substituted for freshly cooked beets in most recipes.

HARVARD BEETS

1½ pounds beets, cooked or canned
¼ cup sugar
    1 teaspoon cornstarch
¼ cup water drained from cooking beets
¼ cup vinegar
½ teaspoon salt
    2 tablespoons butter or margarine

Drain beets, reserving ¼ cup liquid; dice beets. Combine sugar and cornstarch, add beet liquid, vinegar and salt. Bring to a boil and cook, stirring, until thick and smooth. Add the beets and cook over low heat for 20 minutes. Add butter. Makes 6 servings.

PICKLED BEETS

1½ cups vinegar
½ cup water
1 cup sugar
1 stick cinnamon
6 whole cloves

6 peppercorns
4 cups cooked or canned beets

Mix vinegar, water, sugar and spices in a saucepan and heat until sugar dissolves. Add beets and simmer in syrup about 15 minutes. Cool and chill. Makes about 1 quart.

RED-FLANNEL HASH

6 beets, cooked
6 potatoes, cooked
2 cups chopped cooked beef or corned beef
  Salt, pepper
1 to 3 tablespoons light cream or milk
2 tablespoons bacon fat

Chop beets and potatoes; combine with chopped meat and salt and pepper to taste. Moisten mixture with cream as needed to hold it together. Heat fat in a heavy skillet. Spread hash mixture evenly in pan and cook over low heat, without stirring, until the bottom is well browned. Fold like an omelet. Makes 6 servings.

BEETS WITH ORANGE SAUCE

2 pounds beets, cooked or canned
¼ cup butter or margarine
⅓ cup orange juice
1 teaspoon grated orange rind
¼ teaspoon ground cloves

Slice beets. Heat the butter in a skillet, add beets. Combine orange juice, rind and cloves and add. Heat until just simmering. Makes 6 servings.

STEAMED BROCCOLI

Select dark-green broccoli with compact buds. Wash broccoli and trim ends. Slash thickest stalks lengthwise to speed cooking. Place flat in skillet, or tie the stalks together and stand the bunch upright in boiling salted water in a deep saucepan. Cover and steam until stalks are tender, about 10 to 15 minutes. Serve with salt, pepper, and butter or sour cream; or Hollandaise Sauce (page 173) or grated Parmesan cheese. One pound will serve 3 to 4.

BROCCOLI WITH LEMON BUTTER

1 pound fresh broccoli
  Salt
¼ cup butter or margarine
1 tablespoon lemon juice

Wash broccoli, cut flowerets into bite-size pieces. Peel stalks, cut into 1-inch slices. Put stalks and flowerets in a skillet, add ¼ inch boiling salted water, cook 3 minutes uncovered. Cover and cook until just tender, 5 to 10 minutes longer. Melt butter with lemon juice. Drain broccoli and place in serving dish, drizzle with lemon butter. Makes 3 to 4 servings.

BROCCOLI PUFF

2 eggs, separated
½ teaspoon lemon juice
½ teaspoon salt
  Dash pepper
2 tablespoons flour
1 cup sour cream
1 package (10 ounces) frozen chopped
    broccoli, cooked and drained
¼ cup wheat germ
¼ cup grated Cheddar cheese

Beat egg whites with lemon juice until stiff. Beat together egg yolks, salt, pepper, flour and sour cream. Stir in broccoli. Fold in egg whites. Turn into a buttered 6-cup casserole and sprinkle with combined wheat germ and cheese. Bake in a moderately hot oven (375°F) 30 to 35 minutes, or until set. Makes 6 servings.

STEAMED BRUSSELS SPROUTS

Look for firm, compact heads with fresh green color. Wash 1 pound Brussels sprouts, remove any wilted outer leaves, trim stem. Cut an "X" in bottom to speed cooking. Place sprouts in a steamer over a small amount of boiling water in a saucepan. Cover and cook about 10 minutes, or until just tender. Each pound makes 4 to 6 servings.

SKILLET BRUSSELS SPROUTS

Prepare Brussels sprouts for cooking as above. Heat 2 tablespoons butter or margarine in a skillet over medium heat, add sprouts. Cover and cook about 10 minutes, until tender. If desired, add 2 tablespoons lemon juice and heat through.

SKILLET SPROUTS WITH BACON

Brown 4 strips bacon in a skillet; drain, saving 2 tablespoons bacon fat in pan. Add 1 pound trimmed Brussels sprouts to hot bacon drippings. Cook over medium heat until tender. Garnish with crumbled bacon. Makes 4 to 6 servings.

CABBAGE

The most familiar cabbage, a compact, solid ball with smooth whitish leaves, is available all the year round, but other cabbages—crinkly-leafed savoy and long-leafed celery, or Chinese, cabbage—make a welcome change, as does red cabbage. All these can be eaten raw, in salads and slaws, or briefly cooked until just tender.

Look for solid heads, heavy for their size, with blemish-free leaves. The outer leaves of young cabbages are firmly attached to the base.

GREEN CABBAGE WITH CARAWAY AND APPLE

3 tablespoons oil
1 pound cabbage, shredded
2 tart red apples, sliced
   Salt
1 tablespoon caraway seeds

Heat oil in large skillet or Dutch oven. Add cabbage, cook 5 minutes over medium heat, stirring occasionally. Add apples, cook a few minutes longer. Reduce heat. Add salt and caraway seeds, cover, cook about 20 minutes. Makes 6 servings.

STUFFED CABBAGE

   1 medium head cabbage with
      unbroken leaves
   1 pound ground beef
1½ cups cooked rice
   2 tablespoons grated onion
   1 teaspoon salt
¼ teaspoon pepper
   2 tablespoons oil
   1 medium onion, sliced
   1 can (16 ounces) tomatoes
½ cup water
   2 tablespoons lemon juice
   2 tablespoons brown sugar
¼ cup crushed gingersnaps
   1 bay leaf

Plunge cabbage into large pot of boiling salted water, cook about 10 minutes. Drain, cut out center core and carefully separate leaves, cutting away hard portion at bottom of leaf. Combine beef, rice, grated onion, salt and pepper. Put about ¼ cup mixture on each cabbage leaf and roll up, tucking in ends. Shred any remaining cabbage. Heat oil in large heavy saucepan or Dutch oven. Cook sliced onion and shredded cabbage until ten-der. Gently place cabbage rolls in pan. Add remaining ingredients, cover pan and simmer about 2 hours, adding a little water if necessary. Makes 16 appetizer cabbage rolls or 8 main-dish servings.

SWEET-AND-SOUR CABBAGE

   1 onion, chopped
   3 tablespoons butter or margarine
   6 cups shredded red or green cabbage
   1 cup finely shredded carrot
½ cup seedless raisins
   1 large tart apple, diced
   3 tablespoons cider vinegar
   1 cup water
   3 tablespoons brown sugar
      Salt, pepper to taste

Cook onion in butter in a skillet or Dutch oven until wilted. Add cabbage, cover and cook 5 minutes longer. Add remaining ingredients, cover and simmer 10 minutes. Makes 6 to 8 servings.

CABBAGE WITH CHEESE AND BACON

   1 medium head cabbage
¼ pound bacon or salt pork
¼ cup flour
   2 cups milk
¼ pound sharp Cheddar or American cheese,
      grated (1 cup)
      Salt and pepper to taste

Cut cabbage into wedges, cook in small amount of boiling salted water 10 minutes or until tender. Meanwhile, fry bacon or salt pork until crisp, remove from pan. Drain off all but ¼ cup fat from pan, stir in flour. Gradually add milk and cook over low heat, stirring constantly, until sauce is smooth and thick. Add cheese and heat until melted. Season with salt and pepper. Drain cabbage and place on serving platter; cover with cheese sauce and sprinkle with crumbled bacon. Makes 4 servings.

RED CABBAGE AND PINEAPPLE

   6 cups shredded red cabbage
   1 tablespoon lemon juice
½ cup boiling water
   2 tablespoons vinegar
   2 tablespoons brown sugar
   1 tablespoon cornstarch
½ teaspoon salt
   1 can (9 ounces) pineapple tidbits
   1 tablespoon butter or margarine
½ cup coarsely chopped walnuts

Vegetable casseroles in edible shells—a delicious main course. The green peppers are stuffed with canned corned-beef hash. The fillings for other vegetables include their own scooped-out centers, plus sausage and stuffing mix for the eggplant, bread crumbs, cheese and butter for the tomatoes, rice and onions for the yellow summer squash.

Put cabbage, lemon juice and boiling water in a skillet. Cover and cook 10 minutes, stirring occasionally. Combine vinegar, brown sugar, cornstarch and salt. Drain juice from pineapple and blend into cornstarch mixture, add to cabbage with pineapple bits. Add butter. Cook, stirring, until mixture thickens and bubbles. Garnish with walnuts. Makes 6 servings.

CHINESE-CABBAGE DISH

2 tablespoons oil
1 pound pork, slivered
1 teaspoon salt
½ teaspoon pepper
1 clove garlic, minced
1 onion, finely chopped
1 cup chicken bouillon
1 head Chinese cabbage, shredded
1 pound tomatoes, quartered
2 tablespoons cornstarch
1 tablespoon soy sauce
¼ cup water

Heat oil in large skillet or wok. Add pork, seasonings, garlic and onion, cook until pork is completely cooked and no longer pink. Add bouillon, cabbage and tomatoes. Cover, cook 10 to 15 minutes, until cabbage is tender. Blend cornstarch, soy sauce and water, add to pan. Stir over low heat until sauce is thick. Makes 4 servings.

CARROTS

Choose long, firm, uniform carrots with bright color.

Carrot Sticks: Scrub carrots with a brush, scrape if desired. Cut into sticks and serve well chilled.

Carrot Curls: Cut thin lengthwise strips with a vegetable peeler, roll up and secure with a pick. Place in ice water and chill several hours. Remove picks and curls will hold shape.

Boiled Carrots: Scrub carrots, peel or scrape if desired, and cut into strips, slice or dice. Small carrots may be left whole. Cook in a small amount of rapidly boiling salted water, covered, 10 to 25 minutes, until tender. Drain. Drop into cold water and rub off skin if necessary. Season to taste with butter or margarine and minced parsley or mint. Each pound of carrots makes 3 to 4 servings.

Or steam young carrots over boiling water, 25 to 30 minutes.

Fried Carrots: Boil whole baby carrots or carrot slices or strips until almost tender. Rub off skins under cold water. Dry. Fry in hot (375°F) deep fat until browned. Drain on paper. Tuck a small sprig of parsley in top of each fried carrot.

MINTED CARROTS WITH PEAS

1 pound carrots
½ teaspoon sugar
1 teaspoon salt
3 cups fresh green peas
¼ cup butter or margarine
1 tablespoon chopped fresh mint leaves

Peel and slice carrots. Cook carrot slices in boiling water with sugar and salt about 15 minutes. Add peas and cook 10 minutes longer, or until carrots and peas are tender. Melt butter and stir in mint leaves. Drain vegetables and toss with minted butter. Makes 8 servings.

Tip: Use 2 packages (9 ounces each) frozen peas instead of fresh.

PICKLED CARROTS

1½ pounds carrots
1 cup vinegar
¾ cup sugar
¾ cup water
8 whole cloves
2 sticks cinnamon, in small pieces
2 teaspoons salt

Peel carrots and cut into slices or sticks. Cook in boiling salted water until barely tender, 5 to 10 minutes, no longer. Drain. Combine remaining ingredients, bring to a boil, simmer 3 minutes. Pack carrots in a sterilized 1-quart jar or 2 pint jars. Add hot syrup and cover. Cool, refrigerate for several days. These pickles keep up to 2 weeks. Makes 6 to 8 servings.

CAULIFLOWER WITH CHEESE

1 medium head of cauliflower
3 tablespoons butter or margarine
3 tablespoons flour
¼ teaspoon salt
1½ cups milk
4 ounces Cheddar cheese, grated (1 cup)
¼ cup fine dry bread crumbs

Select a white, tightly packed head. Wash cauliflower, remove outside leaves, and cook in boiling salted water about 15 minutes, until tender-crisp. Drain. Melt butter in small saucepan. Stir in flour and salt, blend. Add milk and cook, stirring constantly, until mixture thickens. Add half the grated cheese and stir until cheese melts. Arrange the cauliflower in a baking dish and cover with cheese sauce. Sprinkle with mixture of remaining cheese and bread crumbs. Bake in a moderate oven (350°F) until topping browns. Makes 4 to 6 servings.

PICKLED CAULIFLOWER

1 head cauliflower, broken into flowerets
1 teaspoon salt
1 cup wine vinegar
1 cup water
½ cup brown sugar
¼ teaspoon ground mace
1 tablespoon mustard seed
½ teaspoon dried tarragon
¼ teaspoon celery seed

Place cauliflower in a bowl; sprinkle with salt, cover and let stand 2 hours. Rinse and dry well. Bring remaining ingredients to a boil, simmer 2 minutes. Add cauliflower and bring just to a boil. Remove from heat at once, cool, chill for several hours. Serve cold. Will keep in the refrigerator up to 2 weeks. Makes 4 to 6 servings.

To Pickle Other Vegetables: Use recipe above for carrots, green beans, small white onions or cucumbers; or use any combination.

CELERY

If you've never tried cooked celery, discover how good it is braised, alone or with other vegetables.

CELERY WITH CORN

¼ cup butter or margarine
3 cups thinly sliced celery
1 package (10 ounces) frozen corn
1 can (16 ounces) tomatoes
Salt, pepper, dash nutmeg

Melt butter in saucepan or large skillet. Add celery, cover and cook 5 minutes. Add corn and tomatoes, season and cook 10 minutes, until corn is tender. Season to taste. Makes 6 servings.

CELERY AND CARROTS

10 stalks celery
1 pound carrots
¼ cup butter or margarine
1 teaspoon marjoram leaves
Salt and pepper

Clean celery and cut into 2-inch lengths; peel carrots and cut into chunks. Cook celery and carrots in boiling salted water about 20 minutes, until just tender. Drain. Melt butter with marjoram and pour over vegetables. Season with salt and pepper. Makes 6 servings.

CHESTNUTS

To prepare fresh chestnuts, make a cross on the flat side of each nut with a sharp knife. Place in a shallow pan, sprinkle with a small amount of oil, if desired, and roast in a moderate oven (350°F) until the inner brown skin is toasted and is easy to remove, about 20 minutes. Peel nuts when they are barely cool enough to handle. Or boil the slashed chestnuts 15 to 25 minutes, cool very slightly, peel. The chestnuts will be more tender than they are after roasting.

To serve chestnuts as a snack, roast as above and remove the skins, but continue to bake until the nuts are tender when pierced with a skewer. Or brown the skinned chestnuts lightly in melted butter or margarine.

CHESTNUT PURÉE

2 pounds chestnuts
2 cups beef or chicken stock
2 tablespoons butter or margarine
2 tablespoons cream
Salt, pepper

Peel chestnuts as described above. Boil in stock until very tender, about 30 minutes. Drain and put through a food mill or potato ricer. Blend in butter and cream, adding more cream or some cooking liquid to make desired consistency. Season with salt and pepper. Makes 6 servings.

CORN ON THE COB

Select well-filled ears. Some like corn very young and small; others enjoy larger, mature kernels. Husk and remove silks just before cooking. Drop into boiling salted water to cover, cook 5 to 10 minutes, or until just tender. If desired, add a small amount of sugar to the boiling water. Drain and serve at once with butter or margarine, salt and pepper.

BARBECUED GRILLED CORN

Pull back husks and remove silks. Replace husks and tie them in place with a strip from husk. Soak in salted water 5 minutes. Drain and roast on grill over hot coals 10 to 15 minutes, turning frequently. Peel back husks; cut off ends and use stalks for a handle. Corn may also be prepared in this manner in an oven—bake in a hot oven (400°F) 20 to 25 minutes.

BUTTERED CORN

Husk corn and remove silks. Slice kernels of corn from ears with a sharp knife. Place corn in a saucepan with a very small amount of boiling salted water. Simmer 3 to 5 minutes, drain and season with salt, pepper, and butter or margarine to taste. If desired, add a little paprika, garlic, chives, onions or horseradish.

CORN PUDDING

4 eggs
2 cups corn kernels, fresh, canned or frozen
3 tablespoons flour
1 tablespoon sugar
1 teaspoon salt
  Dash of pepper
1 cup milk or light cream
1 tablespoon melted butter or margarine

Beat eggs until thick, add corn. Combine flour, sugar, salt and pepper, slowly stir in milk or cream, blend in butter. Combine with corn mixture, blend well. Pour into greased 1½-quart casserole. Bake in a moderately slow oven (325°F) 1 hour and 20 minutes, until knife inserted near center comes out clean. Makes 4 servings.

MEXICAN CORN

  1 tablespoon butter or margarine
  1 onion, minced
¼ cup chopped green pepper
1 can (16 ounces) tomatoes
2 tablespoons chili powder
3 cups fresh corn kernels (about 6 ears)
  Salt and pepper

Heat butter in a skillet, add onion and cook until golden. Add green pepper, tomatoes and chili powder; cook 5 minutes, until green pepper is tender. Add corn kernels, cover and cook 10 minutes over low heat. Season with salt and pepper. Makes 6 servings.

CORN "OYSTERS"

  2 cups corn kernels, fresh, canned, or frozen
  2 eggs, separated
½ teaspoon double-acting baking powder
½ teaspoon salt
¼ teaspoon nutmeg

½ cup flour
⅓ cup butter or margarine

Combine corn with egg yolks. Toss baking powder, salt and nutmeg with flour. Blend into egg-corn mixture. Beat egg whites until stiff, fold in. Heat butter in a heavy skillet. Drop mixture from a tablespoon into skillet to form small "oysters." Turn to brown both sides. Makes 4 servings.

FRIED EGGPLANT

Eggplant should be firm and heavy for its size, with a smooth, shiny skin. Wash an eggplant and cut into ½-inch slices. Do not peel. Dredge with seasoned flour, dip in beaten egg, and coat with seasoned fine dry bread crumbs. Fry in a small amount of oil in a skillet. Serve as is, or with your favorite tomato sauce. Each eggplant makes 4 to 6 servings, depending on its size.

BAKED EGGPLANT

  1 eggplant
  1 tablespoon lemon juice
½ cup oil
  1 teaspoon salt
  1 clove garlic, crushed

Peel eggplant and cut into ½-inch slices. Arrange slices in a single layer in an oiled shallow baking pan. Sprinkle with lemon juice. Heat oil with salt and garlic for 2 or 3 minutes, pour over eggplant slices. Bake in a moderate oven (350°F) 30 to 40 minutes. Makes 4 to 6 servings.

EGGPLANT PARMIGIANA

  2 eggplants, about 1 pound each
  Salt
  Seasoned flour
  Oil for frying
  2 cans (8 ounces each) tomato sauce
½ teaspoon thyme
½ teaspoon garlic powder
½ pound mozzarella cheese, sliced
½ cup grated Parmesan cheese

Peel eggplants and cut into ½-inch slices. Spread slices in a single layer, sprinkle with salt, let stand 20 to 30 minutes to remove excess moisture. Pat dry. Dip slices in seasoned flour and brown quickly in hot oil in skillet. Drain. Combine tomato sauce with thyme and garlic powder. Arrange layers of eggplant, tomato sauce, mozzarella and Parmesan in a 2-quart casserole, ending with Parmesan. Bake in a moderate oven (350°F)

30 minutes, until topping browns. Makes 6 to 8 servings.

RATATOUILLE

1 eggplant
⅓ cup flour
2 tablespoons oil
2 tablespoons Worcestershire sauce
3 onions, sliced thin
3 cloves garlic, minced
3 green peppers, seeded and quartered
2 zucchini squash, cut in chunks
4 medium tomatoes, cut in chunks
  Salt, pepper

Slice eggplant ¼ inch thick. Do not peel. Dredge slices with flour. Heat oil and Worcestershire in a large pot, cook onion and garlic until onion is soft. Brown eggplant lightly. Add remaining vegetables and seasonings, toss gently. Cover and cook 20 minutes, or until vegetables are tender. Makes 10 or more servings.

STUFFED EGGPLANT

1 eggplant
1 pound bulk sausage
1 tablespoon minced onion
2 cups seasoned bread stuffing mix
1 can (8 ounces) tomato sauce

Cut eggplant in half and scoop out the pulp, leaving a shell about ¼ inch thick. Chop the eggplant pulp. In a skillet brown sausage with onion and chopped eggplant pulp, stirring with a fork. Add stuffing mix and stir to blend. Fill eggplant shells with the mixture and cover with tomato sauce. Bake in a moderate oven (350°F) 15 minutes, until bubbling hot. Makes 4 servings. (See photo, page 143.)

GREENS

Leafy green vegetables need thorough cleaning. Wash in several changes of water, lifting the leaves from the water to let soil sink to the bottom. Discard tough stems and bruised leaves. Although in the South greens are traditionally simmered for hours with pork or bacon, they retain more nutrients and better color if cooked until just tender.

To Steam: Place in a steamer over boiling water and cook about 30 minutes.

To Boil: Use a small amount of boiling salted water, cook 5 to 25 minutes, depending on variety and maturity. For especially strong-flavored greens, change the cooking water after 5 minutes of cooking, cook until tender in fresh boiling salted water. After cooking, greens may be chopped and seasoned with butter or margarine, vinegar or a cream sauce.

GREENS AND SALT PORK

3 pounds mustard greens, turnip greens or
   collard greens
1 onion
½ pound salt pork
  Salt and black pepper to taste

Clean greens as above and put in a large pot. Add 1 to 2 cups of water, the lesser amount if greens are young and tender. Add remaining ingredients and bring to a boil. Cook just until greens are tender, or cook them 1 hour or longer. Discard pork and onion. Drain greens, serve with corn bread. Makes 6 to 8 servings.

SPINACH

To prepare spinach, remove stems, wash leaves thoroughly in several changes of water. Spinach will cook in the water that adheres to the leaves. Cook over medium heat until wilted, about 4 minutes. Season with salt and pepper, and butter or vinegar, if desired. One pound of spinach makes about 4 servings.

Creamed Spinach: Whirl in blender, purée or chop cooked, drained spinach, mix with Cream Sauce (page 174) and a dash of nutmeg.

Spinach with Sour Cream or Yogurt: Add ½ cup sour cream or yogurt to cooked, drained spinach, season to taste, heat to serving temperature. Do not boil.

CREAMED KOHLRABI

2 pounds kohlrabi
3 tablespoons butter or margarine
3 tablespoons flour
1 cup milk
  Salt, pepper
½ teaspoon chervil

Remove tops from kohlrabi, set aside for another use. Peel bulbs, cut into cubes or slices. Cook in ½ cup boiling salted water about 20 minutes, until tender. Drain, reserving liquid. Melt butter, stir in flour. Add milk and reserved kohlrabi liquid. Cook, stirring, until smooth and thickened. Season with salt, pepper and chervil. Add cooked kohlrabi and heat. Makes 6 servings.

LEEKS

Trim roots and green tops from leeks, wash thoroughly in several changes of water to remove grit from between layers. To steam, place leeks in a steamer over boiling water and cook 15 to 25 minutes, or until tender. To braise, melt a small amount of butter or margarine in a heavy skillet, add leeks with the water clinging to the leaves, cover and simmer 10 to 15 minutes, or until tender. An average bunch of leeks makes 2 servings.

MUSHROOMS

Fresh and canned mushrooms can be used interchangeably, allowing for the firmer, crisper texture of the fresh vegetable. A pound of fresh mushrooms (20 to 24) is the equivalent of a 6- or 8-ounce can of mushroom caps. Use the mushroom liquid whenever possible and take advantage of the savings offered by using canned sliced mushrooms, or stems and pieces, rather than the whole caps.

Look for light-colored, unbruised raw mushrooms. Wipe caps and stems with a damp cloth—do not wash or soak in water. Trim dry base from stems and slice mushrooms down through cap. Or remove stems for another use when the recipe calls for only the caps.

MUSHROOMS BRAISED IN BUTTER

¾ pound fresh mushrooms
4 tablespoons butter or margarine
1 teaspoon salt
  Freshly ground black pepper
1 tablespoon lemon juice or white wine
  Light or dark Swedish crisp bread slices
  Chopped fresh dill for garnish

Slice mushrooms thinly. Melt butter in skillet, add mushroom slices and cook over medium heat until golden and tender, but still firm. Sprinkle with salt, pepper and lemon juice or wine. Spoon onto crisp bread slices and sprinkle with fresh dill. Makes 4 servings.

MUSHROOMS BRAISED IN CREAM

1 pound mushrooms
¼ cup butter or margarine
2 tablespoons grated onion
⅓ cup light cream
½ teaspoon celery salt
  Salt, pepper

Slice mushrooms thinly. Melt butter in skillet, add onion and cook over low heat until transparent. Add mushrooms and cook 10 minutes longer. Stir in cream and celery salt, heat through. Season with salt and pepper and serve on toast. Makes 6 servings.

OKRA WITH TOMATOES AND RICE

4 slices bacon
½ cup chopped onion
2 cups sliced okra or 1 package (10 ounces) frozen okra
1 cup rice
2 cans (1 pound each) tomatoes
½ cup water
1 teaspoon salt
  Dash ground cloves

Fry bacon in large Dutch oven until crisp, remove. In bacon fat, cook onion and okra until onion is soft. Stir in rice, tomatoes, water, salt and cloves. Simmer, covered, 20 to 25 minutes, or until rice is tender. Sprinkle with crumbled bacon. Makes 6 to 8 servings.

BOILED ONIONS

Cut ends from small to medium onions, peel. Leave whole or cut in half. Cover onions with boiling salted water and cook until tender. Small onions or halves will require 10 to 20 minutes' cooking time; larger ones, 20 to 30 minutes. Serve with butter, salt and pepper. Each pound makes about 3 servings.

STEAMED ONIONS

Place unpeeled whole onions in a rack or steamer over boiling water. Cover and cook 30 to 40 minutes, until the onions are tender. Peel and serve as above.

CREAMED ONIONS

2 pounds small white onions
2 tablespoons butter or margarine
2 tablespoons flour
¼ teaspoon salt
1½ cups milk
¼ teaspoon ground nutmeg

Cover whole onions with water, bring to a boil, and cook 5 minutes. Run cold water over onions and skin will slip off easily, without tears. Cook in boiling salted water, covered, about 20 minutes, until tender. Drain. Melt butter, blend in flour and salt. Add milk, cook and stir until sauce is thickened. Stir in nutmeg, add cooked onions, heat. Makes about 6 servings. (See photo, page 94.)

ONION-TOMATO CASSEROLE

5 onions
½ cup chopped celery
1 can (1 pound) tomatoes
1 teaspoon salt
 Pepper to taste
1 tablespoon butter or margarine

Peel and slice onions. In a greased 1-quart casserole, arrange onions and celery in layers. Cover with tomatoes, sprinkle with salt and pepper, and dot with butter. Cover casserole and bake in a moderate oven (350°F) about 1 hour, or until onions are tender. Makes 4 servings.

FRIED ONION RINGS

1 pound Bermuda onions
1 cup milk
½ cup flour
 Shortening or oil for deep-frying
 Salt

Peel onions, cut into ¼-inch slices and separate into rings. Soak in cold milk in refrigerator for ½ hour. Drain and dry. (Use the milk for cream soup.) Dredge onion rings with flour and fry a few at a time in hot deep fat or oil, about 370°F, 2 to 3 minutes. Drain, sprinkle with salt. Makes 4 to 6 servings.

SAUSAGE-STUFFED ONIONS

1 pound small white onions (14 to 16)
½ pound sausage
⅛ teaspoon salt
⅛ teaspoon pepper
¼ teaspoon sage
2 tablespoons sherry
⅔ cup crisp cracker crumbs
2 tablespoons butter or margarine

Cook onions, unpeeled, in boiling salted water for 10 minutes. Drain and peel. Hollow out onions, chop centers. Cook sausage over moderate heat, stirring with a fork until brown. Add chopped onion, cook until golden. Blend with seasonings, sherry and cracker crumbs. Fill onion hollows, dot with butter or margarine. Bake in a buttered shallow pan in a moderate oven (350°F) for 20 minutes. Makes 4 servings.

PARSNIPS

Parsnips, a sweet and flavorful white root, may be peeled before or after cooking. Cook them, whole or sliced, in boiling salted water 25 to 30 minutes, or until tender. Brown the cooked, peeled parsnips in butter. If the core of the vegetable is woody, it should be removed either before or after cooking. Each pound of parsnips makes 3 servings.

GLAZED PARSNIPS

2 pounds parsnips
3 tablespoons butter or margarine
2 tablespoons honey
¼ cup orange juice
1 teaspoon grated orange rind
¼ teaspoon ginger

Peel parsnips, cut into slices and cook in boiling salted water until tender, about 10 minutes. Drain well. Melt butter in small saucepan, add honey, orange juice, orange rind and ginger. Cook, stirring, until sauce is hot and well combined. Add parsnips, coat well with the glaze. Makes about 6 servings.

PEAS

Even in summer, when fresh peas are most plentiful, frozen peas may be a better buy. It pays to compare prices. If you use canned peas in these recipes, do not cook them; simply add at the last moment and heat briefly.

MINTED PEAS

2 packages (10 ounces each) frozen peas, or
 2 pounds fresh peas
1 teaspoon salt
½ teaspoon sugar
1 sprig fresh mint, or ½ teaspoon dried mint
¼ cup butter or margarine, melted
1 tablespoon lemon juice

Cook peas in boiling water with salt, sugar and mint, about 10 minutes, or until peas are tender. Drain. Combine butter and lemon juice, pour over drained peas. Makes 6 servings.

PEAS AND BACON

¼ pound sliced bacon
1 small onion, minced
2 packages (10 ounces each) frozen green peas
 peas
 Salt and pepper
 Dash each sugar, chervil, marjoram

Fry bacon until crisp, remove and drain. Pour off all but 2 tablespoons fat. Cook onion in bacon fat until golden. Add peas, salt and pepper, sugar, chervil and marjoram. Cover and cook over low heat about 10 minutes, until peas are tender. Garnish with crumbled bacon just before serving. Makes 6 to 8 servings.

FRENCH PEAS

1 small onion, minced
2 tablespoons butter or margarine
2 tablespoons water
1 package (10 ounces) frozen peas
   Salt, pepper
2 lettuce leaves, shredded

Cook onion in butter in skillet until translucent. Add remaining ingredients, cover pan, bring to boil. Reduce heat, cook about 5 to 8 minutes, until peas are just tender. Makes 3 servings.

PEPPERS

You will find two kinds of peppers in the produce department, sweet and hot. Both varieties range in color from yellow-green through deep green to red (depending on ripeness), but the hot peppers are generally smaller than the sweet variety. Sweet peppers are used as a vegetable, hot peppers as a seasoning, or in pickles and relishes. Look for smooth, unblemished peppers with glossy, firm skins, heavy for their size.

ROASTED PEPPERS

6 sweet green or red peppers
½ cup oil
2 tablespoons lemon juice
1 teaspoon salt
1 small clove garlic, sliced

Wash peppers and dry well. Place peppers on a baking pan 5 inches from the broiler heat. Broil, turning with tongs frequently, until skin of peppers is black and blistered, about 15 to 20 minutes. Place peppers in a saucepan or bowl and cover while still hot. Let stand 10 to 15 minutes, until steam loosens skins. Peel away the charred skins and cut peppers into strips, discarding seeds and membranes. Mix together oil, lemon juice, salt and garlic; combine with peppers. Place in a covered container and refrigerate for several hours. Use as an appetizer, as part of Antipasto (page 39), as a main-dish accompaniment or as a salad.

PEPPERS WITH TOMATOES

2 green peppers
3 tablespoons butter or margarine

1 onion, chopped
2 stalks celery, sliced
1 can (1 pound) tomatoes
½ teaspoon oregano or thyme
   Salt and pepper to taste

Wash peppers, cut off tops. Discard seeds and pith. Cut into strips. Heat butter in a skillet, add peppers, onion and celery, cook about 3 minutes. Add tomatoes and seasonings, cover, cook 10 minutes, or until vegetables are tender. Makes 4 servings.

STUFFED PEPPERS

4 green peppers
1 can (15 ounces) corned-beef hash

Cut tops from green peppers, remove seeds and membranes. Place shells in boiling water for 5 minutes. Drain well. Stand peppers in muffin tins or custard cups and fill with hash. Bake in a moderate oven (350°F) about 25 minutes. Makes 4 servings. (See photo, page 143.)

POTATOES

You can find a variety of potatoes in the supermarket year round. Select clean, smooth, firm potatoes, fairly regular in shape. A bag of varied sizes suitable for different uses may offer economy in price.

Different varieties of potatoes have different cooking qualities. Mealy older potatoes, or dry Idahos or russets, are better for baking, mashing and French-frying. Waxy new potatoes are better for boiling, for salads, for scalloping and creaming.

Potatoes keep well, so it pays to buy the large bags sometimes featured as specials if a cool, dry place is available for storage. One pound of potatoes makes 3 servings.

BOILED NEW POTATOES

2 pounds new potatoes
2 tablespoons butter or margarine
2 tablespoons chopped parsley

Wash new potatoes; peel a narrow strip around the equator of each potato. Cook in boiling salted water until tender, about 15 minutes. Drain and keep hot. Melt butter with parsley, pour over potatoes. Makes 6 servings.

DILLED POTATOES

Prepare new potatoes as above, using chopped fresh dill or 2 teaspoons dried dill to replace the parsley.

CREAMED POTATOES

Cook small new potatoes whole, or quartered, peeled medium potatoes in boiling salted water until tender. Cover with well-seasoned Cream Sauce (page 174).

FRENCH-FRIED POTATOES

Peel potatoes; cut in strips about ⅜ inch thick. Soak in cold water about 15 minutes. Drain, dry thoroughly. In skillet, heat 1 inch oil to 375°F. Place just enough potato strips in skillet to cover bottom. Cook until lightly browned, 6 to 8 minutes. Drain on paper towels. Salt to taste.

MASHED POTATOES

  2 pounds "old" potatoes
½ **cup milk**
  2 tablespoons butter or margarine
  Salt and pepper

Peel potatoes, cut into quarters. Cook in boiling salted water until tender, about 15 to 20 minutes. Drain potatoes and mash in pan. Push potatoes to one side of pan. Add milk and butter, heat in same pan with potatoes for a few minutes. Beat milk and butter into potatoes, adding more of each to taste. Season with salt and pepper. Makes 4 to 6 servings.

Variations: Cook 1 onion, sliced, with the potatoes and mash it with them. Or add ½ cup grated sharp cheese to the potatoes with the milk and butter.

Duchesse Potatoes: Add 1 egg yolk to hot mashed potatoes and form into small balls, or pipe through a pastry tube to make decorative shapes. Bake on a buttered baking pan in a very hot oven (450°F) until browned.

POTATO-SPINACH PUFF

2½ **cups cooked mashed potatoes**
  1 package (10 ounces) frozen chopped spinach, thawed and drained
  4 tablespoons melted butter or margarine
  1 teaspoon salt
  Dash each pepper, paprika
  4 eggs, separated

Combine mashed potatoes, spinach, butter and seasonings. Blend in 4 egg yolks; beat 4 egg whites until stiff, fold into vegetable

mixture. Pile lightly in a greased 1½-quart casserole. Bake in a moderately hot oven (375°F) 30 to 40 minutes until puffed and golden. Makes 6 servings.

Try substituting other vegetables for potatoes and spinach in above recipe.

Sweet Potato or Yam Puff: Use 3 cups cooked mashed sweet potatoes or yams and 1 cup flaked coconut.

Pumpkin Puff: Use 4 cups cooked mashed pumpkin; add 1 teaspoon fresh chopped dill or dill seed, or add 1 teaspoon nutmeg.

Squash Puff: Use 4 cups cooked mashed butternut or Hubbard squash, or 2 packages (10 ounces each) frozen squash, heated as directed on package.

Turnip or Rutabaga Puff: Use 4 cups cooked mashed turnips or rutabagas; add 1 teaspoon fresh chopped dill, or dill seed, or 1 teaspoon fennel or anise.

Carrot Puff: Use 4 cups cooked mashed carrots; add 2 tablespoons minced parsley.

Parsnip Puff: Use 4 cups cooked mashed parsnips; add 1 teaspoon cinnamon.

OVEN-BROWNED POTATOES

Peel and quarter potatoes; cook in boiling salted water about 10 minutes. Remove from water and dry thoroughly. Brush with oil or meat drippings, sprinkle with salt and paprika. Bake in a moderate oven (350°F) about an hour, until tender and brown.

BAKED POTATOES

Baking potatoes
Butter or margarine, or sour cream and chives
Salt, freshly ground pepper

Scrub potatoes, pierce several times with a skewer. Bake in a moderately hot oven (375°F) 1 hour, until tender. Cut an X in the flat side, press to push potato pulp up through the cut X. Serve with butter, or with sour cream and minced chives. Pass salt and the pepper grinder.

CHEESE-BAKED POTATOES

  4 baking potatoes
¼ **pound grated cheese (1 cup)**
¼ **cup butter or margarine**
  Salt
¼ **teaspoon freshly ground black pepper**

Bake potatoes as above, cut a thin slice from

the long side of each potato and reserve. Carefully scoop out the potato, leaving the shell intact. Mash potatoes, add cheese, butter, salt and pepper to taste, beat until fluffy. Pile into shells and cap with reserved slice. Bake 10 minutes, until piping-hot. Makes 4 servings.

SCALLOPED POTATOES

Peel and slice thinly 4 medium-large potatoes. Butter a 1½-quart baking dish well, fill with layers of potatoes sprinkled with salt and pepper and dotted with butter or margarine. Add milk almost to cover, dot with butter or margarine. Cover baking dish and bake in a moderately hot oven (375°F) 30 minutes. Remove cover, continue cooking until potatoes are tender. Makes 4 servings.

Herbed Scalloped Potatoes: Sprinkle each layer with seasonings, chopped parsley and snipped chives.

Curried Scalloped Potatoes: Fill dish with alternate layers of potatoes and onions. Mix 2 teaspoons curry powder with milk, pour it over the potatoes.

SWISS FRIED POTATOES (ROESTI)

Wash 1 pound potatoes, grate them with a medium grater, with or without the skins. Melt ¼ cup butter or margarine in a large skillet, add grated potatoes, cover. Cook over medium heat without stirring until bottom of cake is brown and potatoes are tender. Add salt and pepper to taste. Turn potato cake, brown other side. Makes 4 servings.

PUMPKIN

To prepare pumpkin for cooking, cut it in half and remove seeds and stringy pulp. Cut into pieces, peel. Cook in a small amount of boiling salted water until tender, about 25 minutes.

Puréed Pumpkin: Make a purée of the cooked pumpkin by forcing it through a food mill. Or whirl cooked pumpkin in a blender with about ½ cup of the cooking liquid until very smooth. Season with salt and pepper.

Mashed Pumpkin: Mash the cooked pumpkin. Beat in a little butter or margarine and enough milk to bring mixture to desired consistency. Sweeten with brown sugar, honey or maple syrup; add a dash of nutmeg.

SUMMER SQUASH

Summer squash are available in many shapes, sizes and colors: bright-yellow crookneck and straightneck; long, deep-green zucchini; mottled cocozelle and caserta; flat, scalloped patty pan, scallop and cymling; and the pear-shaped chayote.

BOILED SUMMER SQUASH

To prepare summer squash, wash thoroughly and remove stem and blossom ends. Slice or cut into chunks. Peeling is unnecessary. Squash may be cooked in a small amount of boiling salted water 8 to 10 minutes, or until tender. One pound of summer squash makes 2 to 3 servings.

Skillet Summer Squash: Cook squash slices in melted butter or margarine with a garlic clove. For a delicious accent, add sliced onion.

STUFFED SUMMER SQUASH

4 medium summer squash
2 tablespoons butter or margarine
1 onion, chopped
1 cup cooked rice
Salt and pepper

Wash squash well, cook whole in boiling salted water until just tender, about 10 minutes. Split squash in half lengthwise. Scoop out center with the tip of a spoon and chop. Turn shells upside down to drain. Heat butter in skillet, add onion and chopped squash, cook until tender. Stir in rice. Season with salt and pepper to taste. Arrange squash shells in a greased baking dish and fill with rice mixture. Bake in a moderate oven (350°F) 30 minutes. Makes 8 servings. (See photo, page 143.)

BAKED SUMMER SQUASH

2 pounds summer squash
2 tablespoons melted butter or margarine
Salt, pepper, rosemary
¼ cup water or chicken broth

Wash squash and cut into slices or strips. Arrange in a buttered casserole, sprinkle with melted butter. Season with salt, pepper and rosemary. Pour liquid around squash, cover, and bake in a moderate oven (350°F) about

30 minutes, or until squash is tender. Makes 6 servings.

SUMMER-SQUASH CASSEROLE

2 pounds summer squash
2 onions
½ cup sour cream
1 egg, beaten
¼ cup grated cheese
½ teaspoon salt

Wash and slice squash. Peel and slice onions. Cook onions and squash in boiling salted water about 15 minutes, or until just tender, drain. Combine sour cream, egg, cheese and salt. Add squash and onions. Pile into a greased baking dish and bake in a moderate oven (350°F) 30 minutes. Makes 6 servings.

ZUCCHINI-TOMATO SKILLET

1 tablespoon oil
1 clove garlic, minced
1 can (1 pound) tomatoes
2 pounds zucchini, sliced
1 onion, sliced
1 teaspoon oregano
¼ cup grated Parmesan cheese

Heat oil in skillet, add garlic and cook 3 minutes. Add tomatoes, zucchini, onion, oregano, salt and pepper, and cook over moderate heat until zucchini is tender. Turn into a serving dish and sprinkle with grated Parmesan cheese. Makes about 6 servings.

WINTER SQUASH

Winter squash is characterized by a hard, rough rind, and by dry flesh more like that of sweet potatoes than that of soft and juicy summer squash. Look for tough, thick skin and heavy weight in relation to size. The heavier the squash, the more edible flesh it provides. Store winter squash as you would potatoes, in a cool dry place. The green oval acorn and the cylindrical yellow to blue-gray Hubbard squash are available the year round. Others, like butternut, buttercup, and turban, peak during the winter months.

All winter squash may be baked, steamed or boiled, to use as a vegetable or as a dessert. Recipes for pumpkin and sweet potatoes may be adapted for use with winter squash.

BAKED WINTER SQUASH

Wash acorn, butternut or Hubbard squash, cut in half and remove seeds. Place squash upside down in a baking pan with ¼ inch water. Bake in a hot oven (400°F) 30 minutes. Turn squash over, brush lightly with melted butter or margarine. Sprinkle with salt and pepper and add a little brown sugar, honey or molasses, if desired. Return to the oven and bake 30 minutes longer or until tender.

STUFFED ACORN SQUASH

2 acorn squash
1 pound bulk sausage, lightly browned
   and drained
1 teaspoon salt
¼ teaspoon pepper
1 tablespoon minced onion
½ teaspoon poultry seasoning
1 cup bread crumbs
1 egg, well beaten
1 can (8 ounces) tomato sauce
1 teaspoon Worcestershire sauce

Wash squash, cut in half and remove seeds. Cut thin slice from base of shells so squash will stand level. Pour ¼ inch water into baking pan, place squash upside down in pan and bake in moderate oven (350°F) 30 minutes. Mix together cooked sausage, salt, pepper, onion, poultry seasoning, bread crumbs, beaten egg and ½ cup tomato sauce. Mound into hollow of each squash half. Bake in a moderate oven (350°F) 30 minutes. Combine Worcestershire sauce and remaining tomato sauce and use to baste squash occasionally while baking. Makes 4 servings.

SWEET POTATOES AND YAMS

Sweet potatoes and yams are used interchangeably in most recipes, although they are quite different botanically. For cooking purposes, sweet potatoes and yams are similar. The yam is slightly sweeter and moister, and darker in color, than the sweet potato.

BAKED SWEET POTATOES OR YAMS

To bake, scrub the sweet potatoes or yams, grease the skins lightly, and bake in a moderately hot oven (375°F) 45 to 55 minutes, or until tender.

MASHED SWEET POTATOES

2 pounds sweet potatoes
3 tablespoons butter or margarine
2 eggs
½ teaspoon grated orange rind to taste
Salt to taste
Nutmeg

Boil sweet potatoes in salted water until tender, drain, peel and mash. Beat in butter, eggs, orange rind and salt. Spoon potato mixture into a buttered casserole. Sprinkle with a little nutmeg. Bake in a moderate oven (350°F) about 45 minutes, or until browned. Makes 6 servings. (See photo, page 94.)

CANDIED SWEET POTATOES

6 medium sweet potatoes
¼ cup butter or margarine
½ cup brown sugar
½ teaspoon cinnamon
¼ cup water

Wash sweet potatoes and cook in boiling salted water about 30 minutes, or until tender, but firm. Drain, peel and quarter. Melt butter or margarine in a small pan. Add brown sugar, cinnamon and water, and cook, stirring, until sugar is dissolved. Dip sweet potatoes in sugar mixture to coat, place in a buttered baking pan. Cover with remaining syrup. Bake in a slow oven (300°F) 30 to 45 minutes. Makes 6 servings.

Marshmallow Sweets: After baking candied sweet potatoes, cover them with a single layer of marshmallows and brown under the broiler. Or use marshmallow to top Mashed Sweet Potatoes (above).

Nutted Sweet Potatoes: Sprinkle Candied Sweet Potatoes or Mashed Sweet Potatoes with ½ cup chopped walnuts or pecans before baking.

Maple Candied Sweet Potatoes: Prepare sweet potatoes as above, substituting ½ cup maple syrup for brown sugar and water.

Peach Candied Sweet Potatoes: Drain a can (1 pound 13 ounces) peach halves, reserving syrup. Prepare sweet potatoes as above, using ½ cup peach syrup to replace brown sugar and water. Bake sweet potatoes and peaches together.

TOMATOES

Tomatoes are available all the year round, but look for the seasonal varieties for special uses. Large beefsteaks make beautiful salads, as do the tiny cherry tomatoes and the egg- or plum-shaped tomatoes, red and yellow.

Buy smooth-skinned, unblemished tomatoes of various degrees of ripeness. Store ripe, ready-to-eat tomatoes in the refrigerator; keep the others at room temperature, stem end down, until they redden.

To peel tomatoes, dip them into boiling water for half a minute. Plunge into cold water, slip the skin off. Or you can pierce the tomato with a fork and hold it over an open flame until the skin splits and will peel off readily.

STUFFED TOMATOES

6 large, firm tomatoes
½ cup soft bread crumbs
¼ cup chopped onions
1 teaspoon salt
1 teaspoon oregano
6 tablespoons grated Parmesan cheese
2 tablespoons fine dry bread crumbs
2 tablespoons butter or margarine

Cut tops from tomatoes, scoop out pulp and turn tomato shells upside down to drain. Combine tomato pulp with soft bread crumbs, onions, salt, oregano and 4 tablespoons Parmesan cheese. Stuff this mixture into the tomato shells; top with a mixture of remaining 2 tablespoons Parmesan cheese and dry bread crumbs; dot with butter. Place close together on a rack over ½ inch of water in a shallow pan. Cook in a moderate oven (350°F) 20 minutes, or until tops are browned. Makes 6 servings. (See photo, page 143.)

STEWED TOMATOES

Wash and peel tomatoes; place in a saucepan with salt and pepper to taste. No water is needed. Cook over medium heat 10 to 15 minutes, or until tomatoes are tender. If desired, continue cooking until thick, or thicken with soft bread crumbs.

SCALLOPED TOMATOES

Season cooked tomatoes (fresh or canned) with basil, salt, pepper, sugar and grated

Take a tip from the Orient—vegetables look and taste their best when they are artistically cut and cooked very briefly to retain color, crispness and vitamins. Here, mushrooms, broccoli, water chestnuts, celery, scallions and tomatoes are arranged in a skillet, ready to stir-fry, with soy sauce added for extra flavor. (See page 156.)

onion to taste. Layer tomatoes and soft bread crumbs in a baking dish, ending with a generous layer of crumbs. Dot with butter or margarine. Bake in a hot oven (400°F) until hot and bubbling, 20 to 30 minutes.

FRIED GREEN TOMATOES

2 large green tomatoes, sliced thick
2 tablespoons flour
1 egg, beaten
½ teaspoon salt
Dash pepper
Fine bread crumbs
Oil
Parmesan cheese

Coat tomato slices with flour, dip them into egg seasoned with salt and pepper and then into bread crumbs. Brown on both sides in a lightly oiled skillet over medium heat. Sprinkle with Parmesan cheese and serve hot.

TURNIPS AND RUTABAGAS

Purple-collared turnips are available the year round. The green tops are sometimes removed to be sold separately. The condition of the tops, if they are still attached, is an index to the youth and freshness of the roots, as is the roots' smoothness and heaviness. The flesh of the rutabaga is deep yellow in color and has a stronger flavor than that of turnips. Look for smooth, firm roots, heavy for their size.

Turnips and rutabagas may be used interchangeably in recipes.

MASHED TURNIPS

Wash and peel turnips. Slice or quarter them, and cook in boiling salted water until tender, about 15 minutes. Drain and mash, adding butter or margarine, and milk to moisten, and season with salt and pepper.

Variation: Use half potatoes and half turnips; prepare as above.

Mixed-Vegetable Dishes

Let your imagination roam when combining an assortment of vegetables. Vary both colors and textures to create interesting, appetizing effects.

SCALLOPED VEGETABLES

2 to 3 cups cooked or canned vegetables, drained
1½ cups medium Cream Sauce (page 174) or 1 can (10½ ounces) condensed cream of mushroom soup plus ¼ cup milk
½ cup buttered crumbs
Paprika

In a greased casserole, layer vegetables (use corn, carrots, green beans, peas, in any desired combination) and cream sauce. Top with buttered crumbs and sprinkle with paprika. Bake in a moderate oven (350°F) about 25 minutes, until brown. Makes 4 to 6 servings.

VEGETABLES WITH CHEESE SAUCE

1 to 2 cups leftover cooked vegetables*
1 tablespoon butter or margarine
1 tablespoon flour
½ cup milk
½ cup grated cheese (Swiss, Cheddar, Parmesan)
Dash Worcestershire sauce
Salt and pepper

Heat vegetables in a steamer, or simmer them in a small amount of water for a few minutes. Meanwhile, melt butter, stir in flour. Add milk slowly, cook, stirring, until sauce is smooth and thickened. Add cheese, Worcestershire sauce, and salt and pepper to taste. Cook until cheese melts. Pour cheese sauce over heated vegetables. Makes 2 to 4 servings.

STIR-FRIED VEGETABLES

1 medium bunch broccoli
2 tomatoes
½ pound mushrooms
1 can (5 ounces) water chestnuts
4 stalks celery
1 bunch scallions
2 tablespoons oil
½ teaspoon salt
½ teaspoon sugar
¼ cup water
1 tablespoon light soy sauce
1 teaspoon cornstarch
1 tablespoon water

Wash vegetables. Cut broccoli into stems and flowers, then cut flowers into bite-size pieces.

* Use a single vegetable or a combination of leftovers. Especially good are green beans, broccoli, cauliflower, summer squash, potatoes, Brussels sprouts, celery and cabbage.

Vegetables at their crisp and flavorful best: green beans, carrots, cauliflower and chick-peas, briefly boiled or steamed, then baked in a rich cheese sauce. Use your own choice of vegetables, fresh, frozen or canned, to make a vegetable casserole to please the whole family, even those who need vegetables most and like them least! (See page 158.)

Quarter the stems lengthwise, then slant-cut into small pieces. Cut tomatoes into wedges. Slice mushrooms and water chestnuts. Slant-cut celery and scallions. Heat oil in large skillet over medium heat. Add vegetables; cook, stirring constantly, about 2 minutes. Add salt, sugar and water, cover, cook 1 minute. Mix soy sauce, cornstarch and water, add. Cook, stirring, about 30 seconds, until sauce is thick and clear. Makes 6 to 8 servings. (See photo, page 155.)

COUNTRY CASSEROLE

½ pound fresh green beans
1 pound fresh carrots
1 small head cauliflower
½ cup cooked or canned chickpeas
Salt and pepper
½ pound Cheddar cheese, grated (2 cups)
¼ cup butter or margarine
½ cup milk

Trim ends of beans, scrape carrots and slice, break cauliflower into flowerets. Cook vegetables separately in boiling water, or steam them separately, until barely tender. Arrange vegetables and chickpeas in a large buttered casserole, sprinkle with salt and pepper and grated cheese. Dot with butter and add milk. Bake in a moderate oven (350°F) about 20 minutes, or until bubbly. Makes 8 servings. (See photo, page 157.)

Tip: Substitute frozen vegetables or canned vegetables, in any desired quantity.

SEVEN-LAYER DINNER

2 cups sliced raw potatoes
2 cups sliced celery
1½ pounds ground beef
1 cup chopped onion
½ cup chopped green pepper
1 can (1 pound) tomatoes
Salt and pepper
2 cups grated cheese

In a greased 2½-quart casserole, arrange layers of potatoes, celery, meat, onion, green pepper and tomatoes. Sprinkle potato and beef layers with salt and pepper. Bake in a moderate oven (350°F) 2 hours, or until potatoes are tender. Add cheese about 15 minutes before casserole is ready to remove from oven. Makes 6 servings.

Variation: To make this a vegetarian casserole, replace the beef layer with 3 cups raw carrots or drained, canned or frozen green beans, peas, or kidney or other beans. Dot layers with butter or margarine.

FRUIT ADDS A FRESH NOTE

Count on fruit, fresh, canned, dried or frozen to add pleasure (plus a bonus of vitamins and minerals) to your meals. Fresh fruit in season is often a good buy, as well as good food value. Balance plentiful seasonal supplies with canned, frozen and dried fruit to round out menus and fulfill your nutritional needs economically.

Most fresh fruits are "convenience" foods, ready to serve as is or to add their distinctive flavors to other foods. Many vegetables, meats, poultry, even fish are more interesting when they are cooked or served with fruit.

Savings in Season

Watch for advertised fruit specials. The harvest depends on weather and on nature's whims, so it pays to check the market carefully. You may find an occasional out-of-season treat, imported or shipped from a distance, that is plentiful and therefore a bargain.

Remember that all fruits taste sweeter when they are fully ripe. If you shop only once a week, buy some fruits for immediate use and some that will ripen during the week.

When favorite fruits are on sale, discover the special pleasure of an extra pie in your freezer, or a jar of delectable homemade preserves made with a single basket of berries bought ripe at the height of the season.

Some small fruits, particularly cranberries and blueberries, may be simply frozen as is, to use as wanted.

Economy Tip: Very ripe, or even slightly overripe, fruit, specially low-priced at the supermarket, can provide sweet, rich flavor for cooking and baking.

Produce Values

Some produce is sold by the piece, some by the pound. When you select items such as pineapple, usually sold by the "each," pick out two or three of the size and ripeness that best suit your needs. Then weigh them on the customers' scale provided in the produce section, to determine which is the best buy.

Advertisements for produce include a small number, e.g., "cantaloupe 16's, 39 cents each." The 16 means that 16 pieces of this fruit fit into a standard packing crate. The larger the number, the smaller the fruit. Cantaloupe 16's are thus larger than 24's, and if offered at the same price, are a better value.

Prepacked produce sold by the pound has the unit price as well as the cost of the package on the price sticker. When you buy prepacked produce sold by the piece, use the customers' scale to determine which package gives you the most weight for your money.

Canned, Frozen and Dried Fruits

In an earlier era, harvest time meant a flurry of work for the housewife who had to preserve her own fruits and vegetables for the winter months ahead. Our grandmothers stirred their own jellies and jams, canned their own fruits and vegetables, spread their own grapes and prunes on trays in the sun to dry.

Now all this preserving—canning, drying and freezing—is done for us, under circumstances that maintain optimum quality. A large cannery or freezer plant can process the harvest of hundreds of acres before any of the fruit reaches your market.

Canned, frozen and dried fruits are ready to serve as they come from their containers, or to use as ingredients in appetizers, salads, sauces, desserts and other dishes.

Take advantage of the different qualities available to you. Read the label to determine quality, form of the contents, method of packing, additional ingredients and weight.

Shopping for Frozen Fruits

Frozen fruits should be hard-frozen when you buy them. If fruits in a package are not firm, they may have lost quality. Avoid packages stained with fruit juice—the fruit may have been defrosted at some point. Buy frozen fruits last, have them bagged with other frozen items, and put them in your freezer as soon as possible. Frozen fruits are best used immediately upon defrosting; they should not be completely thawed.

Dried Fruits

Dried fruits come in varied packs and sizes, for snack and cooking uses. Modern dried fruits are packed in moisture-retaining containers and rarely require soaking before cooking. Refrigerate packages after opening. To cook, cover with cold water, bring to a boil and simmer until tender. Or, pour boiling water over the fruit, let it stand overnight to plump, add more boiling water to cover, and refrigerate until ready to use.

Make the Most of Fresh Fruits

Enjoy the fresh fruits of each season. Never cut fresh fruit until ready to eat or cook. After cutting, sprinkle bananas, avocados, apples and peaches with lemon juice to prevent browning. Ripen at room temperature, and enjoy your fruits in attractive arrangements as they ripen. Refrigerate ripe fruits, except bananas. Wash before serving.

The following pages are designed to help

you buy and use fruits to best advantage. Prepackaged fruits generally are offered at a lower price per pound.

Apples

Choose varieties according to flavor, flesh characteristics, seasonal availability, suitability for various uses, and appearance. Remember that you pay more for larger, more perfectly colored fruit. Sometimes smaller, off-shaped apples have excellent flavor and are a better value, especially for cooking and for eating raw in families with small children.

BEST FOR EATING
(early season, juicy varieties)

McIntosh	Jonathan
Stayman	Winesap
Delicious	Granny Smith

PIES AND APPLESAUCE
(tart, slightly acid varieties)

Gravenstein	Greening
Grimes Golden	Early McIntosh
Jonathan	Granny Smith
Newton	

BAKING
(firmer-fleshed varieties)

Rome Beauty	Winesap
Northern Spy	York Imperial
Greening	

Flavor varies in apples and is affected by the stage of maturity at the time the fruit is picked, as well as at the time you buy it. Apples must be mature when picked to have a good flavor, texture and good storage life. Immature apples lack color and are usually poor in flavor.

Three or 4 medium-sized apples make a pound. Two pounds make 5 to 6 cups diced apples, 3 cups of applesauce or one 9-inch apple pie.

Look For: Solid, smooth, brightly colored apples. Examine the blossom end for firmness.

Avoid: Discolored fruit with brown spots that are soft to the touch. "Scald," irregular tan or brown patches on the skin, may not affect eating quality.

EASY APPLESAUCE

Wash and remove stem and blossom ends from apples, but do not peel. Cut into wedges, directly into cooking pan. Add about 1 inch water. Cook until apples are soft. Force through a food mill, thus eliminating skins and seeds. Season to taste with sugar, lemon juice and cinnamon; stir to dissolve. This makes a pink and flavorful sauce to serve as dessert or as an accompaniment to meat or poultry. Four pounds of apples will make 1 quart or more sauce.

BAKED APPLES

6 large baking apples
**½ cup raisins and/or chopped dried or
    candied fruit**
¼ cup chopped walnuts
¼ cup melted butter or margarine
6 tablespoons brown sugar, packed
2 tablespoons lemon juice or white wine
1½ cups water

Wash and core apples. Peel off strip of skin around center. Arrange apples in a baking dish. Mix raisins and nuts and pack into center of fruit. Combine butter, sugar and lemon juice or wine. Pour mixture into and over apples. Add water to baking dish. Bake in a moderate oven (350°F) 45 to 60 minutes, basting occasionally with syrup in pan. Spoon syrup over apples before serving. Makes 6 servings.

FRESH APPLE CHUTNEY

Cut 1 Delicious apple into shreds, add 1 minced onion, moisten with vinegar and sprinkle with chopped parsley and 1 chopped green chili. Serve as a relish with curry, stews or pot roast.

FRIED APPLE SLICES

2 large cooking apples
3 tablespoons butter or margarine
2 tablespoons cinnamon sugar
¼ teaspoon nutmeg

Core and slice apples. Melt butter in a skillet, add apples, sprinkle with cinnamon sugar and nutmeg. Brown lightly, basting with pan syrup. Serve hot, with roast pork or pork chops. Makes 4 servings.

APPLE-POTATO SCALLOP

4 cups thin potato slices
1 onion, sliced thin
2 tablespoons flour
  Salt, pepper, nutmeg
3 tablespoons butter or margarine
1½ cups applesauce

Put a layer of one-third the potato slices in a greased 1½-quart casserole, top with half the onion slices. Sprinkle with 1 tablespoon flour, dust with salt, pepper and nutmeg, dot with 1 tablespoon butter, add ½ cup applesauce. Repeat. Top with remaining potato slices, dot with remaining butter, top with remaining applesauce. Cover and bake in a moderate oven (350°F) 45 minutes. Uncover, bake 15 minutes longer. Makes 4 servings.

Apricots

Most fresh apricots are marketed in June and July; a limited supply of imported apricots is available in larger cities during December and January.

Serving Suggestions: Serve fresh apricots chilled, a joy to savor. Or stew dried apricots and serve with ice cream, or purée and blend into equal parts of whipped cream, for a heavenly dessert.

Look For: Plump, juicy-looking fruit, with uniform golden-orange color. Ripe apricots will yield to gentle pressure on the skin.

Avoid: Dull-looking, soft or mushy fruit; very firm pale or greenish-yellow fruit.

Avocados

Avocados, grown in California and Florida and available year-round, range in color from green to purple-black, from rough-textured skin to smooth, from pear-shaped to almost spherical. Avocados are generally sold individually.

For immediate use, look for slightly soft avocados. Or buy avocados in advance and let them ripen 3 to 5 days at room temperature before storing them in the warmest part of the refrigerator.

Tip: To avoid discoloration when preparing avocados, brush the exposed surfaces with lemon juice, use as quickly as possible.

Serving Suggestion: For delightful flavor, float thin slices of avocado in chicken soup.

Look For: Bright, glossy-looking fruit, heavy for its size.

Avoid: Wilted or bruised fruit with dark, sunken spots or a cracked surface.

Bananas

Bananas develop good eating qualities after they are harvested, which is fortunate, since they travel great distances to reach us. Our supply comes year round from Central and South America.

Bananas ripen best between 60° and 70°F; higher temperatures cause them to ripen too rapidly. They are injured at temperatures below 55°F, and should not be kept in the refrigerator.

One pound, about 3 medium bananas, makes about 2 cups sliced fruit.

Look For: Firm bananas, bright in appearance and free from bruises. Best eating quality is reached when the yellow of the skin is flecked with brown. Firm, partly green bananas are best for frying or baking. Red bananas, occasionally found in our markets, are excellent for frying or baking. Bananas too ripe for eating plain may be used to make banana cake or bread. (See pages 198 and 203.)

QUICK BANANA DESSERT

Peel bananas, discard fibers, slice fruit and serve topped with sweet cream, sour cream or yogurt. Sprinkle with sugar or honey if desired.

BANANAS IN SALAD

Bananas make a delicious accent for fruit salads. Dip in lemon juice to prevent discoloring.

BANANA VERSATILITY—AND STYLE

Bananas top cereals, shortcake or ice cream with sweet flavor. For a decorative edge, run the tines of a silver fork down the length of a peeled banana, slice crosswise.

BAKED BANANAS

Peel unripe bananas; leave whole or split in half lengthwise. Brush with melted butter or margarine, sprinkle with brown sugar and a little lemon juice. Bake in a moderately hot oven (375°F) about 10 minutes, until fruit is golden and soft. If desired, warm a little brandy or rum, ignite and pour flaming over bananas. Spoon sauce over bananas and serve.

PAN-BROWNED BANANAS

Peel firm, underripe bananas; split in half lengthwise. Brown in hot butter, margarine or bacon fat to serve as accompaniment for meat. Or use butter or margarine, sprinkle bananas in the pan with brown sugar and dash of cinnamon and serve for dessert. To serve aflame, add a little rum or brandy to pan as bananas finish cooking, ignite, baste the bananas with flaming sauce. Serve at once.

BANANA FRITTERS

Cut peeled, firm, unripe bananas into 1-inch lengths; dip in slightly beaten egg mixed with 1 tablespoon milk, then in bread crumbs or pancake mix. Fry in hot (370°F) deep fat until golden brown. Drain on paper.

Berries

Store berries in the refrigerator without washing them. To serve, run cold water over the berries, hull, drain and sprinkle with sugar if desired.

One pint of berries makes 3 to 4 servings.

Serving Suggestions: Serve berries topped with plain, sour or whipped cream or with yogurt, or in Shortcake (page 200), pies, salads and fruit cups. If desired, flavor with a little Kirsch, sherry or liqueur. Large strawberries may be washed, drained and served, with the hulls, around a mound of powdered sugar for dipping.

Look For: Unblemished, ripe berries.

Avoid: Soft, moldy fruit.

PERFECT BERRY PRESERVES

Wash berries, hull. Cut imperfect fruit in pieces, leave rest whole. Sprinkle with an equal volume of sugar. Let stand in an enamel or porcelain pan until sugar forms a syrup. Bring to a brisk boil, remove from heat for a moment, bring to a boil again. Skim off foam. Cook rapidly until syrup bubbles around the edge of the pan. Test by pouring the syrup from the side of a spoon. The last two drops should run together. Skim and cool slightly, stirring occasionally to prevent fruit from floating. Pour into sterilized jar or glasses. Refrigerate for immediate use. To seal for storage, cover jars with ¼-inch layer of melted paraffin immediately after filling.

Cantaloupes (Muskmelons)

Look For: Full maturity—the stem should be gone, leaving a smooth, symmetrical shallow ridge called a "full slip." The netting, or veining, should be thick, coarse and corky, and should stand out over some part of the surface. The skin color (ground color) between the veins should have changed from green to yellowish buff or pale gray. The delicate cantaloupe aroma is the best indication of ripeness.

Avoid: Overripeness, shown by pronounced yellow color and softening of the rind. Mold growth on the cantaloupe, particularly in the stem scar, is a sign of decay. The flesh of overripe melons is soft and watery.

Casabas

These are a late-season melon, running from July through November. Casabas are sweet, juicy, normally pumpkin-shaped, sometimes pointed at the stem end. Not netted, but with shallow, irregular furrows running from stem to blossom end. Rind is hard, light-green or yellow in color. (For more information, see Melons.)

Look For: Ripe melons with gold-yellow rind and slight softening at the blossom end. Casabas have no aroma.

Avoid: Melons with dark, sunken spots.

Crenshaws

Crenshaws have a more pointed stem end than casabas, with a smooth, green-gold rind. Blossom end is soft, rind is dark and aroma is pleasant when fruit is ripe. (For more information, see Melons.)

Cherries

Look For: Smooth skins, bright color. Sweet cherries range in color from the pink and gold of the Queen Anne to the deep purplish-red of Bing cherries. Sweet cherries should be firm; sour cherries, a lighter orange-red color, are somewhat softer. If cherries are small or hard, or if they have poor color, they will be less juicy.

Avoid: Softness, dull color or leaking juices. Cuts or marks indicate decay.

A BOWL OF CHERRIES

For a dessert that is a symbol of good living, simply wash sweet cherries, chill and serve.

STEWED SOUR CHERRIES

1 quart sour cherries
1 cup water
1 cup sugar

Wash cherries, pick over and stem. Remove pits. Combine water and sugar, stir over low heat until sugar is dissolved. Bring to a boil and boil 5 minutes. Add cherries and simmer 5 minutes, or until cherries are tender.

Cranberries

Cranberries will keep in the refrigerator for 1 to 4 weeks, or store the unopened package in the freezer.

Look For: Plump, firm berries with a lustrous, bright color.

Avoid: Discolored, mushy, moldy berries.

CRANBERRY-ORANGE RELISH

2 small oranges
1 pound (4 cups) fresh cranberries
1¼ cups sugar

Quarter oranges and discard center pith and seeds, but do not peel. Grind, using the medium blade of the food chopper. Grind cranberries. Add sugar and mix well. Chill thoroughly. Makes 1 quart. (See photo, page 94.)

FRESH CRANBERRY SAUCE

1 pound (4 cups) fresh cranberries
2 cups sugar
1½ cups water

Combine cranberries, sugar and water in a saucepan. Heat to boiling, stirring until sugar dissolves. Boil rapidly until berries pop open, about 5 minutes. For a thicker sauce, continue cooking until cranberries are soft. Makes about 1 quart cranberry sauce. (See photo, page 94.)

Jellied Cranberry Sauce: Make cranberry sauce, above, and press through a food mill or a sieve. Discard skins. Cook until mixture reaches the jellying stage—when a little is poured from the side of a spoon the last two drops run together and fall in a "sheet."

Figs

Fresh figs come to the market only infrequently, during the summer months.

Buy only as many as you will use at once—they are very perishable. Store in the refrigerator.

Serving Suggestions: Wash figs, trim stems. Serve whole or cut in half or in quarters, with cream and a little sugar, or with cheese, as dessert. Or serve with thin-sliced ham as an appetizer.

Look For: Firm, ripe fruit free from blemishes, bruises or mold.

Fruit Cocktail

Buy canned or frozen fruit cocktail, or make your own combination of fresh, canned and dried fruits. Serve as appetizer or dessert.

Reserve juices drained from canned fruits and fruit cocktail to flavor other desserts or use in mixed drinks.

TREASURE BROWNIES

1 package brownie mix
1 can (16 ounces) fruit cocktail, drained

Prepare brownie mix as directed on package. Fold fruit cocktail into batter. Bake according to package directions.

Grapefruit

Grapefruit is available all year (with best supplies and lowest prices from December through March) from Florida, Texas, California and Arizona. "Seedless" grapefruit has few or no seeds. White-fleshed grapefruit is the most common; pink- or red-fleshed varieties are somewhat sweeter.

Grapefruit is picked ripe and is ready to eat when you buy it; however, a grapefruit stored a few days at room temperature may develop sweeter flavor.

One large to medium grapefruit will yield about 1¼ cups of sections.

Look For: Firm fruit, heavy for its size. Thin-skinned fruits have more juice than the coarse-skinned. Color ranges from yellow and yellow-green to pink. Small marks on the skin, scale, and discoloration don't affect quality. In fact, some of the sweetest grapefruit are spotted with brown.

Avoid: Fruit with soft, discolored areas on the peel at the stem end, dull color, soft and tender peel that punctures easily.

HALF GRAPEFRUIT

Cut grapefruit in half crosswise, remove seeds, cut out core with a sharp scissors or a grapefruit corer. Loosen each section within its membrane with a sharp, pointed knife. Chill thoroughly. Serve plain or sprinkled

with powdered sugar or honey. If desired, place a fresh berry, a stewed prune or a cherry in the center of each half.

BROILED GRAPEFRUIT

Prepare halves of grapefruit as directed above. Sprinkle each half with brown sugar (about 1 tablespoon) and dot with butter or margarine. Broil slowly 15 to 20 minutes, or until heated through and bubbling. Serve piping-hot.

Variation: Instead of brown sugar, use orange marmalade or honey.

GRAPEFRUIT WITH ORANGE OR APPLE

Prepare halves of grapefruit as above, but remove membrane entirely. Insert orange or apple sections between the grapefruit segments.

Grapes

Common varieties are Thompson, seedless early green grapes; Tokay and Cardinal, early bright-red grapes; and Emperor, late deep-red grapes. All have excellent flavor. Ribier, a dark grape, is very sweet. All these are of European origin.

Native American grapes are juicier than the European and have softer flesh. The outstanding variety for flavor is the Concord, which is blue-black when well matured. Delaware and Catawba are also popular.

Serving Suggestions: Wash grapes, drain, and chill, if desired. Serve in bunches, or cut large grapes in half, remove seeds, use in fruit cups or salads.

Look For: Clusters of grapes that are well formed, bright in color and firmly attached to the stem. White or green grapes are sweetest when the skin has a yellowish cast or a tinge of amber. Red varieties are sweetest when the red color predominates on all or most of the berries.

Avoid: Soft, wrinkled, or leaking grapes or grapes with bleached areas around the stem end.

CRYSTALLIZED GRAPES

Select 1 pound perfect bunches of red or purple grapes, wash and dry well. Cut into small clusters. Combine ½ cup water and 1 cup sugar; boil for 5 minutes. Dip bunches of grapes into the syrup, one bunch at a time.

Drain excess syrup, sprinkle with granulated sugar. Place on a cake rack to harden. The coating will crystallize more rapidly if the grapes are placed in the refrigerator. Use as a garnish for cold meats or cake or dessert.

Honeydews

Outstanding sweet flavor makes honeydews highly prized for dessert. The melon is generally large (the smaller, round variety is the Honey Ball), bluntly oval in shape, generally smooth-skinned, with occasional traces of surface netting. The rind is firm, ranges in color from creamy white with a faint green tinge to creamy yellow, depending on the stage of ripeness. Stem does not separate from the fruit. (For more information, see Melons.)

Look For: Mature fruit that feels soft, velvety. A slight softness at the blossom end shows ripeness. Aroma is sweet but very faint.

Avoid: Hard, smooth melons with dead-white or greenish-white color and large bruised areas. Small, superficial spots do not affect quality.

Kiwis

The pale-green interior of this egg-shaped, fuzzy, brown-skinned fruit from New Zealand has a flavor reminiscent of pineapple, strawberries or papaya.

Serving Suggestions: Serve chilled on the half shell, or peeled and sliced with custard or ice cream.

Look For: Fruit that is soft to the touch, which indicates ripeness.

Kumquats

This sour, small, orange, thin-skinned citrus fruit is shaped like an oversized pecan. It is generally sold in quart baskets. Kumquats are usually cooked and sweetened before eating. Both rind and pulp are eaten.

GLAZED KUMQUATS

1 quart kumquats
Water to cover
1 cup water
2 cups sugar

Wash kumquats and cut an X in the stem

ends. Cover with water, bring to a boil. Drain, cover with fresh cold water, boil about 15 minutes, until almost tender. Drain. Boil 1 cup water with 2 cups sugar for 5 minutes. Add kumquats and cook in syrup 5 minutes, until well glazed and tender. Chill in syrup. Serve as dessert, or as a garnish for meat. Delicious with turkey and cranberry sauce.

Lemons

Lemons are a popular seasoning agent for everything from fish to a cup of tea, low in calories, high in vitamin C. Try fresh lemonade for an old-fashioned refresher; use lemon juice in salad dressings and in sauces from mayonnaise to Hollandaise.

Look For: Rich yellow color and reasonably smooth-textured, slightly glossy skin, firm fruit that feels heavy for its size. A pale or greenish color means very fresh fruit with slightly higher acidity. Coarse or rough skin texture is a sign of thick skin and less flesh or juice.

Avoid: Darker yellow or dull color, or hard or shriveled skin (signs of age). Soft spots and punctures of the skin indicate decay.

LEMON CHEESE

6 tablespoons butter or margarine
¾ cup granulated sugar
2 teaspoons grated lemon rind
¼ cup lemon juice
3 eggs, beaten

Put butter into top of double boiler, add sugar, lemon rind and juice. Strain eggs into pan. Stir constantly over moderate heat until thickened. Do not boil. Pour into a jar. The lemon cheese thickens further as it cools. Store in a cool place. Makes 1¼ cups. Use as a filling for pies and tarts and as a spread for tea sandwiches.

FRESH LEMONADE

3 lemons
1 cup sugar (about)
12 to 14 ice cubes
Water to make 1½ quarts

Scrub lemons and roll on the counter to soften slightly. Trim ends, cut fruit into very thin slices, discard seeds. Place slices in a wide-bottomed pitcher, cover with sugar. Let stand briefly until sugar begins to dissolve; press hard with the back of a wooden spoon to hasten the process. Add ice cubes and water, stir. Strain into glasses. Makes 6 to 8 servings.

Pink Lemonade: Prepare as above but use a little less sugar. Add grenadine, raspberry syrup or maraschino cherry juice to taste.

Limes

Limes are used to flavor food and drinks, for tang similar to that of lemon, but sharp rather than sour.

Look For: Firm and glossy fruit, with thin, smooth skins. Limes are juiciest when they are heavy for their size.

Mangoes

Mangoes are a tropical fruit, large, pear-shaped, fleshy, with smooth skin. They may resemble apricots in color, or have a rosier hue. They are available April through June.

Serving Suggestions: Wash fruit, cut it lengthwise, flat along both sides of the seed, shaping two half ovals. Mark the flesh in a crosshatch pattern, turn inside out, cut from skin. Peel skin from attached portion of mango, slice strip from the seed.

Or wash the fruit, cut wedge-shaped pieces, detach from seed. Serve like melon.

Look For: Heavy fruit, slightly soft to the touch when ripe. Skin may be spotted with black when ripe.

Melons

Different varieties of the melon family offer a good supply from May until December. Melons are refreshing and cool in summer, ideal as a first course, salad or dessert. Always serve melons very ripe. If necessary, hold them at room temperature several days to ripen.

For more information, see specific melons.

Melon Tips: Serve all melons chilled. Cut small melons in half or quarters, large melons in wedges. Serve as appetizer with peppered ham, or salt or lemon wedge; fill cantaloupe "bowl" with breakfast cereal, cottage cheese for salad, or ice cream for dessert.

Cut a strip from top of watermelon or other large melon with a scalloped or saw-toothed edge and fill with melon balls, berries, other fruits. The melon becomes a serving container and centerpiece in one.

Nectarines

This smooth-skinned fruit looks and tastes like a peach without fuzz, has the texture of a plum.

Bright-looking, firm fruits ripen within 2 or 3 days at room temperature.

Look For: Rich color and plumpness, and a slight softening along the "seam."

Avoid: Hard, dull fruits and soft or over-ripe fruits. Russet coloring is only skin deep and does not detract from the flavor of the nectarine.

Oranges

Navel oranges, from California and Arizona, have thick, somewhat pebbled skin and no seeds. They peel readily by hand. Valencia oranges have thin skin, are excellent for juice or for salads.

Florida oranges include excellent juice varieties. The Pineapple orange makes good eating; the Temple orange, somewhat like the California Navel, peels easily, separates into segments readily, has excellent flavor.

Look For: Firm fruit, heavy for its size, without soft or discolored spots, cuts or skin punctures. Skin color is not a guide to ripeness; green spots may occur even on ripe oranges and Valencias sometimes turn green again late in the season.

"Russeting" is often found on Florida and Texas oranges. This dark mottling of the skin does not affect eating quality and in fact often occurs on oranges with thin skin and superior eating quality.

CHILLED ORANGE DELIGHT

Cut and reserve a thin slice off the top of a Navel or Temple orange and peel the skin in a long spiral, cutting through the white membrane to the orange pulp. Cut the fruit crosswise into slices, reassemble. Rewind the peel around the fruit, replace top, and chill in the refrigerator or, briefly, in the freezer. Serve very cold, as refreshing dessert.

AMBROSIA

Peel and slice Navel or Temple oranges. Layer in shallow bowl. Sprinkle lightly with confectioners' sugar and generously with grated coconut. Chill thoroughly and serve for dessert.

Festive Ambrosia: Marinate orange slices in orange liqueur, with thin slices of orange peel and a few cloves. A great party treat!

Papayas

These tropical melons are pear-shaped, with a smooth skin of pale green mottled with orange. The flesh is orange, like that of a cantaloupe. Papaya seeds, which have a sharp mustard flavor, are the base of meat tenderizer. A refreshing breakfast fruit or salad. Serve with salt, or with lemon or lime juice.

Peaches

The many local varieties of peaches fall into two general types: freestone (flesh readily separates from the pit) and clingstone (flesh clings tightly to the pit). Freestones are usually preferred for eating fresh or for freezing, while clingstones are used primarily for canning, although they are sometimes sold fresh.

Ripen peaches at room temperature; store unwashed in the refrigerator. Wash before serving.

Tip: To peel peaches, dip fruit into boiling water for a few minutes, plunge into cold water. Skins can then be slipped off.

Look For: Peaches that are fairly firm or becoming a trifle soft. The skin color between the red areas (ground color) should be yellow or at least creamy.

Avoid: Badly bruised or mushy fruit, very green fruit.

STEWED PEACHES

2 pounds peaches
2 cups water
1 cup sugar (or to taste)
  Pinch salt or lemon slice

Select firm, ripe peaches. Plunge into boiling water for a few minutes. Peel, leave whole or cut in half. (If the fruit is halved, cook the peach stones with the peaches for added flavor.) Combine water, sugar and salt or lemon slice. Stir over low heat until sugar is dissolved. Bring to a boil. Add peaches, cover, boil gently about 10 minutes, or until peaches are tender. Cool and chill. Makes 8 servings.

SPICED PEACHES

Prepare peaches as above, but stud each peach with 3 whole cloves and add a small piece of cinnamon stick to the syrup while cooking.

QUICK-BRANDIED PEACHES

When peaches have been stewed (above), remove them from the syrup. Boil syrup for 10 minutes to thicken it. Pour over peaches, cool. Add 4 tablespoons brandy and 2 teaspoons white wine vinegar. Cover tightly and chill. Let stand overnight or longer before using.

Pears

There are two general types of pears: summer pears, sweet, juicy, yellow pears such as Bartletts; and winter pears, firm-fleshed and russet-skinned. Serve the yellow pears fresh, alone or with cheese or nuts; the firmer varieties store well and are good for cooking. Seckel pears are small reddish pears, good for eating out of hand when very ripe, or for cooking and canning when still firm.

Summer pears are perishable and therefore best bought in small quantities and allowed to ripen at room temperature.

There are 3 to 4 pears to a pound.

Look For: Firm, but not hard, fruit, clean and bright in color, free from bruises.

STEWED PEARS

2 pounds pears
2 cups boiling water, or 1 cup water,
  1 cup red wine
1 cup sugar
  Dash nutmeg or ginger

Peel firm cooking pears, leaving stems intact, or cut in half and core. Cook in boiling water, covered, for 10 minutes. Add wine if used, sugar, nutmeg or ginger. Stir until sugar dissolves. Cover and cook 10 to 20 minutes, or until fruit is tender. Makes 6 to 8 servings.

Persian Melons

Persian melons resemble cantaloupes, but have finer netting and are about the same size as honeydews. The flesh is thick, fine-textured, and orange in color.

Look For: Heavy weight for size, pleasant aroma, same characteristics as cantaloupes.

Persimmons

Persimmons are bright Chinese red in color, smooth-skinned, with a broad green cap at the stem end. Choose fully ripe fruit, or let them ripen in your fruit bowl until they are quite soft to the touch. At this point they may develop dark streaks in the skin.

Serving Suggestions: Wash and dry, cut off stem and chill fruit if desired. Cut in half vertically and serve as appetizer or dessert. Or cut into sections and use as part of fruit salad or fruit cup.

Pineapples

Pineapples are available most of the year, but their peak season runs from April through June. Pineapples are fully grown but still green when they are harvested.

Ripen at room temperature, refrigerate before serving.

Look For: Good orange color, rather than greenish tone, and fragrant, spicy aroma. Choose fruit heavy for its size—the larger the pineapple, the greater proportion of edible flesh. Check the bottom for signs of decay.

Avoid: Fruit with soft spots or sunken spines.

Serving Suggestions: The pineapple shell and its leafy frond make a handsome serving container; use it to serve the fruit, or a chicken-and-pineapple salad, or a pineapple-and-ice-cream dessert.

To prepare the pineapple for serving, lay it on a cutting board. Cut it in half lengthwise, through the frond as well as the fruit, using a sharp serrated knife. Cut into lengthwise quarters. Slice off the hard core from each quarter. Slice the flesh from the shell, cut it into chunks, serve in the shell with picks if desired. Garnish with strawberries or cherries, to taste.

PINEAPPLE WEDGES WITH CHEESE

When pineapple is cut, as above, alternate chunks in the shell with thin slices of cheese. Guests use picks to lift out fruit and cheese together.

PINEAPPLE NINON

1 large pineapple
1 jar (8 ounces) guava jelly
¾ cup strawberries, sliced
½ cup melon cubes, tangerine sections,
   other fruits in season

Split pineapple and fronds in half lengthwise. Discard core, scoop out and cut meat into cubes. Stir guava jelly with a fork to break it up, mix with pineapple and other fruit. Pile into pineapple shells. Makes 8 servings.

FROZEN PINEAPPLE SLICES

Drain canned pineapple slices, reserve juice for use in beverages. Arrange slices in a single layer on a cookie sheet or a piece of heavy-duty foil. Freeze. Serve as a refreshing summer treat.

Plums and Fresh Prunes

Plum varieties differ in color—green, yellow, red, blue, purple or purplish-black—and in flavor, from tart to sweet. All are delicious to eat out of hand.

Ripen at room temperature, then store, covered, in the refrigerator.

Serving Suggestions: Most plums are excellent briefly stewed with a little sugar, or baked into old-fashioned pies, cobblers or coffee cakes.

Look For: Plump, clean, fresh-looking plums with good, deep characteristic color and soft bloom on the skin. Ripe plums are fairly firm to slightly soft, with no cracks.

FRESH PRUNE JAM

4 cups prune plums, pitted and quartered
2 cups sugar
½ lemon, juice and grated rind
½ cup water

Bring all ingredients to a boil, reduce heat, and simmer slowly, stirring often, until jam thickens. To test for thickness, pour a little syrup onto a cold plate and draw a path through it with a spoon. The path should remain clear. Fill hot sterilized 6-ounce jars, cover, and invert. Or seal with paraffin. Makes 4 jars.

BRANDIED PRUNE COMPOTE

2 cups pitted dried prunes
1 cup dried apricots
1 stick cinnamon
   Boiling water
2 lemon slices
6 cloves
   Brandy

Put dried fruits into glass jar, add cinnamon and boiling water to cover. Pierce lemon slices with cloves and add. Add ¼ cup brandy. Let the fruit stand overnight to plump. Add more brandy to replenish liquid that has been absorbed, let stand overnight again. Repeat for third time. Discard lemon slices, cloves and cinnamon stick, chill. Serve as meat accompaniment or dessert. Keeps well in the refrigerator.

Rhubarb

Strictly speaking, rhubarb is a vegetable, but it is served as a fruit. Rhubarb leaves are not edible; discard them.

Store fresh rhubarb in the refrigerator and use within 2 days.

One pound of rhubarb stalks will make about 2 cups cooked rhubarb.

Look For: Crisp stalks, red or pink and fairly thick.

BAKED RHUBARB

Wash, trim and cut 2 pounds of rhubarb into 1-inch pieces, discarding coarse strings. Toss in a greased casserole with ⅔ cup sugar. Bake in a hot oven (400°F) about 20 minutes, until rhubarb is tender but not mushy. Makes 6 servings.

STEWED RHUBARB

Prepare rhubarb as above. Mix in saucepan with ½ cup water and ⅔ cup sugar. Let stand until some juices are released. Cover, bring to a boil, and simmer over low heat about 10 minutes, until pieces are tender but not mushy. Makes 6 servings.

Tangelos

This easy-to-peel fruit is a hybrid, a cross between the tangerine and the pomelo, or grapefruit.

Tangerines

Refrigerate, use as soon as possible.

Look For: Fruit that feels heavy for its size. The slip-skin should be brightly lustrous, from deep orange to near red in color. The skin may seem puffy, but the fruit beneath it should feel firm to pressure.

Tomatoes

Botanically a fruit, tomatoes are used as vegetables. See vegetable chapter.

Watermelons

Look For: Solid-green or striped-grayish, rather dull, rind. The surface should be relatively smooth. The ends of the melon should be filled out. The underside, or "belly," of a ripe melon is creamy in color, almost light yellow. In cut melons, look for firm, juicy flesh with good red color, free from white streaks, and with dark-brown or black seeds.

SALADS

Salads play a number of roles in menu planning. A salad can be a meal in itself or an accompaniment to the main dish. Or it can begin a meal, California style, or end one, French style. It can cleanse the palate between courses.

Use these salads as a starting point for your own inventive recipes, based on what you find at the market or what you have on hand. See pages 175–176 for salad dressings.

Add variety to all salads—but particularly to green salads—by using all the different kinds of salad greens you find on the market: buttery Bibb and Boston lettuce, as well as firmly packed heads of crisp iceberg; cos, or romaine, with its long, stiff leaves; feathery chicory and its kin, curly endive and wavy-leafed escarole; Belgian endive, green-tipped white leaves tightly packed in a cylinder no larger than your hand; watercress; and not least, spinach.

Some of these greens can be used alone; others, like chicory, endive and escarole, have a characteristic bitterness that adds interest to mixed green salads.

Rinse salad greens thoroughly in running cold water and wrap them for refrigerator storage in foil or plastic wrap. Dry greens well before using.

BASIC GREEN SALAD

Tear lettuce or other salad greens into bite-size pieces. Toss with any combination of raw vegetables—tomatoes, radishes, carrot slices, celery slices, sliced onions or scallions, cucumber, green pepper, olives, even cauliflowerets or turnip slices. Add crumbled or grated cheese and croutons, if desired. Just before serving, toss with your favorite salad dressing (see page 175).

ELEGANT GREEN SALAD

  4 cups lettuce (romaine, iceberg, Bibb, Boston)
  2 heads Belgian endive
  1 cup watercress
  1 red onion, sliced
½ pound fresh mushrooms, thinly sliced
  4 to 5 radishes, thinly sliced
    Favorite salad dressing
    Salt and pepper

Wash and dry salad greens and tear into bite-size pieces. Pile into a salad bowl. Add onion, mushrooms and radishes; toss with dressing and season with salt and pepper. Makes 6 servings.

SPRING SALAD

1 bunch watercress
2 tomatoes
3 new potatoes, cooked and cooled
6 green onions, with tops
2 medium cucumbers
6 radishes
  Favorite salad dressing

Trim stems from watercress; cut tomatoes into wedges; slice potatoes; cut green onions into 2-inch lengths; score cucumbers with a fork and slice; trim and shape radish roses with sharp knife. Combine the vegetables in a salad bowl, toss. Top each serving with dressing. Makes 3 hearty servings.

RED-AND-GREEN-CABBAGE SALAD

½ cup mayonnaise
1 apple, grated
1½ tablespoons grated horseradish, drained
¼ cup cider vinegar
1 tablespoon sugar
   Salt, pepper to taste
2 cups finely shredded red cabbage
2 cups finely shredded green cabbage
   Lettuce

Blend mayonnaise with apple, horseradish, vinegar, sugar, salt and pepper. Add half of dressing mixture to cabbage of each color and mix lightly. Put red mixture on a bed of lettuce, top with green mixture. Makes 4 servings.

OLD-FASHIONED COLESLAW

1 small head of cabbage, shredded
3 tablespoons grated onion
1 teaspoon salt
2 tablespoons each sugar and vinegar
2 cups sour cream
½ green pepper, shredded

Combine ingredients and toss well. Add 1 tablespoon caraway seeds, if desired. Makes about 8 servings.

GREEK SALAD

1 head escarole
2 tomatoes, in wedges
1 bunch radishes, sliced
1 red onion, sliced
1 green pepper, cut in rings
1 can (8 ounces) black olives, drained
1 hard-cooked egg, quartered
1 small can flat anchovies, drained
4 ounces feta or farmer cheese, crumbled
½ cup olive oil or other salad oil
¼ cup lemon juice

Line a large platter with escarole. Arrange tomatoes, radishes, onion, green pepper, olives, egg, anchovies and cheese on escarole. Just before serving, sprinkle with mixed olive oil and lemon juice. Makes 4 to 6 servings. (See photo, page 177.)

HEARTY SPINACH SALAD

1 pound spinach
1 cup fresh or canned bean sprouts, drained
1 can (5 ounces) water chestnuts, drained and sliced
½ pound fresh mushrooms, sliced
3 hard-cooked eggs, sliced
6 slices bacon, cooked and crumbled
½ cup salad oil
3 tablespoons bacon fat
¼ cup ketchup
¼ cup vinegar
1 tablespoon Worcestershire sauce
3 tablespoons sugar
½ onion, grated

Wash spinach thoroughly, tear into bite-size pieces. Toss spinach with bean sprouts, water chestnuts, mushrooms, eggs and bacon in a large salad bowl. Combine remaining ingredients in a skillet or saucepan and heat just to simmering. Pour hot dressing over salad and serve at once. Makes 8 servings.

SALAMAGUNDI

1 head Boston or iceberg lettuce
1 head romaine lettuce
6 slices day-old bread, crusts removed
6 tablespoons salad or olive oil
2 cloves garlic, minced
1 pound cooked or canned ham, cubed
½ pound Swiss cheese, cubed
4 tomatoes, in wedges
3 hard-cooked eggs, in wedges
2 cans (2 ounces each) flat anchovies, drained, minced
1 cup pitted black olives
1 can (4 ounces) pimiento, drained, sliced
1 cup oil
⅓ cup wine vinegar
   Salt, pepper to taste

Tear lettuce into bite-size pieces, pile into salad bowl. Cut bread into dice. Heat oil in skillet with garlic, brown bread cubes lightly, sprinkle on lettuce. Arrange rows of ham, cheese, tomatoes and eggs around the edge of the bowl, with anchovies, olives and pimientos between the rows. Mix oil and vinegar with seasonings to taste, pour over salad. Toss at the table, just before serving. Makes 6 to 8 servings.

CAESAR SALAD

½ cup Ann Page Caesar Dressing
4 slices white bread, crusts removed
4 cups romaine, in bite-sized pieces
¼ pound blue or Swiss cheese, cut up
¼ cup pitted black olives
1 can (2 ounces) flat anchovy fillets, drained and cut up
2 firm tomatoes, cut in wedges

Heat 3 tablespoons Caesar Dressing in a skillet. Cut bread into ½-inch cubes. Add to skillet and toss until crisp and golden. Set aside. Put romaine into a salad bowl, add bread cubes and remaining ingredients. Toss with rest of dressing. Makes 4 to 6 servings.

THREE-BEAN SALAD

1 can (1 pound) cut green beans
1 can (15½ ounces) red kidney beans
1 can (16 ounces) wax beans
¾ cup oil
   Juice of 2 lemons (6 tablespoons)
1 clove garlic, crushed
¼ teaspoon basil
¼ teaspoon thyme
   Salt and pepper
1 small sweet red onion, sliced and separated
   into rings

Drain beans and combine in a small bowl. Mix together oil, lemon juice, garlic and seasonings, toss with beans. Garnish with onion rings. Makes 6 to 8 servings. (See photo, page 178.)

CARROT SALAD

3 cups shredded carrots
½ cup shredded coconut
½ cup raisins
½ cup sour cream
½ cup mayonnaise
1 tablespoon lemon juice
   Salt to taste

Mix together carrots, coconut and raisins. Combine remaining ingredients, stir in. Makes 6 servings.

POTATO SALAD

2 pounds potatoes, washed and peeled
¼ cup salad oil
2 tablespoons vinegar
1 teaspoon salt
   Dash pepper
2 hard-cooked eggs, chopped
½ cup finely chopped celery
1 cup chopped black olives
1 cup chopped pickles (dill or sweet)
1 onion, diced
½ cup mayonnaise

Cook potatoes in boiling salted water until tender. Slice. Mix oil, vinegar, salt and pepper, pour over the hot potatoes. Cool.

Add remaining ingredients and combine well. Chill until serving time. Makes 6 to 8 servings.

RICE SALAD

⅔ cup rice
3 tablespoons oil
1 tablespoon vinegar
   Salt and pepper to taste
½ teaspoon tarragon
¼ cup finely chopped celery
¼ cup sliced black olives
   Cherry tomatoes

Cook rice as directed on package, or use 2 cups cold cooked rice. Mix oil, vinegar, salt, pepper and tarragon to make dressing. Add to rice, stir. Add celery and olives. Serve cold, garnished with cherry tomatoes. Makes 3 to 4 servings.

MACARONI SALAD

2 cups macaroni
2 tablespoons minced onion
2 tablespoons diced green pepper
2 tablespoons chopped pimiento
¼ cup sour cream
¼ cup mayonnaise
   Salt, pepper

Cook macaroni in boiling salted water until just tender, drain and chill. Toss with remaining ingredients, adding seasonings to taste. Makes 4 to 6 servings.

CALIFORNIA FRUIT SALAD

Arrange cut-up fruits in season attractively on a serving plate. Add your favorite nuts and a scoop of cottage cheese. Enjoy this salad as a light meal or as a dessert. (See photo, page 178.)

WALDORF SALAD

2 cups red Delicious apples, cored and diced
2 tablespoons lemon juice
1 cup diced celery
½ cup mayonnaise
⅓ cup broken walnut meats

Sprinkle diced apples with lemon juice. Combine with celery and mayonnaise to moisten. Stir in walnut meats just before serving. Serve on salad greens. Makes 4 servings.

SAUCES AND SALAD DRESSINGS

You can do your own thing and make your own sauces and dressings according to the recipes in this chapter and others you will find throughout the book.

Or, your A&P offers a wide and all-encompassing assortment of sauces, in bottles, cans and dry-mix packets, from brown gravy to steak sauce to spaghetti sauce. The range of salad dressings is equally appealing: Ann Page Mayonnaise, bottled dressings, packets of dressing mixes to use as is or combine in your own inventive ways.

Sauces

Some sauces are served hot, some are served cold; some are blended with the other ingredients, some are simply poured over the dish they are meant to complement, and some may be served separately, to be used as each diner prefers.

HOLLANDAISE SAUCE

¾ cup butter or margarine
3 egg yolks
1½ tablespoons lemon juice
¼ cup boiling water
Salt, pepper

Let butter soften in the top of a double boiler, off the heat. Whisk in egg yolks and lemon juice. Place pan over simmering water. Slowly whisk in boiling water and cook, whisking constantly, until sauce thickens. Add salt and pepper to taste, remove from heat and whisk again. Serve with poached, baked or broiled fish and with vegetables. Makes 1 cup.

BLENDER HOLLANDAISE

Put into the container of an electric blender 4 egg yolks, 2 tablespoons lemon juice, and dashes of salt and cayenne pepper to taste. Melt 1 cup butter or margarine in a saucepan. Cover the blender container, switch on, and add melted butter in a steady stream until all is combined. Makes 1¼ cups.

MOUSSELINE SAUCE

Heat in a double boiler 1 cup Hollandaise Sauce (above) mixed with ⅓ cup heavy cream, whipped stiff. Season with salt and pepper, and serve with vegetables, or with poached or baked fish, fish soufflés. Makes 1⅔ cups.

BÉARNAISE SAUCE

Flavor 1 cup Hollandaise Sauce (above) with 1 teaspoon each onion juice and tarragon vinegar, 1 teaspoon each finely chopped fresh tarragon and parsley. Serve with steak, and poached or baked fish. Makes 1 cup.

FIGARO SAUCE

Heat 1 cup Hollandaise Sauce (above) with ¼ cup tomato purée, stirring constantly. Serve with cold meats, fish. Makes 1¼ cups.

SPICY COCKTAIL SAUCE

To 1 cup mayonnaise add 1 tablespoon tarragon vinegar, ¼ cup chili sauce, 1 teaspoon onion juice, 1 tablespoon Worcestershire sauce and 2 dashes Tabasco sauce. Serve with raw oysters, seafood cocktails. Makes 1¼ cups.

CUCUMBER MAYONNAISE

Mix 1 cup mayonnaise with 1 cup sour cream and 1 teaspoon dry mustard. Add 2 cucumbers, peeled, seeded and chopped, and 2 tablespoons minced chives. Season with salt, pepper and ½ teaspoon grated onion. Serve with cold poached fish or seafood. Makes 2 cups.

CURRY DRESSING

Mix ½ cup mayonnaise with ½ cup chili sauce and blend well. Blend 2 tablespoons sauce with 2 tablespoons curry powder, combine with dressing. Chill well and serve with cold poached fish or seafood, or poultry. Makes 1 cup.

TARTAR SAUCE

To 1 cup mayonnaise add 1 teaspoon each finely chopped chives, parsley, onions and capers, 1 tablespoon each finely chopped gherkins and green olives. Serve well chilled with fried fish and seafood or cold poached fish or seafood. Makes 1 cup.

MAYONNAISE CAPER SAUCE

Heat 1 cup mayonnaise gently and blend in 2 tablespoons lemon juice and 2 tablespoons capers. Serve hot over poached or baked fish, or with vegetables. Makes 1 cup.

MUSTARD SAUCE

Mix well 1 cup sour cream with ½ cup prepared mustard. Blend well and serve well chilled with cold fish, seafood cocktails, ham, cold roast beef. Makes 1½ cups.

CHINESE FRUIT SAUCE

Combine in a saucepan ½ cup cider vinegar, 1 tablespoon finely minced green pepper, ¼ cup drained crushed pineapple. Cook, stirring, for 2 minutes. Add 2 teaspoons cornstarch mixed with ½ cup water and cook until the mixture is clear and glossy. Season with salt and finish with 1 tablespoon finely chopped pimiento. Serve well chilled, as a dip for deep-fried shrimp or fish, or with pork or ham. Makes about 1 cup.

ANCHOVY BUTTER

Blend ½ cup softened butter or margarine with 1 teaspoon anchovy paste, ⅛ teaspoon finely grated onion and ¼ teaspoon lemon juice. Spread over hot broiled fish, use as a sandwich spread and for appetizer canapés. Makes ½ cup.

HERB BUTTER

Blend 1 cup soft butter or margarine with 3 tablespoons mixed herbs: parsley, chives, and basil or chervil. Season with salt and pepper and spread on fish to be broiled. Use with vegetables. Makes 1 cup.

BROWNED BUTTER SAUCE

Melt ½ cup butter or margarine in a saucepan and cook it over low heat until lightly browned. Season with lemon juice, salt and pepper, and a few drops of Worcestershire sauce. For broiled or fried fish and seafood, vegetables, calf brains. Makes ½ cup.

ALMOND BUTTER SAUCE

Brown ½ cup butter or margarine, as above. Add ¼ cup slivered almonds and stir until the almonds are crisp. Add the juice of ½ lemon. For pan-browned, broiled or baked fish, vegetables. Makes ¾ cup.

LEMON BUTTER SAUCE

Brown ½ cup butter or margarine, as above. Season with 2 tablespoons lemon juice, salt and pepper. Serve with broiled or pan-browned fish, chicken. Makes ½ cup.

PAPRIKA BUTTER SAUCE

Brown ½ cup butter or margarine, as above. Add juice of ½ lemon and 1 tablespoon paprika. Serve with hot boiled seafood, broiled fish, veal scaloppine, chicken. Makes ½ cup.

CREAM SAUCE
(WHITE SAUCE)

Melt 2 tablespoons butter or margarine over low heat. Add 2 tablespoons flour, stir until smooth. Stir 1 cup milk or cream into the butter-flour mixture. Season with salt and pepper and cook, stirring constantly, until sauce is smooth and thickened. Makes 1 cup. This is a basic sauce which can be varied in many ways.

ALLEMANDE SAUCE

Make the basic Cream Sauce (above), reducing the flour to 1½ tablespoons. Just before serving, season the sauce with ½ teaspoon Worcestershire sauce and 1 teaspoon lemon juice, and beat in very slowly, drop by drop, the beaten yolk of 1 egg. Heat, stirring constantly, but do not allow the sauce to come to a boil. Serve immediately with poached or baked fish, poached chicken. Makes 1 cup.

HOT ANCHOVY CREAM SAUCE

Season 1 cup Cream Sauce (above) with 1 teaspoon anchovy paste and a little paprika. Serve with poached or baked fish.

CAPER CREAM SAUCE

Flavor 1 cup Cream Sauce (above) with 1 tablespoon white wine, 2 tablespoons capers and ½ teaspoon sugar. Serve with boiled or baked fish.

CHEESE SAUCE

Add to 1 cup Cream Sauce (above) ½ cup grated Swiss or American cheese and heat, stirring, until the cheese melts. Season with paprika and a few drops of Worcestershire sauce. Serve with poached or baked fish, noodles, vegetables.

HORSERADISH CREAM SAUCE

Add to 1 cup Cream Sauce (above) 2 tablespoons drained, grated horseradish and 1 teaspoon lemon juice or a little mustard. Serve with corned beef, boiled beef or lamb.

OYSTER SAUCE

Season 1 cup Cream Sauce (above) with salt and Worcestershire sauce. Just before serving add 1 cup finely chopped oysters, 1 tablespoon chopped parsley and a few drops of lemon juice. Heat through and serve with poached or baked fish.

MUSHROOM SAUCE

Make Cream Sauce (above). Brown ½ cup thinly sliced mushrooms in 3 tablespoons butter, add to sauce and season with salt, pepper and Worcestershire sauce. Serve with poached or baked fish, pasta, meat loaf, vegetables.

CREOLE SAUCE

Sauté 1 tablespoon chopped onion and ½ chopped green pepper in 2 tablespoons butter or margarine until the vegetables are just tender. Add 1½ cups tomatoes, peeled and quartered, and cook until the sauce is thick. Season with salt, pepper, 1 teaspoon sugar and a few grains of cayenne pepper. Serve with fish, vegetables, rice, pasta, chicken. Makes about 1 cup.

EGG SAUCE

Dice 6 hard-cooked eggs and mix with 1 cup light cream and 1 tablespoon butter or margarine. Season with salt and pepper and heat in the top of a double boiler. Just before serving, add 2 tablespoons finely minced parsley. Pour hot over boiled or baked fish. Traditional in New England as a sauce for poached salmon on Independence Day. Makes about 2 cups.

JAPANESE SOY-SAUCE DIP

Combine in a saucepan ½ cup beef broth, 2 tablespoons soy sauce, 2 tablespoons sherry and 1 teaspoon drained, grated horseradish. Bring to a quick boil. Serve hot as a dip for batter-fried seafood and vegetables. Makes about ⅔ cup.

Salad Dressings

There is such a broad range of salad dressings so easily obtainable that few people bother to make their own. Yet home-made dressings, especially mayonnaise, add a special quality to your salads and take little time.

MAYONNAISE

1 egg or 2 egg yolks
½ teaspoon prepared mustard
½ teaspoon salt
2 tablespoons lemon juice or wine vinegar
1 cup salad oil

With the beater of an electric mixer at medium speed, or with a hand beater, blend egg, seasonings and vinegar. Add oil, drop by drop at first, then in a slow, steady stream, beating constantly until mayonnaise is thick and fluffy. Egg yolks alone make a thicker mayonnaise than whole egg. Makes 1¼ cups.

Russian Dressing: To 1 cup mayonnaise, add ⅓ cup chili sauce. Optional additions: 2 tablespoons chopped stuffed olives or drained pickle relish; or 1 tablespoon grated horseradish and 1 teaspoon grated onion.

Thousand Island Dressing: To 1 cup mayonnaise, add ⅓ cup chili sauce; 1 hard-cooked egg, chopped; 2 tablespoons chopped stuffed olives; 1 tablespoon chopped green pepper.

Chutney Dressing: To 1 cup mayonnaise, add 2 tablespoons drained chutney, finely chopped.

Mustard Mayonnaise: To 1 cup mayonnaise, add 1 tablespoon or more prepared mustard, to taste.

BLENDER MAYONNAISE

Using Mayonnaise recipe (page 175), put ½ cup salad oil and remaining ingredients in blender container. Blend until smooth. Add remaining oil in a slow, steady stream, blending at low speed until all the oil is added. Makes 1¼ cups.

CLASSIC FRENCH DRESSING

⅓ cup cider vinegar
1 cup salad oil
1 teaspoon salt
¼ teaspoon pepper

Combine ingredients in a jar or bowl; shake or whisk well. Shake again before using. Makes 1⅓ cups. For a less rich dressing, use ½ cup vinegar.

Italian-Style Dressing: Use wine vinegar and olive oil; add 1 clove garlic, finely chopped, and ½ teaspoon crushed basil.

Caper French Dressing: Add 2 teaspoons chopped capers, half a garlic clove and 1 mashed anchovy fillet.

Ketchup French Dressing: Add 3 tablespoons ketchup, 1 green onion, finely chopped, and 1 stalk celery, finely chopped.

PARMESAN SALAD DRESSING

3 tablespoons wine vinegar
½ cup salad oil
¼ teaspoon Worcestershire sauce
3 tablespoons Parmesan cheese
½ teaspoon salt
Dash pepper
Dash paprika

Combine ingredients in a jar or bowl; shake or whisk well. Makes about ¾ cup.

TOMATO-SOUP DRESSING

¼ cup sugar
1 teaspoon salt
1 teaspoon dry mustard
1 tablespoon paprika
1 can (10½ ounces) condensed tomato soup
1 cup salad oil
½ cup cider vinegar
1 teaspoon Worcestershire sauce

Combine sugar, salt, mustard and paprika; stir into tomato soup. Add remaining ingredients, mix well. Makes about 3 cups.

BUTTERMILK SALAD DRESSING

¼ cup salad oil
1 tablespoon grated onion
¼ teaspoon prepared mustard
Salt, pepper
1 cup buttermilk

Blend oil, onion, mustard, salt and pepper. Gradually stir in buttermilk. Chill before serving. Makes 1¼ cups.

BLUE-CHEESE DRESSING

2 ounces blue cheese (½ cup crumbled)
4 ounces cream cheese
½ cup sour cream
Pepper

Blend ingredients, adding more sour cream as desired to thin mixture. Season to taste, serve chilled. Makes 1½ cups.

SOUR-CREAM DRESSING

½ cup sour cream
¼ teaspoon prepared mustard
2 teaspoons cider vinegar
Salt and pepper
¼ cup mayonnaise
Chopped chives (optional)

Combine sour cream with mustard, vinegar, salt and pepper to taste. Fold in mayonnaise. Add chopped chives if desired. Makes ¾ cup.

Enjoy a hearty supper of Greek Salad—fresh, raw vegetables, including escarole, tomatoes, radishes, red onions and brined black olives, nutritionally supplemented with soft white cheese, hard-cooked egg and nippy anchovies. Use a home-blended oil-and-vinegar dressing, or a prepared bottled dressing for extra convenience. (See page 175.)

Two kinds of salads: one a high-protein dish to enjoy as salad or main course, the other a luncheon salad, fresh and appealing. The Three-Bean Salad includes kidney beans, green beans and wax beans, for contrast in color, flavor and texture. Thin rings of sweet red onion add snap. The fruit salad includes bananas, oranges, pears and grapes, and nuts for crunch. Make your choice of fruits seasonal. Cottage cheese, in a variety of styles to suit every taste, is always in season—a favorite for calorie counters. (See page 172.)

CONVENIENCE FOODS—GOOD AND EASY

You'll particularly appreciate having the makings of a variety of quick-cook meals on your shelves when you have little time to shop . . . and less time to cook. When you must count pennies, canned and frozen foods and prepared dinners can help you to save money as well as time.

One practical way to use convenience foods is to combine them with leftovers to make nutritious and satisfying meals. Fresh savory vegetables such as onion, celery or green pepper perk up flavors of prepared foods, and add texture and color contrast. Small amounts of fish, meat, poultry, eggs and cheese help extend protein values—economically.

Use your ingenuity in adding sauces and combining ingredients to achieve your own individual flavor effects. One cream-style soup may be substituted for another in most recipes; other ingredients and toppings can be varied as you like them.

There are times when "prepare as the package directs" is the best way to solve a mealtime problem. Add your own fresh accent for extra satisfaction . . . something as simple as a sprinkling of parsley or cheese to top a prepared casserole.

Be creative!

MAYONNAISE-ONION PUFFS

12 thin onion slices
12 slices round "cocktail" bread
6 tablespoons mayonnaise

Put an onion slice on each bread round and cover with ½ tablespoon mayonnaise. Broil 3 to 5 minutes, until mayonnaise is puffy and lightly browned. Makes 4 to 6 servings.

Tip: Trim crusts from regular bread slices, cut into quarters, use as base for puffs.

MAYONNAISE-CHEESE PUFFS

Substitute 12 round slices of American cheese for onion slices in above recipe.

FRESH VEGETABLES WITH ONION DIP

1 envelope (1⅛ ounces) toasted onion party dip mix
1 pint sour cream
  Raw vegetables (carrot sticks, celery sticks, cucumber sticks, cauliflowerets, cherry tomatoes)

Combine contents of envelope with sour cream. Chill. Place bowl of toasted onion party dip in center of platter. Makes about 2 cups. Surround with raw vegetables for dipping.

BEAN DIP

  1 can (1 pound) vegetarian beans with tomato sauce
  1 teaspoon dry mustard
¼ teaspoon chili powder

Combine all ingredients in blender container and whirl until puréed; or force through a sieve. Makes about 1¼ cups. Serve with raw vegetables as above.

CHEESY BISCUIT STICKS

  2 cups biscuit mix
½ cup grated sharp Cheddar cheese
½ cup cold water

Combine biscuit mix and cheese, mix with water according to package directions. Roll dough into a 6-inch-by-10-inch rectangle. Cut into 24 strips, about ½ inch by 3 inches. Bake in a very hot oven (450°F) 10 to 12 minutes, until browned and crusty.

SPICY BISCUIT STICKS

Prepare as above, but substitute 1 teaspoon Italian Seasoning for the cheese.

HAM-AND-EGGS CRESCENT PIZZA

This quiche-like meal or snack won a prize in the Pillsbury Bake-off, 1975.

¼ **cup chopped onion, or 1 tablespoon instant minced onion**
1 **tablespoon butter or margarine**
1 **cup (4 ounces) cubed cooked ham**
1 **can (8 ounces) refrigerator quick crescent rolls, any flavor**
4 **eggs**
1 **teaspoon salt**
¼ **teaspoon pepper**
½ **cup milk**
1 **cup (4 ounces) shredded Swiss or Monterey Jack cheese**
1 **tablespoon chopped chives or ripe olives**

Cook onion in butter until transparent. Remove from heat, stir in ham. Separate crescent dough into 4 rectangles. Place in ungreased 12-inch pizza or 13-inch-by-9-inch pan; press over bottom and ½ inch up sides to form crust, sealing perforations. Spread ham mixture over dough. Beat eggs, blend in seasonings, milk and cheese. Pour over ham. Sprinkle with chives or olives. Bake in a moderate oven (350°F) 25 to 28 minutes, until golden brown. Serve immediately. Makes 6 to 8 main-dish servings or about 2 dozen snacks.

Note: To make ahead, prepare, cover and refrigerate up to 2 hours; bake as directed.

Refrigerate any leftovers. To reheat, wrap in foil; heat at 350°F 10 to 12 minutes.

BEEF POT

2 **tablespoons butter or margarine**
¼ **cup chopped onion**
1 **clove garlic, finely chopped**
2 **cups cubed cooked beef**
1 **can (10¾ ounces) condensed vegetable soup**
¼ **cup water**

Heat butter in a saucepan and cook onion and garlic until softened. Add beef and cook, stirring occasionally, until lightly browned. Add soup and water and heat until bubbling. Makes 3 to 4 servings.

CREAMED CHICKEN

2 **tablespoons butter or margarine**
¼ **cup finely chopped onion**
½ **cup finely chopped celery**
1 **can (10½ ounces) condensed cream of mushroom soup**
½ **cup milk, light cream or sour cream**
2 **cups cubed cooked chicken**

Melt butter in a saucepan and cook onion and celery until softened. Stir in soup and milk. Heat to the boiling point. Add chicken, simmer 5 minutes. Serve over toast or waffles. Makes 4 servings.

BEANS HAWAIIAN

2 **tablespoons oil**
½ **green pepper, slivered**
1 **small onion, thinly sliced and separated into rings**
¼ **cup thinly sliced celery**
1 **clove garlic, minced**
1 **can (1 pound) beans and pork with tomato sauce**
1 **can (8¼ ounces) pineapple tidbits, drained**
1 **teaspoon prepared mustard**

Heat oil, cook green pepper, onion, celery and garlic until just tender. Add beans, pineapple and mustard, stir and heat through. Makes 2 to 3 servings.

BEANS AND BEEFBURGERS

1 **tablespoon oil**
2 **tablespoons chopped onion**
4 **frozen beefburgers**
1 **can (1 pound) vegetarian beans with tomato sauce**

Heat oil in skillet and cook onions until softened. Push onions to side of pan and brown burgers on one side. Turn burgers. Drain excess fat, add beans to pan. Cook until beans are heated through and burgers are done to taste. Makes 4 servings.

CHILI-CHEESE BEANS

1 **package (8 ounces) chili tomato dinner mix**
1 **pound ground beef**
4 **cups hot water**
1 **can (1 pound) vegetarian beans with tomato sauce**
½ **cup shredded American cheese**
¼ **cup finely chopped raw onion**
2 **tablespoons ketchup**

Prepare mix with beef and water as directed. After mixture has simmered, add beans and cheese. Heat, stirring occasionally, until cheese melts. Stir in onion and ketchup. Makes 4 servings.

Beans—economical, hearty, good eating, high in protein—belong in family meals, on their own or as meat extenders. In the Southwest they take on Mexican zest with chili and corn chips. In New England the beans are sweetened with molasses, spiced with mustard. Begin with dried beans, or par-cooked beans, or canned beans available in a variety of styles, ready to eat as is or to be transformed into deliciously different casseroles. (See page 128.)

BEANS-AND-FRANK STEW

**1 can (1 pound) vegetarian beans with
     tomato sauce**
1 can (1 pound) mixed vegetables
4 frankfurters, sliced in rounds
2 tablespoons instant minced onion

Empty beans into saucepan. Drain vegetables,
save juice. Add vegetables, ¼ cup vegetable
juice, frankfurters and onion to pan. Bring to
boil and simmer 5 minutes. Makes 2 to 4
servings.

SALISBURY PATTIES AND
RED EYE GRAVY

**1 envelope (1⅛ ounces) ground beef
     seasoning mix with onions**
¼ cup dry bread crumbs
¼ cup water
1 egg, beaten
1 pound ground beef
1 tablespoon oil
½ cup strong coffee
2 tablespoons ketchup

Combine contents of envelope, bread crumbs,
water and egg with ground beef. Let stand 10
minutes. Form into 4 patties. Heat oil in large
skillet, pan-fry patties to desired doneness.
Drain off excess fat. Add coffee and ketchup
to pan, bring to boil, stirring often, and spoon
over patties. Makes 4 servings.

SOYBURGER AU JUS

1 pound ground beef with soy extender
½ teaspoon salt
⅛ teaspoon pepper
1 tablespoon grated onion
1 envelope (¾ ounce) au jus gravy mix
2 cups water

Combine meat and soy mix with salt, pepper
and onion. Form into 4 patties. Pan-fry in
lightly greased heated skillet on both sides to
desired doneness, remove from pan and keep
warm. Drain excess fat from pan. Add au jus
gravy mix and water to pan. Bring to boil,
stirring often. Pour 2 to 3 tablespoons gravy
over each burger and serve the rest in a gravy
boat, to spoon over potatoes or rice. Makes 4
servings.

MEATBALL STEW

**1 package (10 ounces) frozen mixed
     vegetables**
1 can (16 ounces) meatballs in gravy
1 tablespoon instant minced onion
½ cup sour cream, at room temperature

Thaw frozen vegetables just enough to separate. Combine with meatballs and minced
onion; cook, stirring occasionally, until vegetables are tender. Stir in sour cream and heat
just to boiling point. Makes 3 to 4 servings.

BAKED RAVIOLI MARINARA

**2 packages (12 ounces each) frozen meat or
     cheese ravioli**
3 cups prepared marinara spaghetti sauce
¼ cup grated Parmesan cheese

Following package directions, cook ravioli for
12 minutes; drain. In a shallow baking pan,
layer sauce, ravioli and Parmesan cheese, ending with sauce and cheese. Bake in a moderately hot oven (375°F) about 30 minutes,
until bubbling and browned. Makes 4 to 6
servings.

SPAGHETTI AND SALAMI

**1 package (8 ounces) spaghetti dinner,
     Italian style**
1 can (2 ounces) sliced mushrooms, drained
¼ pound salami, sliced
1 teaspoon minced parsley
½ teaspoon oregano
Parmesan cheese

Prepare spaghetti and sauce as directed. Place
spaghetti in a greased 1½-quart casserole, add
sauce. Top with mushrooms and salami,
sprinkle with parsley, oregano and Parmesan
cheese. Bake in a moderately hot oven
(375°F) 15 minutes, or until cheese browns
slightly. Makes 4 servings.

SPAGHETTI IN PEPPER SHELLS

2 large green peppers
¼ cup chopped onion
1 clove garlic, minced
2 tablespoons vegetable oil
**1 can (15 ounces) spaghetti with
     meatballs in sauce**
2 tablespoons grated Parmesan cheese

Cut peppers in half lengthwise, remove seeds
and pith. Cook in boiling salted water 4 minutes; drain. Cook onion and garlic in oil until
tender. Combine with spaghetti and meatballs
and fill pepper halves. Bake in a moderate
oven (350°F) 10 minutes. Sprinkle with
cheese, bake 5 minutes longer. Makes 4 servings.

QUICK MACARONI SUPPER

**1 package (7¼ ounces) macaroni and
     cheese dinner**

1 can (10½ ounces) condensed cream of
    chicken soup or cream of
    mushroom soup
½ cup milk
1 cup cubed cooked chicken, or 1 can (6½
    ounces) chunk-style tuna, drained
1 cup cooked or canned vegetables

Prepare macaroni and cheese dinner as package directs. Stir in remaining ingredients and heat to boiling point. Makes 4 servings.

MAC SAUSAGE

1 package (8 ounces) macaroni and
    Cheddar dinner
1 tablespoon butter or margarine
2¼ cups boiling water
2 Polish sausages, about ½ pound each,
    sliced

Combine macaroni and sauce mix from dinner with butter and boiling water in a 2-quart casserole. Add Polish sausage. Cover and bake in a moderately hot oven (375°F) 20 to 25 minutes. Stir before serving. Makes 4 servings. (See photo, page 184).

SPAGHETTI-SPINACH BAKE

1 can (15½ ounces) Italian-style spaghetti
1 package (10 ounces) frozen chopped
    spinach, cooked and drained
1 can (3 ounces) sliced mushrooms, drained
1 teaspoon instant minced onion
⅛ teaspoon garlic powder
1 tablespoon butter or margarine
¼ cup dry bread crumbs

Combine spaghetti, spinach, mushrooms, onion and garlic powder in a greased 1-quart casserole. Melt butter, stir in crumbs; sprinkle over casserole. Bake in a moderate oven (350°F) 25 to 30 minutes, until casserole is bubbling and crumbs are browned. Makes 2 to 3 servings.

TUNA TETRAZZINI

1 tablespoon butter or margarine
2 tablespoons chopped onion
2 tablespoons chopped green pepper
1 can (10½ ounces) condensed cream of
    mushroom soup
¾ cup milk or water
1 cup shredded process American cheese
½ pound spaghetti, cooked and drained
2 cans (6½ ounces each) chunk-style tuna

Melt butter in a saucepan and cook onion and pepper until softened. Stir in soup, milk and cheese. Cook over low heat, stirring often, until cheese is melted. Add spaghetti and tuna, heat through. Makes 4 to 6 servings.

TUNA-MACARONI BAKE

1 package (8 ounces) macaroni and
    Cheddar dinner
1 tablespoon butter or margarine
2¼ cups boiling water
1 can (6½ ounces) chunk-style tuna,
    drained
1 can (3 ounces) mushrooms, drained
1 cup crushed potato chips

Combine macaroni, sauce mix from package, butter and water in a 2-quart casserole. Add tuna and mushrooms. Cover and bake in a moderately hot oven (375°F) 20 minutes, stir. Top with potato chips and bake, uncovered, 5 minutes longer. Makes 4 servings.

FISH STICKS CACCIATORE

1 package (1 pound) frozen fish sticks
1 can (8 ounces) tomato sauce
1 teaspoon parsley flakes
¼ teaspoon oregano
⅛ teaspoon garlic powder

Place fish sticks in a shallow pan. Combine remaining ingredients and pour over fish sticks. Bake in hot oven (400°F) 12 minutes. Makes 4 servings.

SWEET-AND-PUNGENT FISH STICKS

2 tablespoons oil
1 package (1 pound) frozen fish sticks
1 can (15¼ ounces) pineapple tidbits,
    undrained
½ cup diced green pepper
¼ cup soy sauce
1 teaspoon vinegar
1 teaspoon cornstarch

Heat oil in a large skillet and brown fish sticks on both sides. Combine remaining ingredients, mix well, add to pan. Cook about 5 minutes, until sauce has thickened slightly. Makes 4 servings.

BEANY FISH BAKE

2 cans (1 pound) beans with tomato sauce
1 tablespoon instant minced onion
1 package (1 pound) frozen breaded cod fillets
6 slices American cheese

Combine beans with onion and pour into a baking pan. Place fillets on beans and bake in

Quick-to-prepare macaroni and Cheddar casserole is more than just convenient. It is a practical, sensible way to provide important nutrients at low cost. And it's a crowd-pleaser, on its own or as a menu supplement. Sliced Polish sausage has been added to this casserole; you may use frankfurters or ham or other meats, or more cheese, for more portions. (See page 183.)

a hot oven (400°F) for 15 minutes. Top each fish portion with a slice of American cheese, bake 10 minutes longer. Makes 6 servings.

TUNA BURGERS

1 can (6½ ounces) chunk-style tuna
3 tablespoons mayonnaise
¼ cup chopped celery
1 tablespoon instant minced onion
3 hamburger buns, split and buttered
6 thin slices tomato

Combine tuna, mayonnaise, celery and minced onion. Spread buns with mixture, broil 6 inches from heat about 3 minutes, until hot. Garnish with tomato. Makes 6 open-faced burgers, 3 main-dish servings.

QUICK SHRIMP CREOLE

1 envelope (1½ ounces) spaghetti sauce mix
2 tablespoons oil
1 small onion, chopped
¼ green pepper, chopped
1 package (12 ounces) frozen peeled shrimp

Prepare sauce as directed. Heat oil in saucepan and cook onion and green pepper until softened. Add sauce and shrimp. Bring to a boil, cook 5 minutes. Makes 4 servings.

MACKEREL SPANISH STYLE

1 can (1 pound) mackerel
1 can (8 ounces) Spanish-style tomato sauce
2 cups hot cooked rice

Drain mackerel and separate into large flakes. Heat sauce just to boiling, add mackerel, heat through. Serve over rice. Makes 4 servings.

CRUSTY SARDINES IN TOMATO SAUCE

2 cans (15 ounces each) sardines in tomato sauce
2 tablespoons water
1 cup packaged stuffing mix
2 tablespoons butter or margarine

Empty sardines into a greased 1-quart casserole. Add water, top with stuffing mix and dot with butter. Bake in a moderately hot oven (375°F) 15 to 20 minutes, until bubbling and browned. Makes 4 servings.

SPEEDY JAMBALAYA

2 tablespoons oil
1 package (8 ounces) beef-flavored rice dinner

1¾ cups hot water
1 can (8 ounces) Spanish-style tomato sauce
2 cups cubed cooked ham
1 can (4½ ounces) shrimp, rinsed and drained

Heat oil in a large deep skillet. Add rice and vermicelli from package and brown lightly. Add water, tomato sauce and contents of seasoning packet. Bring to a boil, reduce heat, cover and cook about 15 minutes, until liquid is absorbed and rice is tender. Stir in ham and shrimp and heat through. Makes 6 servings.

QUICK ARROZ CON POLLO

2 tablespoons vegetable oil
1 medium onion, diced
½ green pepper, diced
1 package (8 ounces) chicken-flavored rice dinner
2¾ cups hot water
3 cups cubed cooked chicken or turkey
¼ cup slivered pimiento

Heat oil in a deep skillet. Add onion and green pepper, cook until soft and just browned. Add rice-vermicelli mixture and cook, stirring often, until vermicelli is light brown. Slowly add water to skillet, stir in contents of seasoning packet. Cover skillet and simmer about 15 minutes, until liquid is absorbed and rice is tender. Stir in chicken or turkey and heat through. Garnish with pimiento. Makes 6 servings.

SPANISH RICE AND CHICKEN

Substitute 2 cups tomato juice and ¾ cup hot water for water in above recipe.

QUICK RICE AND BLACK BEANS

4 slices bacon, diced
¼ cup chopped onion
1 clove garlic, minced
2 cups cooked rice
1 can (1 pound) black beans, drained
1 teaspoon salt

Fry bacon until crisp, remove from pan. Cook onion and garlic until golden in fat remaining in pan. Stir in rice, beans and salt to taste, and heat through. Sprinkle with crumbled bacon. Makes 4 servings.

QUICK CHOP SUEY

2 tablespoons oil
1 small onion, thinly sliced
½ green pepper, slivered
1 clove garlic, minced

1 can (1 pound) Chinese mixed vegetables, drained
1 teaspoon cornstarch
¼ cup water
2 tablespoons soy sauce
2 cups diced cooked chicken, ham or pork

Heat oil, cook onion, green pepper and garlic, stirring occasionally, until softened. Add Chinese mixed vegetables, bring to boil. Mix cornstarch with water and soy sauce and stir into pan. Cook 2 minutes longer, until sauce bubbles and thickens. Add chicken, heat. Makes 4 servings.

SPANISH HASH

¼ cup oil
1 onion, sliced
1 small green pepper, diced
1 can (8 ounces) potatoes, drained and diced
1 can (12 ounces) luncheon meat, diced
¼ teaspoon salt
⅛ teaspoon marjoram

Heat oil and cook onion and green pepper until softened. Add potatoes, luncheon meat and seasonings. Cook, stirring occasionally with a fork, until meat and potatoes are lightly browned. Makes 4 servings.

HASH FLORENTINE WITH POACHED EGGS

1 can (15 ounces) corned-beef hash
1 tablespoon vegetable oil
4 eggs
1 package (9 ounces) frozen creamed spinach

Remove corned-beef hash from can and cut into 4 slices. Heat oil in a large skillet and brown slices on both sides. Make a hollow in each slice with a tablespoon. Drop an egg into each hollow, cover pan, cook until whites are set. Meanwhile, prepare creamed spinach according to package directions. Spoon spinach around hash and egg on serving plates. Makes 4 servings.

SAUERKRAUT AND SAUSAGE

1 can (1 pound) sauerkraut, rinsed and drained
1 medium onion, thinly sliced
1 Polish sausage, about ½ pound, sliced
⅛ teaspoon pepper
1 cup chicken bouillon

Combine all ingredients in a saucepan and bring to boil. Simmer 10 minutes. Makes 4 servings.

Variation: Substitute 2 cups cubed cooked ham for sausage.

CREOLE FRANKS

2 tablespoons oil
1 small onion, finely chopped
¼ green pepper, diced
1 can (10½ ounces) condensed tomato soup
2 teaspoons sugar
2 teaspoons lemon juice
¼ teaspoon garlic powder
¼ teaspoon cayenne pepper
8 to 12 frankfurters, split

Heat oil in a saucepan and cook onion and green pepper until softened. Add soup and seasonings, simmer 10 minutes. Add frankfurters and cook 10 minutes more. Makes 4 to 6 servings.

QUICK HAM CUMBERLAND

1 jar (12 ounces) currant jelly
½ orange, juice and grated rind
½ lemon, juice and grated rind
1 teaspoon instant minced onion
½ teaspoon dry mustard
¼ teaspoon ground ginger
2 pounds sliced ham

Melt jelly in saucepan over low heat, add other ingredients except ham and heat slowly just to boiling point, stirring occasionally. Add ham slices and heat through. Makes 8 servings.

HAM-AND-POTATO SCALLOP

2 cans (1 pound each) sliced potatoes, drained
1 small onion, thinly sliced
½ pound sliced ham
1 can (10½ ounces) condensed cream of chicken soup
½ cup milk
¼ cup dry bread crumbs
2 tablespoons melted butter or margarine
½ teaspoon paprika

Layer potato, onion and ham slices in a greased shallow baking pan. Combine soup and milk, add. Sprinkle with bread crumbs mixed with melted butter and paprika. Bake in a hot oven (400°F) 25 to 30 minutes, until bubbling and browned. Makes 4 servings.

HAM STRIPS AND MACARONI BAKE

1 package (8 ounces) macaroni and Cheddar dinner
1 tablespoon butter or margarine

2 cups boiling water
1 can (8 ounces) canned tomatoes
1 cup cooked ham strips

Combine macaroni, sauce mix from package, butter and water in a 2-quart casserole. Add tomatoes and ham strips. Cover and bake in a moderately hot oven (375°F) 35 minutes. Makes 4 servings.

TONGUE IN MUSTARD SAUCE

2 tablespoons butter or margarine
1 tablespoon flour
1 tablespoon prepared mustard
1 teaspoon salt
¾ cup milk
1 tablespoon lemon juice
1 teaspoon Worcestershire sauce
1 pound cooked tongue, sliced

Melt butter over low heat, stir in flour, mustard and salt. Cook 1 minute. Gradually add milk and cook, stirring, until sauce thickens. Remove from heat, stir in lemon juice and Worcestershire. Spoon over tongue slices. Makes 4 servings.

TONGUE SALAD VINAIGRETTE

1 can (about 6 ounces) tongue
1 jar (2 ounces) pimientos, drained
¼ pound Swiss cheese, cut into strips
1 small onion, sliced and separated into rings
1 can (8 ounces) mixed vegetables, drained
½ cup bottled Italian dressing

Cut tongue and pimientos into slivers. Toss all ingredients with salad dressing. Makes 2 to 3 servings.

BEEF-STEW PIE

2 cups diced cooked beef
1 can (16 ounces) mixed vegetables, undrained
1 can (8 ounces) cooked potatoes, drained
1 envelope (¾ ounce) mushroom gravy mix
¼ cup water
1 package (8 ounces) refrigerator biscuits

Combine beef and vegetables in a saucepan. Blend gravy mix with water and add to pan. Heat, stirring occasionally, just to the boiling point. Pour into 8-inch square pan. Top with biscuits and bake in a very hot oven (450°F) 8 minutes, or until biscuits brown. Makes 4 servings.

POTATO-TOPPED LUNCHEON MEAT

1 can (12 ounces) luncheon meat, sliced
1 tablespoon instant minced onion
1 teaspoon parsley flakes
2½ to 3 cups mashed potatoes (prepared with instant mashed potatoes)
1 tablespoon butter or margarine
Paprika

Arrange meat slices in shallow pan. Stir instant minced onion and parsley flakes into mashed potatoes and spread on meat. Dot with butter and sprinkle with paprika. Bake in a moderately hot oven (375°F) about 25 minutes, until heated through and browned. Makes 4 servings.

DEEP-DISH TURKEY PIE

1 can (8 ounces) mixed vegetables
Milk
1 can (10½ ounces) condensed cream of mushroom soup
2 cups cubed cooked turkey
1 teaspoon instant minced onion
¼ teaspoon thyme
1 cup biscuit mix
¼ cup water

Drain vegetables, pouring liquid into a measuring cup. Add enough milk to make ½ cup. Combine with soup in round 1½-quart baking dish. Stir in cubed turkey, vegetables, onion and thyme. Combine biscuit mix and water as package directs. Roll dough into a circle 1 inch smaller in diameter than the baking dish. Cut into 8 pie-shaped wedges, arrange on top of turkey mixture. Bake in a very hot oven (450°F) 15 to 20 minutes, until browned. Makes 4 servings.

GARDEN CASSEROLE BAKE

1 package (9 ounces) frozen cut green beans
1 package (10 ounces) frozen kernel corn
1 can (10½ ounces) condensed cream of mushroom soup
1 cup shredded Swiss or Cheddar cheese
¼ teaspoon marjoram
1 can (3½ ounces) French-fried onions

Cook vegetables according to package directions. Drain, reserving liquid. Combine mushroom soup and ½ cup of vegetable liquid in a 1-quart casserole. Stir in vegetables, cheese, marjoram and half the onions. Bake in a moderate oven (350°F) 25 minutes. Top with remaining onions, bake 5 minutes longer. Makes 4 to 6 servings.

HAWAIIAN FRANKS IN WRAPS

**1 package (8 ounces) refrigerator
    crescent rolls**
4 teaspoons prepared mustard
½ cup shredded Cheddar cheese
**1 can (8 ounces) pineapple chunks,
    drained**
8 frankfurters

Separate triangles of dough and flatten
slightly. Spread lightly with mustard. Sprinkle
1 tablespoon cheese along wide end of each
triangle. Top with 2 pineapple chunks and a
frankfurter, roll up. Bake seam side down on
a baking sheet in a very hot oven (450°F) 8
minutes, until brown. Makes 8 servings.

FRANKS WITH CANNED YAMS AND TOMATOES

1 can (1 pound 2 ounces) yams
2 firm, large tomatoes, cut in half
4 teaspoons dry bread crumbs
2 tablespoons Italian-style salad dressing
3 tablespoons melted butter or margarine
4 large frankfurters

On broiler pan, arrange yams and tomatoes,
cut side up. Sprinkle tomatoes with bread
crumbs and drizzle with salad dressing. Brush
yams with melted butter. Broil 5 to 6 inches
from heat for 5 minutes. Cut slashes in frankfurters and place on pan with yams and
tomatoes. Broil 5 minutes. Makes 4 servings.

BAKING

THE BREAD BOX

It's always a comfortable feeling to have an adequate supply of bread on hand. Every meal of the day can be supplemented with bread in some form—rolls, biscuits, muffins and sweet breads. Yeast breads take some time to make, but each time the dough is set aside to rise, you are free to do other things. Quick breads can be whipped up in no time at all.

Yeast Breads

Yeast breads are possibly the easiest and the most satisfying product of your home oven. Even a not-quite-perfect home-baked bread can be a joy to eat. If your electric mixer has a bread hook, it will knead the dough for you. Otherwise, you can join devotees who claim that kneading bread is not only good exercise, but a fine way to work off frustrations. Turn the dough out on a lightly floured board, fold it toward you, push it down and away. Make a quarter turn and repeat, keeping the board dusted with flour, until the dough is well blended, smooth, elastic and not sticky to the touch. A novice will need about 15 minutes to achieve this, an expert about 10 minutes, the automatic bread hook about 3 minutes.

Rising is the next step. Roll the ball of dough in a greased bowl to keep the surface from drying; cover with a towel and set the bowl in a warm place, free from drafts, to encourage the yeast to grow and stretch the gluten in the flour. Because of differences in temperature and humidity, rising times given are approximate. When the dough seems to be double in volume, test it by poking it with a finger; if the dent remains, the dough is ready to be punched down, kneaded briefly, and either shaped or set to rise for the second time (as directed in the recipe). Some breads are allowed to rise again after shaping; others go directly into a cold oven and rise in the gradually increasing heat.

WHITE BREAD

1 package active dry yeast
1 cup very warm water
3 tablespoons sugar
2 teaspoons salt
1 cup milk
¼ cup butter or margarine
6 to 7 cups flour

Dissolve yeast in warm water with sugar. Add salt. Warm milk with butter just until butter melts. Add 2 cups flour to yeast mixture, beat well. Add tepid milk and butter, beat again. Add remaining flour to make a soft dough that can be handled. Knead on a floured board until smooth and elastic. Grease a bowl, turn dough in it to coat lightly, cover and let rise until double in bulk, about 1½ hours. Punch down, knead again, let rise until double, about 1 hour. Punch down, divide in half. Shape each half into a loaf, place in greased 9-inch-by-5-inch loaf pan. Let rise until double, about 45 minutes. Bake in a hot oven (400°F) about 45 minutes, until the loaves are well browned. Makes 2 loaves. (See photo, page 193.)

Raisin Bread: After the second rising, knead 1 to 2 cups raisins into the bread dough.

FRENCH BREAD

2 packages active dry yeast
1 tablespoon sugar

2 cups very warm water
1 tablespoon salt
¼ cup oil
5 to 6 cups flour
    Corn meal
1 egg white mixed with 1 tablespoon water

Dissolve yeast and sugar in warm water. Stir in salt and oil. Add flour gradually to make a stiff dough. Knead on a lightly floured board about 10 minutes. Place in a greased bowl, turn to grease top, cover and let rise until doubled, about 1½ hours. Punch down. Turn out onto a floured board and shape into 2 long loaves. Place on a baking sheet that has been sprinkled with corn meal. Slash the loaves diagonally with a sharp knife or cut with scissors; brush with egg-white mixture. Place in a cold oven, turn temperature setting to 400°F and bake 30 to 40 minutes, or until bread is well browned. Makes 2 loaves. (See photo, page 193.)

PUMPERNICKEL BREAD

1½ cups cold water
 ¾ cup yellow corn meal
1½ cups boiling water
1½ teaspoons salt
  2 tablespoons sugar
  2 tablespoons butter or margarine
  1 tablespoon caraway seeds
  2 packages active dry yeast
 ¼ cup very warm water
  2 cups mashed potatoes
  4 cups rye flour
  4 cups whole-wheat flour

Add cold water to corn meal in a saucepan, stir until smooth. Stir in boiling water and cook, stirring constantly, until thick. Add salt, sugar, butter and caraway seeds. Cool to lukewarm. Dissolve yeast in warm water. Add yeast and mashed potatoes to corn-meal mixture. Mix well. Beat in flour. Knead until smooth and satiny. Put into greased bowl, turn once, cover and let rise until doubled, about 1 hour. Punch down, divide dough into 3 portions and form into round loaves. Place on greased pans and let rise until doubled, about 45 minutes. Bake in a moderately hot oven (375°F) for about 1 hour. Makes 3 loaves.

SWEDISH LIMPA BREAD

  2 packages active dry yeast
1½ cups very warm water
 ¼ cup sugar
 ¼ cup molasses

1 tablespoon salt
2 tablespoons oil
2½ cups rye flour
2½ cups white flour
    Grated rind of 2 oranges
1 teaspoon anise seed

Sprinkle yeast on water, add sugar, stir to dissolve. Add molasses and salt. Add oil. Beat in rye flour, beat well. Gradually add enough white flour to make a soft dough. Knead on a lightly floured board until dough is smooth and elastic. Turn in a greased bowl, cover and let rise until double in bulk, about 1½ hours. Punch down, knead again, let rise until double, about 1 hour. Punch down again, add orange rind and anise seed, and knead to distribute evenly. Shape into 2 balls or long loaves, arrange on a baking sheet, let rise until double in bulk, about 45 minutes. Bake in a moderately hot oven (375°F) about 40 minutes, until richly browned. Makes 2 loaves. (See photo, page 193.)

OATMEAL BREAD

  3 cups boiling water
1½ cups regular oatmeal
 ¾ cup molasses
  1 tablespoon salt
 ⅓ cup butter or margarine
  2 packages active dry yeast
 ½ cup very warm water
  7 to 8 cups flour

Pour boiling water over oatmeal in a mixing bowl. Add molasses, salt, butter. Soften yeast in warm water, add to mixing bowl. Beat in flour gradually to make a firm dough. Knead well on a floured board, until dough is smooth and elastic. Roll in a greased bowl to coat, cover bowl, let rise about 1½ hours, until double in bulk. Punch down, knead again, let rise again until double, about 45 minutes. Divide dough in half, shape each half into a 9-inch round, place each in a greased 9-inch layer pan. Let rise until double in bulk, about 30 minutes. Bake in a hot oven (400°F) about 40 minutes, until bread is richly browned. Makes 2 loaves.

EGG TWIST

  2 packages active dry yeast
 ¼ cup sugar
  2 cups very warm water
6½ to 7½ cups flour
  1 tablespoon salt
 ¼ cup oil
  2 eggs, beaten
    Sesame seeds (optional)

Dissolve yeast and sugar in warm water. Add enough flour to make a heavy batter, beat well. Add salt, oil and all but 2 tablespoons of beaten egg. (Reserve remainder of egg to brush on loaves before baking.) Add more flour to make a firm but not hard dough. Knead on a lightly floured board until smooth and satiny. Turn dough in a greased bowl to coat lightly, cover and let rise in a warm place until double in bulk, about 1½ hours. Punch down, knead lightly again, let rise again until double, about 1 hour. Punch down. Divide dough in half. Divide each half into thirds and shape 3 uniform ropes. Braid, press to seal at both ends. Let rise on greased baking sheet until double in bulk, about 45 minutes. Brush with reserved egg, sprinkle with sesame seeds, if desired. Bake in a hot oven (400°F) about 35 minutes, until the loaves are richly browned. Makes 2 twists. (See photo, page 193.)

ENGLISH MUFFINS

   2 packages active dry yeast
   ¼ cup very warm water
   ¼ cup butter or margarine
1¾ cups milk
   2 teaspoons salt
   6 cups flour
      Corn meal

Dissolve yeast in warm water. Melt butter in milk, add salt, cool to lukewarm, add to yeast. Add 4 cups flour, beat batter well. Cover, let rise 1 hour. Punch down, add 2 cups flour or more to make a stiff dough, knead thoroughly on floured board. Let rise until double, about 1 hour. Punch down, pat out ½ inch thick, cut into 3-inch rounds. Dust both sides with corn meal, let rise until double. Heat griddle or heavy skillet, grease lightly, brown muffins slowly on both sides. Makes 12. To serve, split with a fork, toast, then butter and serve hot. (See photo, page 193.)

WHITE BATTER BREAD

   1 package active dry yeast
1¼ cups very warm water
   2 tablespoons sugar
   2 teaspoons salt
   2 tablespoons butter or margarine
   3 cups flour

Dissolve yeast in warm water with sugar and salt. Add butter, stir. Add half the flour, beat well with a mixer or a wooden spoon. Add remaining flour, beat well. Cover and let rise until double in bulk, about 30 minutes. Stir

batter down, spread evenly in greased 9-inch-by-5-inch loaf pan. Let rise again until it reaches within 1 inch of the top of the pan. Bake in a moderately hot oven (375°F) about 45 minutes, until richly browned. Brush top with butter, cool on rack before cutting. Makes 1 loaf.

WHOLE-WHEAT BATTER BREAD

Substitute brown sugar for white, 1 cup whole-wheat flour for 1 cup white flour. Proceed as directed.

ANADAMA BREAD

1½ cups water
   ½ cup corn meal
   1 tablespoon salt
   ½ cup molasses
   ⅓ cup butter or margarine
   2 packages active dry yeast
   ½ cup very warm water
   5 to 6 cups flour
      Melted butter
      Corn meal

Combine 1½ cups water, corn meal and salt. Bring to a boil, cook over low heat, stirring constantly, until thick and smooth. Add molasses and butter, stir well. Cool. Sprinkle yeast on ½ cup very warm water, stir to dissolve. Add cooked corn meal and enough flour to make a soft dough. Knead on a floured board until smooth and elastic. Roll in a greased bowl, cover and let rise until doubled in bulk, about 1½ hours. Punch down, shape into 2 round loaves and arrange on a greased baking sheet. Or divide in half, place in greased 8-inch-by-4-inch loaf pans. Let rise, covered, until double in bulk, about 1 hour. Brush with melted butter, sprinkle with corn meal. Bake in a moderate oven (350°F) 50 to 60 minutes, until browned. Makes 2 loaves.

PITA

5 to 6 cups flour
1 tablespoon sugar
2 teaspoons salt
1 envelope active dry yeast
2 cups very warm water

Mix 2 cups flour, sugar, salt and yeast in a large bowl. Gradually add water and beat until smooth. Add ¾ cup flour and beat until smooth. Add enough additional flour to make a soft dough. Beat well. Turn out onto a lightly floured board, knead until smooth and elastic, about 10 minutes. Turn in a greased bowl, cover and let rise in a warm place until doubled in bulk, about 1 hour. Punch dough down, turn out onto a lightly floured board. Cover and let rest 30 minutes. Divide dough into 12 equal pieces and shape each into a ball. On a lightly floured board, roll each ball into a 5-inch circle. Bake on a pre-heated iron skillet or cookie sheet placed on the lowest rack of a very hot oven (450°F), about 5 minutes. Bottoms will be brown, tops will not. To brown tops, place bread under a hot broiler for about 1 minute. Makes 12.

WINTER FRUIT RING

   1 package active dry yeast
3¾ to 4 cups all-purpose flour
   ½ cup molasses
   6 tablespoons butter or margarine
1¼ cups milk
   1 teaspoon salt
   1 egg
   Grated rind and juice of 1 orange
   1 teaspoon cinnamon
   ¼ cup maraschino cherries,
      drained and halved
   2 tablespoons slivered, blanched
      almonds

Combine yeast with 2 cups flour in mixing bowl. Combine ¼ cup molasses with 4 table-spoons butter, milk and salt in saucepan. Heat until warm (110° to 115°F), stirring constantly. Add to flour mixture with egg and orange rind, beat smooth. Add enough of remaining flour to make a soft dough. Turn onto lightly floured board, knead until smooth and satiny. Place in a greased bowl, cover and let rise until doubled, about 1½ hours. Punch down. Combine remaining molasses and butter with orange juice and cinnamon, stirring until butter melts. Cool. Lightly flour hands and shape uniform balls the size of a golf ball. Roll in molasses syrup and place in layers in a greased 9-inch tube pan. Let rise until doubled, about 1 hour. Toss cherries and almonds in molasses syrup and scatter over top of risen dough. Bake on lowest rack in a moderately hot (375°F) oven 40 minutes. (Cover with aluminum foil if top begins to brown too quickly.) Loosen cake from tube pan and turn out immediately. Brush on remaining molasses syrup. Cool on wire rack. (See photo, page 195.)

BABKA

   1 package active dry yeast
   ¼ cup very warm water
   ½ cup butter or margarine
   ½ cup sugar
   5 egg yolks
   Grated rind of 1 lemon
   1 teaspoon salt
   1 teaspoon cinnamon
   1 cup lukewarm milk
   4 cups flour (about)
   1 cup raisins
   1 cup slivered blanched almonds

Sprinkle yeast on warm water. Cream butter with sugar, add egg yolks, beat until very light. Add yeast, lemon rind, salt and cinnamon. Add milk alternately with flour, using a little more flour if necessary to make a soft dough. Knead dough in bowl, cover and let rise in a warm place until doubled, about 2 hours. Punch down, knead briefly, work in raisins. Butter a 12-cup Bundt pan or tube pan. Sprinkle bottom and sides with almonds. Pile dough into pan evenly. Let rise again, covered, until doubled, about 1½ hours. Bake in a moderate oven (375°F) about 50 minutes, until richly browned.

BASIC SWEET YEAST DOUGH

   2 packages active dry yeast
   ½ cup very warm water
1½ cups milk
   ½ cup butter or margarine
   ½ cup sugar
   2 teaspoons salt
   6 to 7 cups flour
   2 eggs, beaten

Dissolve yeast in warm water. Heat milk with butter until butter melts. Add tepid milk to yeast mixture with sugar and salt. Add 2 cups flour, beat smooth. Add eggs. Add remaining flour to make a soft dough. Knead dough on a floured board until smooth and satiny. Roll in a greased bowl to coat, cover and let rise in a warm place until doubled in bulk, about 1 hour. Punch down, shape (below) and let rise in the baking pan until doubled in bulk. Bake as directed, about 30 minutes in a moderately hot oven (375°F) for cakes, 20 minutes for rolls. Makes about 3 dozen rolls, 2 large coffee cakes.

Parker House Rolls: Roll dough ¼ inch thick, cut into 2½-inch rounds. With a knife handle make a crease across the circle, not quite at the center. Fold the smaller half over the larger, press together. Lay on greased baking sheet, folded side up.

Crescent Rolls: Roll dough into 9-inch circles ¼ inch thick. Cut circles into 12 or 16 wedges. Roll up, beginning at the wide end

Is it more fun to bake bread or to eat it? Try these and see for yourself. Clockwise, beginning at 12 o'clock: White Bread, English Muffins, French Bread, Cranberry-Orange Tea Bread, Rich Blueberry Muffins, Egg Twist, Swedish Limpa Bread. The Cranberry-Orange Tea Bread and Rich Blueberry Muffins are quick breads made with baking powder; the rest are slowly raised with yeast.

of the wedges. Lay on greased baking sheet point down.

Cloverleaf Rolls: Shape dough into chestnut-size balls, put 3 balls into each greased muffin tin.

Fantans: Roll dough ⅛ inch thick, cut into 1½-inch strips. Stack 6 strips; cut into 2-inch squares. Arrange bundles cut side up in greased muffin tins.

Pan Rolls: Roll dough 1 inch thick, cut into squares or rounds. Roll sides in butter, arrange side by side in greased pan.

STOLLEN

½ **Basic Sweet Yeast Dough recipe (above)**
¾ **cup raisins**
¼ **cup finely chopped citron**
¼ **cup chopped candied cherries**
¾ **cup chopped nuts**
2 **tablespoons melted butter or margarine**
　Confectioners' Sugar Icing (page 207)
　Candied fruit and nuts for garnish

After first rising of dough, knead in raisins, citron, cherries and nuts. Shape dough into 2 rounds and allow to rest 10 minutes. Flatten each round into an oval about ¾ inch thick and brush with melted butter. Fold one-third the long side over as for a large Parker House roll. Pinch ends firmly together and place on greased baking sheet, folded side up. Brush with melted butter and allow to rise until doubled in bulk. Bake in a moderate oven (350°F) for 35 minutes. Cool, brush with confectioners' sugar icing and decorate with large pieces of fruit and nuts. Makes 2 Stollen.

HUNGARIAN BUBBLE LOAF

½ **Basic Sweet Yeast Dough recipe (above)**
½ **cup melted butter or margarine**
⅔ **cup sugar**
2 **teaspoons cinnamon**

Glaze:

¼ **cup dark corn syrup**
1 **tablespoon melted butter or margarine**
½ **teaspoon vanilla**

After first rising of dough, punch down, let rest 10 minutes. Shape walnut-size balls. Dip each into butter, then into sugar and cinnamon; arrange in layers in a greased tube pan. Let rise until double, about 1 hour.

Make glaze by mixing corn syrup, butter and vanilla, drizzle over cake. Bake in a moderate oven (350°F) about 40 minutes, until well browned. Makes 1 loaf.

COFFEE BRAID

½ **Basic Sweet Yeast Dough recipe (above)**
½ **cup sugar**
1½ **teaspoons cinnamon**
¼ **teaspoon nutmeg**
½ **cup melted butter**
　Confectioners' Sugar Icing (page 207)
　Cherries and nuts

After first rising of dough, divide dough into 3 equal parts. Roll each into a 12-inch-by-17-inch rectangle. Brush with melted butter. Mix sugar, cinnamon and nutmeg, sprinkle on dough. Roll each piece tightly, beginning from narrow side. Put on greased cookie sheet. Braid rolls tightly, pinching ends together. Brush with melted butter. Let rise again until doubled. Bake in a moderate oven (350°F) about 35 minutes. Cool and decorate with confectioners' sugar icing. Garnish with cherries and nuts, to taste.

CINNAMON PINWHEELS

Make half the Basic Sweet Yeast Dough recipe (above). After the first rising, punch down and allow to rest 10 minutes. Roll out into rectangle ¼ inch thick and 6 inches wide. Brush with melted butter or margarine. Sprinkle with mixture of cinnamon, sugar and ½ cup raisins. Roll up lengthwise, as for jelly roll, sealing edge. Cut into slices and place cut side down on greased cake pan. Brush top with milk and sprinkle with more cinnamon-sugar mixture. Let rise until doubled and bake in a moderate oven (350°F) 25 minutes. Makes 12.

HONEY SNAILS

Make half the Basic Sweet Yeast Dough recipe (above), let rise, punch down, let rest 10 minutes. Roll out dough into a rectangle 6 by 12 inches, ¼ inch thick. Brush with 2 tablespoons melted butter or margarine. Fold dough over with butter surface inward. Cut into 12 strips ½ inch wide and 6 inches long. Twist strips. Hold one end of twisted strip down on greased baking sheet and swirl strip around it. Tuck end firmly underneath. Brush with a mixture of ¼ cup softened butter or margarine, ⅔ cup confectioners'

Enjoy these cakes (clockwise, beginning at 12 o'clock): choose Winter Fruit Ring, Chocolate Cake with Seven-Minute Frosting, assorted Cupcakes, Chocolate Meringue Cake Roll, Snacking Cake, Orange-Coconut Cake. See pages 199–206 for cake recipes that start from scratch or begin with a mix—to do your own thing in baking.

The most celestial of desserts, and one of the simplest. The shortcake biscuit can be your own or a mix, the berries fresh, the topping real whipped cream. Or choose other seasonal fruit for economy, or frozen berries, or even canned fruit. Other toppings (see page 244) can replace the whipped cream. If the biscuit is crisp and hot, the fruit sweet and tart, the topping rich and creamy, shortcake remains the perfect dessert for any season. (See page 200.)

sugar, 1 egg white and 2 tablespoons honey. Let rise until doubled and bake in a moderate oven (350°F) about 20 minutes. Makes 12.

HOT CROSS BUNS

½ **Basic Sweet Yeast Dough recipe (above)**
1 **teaspoon cinnamon**
½ **teaspoon allspice**
1 **cup currants**
Confectioners' Sugar Icing (page 207)

After first rising of dough, punch down and knead in spices and currants. Divide into 18 balls. Place ½ inch apart on a greased baking sheet and allow to rise until doubled in bulk. Bake in a moderate oven (350°F) 20 minutes. Remove at once from baking sheet and make a cross of confectioners' sugar icing on each bun. Makes 18.

KOLACKY

Make half the Basic Sweet Yeast Dough recipe (above). After first rising, punch dough down and let rest 10 minutes. Pinch off pieces the size of walnuts, roll into balls. Place 2 inches apart on greased baking sheet and allow to rise in a warm place about 15 minutes. Press down the center of each to make a hollow, leaving a raised rim about ¼ inch thick. Brush with melted butter or margarine and fill hollows with your choice of jams and preserves. Bake in a moderate oven (350°F) about 25 minutes. Makes about 1 dozen.

YEAST DOUGHNUTS

Make half the Basic Sweet Yeast Dough recipe (above). After first rising, punch down, let rest 10 minutes. Roll out ½ inch thick. Cut with a doughnut cutter. Let rise about 30 minutes. Fry a few at a time in hot (375°F) fat. When doughnuts rise to surface and are browned on the bottom, turn to brown other side. Drain on absorbent paper. Serve plain. Or shake in a paper bag with superfine granulated sugar and cinnamon or nutmeg. Makes about 1 dozen.

JELLY DOUGHNUTS

Prepare and roll out dough as above. Cut into 3-inch rounds with a cookie cutter or a glass. Let rise about 30 minutes, fry as above. Cool. Cut a slit into the center of each doughnut, fill with 1 teaspoon jam, jelly, or apple or prune butter. Dust with confectioners' sugar.

Quick Breads

If you serve hot breads frequently—pancakes and waffles at breakfast, biscuits at dinner, muffins at lunch—you will enjoy the convenience and economy of your own Pantry Hot-Bread Mix, to store on the shelf and use as a base for all these hot breads and more that you may invent. Less frequent users may settle for a prepared mix, or for recipes that begin from scratch. Use whichever method suits your needs, but don't skip the hot breads—take two and butter them while they're hot!

PANTRY HOT-BREAD MIX

12 **cups flour**
2 **tablespoons salt**
6 **tablespoons double-acting baking powder**
1½ **cups shortening**

Toss dry ingredients to mix. Cut in shortening with a pastry blender or two knives until mix looks like coarse meal. Store in a covered container. Makes 14 cups.

PANTRY BISCUITS

To 2⅓ cups Pantry Hot-Bread Mix (above) add ⅔ to ¾ cup milk. Pat out on lightly floured board, cut into shapes. Bake in a hot oven (425°F) about 15 minutes, until biscuits are well browned. Serve hot. Makes 12 or more.

PANTRY WAFFLES

To 2 cups Pantry Hot-Bread Mix (above) add 1⅔ cups milk, 2 eggs, 2 tablespoons melted butter or margarine. Beat well with rotary beater, bake in waffle iron as usual. Serve with butter and syrup. Makes 6 servings.

PANTRY PANCAKES

To 2 cups Pantry Hot-Bread Mix (above) add 1⅔ cups milk, 1 egg. Beat smooth. Heat griddle or large skillet, brush with butter, margarine or bacon fat. Pour ⅓ cup batter onto hot griddle, cook over moderate heat until top is bubbly and beginning to dry; turn over and brown other side. Serve with butter and syrup. Makes 6 servings.

PANTRY MUFFINS

To 2 cups Pantry Hot-Bread Mix (above), add 2 tablespoons sugar, 1 egg, ¾ cup milk.

Mix to moisten. Fill buttered muffin pans two-thirds full. Bake in a hot oven (400°F) 20 to 25 minutes, until richly browned. Serve hot. Makes 1 dozen.

Variety Muffins: Add to Pantry Muffins ½ cup crumbled cooked bacon; or ½ cup shredded Swiss or Cheddar cheese; or ½ cup chopped nuts; or 1 cup chopped dates, prunes or cranberries; or 1 cup whole blueberries. Or give muffin tops a special touch: sprinkle with chopped nuts, crumbled cooked bacon, crushed dry cereal, cinnamon and sugar; or drizzle with honey or maple syrup before baking.

PANTRY BANANA BREAD

 3 cups Pantry Hot-Bread Mix (above)
⅔ cup sugar
⅓ cup flour
 1 egg
½ cup milk
 1 cup mashed bananas
½ cup chopped nuts

Combine mix, sugar and flour. Beat egg and milk, add to mix, beat. Add bananas and nuts, combine well. Bake in greased 9-inch-by-5-inch loaf pan in a moderate oven (350°F) about 1 hour, until bread is richly browned and a skewer inserted at the center comes out clean and dry. Cool on a rack before slicing.

Variations: Use 1 cup canned applesauce instead of bananas; add ½ teaspoon each cinnamon, cloves and nutmeg. Or use 1 cup canned crushed pineapple, well drained, instead of bananas.

CRANBERRY-ORANGE TEA BREAD

 1 cup sugar
 2 cups flour
1½ teaspoons double-acting baking powder
½ teaspoon baking soda
 1 teaspoon salt
¼ cup softened butter or margarine
¾ cup orange juice
 1 egg, beaten
 1 tablespoon grated orange rind
½ cup chopped nuts (optional)
 1 cup fresh cranberries, chopped

Toss sugar, flour, baking powder, baking soda and salt to mix. Cut in butter with a pastry blender or two knives to make very fine

crumbs. Combine orange juice and egg, add all at once, stir to moisten. Fold in orange rind, nuts, if desired, and cranberries. Avoid overmixing. Spread in a greased 9-inch-by-5-inch loaf pan; flatten center slightly. Bake in a moderate oven (350°F) about 1 hour, until loaf is browned and a skewer inserted at the center comes out dry. Cool thoroughly on a rack before slicing. (See photo, page 193.)

NORTHERN-STYLE CORN BREAD

1½ cups flour
 3 teaspoons double-acting baking powder
 1 teaspoon salt
¼ cup sugar
½ cup yellow corn meal
 2 eggs
 1 cup milk
 3 tablespoons melted butter or
    margarine

Toss dry ingredients to mix. Beat eggs and add with milk and butter, stirring just until moistened. Bake in 8- or 9-inch square baking pan in a hot oven (425°F) about 35 minutes, until well browned. Serve hot.

BUTTERMILK CORNSTICKS

1⅓ cups corn meal
⅓ cup flour
 1 teaspoon double-acting baking powder
½ teaspoon baking soda
 1 tablespoon sugar
½ teaspoon salt
 1 cup buttermilk
 1 egg
 2 tablespoons melted shortening

Toss dry ingredients to mix. Combine buttermilk and egg, add all at once, stir until smooth. Add melted shortening. Bake in greased cornstick pans in a hot oven (400°F) about 25 minutes, until richly browned. Serve hot with butter. Makes 1 dozen.

PURI
(INDIAN FRIED BREAD)

 2 cups flour
 1 teaspoon salt
¼ cup oil
 6 tablespoons water

Toss flour and salt, add oil and water, mix well. Knead on a floured board until dough is satiny, about 10 minutes. Roll dough very thin. Cut it into 3-inch circles. Drop circles into moderately hot (360°F) deep fat. When dough begins to puff, turn to brown both sides. Cooking takes about 1 minute. Drain on absorbent paper. Makes about 16.

RICH BLUEBERRY MUFFINS

1½ cups flour
¾ cup sugar
1½ teaspoons baking powder
¼ teaspoon salt
½ teaspoon cinnamon
1 large egg
6 tablespoons butter or margarine, melted
½ cup milk
1½ cups blueberries, fresh or dry frozen

Toss flour, sugar, baking powder, salt and cinnamon to mix. Beat egg with melted butter and milk. Add to flour, stir until smooth. Fold in blueberries. Bake in greased muffin cups in a hot oven (400°F) about 25 minutes, until muffins are well browned. Serve warm or at room temperature, with or without butter. Makes 12. (See photo, page 193.)

BASIC BISCUITS

2 cups flour
2 teaspoons double-acting baking powder
1 teaspoon salt
¼ cup shortening
⅔ to ¾ cup milk

Toss dry ingredients to mix. Cut in shortening until mixture looks like coarse meal. Add milk, stir to form dough. Knead five or six times on lightly floured board, pat out ½ inch thick, cut into shapes. Bake in a hot oven (425°F) about 15 minutes. Makes 1 dozen or more.

Orange Biscuits: Add 2 teaspoons grated orange rind with milk. Dip half a cube of sugar into orange juice, top each biscuit. Bake as usual.

Cheese Biscuits: Add ½ cup grated cheese to mix before adding milk. Bake as usual.

Drop Biscuits: Add 1 cup milk to dry mixture, drop batter from spoon onto greased baking sheet. Bake as usual.

Buttermilk Biscuits: Add ½ teaspoon baking soda, use ⅔ cup buttermilk instead of ordinary milk. Bake as usual.

Herb Biscuits: Add 2 tablespoons finely snipped chives, parsley, dill or other fresh herbs to dry mix. Bake as usual.

CINNAMON BISCUITS

Make dough for Basic Biscuits (above) as directed, roll or pat out into a sheet about ¼ inch thick. Brush dough with 2 tablespoons softened butter, sprinkle with 2 tablespoons sugar, ½ teaspoon cinnamon. Roll up. Cut roll into slices ½ inch thick. Lay on greased pan, cut side down; bake as usual.

CARAMEL PECAN BUNS

Follow recipe for Cinnamon Biscuits (above), but spread dough with 2 tablespoons softened butter or margarine, 3 tablespoons brown sugar and ¼ cup chopped pecans. Roll up, slice and bake as usual.

THE CAKE PLATE

With the availability and range of cake mixes, even the busiest cook need not be without some form of cake to suit her family's tastes. When time allows, produce a cake from scratch for the family's pleasure.

Cake Mixes

When you buy a cake mix, read the label— and not simply for directions on how to prepare the mix successfully. You will also find on the label suggestions for varying the mix in delicious ways, all of them easy and amateurproof.

ORANGE-COCONUT CAKE

1 package (19 ounces) yellow cake mix
1 package (4⅞ ounces) coconut pudding mix
4 eggs
¾ cup oil
1 cup orange juice
1 can (3½ ounces) flaked coconut

Combine all ingredients in a large mixing bowl. Beat by hand or with a rotary beater 4 or 5 minutes, until thoroughly combined and smooth. Bake in a moderate oven (350°F) 50 to 60 minutes, or until cake is firm to the touch. While cake is still warm, drizzle with Orange Glaze (page 200). (See photo, page 195.)

ORANGE GLAZE

Combine 1½ cups confectioners' sugar, 1 tablespoon finely grated orange rind and 2 to 3 tablespoons orange juice. Drizzle over warm cake.

PINEAPPLE UPSIDE-DOWN CAKE

  1 cup brown sugar
½ cup butter or margarine
  1 can (14½ ounces) pineapple slices
     Maraschino cherries
  1 package (19 ounces) honey spice cake
     mix

Heat brown sugar and butter in a 10-inch skillet or layer pan until butter is melted. Arrange pineapple rings on sugar; put a maraschino cherry into the center of each ring. Make cake mix according to package directions, pour carefully over fruit. Bake in a moderate oven (350°F) about 30 minutes, until the cake tests done. Let stand 5 minutes, invert on serving plate.

BANANA UPSIDE-DOWN CAKE

Substitute sliced bananas for pineapple rings in the recipe for Pineapple Upside-Down Cake (above). Use honey spice, devil's food, yellow or lemon cake mix, bake as directed.

VELVET CRUMB CAKE

1⅓ cups Pantry Hot-Bread Mix (page 197),
     or commercial biscuit mix
 ¾ cup sugar
  3 tablespoons butter or margarine
  1 egg
 ¾ cup milk
  1 teaspoon vanilla
 ¼ cup Pantry Hot-Bread Mix
     (or biscuit mix)
  2 teaspoons cinnamon
  2 tablespoons brown sugar
  1 tablespoon butter or margarine

Combine 1⅓ cups hot-bread mix with sugar. Add 3 tablespoons butter and egg, blend. Stir in milk and vanilla gradually, beat 1 minute. Pour into a greased and floured 9-inch round layer pan. Mix ¼ cup hot-bread mix and remaining ingredients with a fork, sprinkle on batter. Bake 40 minutes in a moderate oven (350°F). Serve warm.

Variation: Top hot cake with ½ cup jam or preserves.

QUICK ORANGE CAKE

  2 cups Pantry Hot-Bread Mix (page 197),
     or commercial biscuit mix
½ cup sugar
  2 eggs
  1 tablespoon grated orange rind
½ cup orange juice
  3 tablespoons butter or margarine
  1 teaspoon vanilla

Combine all ingredients in a mixing bowl; beat well, about 5 minutes with an electric mixer. Bake in a greased and floured 9-inch square baking pan in a moderate oven (350°F) about 30 minutes. Serve as is, or top with Broiled Topping (page 208).

SHORTCAKE

To 2 cups Pantry Hot-Bread Mix (page 197), add ¼ cup soft butter or margarine, ⅔ cup milk and 2 tablespoons sugar. Pat 1 inch thick on floured board, cut into 6 large biscuits. Or shape into a single 8-inch round. Bake in a very hot oven (450°F) 10 to 15 minutes for small shortcakes, about 20 minutes for large one. Split while hot, butter. Cover bottom half with sweetened sliced strawberries or peaches; cover with top half, add more fruit. Garnish with whipped cream and whole fruit. Serve at once. (See photo, page 196.)

DOUBLE LEMON CAKE

  1 package (19 ounces) lemon cake mix
  1 package (3 ounces) lemon gelatin
     dessert
 ¾ cup oil
 ¾ cup water
  4 eggs

Toss cake mix and gelatin to mix. Add remaining ingredients and beat with an electric mixer at medium speed for 4 minutes. Fill a greased and floured 9-inch-by-13-inch baking pan. Bake in a moderate oven (350°F) about 30 to 35 minutes, until well browned.

Variation: While cake is still hot, pour over it the juice of 1 lemon mixed with 1 cup confectioners' sugar.

How to Bake a Good Cake

1. Measure as accurately as possible. Use measuring spoons and level measuring cups

for dry ingredients, cups with a pouring spout that begins above the 1-cup line for liquids. The wrappers of margarine and butter are usually marked with tablespoons and cups so you can cut accurate measures. Measure hydrogenated shortenings by level cups and spoons; measure oil like other liquids. Most recipes no longer suggest that you sift flour before measuring it—it is enough simply to toss the flour to lighten it before scooping it into a measuring cup and leveling it off. To mix flour with other dry ingredients, toss together in a bowl, or shake in a covered container.

2. Follow recipe instructions accurately for best results, using mixing methods, pans and baking temperature as prescribed.

3. Unless otherwise specified (for angel food, for instance) always grease the bottom of the baking pan. Put a square of waxed paper in the center of the pan, cover entire bottom with a thin layer of shortening. Cakes rise better if the sides of the pan are not greased. If the recipe suggests flouring the pan, sprinkle the greased pan with flour and shake the pan to distribute flour evenly. Then invert the pan and tap it to get rid of the excess flour.

4. Preheat the oven to the proper temperature; if your oven thermostat is unreliable, an oven thermometer is a good investment. Place the oven rack in the center of the oven. Arrange pans in the center of the rack, not touching the oven walls or each other, or, if you need to use two racks, place pans not directly above or below one another.

5. Test a cake for doneness at the minimum time suggested. A properly baked cake will be browned and will shrink from the sides of the pan. It will spring back from the gentle pressure of a fingertip. Insert a straw or skewer in the center of the cake as a final test. The straw should come out clean and dry.

6. Most cakes should be cooled on a rack, in the baking pan. After 15 minutes or longer, loosen the cake from the pan with a spatula. Cover the cake with a second rack, and invert it, with the rack, to unmold. Invert again, and finish cooling the cake, right side up. Sponge cakes, angel food, or other cakes for which the pan is not greased, should be cooled upside down, hanging free and not touching the rack. Balance the pan on its own tube or ears, if it has them, or on a bottle or two cups. When cake is thoroughly cooled, in about 2 hours, loosen it with a spatula and unmold right side up.

Baking Pans

Your baking-pan wardrobe should include the following basic pans:
8-inch rounds (2) or 9-inch rounds (2)
8-inch squares (2) or 9-inch squares (2)
13-inch-by-9-inch rectangle
8-inch-by-12-inch loaf pan (2) or 8-inch-by-4-inch loaf pan (2)
9-inch tube pan or 10-inch tube pan
10-inch-by-15-inch flat jelly-roll pan
8-inch pie pans (2) or 9-inch pie pans (2)
Cupcake pan, 12 cakes (2)
Cookie sheets (2)

Add these special types to increase your baking power:
A fluted-edge quiche pan
A large, flat pizza pan
A spring-form pan with removable sides
A round pan with a removable bottom
Fluted Bundt pan

Cakes are best baked in the cake pans specified in the recipe. Use the following chart of cake-pan substitutions when the indicated sizes are unavailable. Remember never to fill a pan more than half full.

If a recipe specifies:	You can substitute:
8-inch square	9-inch round
9-inch square	a pair of 8-inch rounds
9-inch-by-13-inch rectangle	a pair of 9-inch rounds
	or
	a pair of 8-inch squares
8-inch-by-12-inch rectangle	a pair of 8-inch rounds

BUTTER CAKE

½ cup butter or margarine
1 cup sugar
2 eggs
2 cups flour
2 teaspoons double-acting baking powder
½ teaspoon salt
1 cup milk
1 teaspoon vanilla

Cream butter, add sugar, cream until light. Beat in eggs, one at a time, beat well. Toss flour, baking powder and salt to mix; add to butter mixture alternately with milk, beginning and ending with flour. Stir in vanilla. Bake in a greased and floured 9-inch square pan in a moderate oven (350°F) about 35 minutes; or in 2 greased and floured 8-inch layer pans in a moderately hot oven (375°F) for about 25 minutes. Cool on a rack and frost as desired; or serve warm from the oven with ice cream or whipped cream or fruit.

White Cake: Substitute 3 egg whites for whole eggs, beat stiff, fold in last.

Gold Cake: Substitute 3 egg yolks for whole eggs, beat until very light with butter and sugar.

Chocolate Cake: Add 2 squares baking chocolate, melted, to butter and sugar. Frost with Seven-Minute Frosting (page 207). (See photo, page 195.)

Spice Cake: Add to flour mixture 1 teaspoon cinnamon, ½ teaspoon each cloves and nutmeg.

Marble Cake: Pour half the batter for Butter Cake into another bowl. Add 1 envelope melted chocolate, ¼ teaspoon soda, 2 tablespoons water. Beat well. Fill baking pan with alternate tablespoons of white and chocolate batter.

Caramel Cake: Substitute 1¼ cups brown sugar for the white sugar.

COCOA MARBLE CAKE

Custard:
  1 egg
½ cup sugar
  3 tablespoons cocoa
½ cup boiling water

Batter:
¾ cup butter or margarine
  1 cup sugar
  2 eggs
  2 cups flour
  2 teaspoons double-acting baking powder
  1 teaspoon baking soda
¼ teaspoon salt
¾ cup milk
  1 teaspoon vanilla

Beat egg, add sugar and cocoa. Add boiling water, cook over low heat, stirring constantly, until custard is thick and smooth. Cool. Cream butter with sugar until light and fluffy, beat in eggs, one at a time, beat well. Toss flour with baking powder, baking soda and salt to mix. Add alternately to butter mixture with milk, beginning and ending with flour. Add vanilla. Pour into greased and floured 7-inch-by-11-inch baking pan. Pour custard over batter, with a knife draw zigzag lines through custard and batter. Bake in a mod-

erate oven (350°F) about 40 minutes, until the cake tests done.

COFFEE DEVIL'S FOOD CAKE

½ cup cocoa
  1 teaspoon instant coffee
  1 cup boiling water
½ cup butter or margarine
1¼ cups sugar
  2 eggs
  2 cups flour
  1 teaspoon baking soda
  1 teaspoon double-acting baking powder
½ teaspoon salt

Stir cocoa and instant coffee in boiling water until mixture is smooth. (Or use leftover brewed coffee.) Cool. Cream butter, add sugar, cream until light. Add eggs, beat well. Toss flour with baking soda, baking powder and salt to mix. Add to batter alternately with cooled cocoa mixture. Bake in a greased and floured 9-inch square pan, in a moderate oven (350°F) about 45 minutes.

PLANTATION CAKE

½ cup shortening
½ cup sugar
  1 egg
½ cup molasses
1½ cups flour
¾ teaspoon baking soda
¾ teaspoon salt
½ teaspoon ginger
½ teaspoon cloves
½ teaspoon cinnamon
½ cup sour milk

Cream shortening, add sugar, beat until light. Add egg, beat well, add molasses. Toss dry ingredients to mix, add alternately with sour milk, beginning and ending with flour. Bake in a greased and floured 8-inch square pan in a moderate oven (350°F) about 45 minutes. Serve warm with Orange Sauce (below).

ORANGE SAUCE

1½ tablespoons cornstarch
½ cup sugar
  2 teaspoons grated orange rind
    Dash salt
¼ teaspoon cinnamon
1¼ cups cold water
¼ cup orange juice
  2 tablespoons lemon juice
  3 tablespoons butter or margarine

Mix dry ingredients and water, stir over low heat until mixture comes to a boil. Boil 5 minutes, stirring occasionally. Add remaining ingredients, serve hot over Plantation Cake.

SNACKING CAKE

- ½ cup butter or margarine
- 1 cup unsulphured molasses
- 1 egg
- 2½ cups flour
- 1 teaspoon each baking soda, salt, cinnamon
- 1 cup applesauce
- ¼ lemon, juice and grated rind
- ¾ cup chopped walnuts (optional)

Cream butter, beat in molasses and egg. Toss dry ingredients to mix, add alternately with applesauce. Stir in lemon juice and rind and walnuts. Bake in a greased and floured 9-inch square pan in a moderate oven (350°F) about 40 to 45 minutes, until cake tests done. Turn out onto a cake rack. Sprinkle with cinnamon sugar, or glaze with mixture of 1½ tablespoons lemon juice and ¾ cup confectioners' sugar, if desired. (See photo, page 195.)

CUPCAKES

- 1 cup sugar
- ½ cup butter or margarine
- 2 eggs
- 1 teaspoon vanilla
- 2 cups flour
- 2½ teaspoons baking powder
- ½ teaspoon salt
- ½ cup milk

Cream together sugar and butter, beating until light and fluffy. Add eggs, one at a time, beating well after each addition. Add vanilla. Toss together flour, baking powder and salt. Add to creamed mixture alternately with milk. Stir only enough to blend thoroughly. Fill muffin tins, greased or lined with cupcake papers, half full. Bake in a moderately hot oven (375°F) for 20 minutes, until golden and springy to the touch. Makes 2 dozen. (See photo, page 195.)

APPLE CAKE

- ⅓ cup butter or margarine
- 1 cup sugar
- 1 egg
- 2 cups chopped apples
- 1½ cups flour
- 1 teaspoon cinnamon
- 1 teaspoon salt
- 1 teaspoon baking soda
- 1 teaspoon vanilla
- ½ cup chopped nuts

Cream butter, add sugar, cream until light. Add egg. Stir in chopped apples. Toss flour with cinnamon, salt and baking soda, stir in. Add vanilla and chopped nuts. Bake in a greased and floured 8-inch baking pan in a moderate oven (350°F) 35 minutes, until the cake tests done.

APPLESAUCE CAKE

- ½ cup butter or margarine
- 1 cup sugar
- 1 egg
- 1½ cups flour
- 1 teaspoon cinnamon
- 1 teaspoon baking soda
- ½ teaspoon salt
- 1 cup thick applesauce
- 1 cup mixed nuts and raisins
- 2 tablespoons flour

Cream butter, add sugar, cream until light. Add egg, beat well. Toss 1½ cups flour with cinnamon, baking soda and salt. Add flour and applesauce to butter mixture alternately, beating to combine after each addition, beginning and ending with flour. Toss nuts and raisins with 2 tablespoons flour, fold into batter. Bake in a greased and floured 9-inch tube pan in a moderate oven (350°F) about 1 hour.

BANANA CAKE

- ½ cup butter or margarine
- 1 cup sugar
- 2 eggs
- 1 teaspoon vanilla
- 2 cups flour
- 2 teaspoons double-acting baking powder
- ½ teaspoon baking soda
- ½ teaspoon salt
- ¼ cup buttermilk
- 1 cup mashed ripe bananas

Cream butter with sugar until very light. Add eggs, one at a time, beat well. Add vanilla. Toss flour with dry ingredients to mix, add alternately with buttermilk and bananas, blending well after each addition. Bake in 2 greased and floured 8-inch layer cake pans, or in a 9-inch ring pan, in a moderately hot oven (375°F) about 25 minutes for layers, 45 minutes for ring, or until cake tests done. Cool. Frost to taste with whipped cream or butter cream.

PUMPKIN CAKE

½ cup butter or margarine
1 cup brown sugar
½ cup white sugar
¾ cup mashed cooked pumpkin
1 egg
2 cups flour
1 teaspoon double-acting baking powder
1 teaspoon baking soda
1½ teaspoons pumpkin-pie spice
½ teaspoon salt
½ cup water

Cream butter, add sugar, cream together, add pumpkin. Add egg, beat well. Sift flour with dry ingredients, add alternately with water, beginning and ending with flour. Bake in a greased and floured 9-inch square baking pan in a moderate oven (350°F) about 45 minutes, until cake tests done.

SARAH'S CALIFORNIA FRUITCAKE

1 pound butter or margarine
2 cups sugar
6 eggs
1 bottle (2 ounces) lemon extract
4 cups flour
1 teaspoon baking powder
  Pinch salt
1 pound pecan nutmeats
1 pound golden raisins
½ pound candied pineapple
½ pound candied cherries

Cream butter and sugar until fluffy. Add eggs, one at a time, beating well after each. Add lemon extract. Toss flour, baking powder and salt to mix. Toss nutmeats and fruits with 1 cup flour, add remaining flour to the egg mixture. Stir batter into fruit, mixing with a spatula or your hands. Grease and line with waxed paper a 10-inch tube pan, or two 9-inch-by-5-inch loaf pans; grease paper, fill pan. Put a pan of water in the oven. Bake in a slow oven (275°F) 2½ hours for tube cake, about 2 hours for loaves.

MOLASSES FRUITCAKE

¼ cup butter or margarine
¾ cup unsulphured molasses
¾ cup applesauce
  Grated rind and juice of 1 orange
1 teaspoon rum or brandy extract
2 eggs
2½ cups all-purpose flour
1 teaspoon baking soda

1 teaspoon baking powder
½ teaspoon salt
1½ teaspoons cinnamon
½ teaspoon each nutmeg, cloves, ginger
1 cup golden seedless raisins
1 jar (8 ounces) maraschino cherries, drained
1 cup walnuts, coarsely chopped

Cream butter with molasses until fluffy. Beat in applesauce, orange rind and juice, extract and eggs. Toss 2 cups of flour with baking soda, baking powder, salt and spices to mix. Add to molasses mixture and blend well. Toss raisins, cherries and walnuts (reserving several cherries and whole nuts to decorate top of cake) with remaining ½ cup flour, fold into batter. Grease a 9-inch tube pan, line bottom with waxed paper, add batter. Garnish with reserved fruit and nuts. Bake in a moderately slow oven (325°F) 1¼ hours, until a cake tester comes out dry. Let stand 20 minutes in pan, turn out of pan, cool on a rack.

FRUIT KUCHEN

1½ cups flour
¼ cup sugar
½ teaspoon salt
½ cup butter or margarine
1 egg yolk
2 tablespoons milk
2 tablespoons flour
4 cups fruit (sliced apples, peaches, pears, halved plums)
½ cup sugar
1 teaspoon cinnamon
1 tablespoon butter or margarine

Toss 1½ cups flour, sugar and salt to mix. Cut in butter with a pastry blender or two knives, until mixture looks like coarse meal. Beat egg yolk with milk, add to flour. Press dough against bottom and sides of a greased 8-inch square baking pan. Sprinkle with 2 tablespoons flour. Spread with fruit, sprinkle with sugar mixed with cinnamon, dot with butter. Bake in a hot oven (400°F) about 45 minutes, until crust is brown and fruit is tender.

Variation: Use 3 cups drained canned fruit, reduce sugar topping to ¼ cup.

Cream Topping: Beat 1 egg yolk with ¼ cup sour cream, pour over fruit after first 10 minutes of baking.

LINZER TORTE

1½ cups butter or margarine
1 cup confectioners' sugar, sifted
1 egg
2¾ cups sifted flour
Pinch salt
½ teaspoon cinnamon
1½ cups ground almonds, hazelnuts, or
a mixture
1½ cups raspberry or apricot jam
2 teaspoons lemon juice

Cream butter with sugar, add egg and beat until light. Work in combined flour, salt and cinnamon alternately with nuts. Form dough into a ball, chill. Press one-half to two-thirds of dough into a greased tart pan or spring-form pan to make a crust ¼ inch thick, ¾ to 1 inch deep. Roll remaining dough between sheets of waxed paper. Chill. Spread crust with a mixture of jam and lemon juice. Cut chilled dough into ½-inch-wide strips, make a lattice top. Bake in a moderately hot oven (375°F) 40 minutes. Cool. Add extra jam between lattice strips if necessary. Sprinkle with confectioners' sugar, if desired.

STREUSEL COFFEE CAKE

½ cup butter or margarine
1 cup sugar
3 eggs
2 cups flour
½ teaspoon salt
1 teaspoon baking soda
1 teaspoon double-acting baking powder
1 cup sour cream
2 teaspoons vanilla
2 tablespoons flour
1 tablespoon cinnamon
1 tablespoon cocoa
½ cup chopped nutmeats
2 tablespoons butter or margarine

Cream butter, add sugar, cream well. Add eggs, beat until light and fluffy. Toss 2 cups flour with salt, baking soda and baking powder. Add to batter alternately with sour cream, beating well after each addition. Add vanilla. Fill greased 9-inch tube pan. Combine 2 tablespoons flour, cinnamon, cocoa and nutmeats with 2 tablespoons butter to make a crumbly mixture, sprinkle on cake. Bake in a moderate oven (350°F) about 1 hour, until cake tests done.

DATE-NUT COFFEE CAKE

½ cup butter or margarine
½ cup sugar
1 egg
½ teaspoon vanilla
1½ cups flour
1½ teaspoons double-acting baking powder
1 teaspoon salt
½ cup milk
½ cup brown sugar
1 tablespoon flour
¼ cup melted butter or margarine
½ cup mixed chopped walnuts and dates

Cream butter, add sugar, cream well. Add egg and vanilla, beat until light. Toss 1½ cups flour with baking powder and salt, add to butter mixture alternately with milk, stirring after each addition only until blended. Pour half the batter into a greased and floured 8-inch square baking pan. Combine brown sugar, 1 tablespoon flour, melted butter, and chopped nuts and dates. Sprinkle half this mixture on batter. Add remaining batter, top with remaining topping mixture. Bake in a moderate oven (350°F) about 50 minutes.

CHIFFON CAKE

2 cups flour
1½ cups sugar
3 teaspoons double-acting baking powder
1 teaspoon salt
½ cup oil
7 eggs, separated
¾ cup water
2 teaspoons vanilla
2 teaspoons grated lemon rind
½ teaspoon cream of tartar

Toss flour, sugar, baking powder and salt in mixing bowl to mix. Add oil, egg yolks, water and vanilla, beat with a spoon until smooth. Add lemon rind. Beat egg whites until foamy, add cream of tartar, beat until very stiff but not dry. Pour batter gradually over egg whites, folding with a gentle over-and-over motion to combine thoroughly. Bake in an ungreased 10-inch tube pan in a moderate oven (325°F) for 55 minutes, until cake is browned. Invert tube on a bottle neck until cake is cold.

CHOCOLATE MERINGUE CAKE ROLL

1 cup less 2 tablespoons flour
1 teaspoon baking powder
¼ teaspoon salt
¼ cup cocoa
3 eggs
1 cup sugar
⅓ cup water

1 teaspoon vanilla
   Confectioners' sugar
   Italian Meringue or sweetened whipped
      cream

Line a 10-inch-by-15-inch jelly-roll pan with waxed paper or aluminum foil, grease well. Toss together flour, baking powder, salt and cocoa. Beat eggs until very thick and lemon-colored, about 5 minutes; gradually beat in sugar. Stir in water and vanilla. Add flour mixture, mixing only until batter is smooth. Spread evenly in prepared pan. Bake in a moderately hot oven (375°F) 12 to 15 minutes. Loosen cake and invert on a towel that has been sprinkled with confectioners' sugar. Remove paper from cake; if edges are crisp, trim them. Roll cake and towel from narrow end while still hot. Cool cake, unroll; remove towel, spread cake with Italian Meringue (page 207) or sweetened whipped cream. Roll up and sprinkle with confectioners' sugar if desired. Makes 10 servings. (See photo, page 195.)

SPONGE ROLL

   4 eggs
   2 cups sugar
   2 teaspoons lemon extract
   2 cups flour
   2 teaspoons double-acting baking powder
   ½ teaspoon salt
   1 cup boiling water
      Confectioners' sugar
      Choice of filling

Beat eggs, add sugar, beat until very light and thick. Beat in lemon extract. Toss flour with baking powder and salt, fold in. Stir in boiling water. Grease a 10-inch-by-15-inch jelly-roll pan, line with waxed paper, grease paper. Spread batter on pan. Bake in a hot oven (400°F) 15 minutes or longer, until cake is browned and tests done. Turn out on a towel dusted with confectioners' sugar, strip off waxed paper, roll cake in the towel. Cool, unroll, spread with jam, or with fruit and whipped topping, or with Chocolate Cream Frosting (page 208), and roll up again.

PAVLOVA CAKE

   6 egg whites
   1½ cups sugar
   1 tablespoon vanilla extract
   1 teaspoon white vinegar

Grease an 8- or 9-inch spring-form pan. Beat egg whites until soft peaks form. Beat in 6 tablespoons sugar, one spoonful at a time.

With the final 2 tablespoons sugar, add vanilla extract and vinegar. Fold in the remaining sugar with a spatula. Pile egg whites in the spring-form, place pan in a cold oven. Set thermostat for 250°F. Bake for 45 minutes. Cool on a rack for 15 minutes. Remove sides of spring-form carefully, transfer Pavlova to cake plate. Fill with unsweetened whipped cream and sweetened strawberries or other fruit. Makes 8 to 10 servings.

FROSTINGS AND FILLINGS

Frostings and fillings may enhance a cake's basic flavor or may lend a flavor of their own.

Frostings

Frosting (or icing or glaze or topping) is the final touch to a cake. In addition to the flavor it imparts, frosting is also a decorative device; there is no end to the patterns you can create with a spatula, a pastry tube, and a little imagination.

How to Frost a Cake

Cool the cake thoroughly before frosting. Arrange three strips of waxed paper so that they cover the rim of the serving plate. Level off the top of one layer with a sharp knife, if necessary, then place it, top side down, on plate. Spread frosting to the edges. The waxed paper will catch stray drips and protect the plate. Wait a few minutes until the frosting is set; place second layer, top side up, on the filling. Brush off any crumbs. Frost the sides of both layers, then the top, making swirls or ripples with a spatula. When the cake is completely frosted, remove the waxed paper.

The following chart shows how much Butter Cream Frosting you need for various sizes of cakes. Note: If you use fluffy frosting, prepare about twice the quantities indicated below.

9-inch layer cake	about 3 cups (including center)
8-inch square	about 1½ cups
9-inch square	about 2 cups
13-inch-by-9-inch cake	about 2½ cups
24 cupcakes	about 2½ cups
10-inch tube cake	about 2 cups

BUTTER CREAM FROSTING

⅓ cup soft butter or margarine
3 cups sifted confectioners' sugar
3 tablespoons milk or cream
1 teaspoon vanilla

Mix butter and sugar together. Stir in milk and vanilla, mix until smooth. If necessary, add more milk to bring to spreading consistency.

Chocolate Cream Frosting: Sift ⅓ cup cocoa with confectioners' sugar before mixing with butter.

Coffee Cream Frosting: Dissolve 2 teaspoons instant coffee in 3 tablespoons hot water; substitute for milk.

Orange or Lemon Cream Frosting: Substitute 3 tablespoons orange or lemon juice and 1 tablespoon grated rind for milk and vanilla.

ALMOND FROSTING

¼ cup butter or margarine
2 cups confectioners' sugar
3 tablespoons milk
   Pinch salt
¼ teaspoon almond extract
¼ cup slivered almonds

Cream butter, add sugar, blend well. Add milk, stir until smooth and light. Flavor with salt and almond extract. Stir almonds into frosting; or sprinkle them on frosted cake.

COOKED BUTTER FROSTING

2½ tablespoons flour
   Pinch salt
½ cup milk
½ cup butter or margarine
½ cup sugar
½ teaspoon vanilla

Blend flour, salt and milk in a small pan, stir over low heat until mixture is thickened and smooth. In a mixing bowl cream butter, add sugar and vanilla. Gradually beat in milk mixture, continue to beat until frosting is fluffy.

CHOCOLATE GLAZE

1 square (1 ounce) unsweetened chocolate
2 tablespoons butter or margarine
2 tablespoons milk
1 cup confectioners' sugar
¼ teaspoon vanilla
⅛ teaspoon salt

Melt chocolate with butter and milk in a small pan. Cool. Add sugar, vanilla and salt, beat until smooth.

CHOCOLATE VELVET FROSTING

½ cup sugar
1½ tablespoons cornstarch
2 tablespoons butter or margarine
1 cup boiling water
1 square (1 ounce) unsweetened chocolate
½ teaspoon vanilla

Combine ingredients except vanilla, stir over low heat until smooth and thick. Add vanilla.

CONFECTIONERS' SUGAR GLAZE

½ cup confectioners' sugar
1 tablespoon hot water
   Few drops vanilla, lemon or
      almond extract

Blend sugar and water, flavor to taste. Or substitute slightly warmed brandy or other liquor for the water.

SEVEN-MINUTE FROSTING

3 egg whites
¼ cup sugar
6 tablespoons corn syrup
   Pinch salt
1 teaspoon vanilla

In the top of a double boiler over boiling water combine egg whites, sugar, corn syrup and salt. Beat with a rotary beater until the mixture holds firm peaks when the beater is lifted. Stir in vanilla. (See photo, page 195.)

SEA FOAM FROSTING

2 egg whites
1½ cups brown sugar (firmly packed)
1 tablespoon dark corn syrup
   Dash salt
⅓ cup cold water
1 teaspoon vanilla

Combine egg whites, sugar, corn syrup, salt and water in top of double boiler. Beat until blended, about ½ minute. Cook over boiling water, beating constantly, until stiff peaks form, about 5 to 7 minutes. Stir from bottom occasionally. Remove from heat and stir in vanilla.

Snowy Frosting: Use white sugar in place of brown sugar, and light corn syrup instead of dark.

ITALIAN MERINGUE

1 cup sugar
⅓ cup water
¼ teaspoon cream of tartar
2 egg whites
1 teaspoon vanilla

Combine sugar, water and cream of tartar in a saucepan, stir over moderate heat until sugar is dissolved. Bring the syrup to a boil and boil until the syrup spins a long thread from the end of a spoon, or registers 232°F on a candy thermometer. Meanwhile, beat the egg whites until they hold soft peaks. Add the hot syrup in a thin stream, beating constantly, until the frosting stands in stiff peaks. Stir in vanilla.

Variations: Add about 1 cup chocolate chips or nuts with the flavoring; or brown sugar may be substituted for the white; or use coffee brew instead of water; or swirl ½ cup preserves, marmalade or jam through the completed frosting.

CHOCOLATE MERINGUE

Fold into completed frosting, above, 3 squares (3 ounces) unsweetened baking chocolate, melted and cooled.

BROWN-SUGAR ICING

3 cups brown sugar
1 cup water
1 tablespoon butter or margarine
1 teaspoon vanilla
  Cream or milk

Boil sugar and water until syrup spins a thread (232°F on a candy thermometer). Add butter and vanilla, remove from heat. Cool. Beat until creamy, add cream or milk to thin icing to spreadable consistency.

CHOCOLATE CREAM FROSTING AND FILLING

⅔ cup sugar
⅓ cup water
3 egg yolks
1 cup butter or margarine, softened
2 ounces semisweet chocolate (⅓ cup morsels)
1 tablespoon double-strength brewed coffee
3 tablespoons brandy or rum

Boil sugar and water in a small saucepan until a few drops of syrup will form a soft ball in cold water or a candy thermometer registers 240°F. Beat the egg yolks until very light. Gradually beat in syrup, in a thin stream. Continue to beat until the mixture is cool to the touch. Gradually beat in butter. Melt the chocolate in coffee and add. Add the brandy or rum and beat until cool.

BROILED TOPPING

3 tablespoons water
3 tablespoons butter or margarine
1 cup finely chopped nuts
¾ cup brown sugar
1 egg, beaten

Combine water and butter in small pan, bring to a boil. Add remaining ingredients, spread on baked butter cake or other plain yellow cake. Place under broiler heat until topping browns and bubbles.

Frosting Mixes

Vary frosting mixes to your taste—anything, or almost anything, goes! To a creamy chocolate frosting, add crushed peppermint candy or a few drops of peppermint extract; or quick-dissolving instant coffee; or spices to taste; or a few drops of almond extract; or chopped nuts or coconut. Or sprinkle the frosted cake with nuts or coconut. Grated lemon or orange rind can be added to chocolate frosting or to creamy lemon frosting, for extra zip, or heated orange juice can be used in place of water.

Fluffy frosting can be flavored with any flavoring extract; or you can fold into the completed frosting 2 envelopes melted baking chocolate; or chocolate chips, nuts or coconut can be folded into the frosting or sprinkled on the frosted cake.

Fillings

Fillings, usually spread between the layers of a cake, may also be used as toppings on single or layer cakes, and in this way take the place of frosting (a timesaver).

PASTRY CREAM

½ cup sugar
⅓ cup flour
½ teaspoon salt
2 cups milk
4 egg yolks, or 2 whole eggs
2 teaspoons vanilla

Stir sugar, flour and salt with milk. Cook over low heat, stirring constantly, until mixture is smooth and thick. Beat a little hot sauce into the egg yolks, return to pan, cook, stirring, until smooth, about 1 minute. Cool, add vanilla. Use to fill pies, tarts, layer cakes. Makes about 2½ cups.

CHOCOLATE-CHEESE FILLING

**1 package (6 ounces) semisweet chocolate
   pieces**
2 tablespoons butter or margarine
3 tablespoons hot water
**1 cup cottage cheese, pressed through a
   sieve, or ricotta cheese**
½ teaspoon almond extract
½ teaspoon lemon juice

Melt chocolate and butter in the top of a double boiler. Add hot water, blend well. Combine cottage cheese or ricotta with the chocolate mixture. Add almond extract and lemon juice, blend until smooth. Makes about 1½ cups.

LEMON FILLING

¾ cup sugar
3 tablespoons cornstarch
   Dash salt
¾ cup water
2 egg yolks
2 tablespoons butter or margarine
2 tablespoons grated lemon rind
¼ cup lemon juice

Combine sugar, cornstarch and salt in saucepan, stir in water. Bring to a boil, stirring constantly, boil 1 minute. Add half hot mixture to egg yolks, return to pan and cook 1 minute longer. Remove from heat, add butter, lemon rind and lemon juice. Cool before filling 8- or 9-inch layer cake.

EASY CAKE FILLING

Prepare any flavor pudding and pie filling mix as directed on the package. Cover with waxed paper, cool. Beat until smooth and creamy. Spread between layers of 8- or 9-inch cake. Leftover filling may be served as a dessert. To use instant pudding mix, simply prepare as directed, use immediately.

PIE TALK

Is there anything that compares to a piece of hot apple pie with a slice of sharp Cheddar cheese? Or blueberry pie à la mode? The tang of lemon chiffon? The rich, sweet chill of Nesselrode? The range of pies is diverse enough to satisfy everyone's tastes.

Pie Pastry

A pie is only as good as its pastry. No matter what the filling is, no matter how good it is, a leathery crust or a soggy crust will ruin the pie. And remember, pie shells, baked and unbaked, are also used in a number of recipes other than for dessert pies.

PASTRY FOR 2-CRUST PIE

2 cups flour
1 teaspoon salt
2 tablespoons sugar (optional)
⅔ cup hydrogenated shortening or lard
¼ cup ice water (approximately)

Toss flour, salt and sugar to mix. Cut in shortening with a wire pastry blender or two knives until mixture looks like coarse meal. Sprinkle with water, using enough to moisten. Gather into a ball with a fork. Divide dough in half, roll out between floured sheets of waxed paper or on lightly floured board to make thin rounds.

PASTRY FOR 1-CRUST PIE

1 cup flour
½ teaspoon salt
1 tablespoon sugar (optional)
⅓ cup hydrogenated shortening or lard
2 tablespoons cold water

Prepare dough as directed for a 2-crust pie (above). Roll between floured sheets of waxed paper or on lightly floured board to make a round 1 inch larger than inverted pie pan. Ease pastry into pan, fold edges under, even with rim. Flute edges. Fill and bake according to recipe. To bake before filling: Prick pie shell with a fork or cover with dried beans or rice to prevent crust from bubbling. Bake in a very hot oven (475°F) 8 to 10 minutes. Remove beans a few minutes before baking is finished. Cool before filling.

LATTICE TOP

To make a lattice top: Roll pastry for top crust of pie, cut into ½-inch-wide strips with a knife or fluted pastry wheel. Place half the pastry strips across filling about 1 inch apart. Weave remaining strips to make lattice. Moisten ends of strips, fold lower crust over ends and press firmly to seal. Flute, if desired. (See photo, page 213.)

PANTRY SHELF PIE CRUST MIX

6 cups flour
1 tablespoon salt
⅓ cup sugar (optional)
**2 cups (1 pound) hydrogenated shortening
   or lard**

Mix ingredients as for 2-crust pie (above). Store on the pantry shelf in a covered container—a 3-pound coffee tin is a good choice. Add about ¼ cup ice water to 2⅔ cups of this mixture to make Pastry for 2-Crust Pie (see above).

OIL PIE PASTRY

2 cups flour
1 teaspoon salt
½ cup vegetable oil
3 tablespoons ice-cold water

Toss flour and salt together, add oil, mix with a fork or a pastry blender until mixture looks like fine crumbs. Sprinkle with enough ice-cold water to moisten, gather into a ball. Makes enough for a 2-crust pie.

COOKIE-DOUGH PIE CRUST

1 cup flour
½ teaspoon salt
2 tablespoons sugar
½ cup butter or margarine

Toss flour, salt and sugar to mix. Add butter and work to a paste. Press paste against bottom and sides of a 9-inch pie plate. Use for open-faced fruit pies. To use for chiffon pies and other cooked fillings, chill, prick and bake in a hot oven (400°F) about 15 minutes, until golden brown.

COOKIE-CRUMB SHELL

1 cup zwieback or graham-cracker crumbs
2 tablespoons confectioners' sugar
¼ cup melted butter or margarine

Mix ingredients, press on bottom and sides of an 8- or 9-inch pie pan. Chill until set before filling; or bake in a moderate oven (350°F) 10 minutes, cool before filling. Baking produces a crisper crust.

TART SHELLS

2 cups flour
½ teaspoon salt
½ cup butter or margarine
½ cup shortening
6 tablespoons ice water

Toss together flour and salt, cut in butter and shortening. Sprinkle with water, gather dough into a ball, chill. Roll out thin on a floured board. Cut small circles, ovals or other shapes. Cut matching shapes out of heavy-duty aluminum foil. Lay dough on foil, turn up dough and foil together and pinch edges to shape tart shells. Prick well, bake on cookie sheet in a very hot (450°F) oven about 10 minutes, until brown. Cool. Just before serving fill with fruit and whipped cream or with cooked pie fillings. This dough can also be used to make 2 pie shells.

Pie Recipes

One-crust pies, 2-crust pies, lattice-topped pies, meringue-topped pies, fruit-filled pies, chiffon pies, tarts, turnovers—the choice is broad and the choice is yours.

VERMONT APPLE PIE

Pastry for 2-crust pie
2½ pounds tart apples
½ cup sugar (approximately)
½ teaspoon cinnamon
⅛ teaspoon salt
¼ cup flour
2 tablespoons butter or margarine

Line a 9-inch pie pan with pastry. Peel and slice apples, taste them and add more or less sugar, as required. Add cinnamon, salt and flour, toss to mix. Fill pie shell, dot with butter. Cover with pastry, flute edges to seal, cut gashes in crust. Bake in a hot oven (400°F) about 45 minutes, until crust is browned and apples are tender. Serve warm or reheated, with cheese or ice cream.

SOUR-CREAM APPLE PIE

Pastry for 2-crust pie
2½ pounds apples
¼ cup flour
½ cup sugar (less if apples are sweet)
½ teaspoon cinnamon
¼ teaspoon salt
½ cup sour cream

Line a 9-inch pie plate with pastry. Peel and slice apples into a bowl. Add flour, sugar, cinnamon and salt, toss to mix. Fill pie plate. Spread sour cream over fruit, arrange top crust, crimp edges. Slash top crust. Bake in a moderately hot oven (400°F) about 35 minutes, until the crust is browned.

FRESH BLUEBERRY PIE

Pastry for 2-crust pie
4 cups blueberries
½ cup sugar (approximately)
¼ cup flour
Cinnamon, cloves, salt
1 tablespoon lemon juice
2 tablespoons butter or margarine

Line a 9-inch pie pan with pastry, fill with berries tossed with sugar to taste, flour, spices and salt. Sprinkle fruit with lemon juice, dot with butter. Adjust top crust, slash to allow steam to escape. Bake in a hot oven (400°F) about 35 minutes, until crust is browned.

Fresh Cherry Pie: Substitute fresh pitted sour red cherries for blueberries. Sweeten fruit with about ¾ cup sugar, eliminate lemon juice. Bake as directed.

CHERRY PIE

   2 cans (1 pound each) unsweetened sour
         pitted cherries
   ¼ cup cornstarch
   1½ cups sugar
   ⅛ teaspoon each salt and powdered cloves
   ½ cup juice drained from cherries
   ½ teaspoon almond extract
   1 tablespoon butter or margarine
      Pastry for 2-crust 9-inch pie

Drain cherries, reserving ½ cup juice. Mix cornstarch, sugar, salt and cloves with reserved juice. Cook over low heat, stirring constantly, until juice is clear and thickened. Add cherries, almond extract and butter. Cool. Fill pastry-lined pie pan with cherries, cover fruit with top crust, press edges to seal, flute. Or cover fruit with lattice strips of pastry. Bake in a hot oven (400°F) about 35 minutes, until crust is browned. Serve warm. (See photo, page 213.)

PEACHES-AND-CREAM PIE

   3 cups fresh peach slices
   ¾ cup sugar
   ¼ cup flour
   ¼ teaspoon salt
   ¼ teaspoon nutmeg
      Unbaked 9-inch pie shell
   1 cup heavy cream

Toss peach slices with sugar, flour, salt and nutmeg. Fill pie shell. Pour cream over fruit. Bake in a moderately hot oven (375°F) for about 40 minutes, until pastry is browned and fruit is tender. Serve chilled.

PRUNE PIE

   2 cups snipped pitted prunes
   ¼ cup honey
   ¼ cup orange juice or sherry
      Baked pie shell
      Meringue Topping (page 214)

Cover finely snipped prunes with honey and orange juice or sherry, let stand 30 minutes.

Fill baked pie shell, spread to edges with meringue topping. Bake in a moderate oven (350°F) about 15 minutes, until meringue is golden.

RAISIN PIE

   2 eggs, lightly beaten
   ¾ cup sugar
   ¼ teaspoon salt
   1 teaspoon cinnamon
   ½ teaspoon nutmeg
   ¼ teaspoon cloves
   1 cup dairy sour cream
   1 cup raisins
      Unbaked 8-inch pie shell

Combine eggs, sugar, salt and spices, mix well. Stir in sour cream and raisins, pour into pie shell. Bake in hot oven (425°F) for 10 minutes. Reduce heat to moderate (350°F) and bake 30 minutes longer, or until knife inserted near center comes out clean. Serve warm or chilled.

RHUBARB PIE

      Pastry for a 2-crust pie
   3 cups sliced rhubarb
   1 cup sugar
   ¼ cup flour
   2 tablespoons butter or margarine

Line pie plate with pastry. Toss rhubarb with sugar and flour, fill pie plate, dot with butter, cover with top crust. Flute edges to seal. Cut gashes in top to allow steam to escape. Bake in a hot oven (400°F) about 35 minutes, until crust is well browned. Taste the juices by inserting a small spoon through a gash into the crust, and add more sugar if necessary.

Strawberry-Rhubarb Pie: Use half rhubarb, half strawberries in above recipe, reduce sugar to ¾ cup, and proceed as directed.

CRUMB-TOPPED MINCE PIE

   4 cups mincemeat
   3 cups chopped tart apples
      Unbaked 9-inch pie shell
   1 cup flour
   ½ teaspoon salt
   ½ cup brown sugar
   ½ cup butter or margarine

Mincemeat may be homemade, canned, or reconstituted dried. Add apples. Fill pie shell. Toss flour, salt and sugar, work in butter with the fingertips to make very coarse crumbs. Sprinkle crumbs on mincemeat. Bake in a hot oven (400°F) about 35 minutes, until pie crust is golden brown.

Variation: Substitute pears for apples; use white sugar in crumb topping instead of brown. Spice topping with cinnamon or clove. (See photo, page 213.)

PUMPKIN PIE

**1 can (1 pound) pumpkin, or 2 cups
   cooked mashed winter squash
½ teaspoon ground ginger
1 teaspoon cinnamon
   Pinch nutmeg
⅔ cup brown sugar
1¾ cups light cream, or 1 can (13 ounces)
   evaporated milk
4 eggs, lightly beaten
   Unbaked 9-inch pie shell, chilled**

Mix 2 tablespoons pumpkin with spices, combine with remaining pumpkin and sugar, blend well. Stir in cream and eggs, pour into pie shell. Bake in a hot oven (450°F) 15 minutes, reduce heat to moderate (350°F) and bake 25 minutes longer, until filling is set and crust is browned. A knife inserted near, but not at, the center should come out dry. Serve at room temperature or chilled.

SWEET-POTATO PIE

**1½ cups mashed cooked sweet potatoes
¾ cup brown sugar, packed
2 teaspoons pumpkin-pie spice
½ teaspoon salt
2 eggs, beaten
1 can (13 ounces) evaporated milk
2 tablespoons melted butter or margarine
   Unbaked 9-inch pie shell**

Mix all ingredients and pour into pie shell. Bake in a hot oven (425°F) 10 minutes. Lower heat to 350°F and bake ½ hour or more, until filling is set. Cool.

FRENCH APPLE TART

**1 recipe Cookie-Dough Pie Crust (page 210)
3 pounds apples
2 tablespoons water
3 tablespoons butter or margarine
1 tablespoon lemon juice
   Sugar to taste
½ cup apple jelly**

Bake pie crust in a hot oven (400°F) for only 10 minutes; cool. Reserve 2 large apples; peel and slice the rest into wedges, put into a skillet with water and half the butter. Simmer

until water evaporates and apple slices are just tender. Add lemon juice and sugar to taste, simmer until sugar dissolves. Cool. Put cooked fruit into tart shell. Peel and slice remaining apples into thin slices. Arrange slices in a spiral pattern on top of cooked fruit. Brush with remaining butter, sprinkle with a little sugar. Bake in a moderately hot oven (375°F) about 15 to 20 minutes, until the apple slices are tender. Melt jelly, pour over fruit. (See photo, page 215.)

STRAWBERRY-APPLE TART

**Unbaked 9-inch pie shell
½ cup cookie crumbs
2½ pounds Rome Beauty or other cooking
   apples
½ cup sugar
½ teaspoon cinnamon
3 tablespoons lemon juice
½ cup strawberry preserves**

Sprinkle pie shell with cookie crumbs. Peel and slice apples, toss with sugar, cinnamon and lemon juice. Heap in pie shell. Bake in a moderate oven (350°F) about 1 hour, until the apples are tender and the crust is browned. Spread with preserves.

CREAM TARTS

**1 package pudding dessert, any flavor
   (about 4 ounces)
1¾ cups milk
½ cup prepared whipped topping
6 Tart Shells (page 210)**

Combine pudding dessert and milk in a saucepan. Cook, stirring, until mixture comes to a boil. Lay a round of waxed paper on surface of pudding, cool and chill thoroughly. Fold in whipped topping (or whipped cream). Fill tart shells, top with shaved chocolate, chopped nuts, coconut flakes, or fresh or canned fruit.

SHOOFLY PIE

**¾ cup molasses
¾ cup hot water
½ teaspoon baking soda
   Unbaked 9-inch pie shell
2 cups flour
½ cup brown sugar
   Pinch salt
⅓ cup butter or margarine**

Stir molasses and hot water with baking soda, cool, pour into unbaked pie shell. Mix flour, sugar and salt, rub in butter with the finger-

Crumb-Topped Mince Pie begins with prepared mincemeat, to which you add fresh apples or pears, and crisp crumb topping. The lattice-topped Cherry Pie is positively bursting with filling—as bountiful as you want to make it for your family. When you present a pie like this, your whole family knows you care. Serve slightly warmed for best-flavored filling, best-textured crust. (See page 211.)

tips to make a crumbly mixture. Sprinkle over molasses. Bake in a hot oven (400°F) for 15 minutes, reduce heat to moderate (350°F), bake about 25 minutes longer, until filling is firm.

PECAN PIE

2 eggs, beaten
1 cup dark corn syrup
⅓ teaspoon salt
1 teaspoon vanilla
1 cup sugar
2 tablespoons melted butter or margarine
1 cup pecan meats
Unbaked 9-inch pie shell

Mix ingredients, pour into unbaked pie shell. Bake in hot oven (400°F) 35 to 40 minutes, until knife inserted near center comes out clean.

ANGEL PIE

4 egg whites
Pinch salt
1 cup sugar
1 teaspoon vinegar
1 teaspoon vanilla

Beat egg whites with salt until frothy, gradually beat in sugar, continue beating until very stiff. Fold in vinegar and vanilla. Spread meringue on a lightly greased pie pan, shaping it like a pie crust, with a high rim and a flat center. Bake in a very slow oven (275°F) about 1 hour, until meringue is dry and crisp, but not colored. Cool, fill with any cooked, cooled pie mixture, cream, custard, or chiffon; or with whipped cream and fruit; or with a can of fruit pie filling.

LEMON MERINGUE PIE

1 package (3⅜ ounces) lemon pudding
   and pie filling mix
2 eggs, separated
2½ cups water
¾ cup sugar
Pinch salt
Baked 9-inch pie shell

Blend pudding mix with egg yolks and ½ cup water in a saucepan. Add ½ cup sugar and remaining water. Cook over moderate heat, stirring, until mixture thickens and comes to a boil. Cool 5 minutes, stirring occasionally. Meanwhile, beat egg whites with a pinch of salt until foamy. Gradually beat in remaining ¼ cup sugar, beat until stiff peaks form. Fill pie shell with lemon mixture. Spread

this meringue topping on filling, touching pie crust edges. Bake in a moderate oven (350°F) about 15 minutes, until meringue is tipped with golden brown.

MERINGUE TOPPING FOR PIE

3 egg whites
Pinch salt
¼ teaspoon cream of tartar
6 tablespoons sugar

Beat egg whites until foamy, add salt and cream of tartar, beat until mixture forms soft peaks. Add sugar, a spoonful at a time, beating constantly, until meringue stands in very stiff peaks when beater is removed. Pile on hot pie filling, spreading to touch edges all around—this prevents shrinking—and swirl with a spatula. Bake in a moderate oven (350°F) about 15 minutes, until the meringue is tipped with golden brown. Cool before serving.

NESSELRODE PIE

1 envelope unflavored gelatin
1½ cups milk
3 eggs, separated
½ cup chopped candied fruit
2 tablespoons slivered almonds
1 cup macaroon crumbs
1 teaspoon vanilla
1 tablespoon rum
⅓ cup sugar
Pinch salt
Baked 9-inch pie shell or crumb crust
Semisweet chocolate

Soften gelatin in ¼ cup milk. Whisk remaining milk with egg yolks in a saucepan over low heat, add gelatin. Cook, stirring constantly, until gelatin is dissolved and custard is smooth and thickened. Do not boil. Add fruit, almonds, crumbs and flavorings. Cool, stirring occasionally, until mixture is stiff enough to mound on a spoon. Beat egg whites until foamy, gradually beat in sugar and a pinch of salt, continue to beat until stiff peaks form. Fold egg whites into cooled custard. Pile into prepared pie shell, garnish with chocolate shaving. Chill until very firm. If desired, decorate with whipped cream before serving. Makes 8 servings.

NESSELRODE PUDDING PIE

2 eggs, separated
1½ cups milk
1 package (3¼ ounces) vanilla pudding
   and pie mix

Handsome enough to grace the pastry table in the most elaborate French restaurant, yet so simple you will want to make it often, so wholesome you will gladly serve it to the children. The crust requires no rolling; simply press the dough into the pan. No guessing about the flavor; the apples are glazed first, seasoned with lemon juice and sugar to taste. Melted apple jelly makes an instant glossy topping. (See page 212.)

1 envelope unflavored gelatin
2 tablespoons sugar
Pinch salt
¼ cup sliced maraschino cherries
¼ cup raisins
¼ cup slivered almonds
¼ teaspoon almond extract
Baked 9-inch pie shell or crumb crust
Sweet chocolate

Stir egg yolks in a saucepan with ½ cup milk, vanilla pudding and gelatin. Add remaining milk, cook over moderate heat, stirring constantly, until pudding reaches the boiling point. Chill until thick enough to mound on a spoon, stirring occasionally. Beat egg whites until frothy, gradually beat in sugar and salt, continue to beat until whites stand in stiff peaks. Fold into thickened pudding. Fold in cherries, raisins, almonds and extract. Fill prepared pie shell, garnish with chocolate shavings. Chill until firm. Serve with whipped cream, if desired.

QUICK JELLIED FRUIT PIE

1 package (3 ounces) fruit-flavored gelatin
1 cup boiling water
¼ cup cold water
1 package (10 ounces) frozen fruit
Baked 8-inch pie shell
½ cup heavy cream, whipped (optional)

Dissolve gelatin (any flavor) in boiling water, add cold water and frozen fruit, stir until fruit separates. Pour into pie shell, chill until firm. Top with whipped cream, if desired.

EASY LEMON CHIFFON PIE

1 envelope unflavored gelatin
¼ cup cold water
½ cup boiling water
⅔ cup sugar
1 can (6 ounces) frozen lemonade
    concentrate
1 cup heavy cream, whipped; or 2 cups
    whipped topping
9-inch cookie-crumb pie shell (page 210)

Soften gelatin in cold water, dissolve in boiling water. Add sugar, dissolve. Add lemonade, stir. Chill until mixture is thickened but not set. Whip cream, fold in. Fill pie shell, chill until firm.

ORANGE CHIFFON PIE

4 eggs, separated
½ cup sugar
½ teaspoon salt

¾ cup orange juice
1 envelope unflavored gelatin
1 tablespoon grated orange rind
½ cup sugar
Baked 9-inch pie shell
Orange slices for garnish

Beat egg yolks with sugar, salt and orange juice in the top of a double boiler. Add gelatin and cook over boiling water, stirring constantly, until gelatin is dissolved and mixture is smooth and thickened. Add orange rind. Cool, stirring occasionally, until mixture is thick enough to mound on a spoon. Beat egg whites until foamy, gradually add sugar, beating until stiff. Fold whites into cooled yolk mixture. Fill pie shell, chill until firm. Garnish with thin orange slices and whipped cream if desired.

Lemon Chiffon Pie: Substitute ½ cup lemon juice and ¼ cup water for the orange juice, 2 teaspoons grated lemon rind for the orange rind; proceed as directed.

PUMPKIN CHIFFON PIE

1¾ cups canned pumpkin
1 cup dark brown sugar
½ teaspoon salt
1 teaspoon cinnamon
½ teaspoon ginger
½ teaspoon nutmeg
¼ teaspoon allspice
1 envelope unflavored gelatin
3 eggs, separated
1 cup heavy cream, or 2 cups whipped
    topping
2 tablespoons sugar
Baked 9-inch pie shell

Combine pumpkin, brown sugar, salt, spices and gelatin; stir in egg yolks. Cook over medium heat until the custard is smooth and thickened, stirring constantly. Cool, chill until on the point of setting. Whip cream; fold half into chilled pumpkin mixture. Beat egg whites until foamy, add sugar, beat until stiff. Fold into pumpkin custard. Pile in baked pie shell, chill until set. Serve topped with remaining whipped cream.

FRIED PIES

Roll out pastry for a 2-crust pie half at a time, cut into 5-inch rounds. On half of each round put a spoonful of applesauce, chopped peaches or apples, or cooked, mashed dried fruits, seasoned to taste with sugar and spices. Fold over, crimp edges with a fork. Fry in hot (365°F) deep fat until delicately brown. Drain on absorbent paper. Serve warm.

APPLE TURNOVERS

½ cup butter or margarine
4 ounces cream cheese
1 cup flour
1 teaspoon sugar
¼ teaspoon salt
2 cups finely chopped apples
1 tablespoon lemon juice
1 teaspoon cinnamon
2 tablespoons sugar
Pinch salt

Cream butter and cream cheese, work in flour, sugar and salt. Blend until smooth, chill until firm. Roll dough very thin, cut into 5-inch squares. Toss apples with seasonings to taste. Divide apples onto half of each square, fold to make triangles, press edges to seal. Bake in a hot oven (400°F) until dough is well puffed and browned, about 15 minutes.

Cream Puff Shells

Cream puff paste is one of the most useful and versatile doughs in the baker's repertory. It can be shaped in an endless variety of ways, from tiny puffs to huge rings, baked and filled with pastry cream, whipped cream, ice cream, or any sweet mixture for dessert. Or the same shells can be filled with savory mixtures and served as appetizers or main dishes.

CREAM PUFF PASTE

1 cup water
½ cup butter or margarine
1 cup flour
½ teaspoon salt
4 eggs

Bring water to a boil with butter. Add flour and salt, beat with a wooden spoon until mixture leaves sides of pan and forms a ball. Remove pan from heat. Beat in eggs, one at a time, beating well after each.

CREAM PUFFS

Shape large cream puffs by dropping tablespoons of Cream Puff Paste (above) onto a greased baking sheet. Bake in a hot oven (400°F) 10 minutes, reduce temperature to 350°F and bake about 30 minutes longer, until the puffs are dry and browned. Pierce them with a skewer for the last 5 minutes of baking time to let steam escape. Makes 16.

Shape small cream puffs with a teaspoon. Bake at 400°F for 10 minutes, at 350°F for 10 minutes. Pierce, bake about 5 minutes longer. Makes about 40.

To make eclairs, use a pastry bag or cookie press with a flat nozzle, or use a spoon and a spatula to shape 16 strips about 4 inches long and 1 inch wide. Bake at 400°F for 10 minutes, at 350°F for 25 minutes. Pierce, bake 5 minutes, until dry and browned.

To Fill: Cut off top, fill with pastry cream, pudding, custard or whipped cream, and replace top. Top with frosting or confectioners' sugar, if desired.

PROFITEROLES

Fill tiny cream puff shells with ice cream, serve 2 or 3 to a portion, pour hot chocolate sauce over them.

THE COOKIE JAR

Keeping the cookie jar full is no problem, even when your time is restricted and the children's appetites unbounded. Choose bar cookies or drop cookies when time is short; refrigerator cookies to keep on hand for emergency baking; shaped and cutout cookies for special occasions . . . and let the children help make them!

Bar Cookies

Bar cookies are baked in one sheet, and then may be cut into any desired shape, but usually squares or rectangles.

COCOA BROWNIES

⅓ cup butter or margarine
⅓ cup cocoa
2 eggs
1 cup sugar
1 teaspoon vanilla
½ cup flour
½ teaspoon baking powder
¼ teaspoon salt
¾ cup chopped nuts (optional)

Melt butter, add cocoa, stir until smooth. Beat eggs with sugar until light. Add cocoa mixture and vanilla. Toss flour, baking powder and salt to mix. Add to batter, beat well. Stir in nuts, if desired. Bake in a greased and floured 8-inch square baking pan in a moderate oven (350°F) about 30 minutes. Cut into 2-inch squares. Makes 16 brownies.

CHEWY RAISIN BARS

½ cup butter or margarine
2 cups brown sugar, packed
2 eggs
1 cup all-purpose flour
2 teaspoons baking powder
½ teaspoon salt
1½ cups raisins
½ cup chopped walnuts

Melt butter, add sugar, stir over low heat until sugar is just dissolved. Cool slightly. Beat in eggs, one at a time; add vanilla. Toss dry ingredients, add to sugar mixture. Combine well. Fold in raisins and walnuts. Bake in a shallow greased and floured 10-inch-by-15-inch pan in a moderate oven (350°F) 25 minutes. Cool, cut into bars, 2 by 1½ inches. Makes 50.

APRICOT-ORANGE BARS

¼ cup water
1 tablespoon flour
½ cup sugar
½ teaspoon grated orange rind
⅛ teaspoon salt
1½ cups chopped dried apricots
¼ cup orange juice
1 cup flour
½ teaspoon salt
¾ cup sugar
⅔ cup butter or margarine
1½ cups rolled oats

Make filling by combining first seven ingredients in a saucepan; cook until thick. Toss 1 cup flour with salt and sugar. Cut in butter with pastry blender or two knives until the mixture resembles coarse meal. Add rolled oats and mix thoroughly. Pat half this mixture into an 8-inch square baking pan. Spread with filling. Cover with remaining flour mixture, pat firmly. Bake in a hot oven (425°F) 25 to 30 minutes, until lightly browned. Cool, cut into 2-inch squares. Makes 16. (See photo, page 219.)

BUTTER PECAN BARS

½ cup butter or margarine
1 cup brown sugar
2 eggs
2 teaspoons vanilla
1 cup flour
1 teaspoon baking powder
¼ teaspoon salt
1 cup finely chopped pecans

Cream butter with sugar, beat in eggs and vanilla. Toss together flour, baking powder and salt, add to butter mixture, mix well. Stir in pecans. Bake in a greased 10-inch-by-15-inch jelly-roll pan in a moderate oven (350°F) 12 to 15 minutes. Cool in pan, cut into bars. Makes 75 2-inch-by-1-inch bars. (See photo, page 219.)

Drop Cookies

Drop cookies are formed by dropping spoonfuls of batter onto a cookie sheet.

PEANUT-BUTTER COOKIES

½ cup peanut butter
½ cup butter or margarine
½ cup brown sugar
1 cup granulated sugar
2½ cups quick-cooking oats
1 egg
¼ cup milk
¼ teaspoon salt
½ teaspoon baking soda
½ cup seedless raisins

Cream peanut butter and butter together, add sugar, blend well. Add oats gradually. Mix together egg, milk, salt and baking soda; add with raisins. Drop dough by teaspoonfuls, 2 inches apart, onto an ungreased cookie sheet. Bake in a moderately hot oven (375°F) 10 to 20 minutes, until lightly browned. Makes 4 to 5 dozen.

CHOCOLATE DROPS

½ cup butter or margarine
1 cup sugar
2 eggs, well beaten
2 squares (2 ounces) unsweetened chocolate, melted
¼ teaspoon salt
½ teaspoon vanilla
¾ cup flour
Pecan or walnut halves

Cream butter with sugar, beat in eggs. Stir in chocolate, salt and vanilla. Add flour and mix well. Drop from a teaspoon onto ungreased baking sheet, top each mound with a nut. Bake in a moderate oven (350°F) 10 to 12 minutes, until firm to the touch. Makes about 2 dozen.

OATMEAL BRITTLE

½ cup butter or margarine
½ cup white sugar
½ cup brown sugar
1 egg

Name your favorite cookie (clockwise, beginning at 12 o'clock): Marble Refrigerator Cookies, Apricot-Orange Bars, Spritz, Sugar Cookie Cutouts, Gingerbread Men, Cocoa-Rum Treats, Chocolate-Chip Cookies, Shortbread, Butter Pecan Bars. Crisp cookies should be stored in airtight tins, soft cookies with an apple slice in the container to keep them moist.

½ teaspoon vanilla
2½ cups oatmeal
½ teaspoon baking soda
½ teaspoon salt
½ cup chopped nuts
½ cup raisins
½ cup chocolate chips

Cream butter with sugar. Beat in egg, add vanilla. Add oatmeal, baking soda and salt. Blend well. Add nuts, raisins, chocolate chips. Drop from teaspoon onto greased cookie sheet 1 inch apart. Bake in a moderately hot oven (375°F) about 10 minutes. Let stand 1 minute before removing from sheet. Makes 4 dozen.

APPLESAUCE HERMITS

½ cup butter or margarine
1 cup light brown sugar, firmly packed
1 egg
2 cups applesauce
2¾ cups flour
1 teaspoon baking soda
½ teaspoon salt
½ teaspoon cinnamon
¼ teaspoon each nutmeg and ginger
1 cup chopped nuts
1 cup raisins

Cream butter, add sugar gradually, beat until fluffy. Beat in egg and applesauce. Toss flour with baking soda, salt and spices to mix, add nuts and raisins. Add to applesauce mixture, mix well. Drop by teaspoonfuls, 2 inches apart, onto greased cookie sheets. Bake about 12 minutes in a moderate oven (350°F). Makes about 6 dozen.

CHOCOLATE-CHIP COOKIES

½ cup butter or margarine
½ cup granulated sugar
¼ cup brown sugar, firmly packed
1 egg
¾ teaspoon vanilla
1 cup + 2 tablespoons flour
½ teaspoon baking soda
¼ teaspoon salt
1 cup chocolate chips
½ cup raisins or nuts

Beat butter and sugar together until fluffy. Beat in egg and vanilla. Gradually stir in flour, baking soda and salt. Add chocolate chips and raisins. Drop by teaspoonfuls onto lightly greased cookie sheets. Bake in a moderately hot oven (375°F) 8 to 10 minutes,

until golden. Makes 4 dozen cookies. (See photo, page 219.)

Oatmeal Chocolate-Chip Cookies: Reduce flour to ½ cup and add 1 cup + 2 tablespoons quick-cooking oatmeal. Proceed as above.

COCONUT MACAROONS

2 egg whites
½ teaspoon salt
1 cup sugar
2 cups cornflakes
1 cup flaked coconut
½ teaspoon almond extract

Beat egg whites and salt until foamy. Add sugar, a tablespoon at a time, beating well after each addition. Continue beating until mixture is stiff and glossy. Lightly stir in cornflakes, coconut and flavoring. Drop from teaspoon onto greased cookie sheets. Bake in moderate oven (350°F) 12 to 15 minutes, or until lightly browned. Remove from cookie sheets immediately. Makes about 3 dozen.

Refrigerator Cookies

The dough for refrigerator cookies is formed into a roll and then refrigerated until thoroughly chilled. You may slice from the chilled roll only as many cookies as you wish to bake. The refrigerated dough will keep for a reasonable length of time.

MARBLE REFRIGERATOR COOKIES

1 cup butter or margarine
1 cup sugar
1 egg
1 teaspoon almond extract
1 teaspoon lemon extract
2½ cups flour
1½ teaspoons baking soda
⅛ teaspoon salt
1 tablespoon cocoa

Cream butter with sugar, add egg and flavorings, beat well. Add flour combined with baking soda and salt. Beat until dough cleans sides of bowl. Divide dough in half. Add cocoa to one part, mix well. Combine 2 portions of dough just until marbled. Form dough into a roll 3 inches in diameter. Wrap in waxed paper and chill several hours. Slice ¼ inch thick. Bake on a greased cookie sheet in a moderate oven (350°F) about 15 minutes. Makes 12 large cookies. (See photo, page 219.)

Molded Cookies

Molded cookies are shaped either by a cookie press or by hand.

SPRITZ

    1 cup butter or margarine
    ¾ cup sugar
    3 egg yolks
    1 teaspoon vanilla or almond extract
    2½ cups flour

Cream butter with sugar, beat in egg yolks and flavoring. Add flour, mix to make dough. Force dough through a cookie press onto ungreased baking sheets. Bake cookies in a hot oven (400°F) about 8 to 10 minutes, until firm to the touch, but not brown. Makes about 6 dozen cookies. (See photo, page 219.)

THIMBLES

    1 cup butter or margarine
    ¾ cup sugar
    2 egg yolks
    1 teaspoon vanilla
    2½ cups flour
    ½ teaspoon salt
    Marmalade or favorite preserves

Cream butter with sugar, add egg yolks and vanilla, blend well. Stir in flour mixed with salt. Chill dough for several hours, until it is firm enough to handle. Mold walnut-size balls, arrange on an ungreased baking sheet. With a thimble or your thumb, make a hollow in the center of each ball, fill with marmalade or preserves. Bake in a moderately hot oven (375°F) about 12 to 15 minutes, until lightly browned. Makes about 4 dozen.

SNICKERDOODLES

    1 cup butter or margarine
    1½ cups sugar
    2 eggs
    2¾ cups flour
    1 teaspoon baking soda
    2 teaspoons cream of tartar
    ½ teaspoon salt
    Sugar, cinnamon

Cream butter and sugar, beat in eggs. Toss flour with baking soda, cream of tartar and

salt, add to creamed mixture. Shape dough into small balls, roll in a mixture of sugar and cinnamon (about 4 parts sugar to 1 part cinnamon). Bake on ungreased cookie sheet in a hot oven (400°F) about 10 minutes, or until lightly browned. Makes 4 to 5 dozen.

RUSSIAN BALLS

    1 cup butter or margarine
    ½ cup sugar
    2¼ cups flour
    ¼ teaspoon salt
    1 teaspoon vanilla
    1 cup finely chopped nuts
    Confectioners' sugar for coating

Cream butter with sugar, work in flour mixed with salt. Add vanilla and chopped nuts. Shape into 1-inch balls. Bake on an ungreased baking pan in a hot oven (400°F) 15 minutes. Roll in confectioners' sugar, cool, roll in confectioners' sugar again. Makes 4 dozen.

Cutout Cookies

Cutout cookies are rolled out and cut into the desired shapes, either with a cookie cutter or a sharp knife, before they are baked.

CHEESE HORNS

    ½ cup butter or margarine
    ½ cup cottage cheese
    1 cup flour
    ½ cup sugar
    ½ cup chopped walnuts
    ½ teaspoon cinnamon

Blend butter, cottage cheese and flour to make a dough. Roll out ⅛ inch thick, cut into 3-inch squares. Mix sugar, nuts and cinnamon, sprinkle on squares. Roll up, corner to corner, bend ends to shape horns. Bake on a greased baking sheet in a moderate oven (350°F) about 20 minutes, until browned. Makes about 18.

SUGAR-COOKIE CUTOUTS

    1 cup sugar
    ¾ cup butter or margarine
    1 egg, beaten
    2 cups flour
    1 teaspoon baking powder
    ½ teaspoon salt
    ¼ cup milk
    ½ teaspoon lemon extract

Cream sugar and butter until light and fluffy. Add egg. Mix together flour, baking powder and salt, add to sugar mixture alternately with milk and extract. Chill. Roll dough ⅛ inch thick on lightly floured board. Cut with cookie cutters. Bake cutouts on ungreased baking sheet in a hot oven (400°F) 6 to 8 minutes, until golden. Makes 4 dozen 3-inch cookies. (See photo, page 219.)

APRICOT HATS

1 cup butter or margarine, softened
1 package (8 ounces) cream cheese, softened
2 cups all-purpose flour
1 cup apricot or other flavor preserves
2 tablespoons apricot or other fruit liqueur
Confectioners' sugar

Cream together butter and cream cheese until light and fluffy. Gradually add flour, blending well after each addition. Form dough into a ball, wrap in waxed paper and chill about 2 hours or until firm enough to roll. Meanwhile, combine preserves with fruit liqueur, heat until slightly thickened; cool. Remove half of chilled dough at a time, roll ¼ inch thick on board sprinkled with confectioners' sugar. Cut into 3-inch squares, spread each with about 1 teaspoon preserves. Fold corners to the center and pinch edges to shape a four-cornered hat. Place on ungreased cookie sheet, slightly apart. Bake in a moderately hot oven (375°F) about 15 minutes, until golden. Sprinkle with confectioners' sugar. Makes about 2 dozen.

SHORTBREAD

1 cup butter or margarine
½ cup confectioners' sugar
2½ cups flour
Pinch salt
¼ teaspoon almond extract (optional)

Cream butter with sugar. Add flour and salt, blend. Add almond extract, if desired. Chill at least 1 hour. Divide dough in half and roll about ⅓ inch thick on a lightly floured board. Cut into squares or diamonds. Bake in a moderately hot oven (375°F) about 15 minutes. Makes about 4 dozen 1½-inch cookies. (See photo, page 219.)

GINGERBREAD MEN

⅓ cup butter or margarine
1 cup brown sugar, firmly packed
1½ cups molasses
⅔ cup milk

7 cups all-purpose flour
2 teaspoons baking soda
1 teaspoon cinnamon
1 teaspoon cloves
1 teaspoon allspice
1 teaspoon ginger
1 teaspoon salt
Raisins for decoration (optional)

Cream butter with brown sugar and molasses until fluffy. Add milk. Toss remaining ingredients to mix, stir in. Chill several hours. Roll dough ¼ inch thick on a floured surface and cut with gingerbread man cookie cutter. Place on a lightly greased cookie sheet. Decorate with raisins for eyes, nose, mouth, etc., if desired. Bake in a moderate oven (350°F) 10 to 12 minutes, until cookies are firm to the touch. Makes about 2½ dozen. (See photo, page 219.)

ALMOND WAFERS

1 egg, well beaten
¾ cup sugar
½ cup ground almonds
¾ cup butter or margarine
2¼ cups sifted flour

Combine egg, sugar and almonds, add butter and mix well. Stir in flour, mixing well. Chill thoroughly. Roll thin and cut in desired shapes. Bake in a moderately hot oven (375°F) about 10 minutes. Makes about 5 dozen.

Unbaked Cookies

Unbaked cookies are just what the name implies. The dough is stiff enough and moist enough to be formed or cut, and the ingredients do not require further cooking.

RUM BALLS

4 cups yellow cake crumbs
2 tablespoons cocoa
½ cup light corn syrup
¼ cup rum
Confectioners' sugar
Chocolate sprinkles

Toss crumbs and cocoa to combine. Add syrup and rum to make a stiff paste. Shape teaspoons of mixture into 1-inch balls, rolling the mixture between hands dusted with confectioners' sugar. Roll in chocolate sprinkles, let stand in a cool place to dry about 1 hour. Makes 3 dozen rum balls.

CHOCOLATE-PEANUT BUTTER DROPS

1 cup peanut butter
½ cup raisins
1 cup (6 ounces) chocolate chips
1 tablespoon butter or margarine

Mix peanut butter with raisins and shape into 18 balls, using a heaping tablespoon for each. Place on waxed paper. Melt 1 cup chocolate bits with butter over hot water. Drizzle over peanut-butter balls. Quick-chill in refrigerator or freezer to harden chocolate. Makes 18.

MARSHMALLOW SQUARES

¼ cup oil
¼ pound marshmallows
1 teaspoon vanilla
4 cups crisp rice cereal

Heat oil in a large saucepan, add marshmallows, stir over low heat until melted. Stir in vanilla, add rice cereal, mix well. Pack into a greased 8-inch square pan, pressing down firmly with the back of a spoon. Cool. Cut into small squares.

BAKE SHOP BONUSES

The best of your local baker's products and the best we can bake in the Jane Parker Bakeries are offered to you at the A&P, with the freshness date stamped on the wrapper or the label.

There are soft sliced breads and crisp Italian loaves, dark breads, rye breads, home-style oatmeal breads, practical sandwich loaves, raisin breads, date-nut breads . . . and more. Choose breads to add variety and interest to meals and snacks—with a bonus in good nutrition and good eating at economical cost.

Rolls, muffins and biscuits come in varied textures and shapes, plain and fruited. Choose rolls that meet your needs and appetites, from muffins for breakfast to hero rolls for hearty lunch sandwiches to soft dinner rolls to set off a favorite meal.

Don't overlook the special values in day-old breads and rolls. They offer real savings with every purchase. To freshen them, remove from wrappings and heat in moistened paper bag or aluminum foil before serving.

If you shop infrequently, store extra breads, rolls and cakes in the freezer, to maintain freshness. If purchases are in moisture/vaporproof wrap, they may be placed directly in the freezer; otherwise, rewrap securely, or place in a plastic freezing bag and close securely. Note the date of purchase on the wrapper, and rotate freezer stocks so that the longest-stored are used first.

If you are watching your budget, bakery products offer good value for the food dollar. In fact, nutritionists suggest that the average family in the United States could get a good diet at a lower cost by using a larger share of each dollar for bakery products, milk and milk products, vegetables and fruit, and less of each dollar for foods in the meat group and other foods such as fats, oils, sugar, sweets, coffee, tea and soft drinks.

Breads and rolls, even when they are stale, can be used to make many quick and thrifty treats.

A Loaf of Bread

Take a loaf of bread and . . . and enhance it with seasonings, herbs, spices. Use stale bread for croutons and bread crumbs.

GARLIC FRENCH BREAD

Split a long French bread in half lengthwise. Spread cut sides generously with Garlic Butter (below). Put halves together, make crosswise slashes in bread to about ½ inch from the bottom crust. Place on foil, bake in a moderate oven (350°F) 10 to 15 minutes, until hot and crusty. If desired, bread may be prepared in advance, wrapped in foil and frozen. Bake in wrapper in a moderate oven (350°F) about 25 minutes to heat.

GARLIC BUTTER

Purée or grate 1 clove garlic, mash with ½ cup butter or margarine.

HERB BREAD

Slice long French bread on the diagonal down to, but not through, the bottom crust. Cream ½ cup butter or margarine with 1 to 2 teaspoons mixed dried herbs. Spread both sides of each slice. Place bread on foil and bake in a moderate oven (350°F) 10 to 15 minutes, until hot and crusty. If desired, prepare in advance, wrap in foil, and freeze. To heat, bake in the wrapper in a moderate oven (350°F) about 25 minutes.

> *White, whole wheat, rye, French—vary the breads you use for crumbs and croutons.*

TASTY CROUTONS

Cut stale bread into ½-inch cubes, toss with oil or melted butter or margarine, and bake in a slow oven (300°F) until lightly browned, stirring once or twice, for about 20 minutes. Add garlic or herbs to the oil for varied flavor.

DRY BREAD CRUMBS

Whirl stale bread cubes in a blender, or crush dry bread with a rolling pin. One bread slice makes about ½ cup dry bread crumbs. For herb-flavored crumbs, whirl parsley and basil flakes with the crumbs. Dry bread crumbs can be stored in a covered container for use as needed.

TOAST BASKET

Remove top and side crusts from a loaf of unsliced bread. Hollow out the center, leaving a shell about ¾ inch thick. (Use a very thin, sharp knife for this, cutting down one side at a time, then across bottom to release.) Brush shell with melted butter or margarine. Toast in a moderately hot oven (375°F) until lightly browned. Fill with creamed meat, fish or vegetables, or with scrambled eggs. Serve immediately.

Tip: Slice center removed from loaf thinly, spread with butter or margarine and use for dainty sandwiches.

TOAST CUPS

Remove crust from thin slices of very soft bread. Spread with softened butter or margarine. Press buttered side down into muffin pans. Toast in a moderately hot oven (375°F) until lightly browned. Fill with salad or creamed chicken.

Sandwiches

Make sandwiches in your choice of shape and style, from a wide variety of breads and rolls. Serve them hot or cold, open or closed, as a meal or as a snack.

TEA SANDWICHES

Make tea sandwiches from white bread, whole wheat, oatmeal, brown, almost any type of bread, for variety. Trim crusts from bread, flatten slightly with rolling pin, sandwich with softened butter or margarine and desired filling. Cut into finger slices, squares or triangles. Or cut the sandwiches into fancy shapes with a cookie cutter. Cover sandwiches with damp towel or foil and store in the refrigerator until serving time.

To make open sandwiches, spread bread with filling and garnish with sliced olives, parsley sprigs, sliced hard-cooked eggs, crumbled bacon, sliced cucumbers or lemon twists. Or decorate with tinted cream cheese. Cut into desired shapes.

ROLLED SANDWICHES

Trim crusts from unsliced day-old bread, cut loaves lengthwise into 5 or 6 slices. Flatten slightly with rolling pin, brush with melted butter or margarine. Spread each slice with ¼ cup of sandwich filling, cut it into two rectangles. At one end of each rectangle, lay a line of pimiento, olive or dill pickle. Beginning at this end, roll up sandwich. Cover rolls with damp towel or foil. Refrigerate 1 hour or more. Cut each roll into 4 slices. Arrange on platter for serving. These may be made in advance and frozen.

RIBBON SANDWICH LOAF

1 loaf unsliced day-old bread
  Butter or margarine

Red Filling:
4 slices boiled ham, minced
3 slices crisp bacon, crumbled
1 pimiento, minced
3 tablespoons mayonnaise

Yellow Filling:
  Mashed yolks of 3 hard-cooked eggs
  Salt, pepper
2 tablespoons mayonnaise

White Filling:
  1 package (3 ounces) cream cheese
½ cup peeled, grated radishes
  Chopped whites of 3 hard-cooked eggs
  2 tablespoons sour cream

Green Filling:
4 small sweet pickles, minced

1 tablespoon chopped parsley
2 tablespoons mayonnaise

Frosting:
   1 package (8 ounces) cream cheese
¼ cup hot milk

Remove crusts from loaf, cut into 5 length-wise slices, butter each slice. Mix fillings in separate bowls. Reshape the loaf, sand-wiching with fillings in the order given. Wrap in a damp towel, chill 3 hours. Beat milk into cream cheese gradually to make frosting, cover top and sides of loaf thickly. If desired, loaf may be decorated with tinted cream cheese, or with carrot curls, radish roses, parsley sprigs. Cut into slices to serve. Makes about 16 slices.

Sandwich Fillings

There is scarcely any food product, in any form, that can't become a sandwich filling on its own or in combinations.

CHICKEN FILLING

   2 cups finely diced cooked chicken
½ cup sour cream
¼ cup chopped toasted almonds
½ teaspoon curry powder

Combine ingredients. Makes 2 cups.

CRESS-AND-CHEESE FILLING

   1 package (8 ounces) cream cheese
¼ cup warm milk
   1 cup grated sharp Cheddar cheese
   1 cup finely chopped watercress
¼ teaspoon salt
   Dash cayenne

Soften cheese at room temperature. Beat in milk gradually. Add remaining ingredients and blend well. Makes about 2 cups.

HAM FILLING

½ pound lean ham, minced
   1 hard-cooked egg, chopped
   1 dill pickle, minced
   1 tablespoon tomato purée or ketchup
¼ cup sour cream
½ teaspoon prepared mustard

Combine ingredients. Makes about 1¾ cups.

AVOCADO FILLING

   1 avocado, peeled and stoned
   2 tablespoons lemon juice

   2 tablespoons sour cream
   2 tablespoons chopped chives
½ teaspoon salt

Mash avocado with remaining ingredients. Makes about 1 cup.

ORANGE BLOSSOM FILLING

   1 package (8 ounces) cream cheese
   1 tablespoon orange juice or milk
¼ cup orange marmalade
   1 teaspoon minced onion

Cream together cream cheese and orange juice. Add remaining ingredients. Makes 1¼ cups.

BANANA SPREAD

   1 large banana
¼ cup peanut butter
   1 teaspoon lemon juice

Mash banana, combine with remaining ingredients, mix well. Makes about 1 cup.

MUSHROOM FILLING

½ cup soft butter or margarine
½ cup mushrooms, finely chopped
½ teaspoon salt
   2 tablespoons chopped ripe olives

In 2 tablespoons of butter, cook mushrooms until soft. Cool. Cream remaining butter with cooked mushrooms, salt and olives. Makes about 1 cup.

Toasted English Muffins

Use toasted English muffins instead of white bread in all your favorite grilled-sandwich recipes.

PIZZA GRILL

Spread toasted muffins with prepared spa-ghetti sauce, sprinkle with grated mozzarella cheese or your own favorite, top with a curled anchovy. Grill until cheese melts.

TUNA PIMIENTO

Cover toasted muffins with flaked tuna fish, spread with mayonnaise, fleck with bits of pimiento. Grill until mayonnaise puffs and browns.

BACON GRILL

Top toasted muffins with a slice of cheese and a strip of cooked bacon. Grill under the broiler until the cheese melts.

Bakery Bonanza

With a loaf of bread or a package of lady-fingers or any other packaged bakery goods as a basis, it's easy to create something different, something good.

BREAD INTO CAKE

1 loaf unsliced day-old bread
Melted butter or margarine
Jelly or marmalade
½ cup sugar
1 tablespoon cinnamon
¼ cup raisins
¼ cup chopped nuts
Brown sugar

Trim crusts from bread, slice loaf lengthwise into 5 thin slices. Flatten slices with a rolling pin, brush with melted butter, spread with a thin layer of jelly or marmalade. Combine sugar, cinnamon, raisins and nuts, sprinkle on bread slices. Roll up like a jelly roll. Generously butter small muffin cups and sprinkle with brown sugar. Cut rolls into ¾-inch pieces. Place cut side down in muffin cups. Brush with melted butter. Bake in a moderate oven (350°F) for 15 minutes. Serve warm. Makes about 25.

MOCK ANGEL FOOD CAKE

Cut unsliced day-old bread into 1-inch cubes. Dip into sweetened condensed milk, then into shredded coconut, coating evenly. Skewer cubes and toast over charcoal, or arrange on foil and broil 4 inches from heat, turning once, until browned.

RAISIN BREAD PUDDING

Prepare 1 package (3 ounces) home-style custard mix as directed on package. Cut 3 slices raisin bread into ½-inch cubes, pile in buttered 1-quart casserole. Pour custard over bread cubes, sprinkle with cinnamon. Let stand 1 hour. Serve chilled. Makes 5 servings.

CHERRY BREAD PUDDING

3 eggs
1½ cups milk
½ cup sugar
2 tablespoons melted butter or margarine
¼ teaspoon salt
¼ teaspoon cinnamon
8 slices bread, cut in ½-inch squares
1 jar (25 ounces) cherry pie filling

Beat eggs until foamy, stir in milk, sugar, butter, salt and cinnamon. Add bread and mix well. Stir in 2 cups cherry pie filling, reserve rest for topping. Pour into greased 8-inch square pan. Bake in a moderate oven (350°F) 45 minutes. Let stand about ½ hour. Gently loosen pudding from sides of pan with a small knife, invert onto a platter. Top with remaining cherry pie filling. Garnish with whipped cream or whipped topping, if desired. Makes 8 to 10 servings.

ELEANOR ROOSEVELT'S HUCKLEBERRY PUDDING

In answer to a request from the Parent-Teacher Association of the Smyth Road School, Manchester, New Hampshire, Mrs. Eleanor Roosevelt graciously sent "one of my favorite recipes" for inclusion in the members' fund-raising *First Lady Cookbook.*

"Line sides and bottom of glass casserole with slices of white bread (not too fresh and remove crusts). Pour in stewed huckleberries to cover bottom. Continue adding alternately bread and berries until dish is filled. Put in ice-box overnight. Serve with plain or whipped cream."

HUCKLEBERRY REFRIGERATOR PUDDING

The recipe that follows is our kitchen-tested interpretation of Mrs. Roosevelt's rule.

2 cups huckleberries or blueberries
1 tablespoon flour
Pinch salt
¼ cup water
¼ cup sugar (approximately)
Dash ground cloves
Lemon juice to taste
Thin-sliced white bread, crusts removed
1 cup whipped cream or whipped topping

Pick over huckleberries and discard stems; wash and drain. Toss with flour and salt. Add to water in a small saucepan, stir. Add ¼ cup sugar. Simmer, stirring constantly, until berries are cooked through but not mushy, 5 minutes or less. Taste and adjust the seasonings with more sugar, cloves and lemon juice. Cool slightly. Butter a 2-quart glass serving dish, cover bottom with bread. Cover bread with one-third of the berries. Fill the dish with alternate layers of remaining bread and berries, ending with the fruit. Chill several hours or overnight. Serve in the bowl, with whipped cream or whipped topping. Makes 6 servings.

Note: If huckleberries or blueberries are not available, use blackberries, raspberries or strawberries.

EASY FRUIT TARTS

    1 can (25 ounces) fruit pie filling
    12 slices fresh white bread, trimmed
        Soft butter or margarine
    ¼ pound cream cheese, softened
    2 tablespoons milk or cream
    1 teaspoon grated lemon rind
    1 tablespoon sugar

Chill pie filling. Spread bread with butter, fit into buttered individual muffin cups. Bake in a hot oven (400°F) about 10 minutes, until petal shells are crisp and golden. Cool. Beat softened cream cheese with milk to make a fluffy mixture. Add lemon rind and 1 tablespoon sugar. Put a spoonful of cheese filling into each shell, top generously with chilled pie filling, serve at once. Makes 12 servings.

Note: If desired, replace slices of white bread with purchased individual dessert shells.

IRISH TIPSY CAKE IN A HURRY

    2 sponge-cake layers
    ¼ cup raspberry jam
    1 cup sweet wine
    1 package (about 3 ounces) instant
        vanilla pudding
    1½ cups milk
    1 cup blanched slivered almonds

Spread the cake layers with jam and arrange in a glass serving bowl. Sprinkle with ¾ cup wine and let stand 1 hour in the refrigerator. Blend instant pudding mix with milk and the remaining ¼ cup wine. Beat with a rotary beater until thickened. Pour the custard over the cake. Stud with blanched almonds. Makes 8 servings.

SPARKLE CROWN CAKE

    3 packages (3 ounces each) fruit-flavored
        gelatin, flavors of different colors
    1 angel food cake (16 ounces)
    1 cup heavy cream or 2 cups whipped topping

Prepare gelatin separately as directed on packages, using ¼ cup less water than directed for each package. Put one flavor in refrigerator to chill until syrupy, set the other two aside. Slice a ½-inch layer from top of cake and set it aside. Cut down into cake ¾ inch from outer edge and ¾ inch from inside edge, stopping ¾ inch from the bottom. Gently pull out the cake between the cuts, leaving a ¾-inch-thick shell. When first gelatin begins to set, spoon a ½-inch layer into the cake. Chill. Pour remainder of this batch of gelatin into a flat plate to set. Set a second flavor of gelatin to chill. When this is syrupy, spoon a ½-inch layer over the solidly set first flavor in the cake. Chill. Pour remainder of this batch of gelatin into a flat plate to set. When second gelatin layer is set, add layer of the third flavor of gelatin and chill remainder in flat plate. Replace top slice of cake. Chill. Frost cake with whipped cream or whipped topping, building up cream on outside and inside edges. Chill. Cut reserved gelatin into diamonds and squares and sprinkle the "gems" on the cake. Makes 10 servings. (See photo, page 237.)

CHOCOLATE ICEBOX CAKE

    1 package (12 ounces) semisweet
        chocolate chips
    2 tablespoons sugar
    3 eggs, separated
    2 cups heavy cream, whipped, or 4 cups
        whipped topping
    1 teaspoon vanilla
    1 angel food cake
        Slivered toasted almonds

Melt chocolate and sugar in top of double boiler. Beat egg yolks well, add to chocolate. Cool. Beat egg whites until stiff, fold into chocolate. Fold in whipped cream and vanilla. Tear cake into small pieces. Place a layer of cake pieces in a buttered 2-quart mold, add a layer of chocolate, sprinkle with almonds. Repeat until mold is full. Chill 12 hours, unmold to serve. Makes 10 servings.

QUICK CHOCOLATE FANCY

    2 tablespoons cognac
    2 tablespoons water
    1 package (12) ladyfingers
    1 cup whipping cream
    ½ cup confectioners' sugar
    ¼ cup cocoa
        Dash salt

Mix cognac and water, dip ladyfingers into mixture, arrange 2 on each dessert plate. Sprinkle with remaining cognac mixture. Combine cream, sugar, cocoa and salt in blender container, whirl until smooth and thick, about 45 seconds, or whip with rotary beater. Pile onto ladyfingers. Makes 6 servings.

STRAWBERRY CHEESE CAKE

1 package (3 ounces) lemon gelatin dessert
1 cup boiling water
1 pound cottage cheese
1 package (8 ounces) cream cheese
24 ladyfingers
1 cup heavy cream, whipped, or 2 cups
   whipped topping
1½ cups Ann Page Strawberry Preserves

Dissolve gelatin in boiling water, cool. Sieve cottage cheese, beat in cream cheese and the cooled gelatin. Chill until thick. Line a 9-inch spring-form pan with 18 ladyfingers, split. Fold whipped cream into thickened cheese. Pour half of mixture into lined pan, cover with remaining 6 ladyfingers and ½ cup strawberry preserves. Top with remaining filling. Chill 3 hours. Remove sides of pan. Spread remaining preserves on cake. Makes 8 to 12 servings. (See photo, page 238.)

DOUGHNUTS

Buy doughnuts in the bakery section of the supermarket and add your own special touches. Frost with a thin layer of Butter Cream Frosting (page 207) and sprinkle with coconut, finely chopped nuts or candy sprinkles. Or spread doughnuts with Chocolate Glaze (page 207) or cover plain doughnuts with Broiled Topping (page 208) and broil as directed.

PIES PLUS

Pies from the bakery section of the supermarket can be a real bonus. Fruit pies are especially good when they are warmed to bring out the natural fruit flavors. They may be heated to serving temperature in about 15 minutes in a moderate oven (350°F). Serve them warm with ice cream, wedges of cheese, or whipped cream, or whipped topping. Or mix together 2 teaspoons of lemon juice and ½ cup confectioners' sugar and drizzle over the warm pie to glaze.

Pumpkin or custard pies may be served at room temperature. Top with whipped cream or your favorite whipped topping, or serve with ice cream. Garnish with chopped nuts, toasted coconut or shaved chocolate.

COOKIE REFRIGERATOR CAKE

Arrange alternate layers of cookies (chocolate wafers, ginger cookies or chocolate-chip cookies) and your favorite whipped topping (see page 246) in a serving dish. Refrigerate several hours. Serve as is, or with a dessert sauce (pages 244–246) if desired.

DESSERTS

Crown your meal or welcome guests with a dessert that complements the occasion . . . a light dessert after a heavy meal, a substantial dessert to round out a light meal. A thrifty dessert glorifies an economical meal, and even the simplest of desserts, quickly prepared, says you care enough to add something special to your menus.

A good dessert offers contrasts of flavor, texture and appearance in relation to the rest of the meal. It can also round out your nutritional plan for the day with fruits, dairy products including ice cream, bread or grains, and protein sources such as eggs or cheese.

A little advance planning can save a lot on your dessert budget. When you buy fruits, include apples or bananas for baking. Stock unflavored gelatin and use it with juices drained from canned fruit, or fresh juices, or chocolate, or even coffee, to make thrifty gelatin desserts. Or use prepared fruit-flavored gelatins for moderate-cost desserts. But if your time is very tight and you can't stir up even a quick-mix pudding, a fully prepared refrigerated or frozen dessert may add the final touch to a home meal at reasonable cost. Compare brands and package sizes of dessert mixes, and check specials, particularly, for moneysaving buys.

Gelatin Desserts

Gelatin desserts are a good follow-up to a hearty meal and are much appreciated during the summer months.

FRUITED GELATIN

　1 envelope unflavored gelatin
　¼ cup cold water
　¼ cup sugar
　　Dash salt
　½ cup boiling water
　1¼ cups cold fruit juice (any, except fresh or frozen pineapple) mixed with lemon juice to taste

Sprinkle gelatin on cold water, let stand to soften. Add sugar, salt and boiling water, stir to dissolve. Add fruit juice. Chill until set, about 2 hours. This makes a jelly firm enough to unmold. For a softer set, use 1½ cups cold fruit juice, including the lemon juice. Makes 4 servings.

QUICK FRUIT GELATIN

Dissolve gelatin as above. Instead of fruit juice, add 1 can (6 ounces) hard-frozen fruit juice concentrate and 6 ice cubes (or ½ cup ice water). Chill until set, about 30 minutes. This makes a jelly firm enough to unmold. For a softer set, use 3 more ice cubes or ¼ cup more ice water. Makes 4 servings.

WHIPPED GELATIN

Make Fruited Gelatin (above), chill until slightly thickened. Beat with a rotary beater until light, fluffy and doubled in volume. Chill until firm.

GELATIN SNOW

Make Fruited Gelatin (above), chill until slightly thickened. Beat until light and fluffy and doubled in volume. Whip ½ cup heavy cream or 1 egg white until thick but not stiff, fold in. Chill until firm.

GELATIN WITH FRUIT

Chill Fruited Gelatin (above) until slightly thickened, fold in 1 cup any cut fruit, to taste. Chill until set.

SPANISH CREAM

   1 envelope unflavored gelatin
¼ cup cold water
   2 cups milk
   3 eggs, separated
½ cup sugar
   Pinch salt
   1 teaspoon vanilla

Sprinkle gelatin on cold water, let stand 5 minutes. Scald milk, add gelatin, stir to dissolve. In the top of a double boiler beat egg yolks until light. Gradually add milk, ¼ cup sugar and salt. Cook over hot water, stirring constantly, until sugar is dissolved and sauce is thickened. Add vanilla. Beat egg whites until soft peaks form, add remaining sugar, beat until stiff. Fold into custard. Fill 6 individual molds, chill until firm. Unmold onto chilled serving dishes. Serve with whipped cream or fruit. This cream separates into two layers: the custard rises to the top and the jelly goes to the bottom. Makes 6 servings.

Note: If you want to keep this dessert uniform in texture, without separating, refrigerate the gelatin-yolk mixture until slightly thicker than unbeaten egg whites. Then add vanilla, beat egg whites with sugar and fold into custard. Chill.

BAVARIAN CREAM

   1 envelope unflavored gelatin
   2 tablespoons cold water
   2 egg yolks
½ cup sugar
   Dash salt
   1 cup milk
   1 teaspoon vanilla
   1 cup heavy cream, or 2 cups
      whipped topping

Sprinkle gelatin on cold water. Beat egg yolks, sugar and salt in the top of a double boiler. Beat until light. Add milk. Cook over boiling water, stirring constantly, until mixture is thick and smooth. Add softened gelatin, dis-

solve. Add vanilla. Cool until thick, stirring often. Whip cream until it is very thick but not stiff, fold into the cooled gelatin mixture. Pour into a 6-cup mold rinsed in cold water, chill until set. Unmold, serve with chocolate sauce. Makes 6 servings.

CHOCOLATE CREAM CHARLOTTE

   1 package (4 ounces) chocolate pudding and
      pie filling mix
   2 envelopes unflavored gelatin
   1 quart milk
   2 eggs, separated
¼ cup sugar
   1 cup heavy cream, whipped, or 2 cups
      whipped topping
   1 package (12) ladyfingers

Blend pudding mix with gelatin, stir in milk. Stir over low heat until mixture comes to a boil. Warm egg yolks with a little hot pudding, stir into pan. Cool, stirring often. Beat egg whites until foamy, gradually add sugar, beat until stiff. Fold into pudding mixture. Fold in whipped cream. Line the bottom and sides of a 2-quart spring-form pan with split ladyfingers. Fill with charlotte mixture, chill until firm. Unmold onto chilled serving plate. Makes 8 to 10 servings.

CHOCOLATE MOUSSE

   2 cups milk
   2 eggs, separated
   1 package (4 ounces) chocolate pudding and
      pie filling mix
   1 envelope unflavored gelatin
   Pinch salt
¼ cup sugar

Combine ½ cup milk and egg yolks in a saucepan. Stir in pudding mix and gelatin. Add remaining 1½ cups milk. Stir over medium heat, just until boiling. Chill until mixture mounds on spoon, stirring occasionally. Beat egg whites with salt until foamy, gradually add sugar. Beat until stiff and glossy, fold into pudding mixture. Chill in serving dish. Makes 6 to 8 servings.

QUICK ICE-CREAM MOUSSE

   1 envelope unflavored gelatin
¾ cup orange juice
   1 pint vanilla ice cream

Sprinkle gelatin on juice, let stand 5 minutes. Stir over low heat until gelatin is dissolved. Remove from heat. Add ice cream, spoonful by spoonful, stirring after each addition. Fill serving dish, chill briefly until firm. Makes 4 servings. Or use the mousse to fill an 8-inch prepared crumb pie shell.

Variations: Use pineapple, cranberry or prune juice instead of orange juice; or use other ice-cream flavors.

COLD LEMON SOUFFLÉ

4 eggs, separated
1 cup sugar
2 lemons, grated rind and juice
1 envelope unflavored gelatin
¼ cup water
2 cups whipped cream or whipped topping

Combine egg yolks and sugar in a saucepan, beat well. Add lemon rind and juice. Soften gelatin in cold water, add to custard. Whisk mixture over low heat until thick and smooth. Do not boil. Cool slightly. Meanwhile, tie a 2-inch standing collar of foil around the top of a 1-quart straight-sided soufflé dish. Beat egg whites until stiff peaks form. Fold whipped cream into egg yolk mixture, fold in egg whites. Pour into soufflé dish, chill until firm. Remove collar to serve. Makes 6 servings.

COLD CHOCOLATE SOUFFLÉ

1 envelope unflavored gelatin
½ cup sugar
Dash salt
2 eggs, separated
1 cup milk
1 cup (6 ounces) semisweet chocolate chips
½ teaspoon vanilla
2 cups whipped cream or whipped topping

Stir gelatin, ¼ cup sugar, salt, egg yolks and milk in a saucepan. Add chocolate, stir over low heat until chocolate is melted. Beat with a whisk or rotary beater to blend. Add vanilla, cool until thick. Meanwhile, tie a standing 2-inch collar of foil around the top of a straight-sided 1-quart soufflé dish. Beat egg whites with remaining sugar until stiff, fold into cooled chocolate mixture. Fold in whipped cream. Fill collared soufflé dish, chill until firm. Remove collar to serve. Makes 6 servings.

COLD STRAWBERRY SOUFFLÉ

2 cups strawberries, fresh or frozen
　　without sugar
¾ cup sugar
1 envelope unflavored gelatin
¼ cup cold water

¾ cup boiling water
1 tablespoon lemon juice
½ teaspoon lemon rind
4 egg whites

Reserve 6 perfect berries for garnish. Mash remaining fruit with ½ cup sugar in a mixing bowl. Sprinkle gelatin on cold water to soften, dissolve in boiling water, add to mashed berries. Add lemon juice and rind. Chill until thickened but not stiff. Meanwhile, tie a 2-inch standing collar of foil around the top of a 6-cup straight-sided soufflé dish. Put the bowl containing the berry mixture into a pan of ice and water and beat with a rotary beater until light and fluffy, about 10 minutes. Beat the egg whites until soft peaks form, add remaining sugar gradually, beat until stiff. Fold egg whites into berries. Pour into collared soufflé dish, chill until firm. To serve, remove collar, garnish soufflé with berries. Makes 6 to 8 servings.

Tip: Taste fruit mixture and adjust sugar and lemon juice to taste.

Variations: Make this soufflé with raspberries, blackberries or loganberries. Mash fruit through a food mill or sieve to remove seeds.

Top-of-the-Range Desserts

TAPIOCA PUDDING

1 egg, separated
⅓ cup sugar
Pinch salt
2 cups milk
3 tablespoons quick-cooking tapioca
½ teaspoon vanilla

Beat egg yolk, 3 tablespoons sugar, salt and milk in a saucepan. Add tapioca, let stand 5 minutes. Cook over moderate heat, stirring constantly, until mixture comes to a boil, about 6 minutes. Beat egg white until it stands in soft peaks, gradually beat in remaining sugar, beat until stiff. Stir the hot tapioca mixture into the beaten egg white. Add vanilla. Cool about 20 minutes, stir again. Chill in a serving dish or in 5 individual dessert serving dishes. Garnish with fruit or toasted coconut, or serve with cream or whipped cream. Makes 5 servings.

TAPIOCA TRIFLETTE

Prepare 1 package (3¼ ounces) vanilla tapioca pudding mix as directed. Cool 30 minutes, stirring occasionally. Cover bottom of glass bowl or 4 to 6 individual glass dishes with cubes of plain cake—yellow or sponge or white cake. Sprinkle with ½ cup orange juice, spread with 2 tablespoons marmalade or preserves, sprinkle with raisins or nuts. Fill dish with tapioca and garnish with whipped topping. Makes 4 to 6 servings.

WINE CUSTARD (ZABAGLIONE)

  4 egg yolks
  4 tablespoons sugar
½ cup Marsala wine or sherry

In the top of a double boiler whisk egg yolks with sugar until light. Place pan over simmering water, add wine. Cook, whisking constantly, until the sauce is thickened and very frothy. Serve warm, as a sauce for pudding, cake or fruit; or chill the sauce, whisk again, and serve as a dessert. In the latter case, ½ cup heavy cream, whipped, may be folded into the cooled custard. Makes 4 dessert servings.

FLOATING ISLAND

  3 eggs, separated
10 tablespoons sugar
  2 cups milk
    Pinch salt
  1 teaspoon vanilla

Beat egg whites until foamy, gradually beat in 6 tablespoons sugar, beat until stiff. Bring milk to a boil with salt, vanilla and remaining ¼ cup sugar in a saucepan. Drop meringue mixture by tablespoons into the milk and poach the "islands" until they are firm, turning them to cook both sides. Remove with a slotted spoon. Beat the egg yolks well, gradually add hot milk used to poach meringues. Cook over low heat, stirring constantly, until thick. Pour custard into a flat dish, cool. At serving time, top custard with poached meringues. Makes 4 to 6 servings.

TOASTED COCONUT MELBA

Prepare 1 package (3¼ ounces) instant toasted coconut pudding mix as directed. Place half a canned peach, cut side down, in each of 6 individual serving dishes. Mound with pudding, chill. Top with a spoonful of frozen raspberries or with raspberry preserves. Makes 6 servings.

DANISH CREAM

¼ cup apricot jam
1 package (3¼ ounces) instant vanilla
    pudding mix
1 cup milk
1 cup sour cream

Spread jam on bottom of decorative 2-cup serving dish. Prepare pudding according to package directions, substituting sour cream for half the milk. Pour into dish, chill until firm. Top with chocolate shavings, if desired. Makes 4 servings.

MARMALADE TOP-RANGE SOUFFLÉ

4 egg whites
1 tablespoon lemon juice
2 tablespoons sugar
3 tablespoons orange marmalade

Beat egg whites until foamy, add lemon juice and sugar, beat until stiff. Fold in orange marmalade. Butter the top of a 1-quart double boiler, add soufflé mixture. Place pan over but not touching hot water in bottom of boiler. Cover, cook over high heat for 45 minutes. To unmold, release soufflé from pan with a knife, turn out onto warmed serving plate. Serve at once with fruit or whipped topping. Makes 4 servings.

PLUM PUDDING

  1 cup flour
  1 teaspoon salt
¼ teaspoon baking soda
¼ teaspoon each cinnamon, ground cloves,
    allspice, nutmeg
¾ cup brown sugar, firmly packed
  1 cup ground beef suet
  1 package (12 ounces) pitted prunes, snipped
¾ cup seedless raisins
¾ cup golden raisins
¾ cup chopped, mixed candied fruit
  2 eggs, beaten
¼ cup orange juice (or brandy)

Toss flour, salt, baking soda and spices in a mixing bowl. Add brown sugar, suet, prunes, raisins and candied fruit. Toss to combine. Stir in beaten eggs and orange juice. Mix well. Pour into greased 1½-quart pudding mold or mixing bowl. Cover mold with lid; or use aluminum foil to cover bowl. Place on rack in pot. Add boiling water to come halfway up sides of mold, cover pot. Steam over medium-low heat (just enough to keep water boiling) for 4 hours. Let pudding cool slightly before unmolding. Serve with Hard Sauce (page 246). Makes 8 servings.

CORNSTARCH PUDDING

  ¼ cup sugar
  ¼ cup cornstarch
    Pinch salt
  ¼ cup cold milk
1¾ cups hot milk
  1 teaspoon vanilla

Mix sugar, cornstarch and salt, stir in cold milk. Add hot milk slowly. Cook over low heat, stirring constantly, until mixture is thick and smooth. Cool, stirring occasionally. Add vanilla. Pour into a 2-cup mold or 4 individual molds, chill. Unmold and serve with cream or fruit, or with chocolate sauce. Makes 4 servings.

Variations: Add ½ cup shredded coconut to pudding with vanilla. Or add 2 teaspoons instant coffee to hot milk. Or substitute ½ cup brown sugar for granulated sugar; add 1 tablespoon butter or margarine to cooked pudding. Or add ½ cup well-drained fruit cocktail to slightly cooled pudding.

PRUNE GRUNT

  1 package (12 ounces) pitted prunes
  3 cups boiling water
  2 apples, peeled and coarsely chopped
    Juice and peel of ½ lemon
  ¼ cup sugar
  ½ teaspoon cinnamon
  ¾ cup flour
  2 tablespoons cornstarch
  ¼ cup sugar
  1 teaspoon baking powder
  ¼ teaspoon salt
  1 tablespoon melted butter or margarine
  ¼ cup milk

Cover prunes in a shallow pan with boiling water; add apples, lemon juice and peel, sugar and cinnamon. Cover the pan, simmer 15 minutes. Meanwhile, toss flour, cornstarch, sugar, baking powder and salt to mix. Add butter and milk, stir to moisten. Drop dough by teaspoons into simmering prune sauce. Cover the pan, simmer 10 minutes, until dumplings are puffed and cooked through. Serve hot. Makes 6 to 8 servings.

BOSTON LEMON PIE

Prepare 1 package (3⅜ ounces) lemon pudding and pie filling mix as directed. Cool until thick. Spread between two 8- or 9-inch cake layers. Make frosting by melting 1 square unsweetened chocolate with 1 teaspoon butter or margarine, stir in 1 cup confectioners' sugar and 2 tablespoons hot water. Spread on top of cake, let drip down sides.

DOUBLE CHOCOLATE PIE

1¼ cups chocolate cookie crumbs
  4 tablespoons melted butter or margarine
  1 tablespoon sugar
  1 package (4 ounces) chocolate pudding
    and pie filling mix
  2 cups milk

Blend cookie crumbs with butter and sugar. Press into 8-inch pie plate with back of a spoon. Chill. Make chocolate pudding, adding milk, according to package directions. Cool, stirring often. Pour pudding into crust, chill. Top with whipped topping, if desired.

CHOCOLATE-GINGER
REFRIGERATOR CAKE

Prepare 1 large package (6 ounces) chocolate pudding and pie filling mix with 3 cups milk, according to package directions. Fill a 5-cup loaf pan or mold with alternate layers of pudding and gingersnaps, beginning with cookies and ending with pudding. Chill several hours. Unmold, slice, serve with whipped cream or whipped topping. Makes 10 servings.

CHERRIES JUBILEE

  1 can (1 pound 14 ounces) pitted Bing
    cherries
  ½ teaspoon cinnamon
  ½ teaspoon cornstarch
  1 tablespoon lemon juice

Drain syrup from cherries into a saucepan, heat to boiling. Stir cinnamon and cornstarch to a paste with lemon juice, add to pan, stir until clear. Add cherries, heat through. Serve plain or over ice cream. Makes 6 plain servings, ice-cream topping for 10 servings.

Flaming Cherries Jubilee: Omit lemon juice. Stir cinnamon and cornstarch with a little water. Heat ¼ cup brandy in a metal ladle or small pan, ignite; pour, blazing, into the cherries.

Top-of-the-Counter Desserts

These desserts are easy on the cook, especially in hot weather, because no cooking is required.

INSTANT "CHEESE" PIE

Pour 1 cup sour cream and ¾ cup cold milk into a bowl. Add 1 package (3¼ ounces) instant vanilla pudding, beat with rotary beater 1 minute, until smooth. Pour into prepared 8-inch graham-cracker pie shell, chill until set.

HEART OF CREAM

 1 pound cream cheese, softened
¼ cup heavy cream
¼ cup sour cream
 2 tablespoons confectioners' sugar
½ teaspoon vanilla

Beat all ingredients together until smooth. Wet a strip of cheesecloth, wring out, and spread as a liner in a 2½-cup heart-shaped mold. Fill with cheese mixture, packing it down well. Cover and refrigerate until firm, several hours or overnight. To serve, invert mold on serving plate. Strip off cheesecloth. Surround heart with fresh or frozen strawberries. Makes about 8 servings.

STRAWBERRIES ROMANOFF

 2 pints strawberries
½ pint vanilla ice cream
 1 cup whipped cream or whipped topping
 Juice of ½ lemon
 3 tablespoons orange liqueur (optional)

Wash, hull and chill berries. Soften ice cream slightly, whip until fluffy. Fold in whipped cream and lemon juice. Add liqueur, for the traditional dessert. Spoon sauce over berries. Makes 6 servings.

Baked Desserts

Choose a light, chilled dessert to top off a filling meal; a hearty, old-fashioned baked dessert to top off a light meal: a spicy fruit betty or cobbler or grunt, best enjoyed warm; or a cakelike pudding in its own rich sauce.

CHOCOLATE TAPIOCA SOUFFLÉ

 2 cups milk
 2 eggs, separated
 1 package (3½ ounces) chocolate tapioca
 pudding mix
 Pinch salt
¼ cup sugar

Combine ½ cup milk and egg yolks in saucepan with pudding mix; stir until smooth. Add remaining milk and stir over medium heat until mixture comes to a rolling boil. Cool 15 minutes. Beat egg whites with salt until foamy, gradually beat in sugar, beat until stiff. Fold into pudding. Pour into greased 1-quart baking dish. Bake in a moderate oven (350°F) about 45 minutes, until puffed and browned. Serve immediately. Makes 4 servings.

CUSTARD

 2 eggs
¼ cup sugar
 Dash salt
 2 cups hot milk

Beat eggs, sugar and salt until light. Gradually whisk in milk. Pour through a strainer into 4 buttered custard cups. Set molds in a baking pan in hot water to reach level of custard in cups. Bake in a moderate oven (350°F) about 30 minutes, until custard is set. A silver knife inserted near the center of the custard will come out clean. Cool. Makes 4 servings.

FLAN

Cook ½ cup sugar over low heat, stirring constantly, until sugar melts and turns golden brown. Divide into 4 buttered custard cups, tip and roll cups to coat evenly. Add Custard and bake as above. Unmold. Serve chilled. Makes 4 servings.

CRÈME BRÛLÉE

Cover custard, made by any method, with a ¼-inch layer of brown sugar. Place under broiler; heat until sugar caramelizes and forms a crusty brown topping. Chill again before serving.

BAKED ALASKA

 4 egg whites
¾ cup confectioners' sugar
 Sponge cake layer, 1½ inches thick
 1 quart hard-frozen ice cream, sliced

Beat egg whites until they stand in soft peaks. Gradually beat in ½ cup confectioners' sugar, beat until stiff. Arrange sponge cake on a board. Cover the cake with ice cream, leaving a 1-inch border all around. Swirl meringue over ice cream and cake to cover completely. Sprinkle with remaining sugar. Bake in a very hot oven (450°F) for about 5 minutes, until the meringue is golden. Serve at once. Makes 8 servings.

LEMON PUDDING SPONGE

2 tablespoons butter or margarine
⅔ cup sugar
2 eggs, separated
2 tablespoons lemon juice
1 teaspoon grated lemon rind
2 tablespoons flour
1 cup milk

Cream butter, add sugar and cream well. Beat egg yolks until thick and lemon-colored; add to creamed mixture with lemon juice and rind. Fold in flour and stir in milk. Beat egg whites until stiff, fold into the yolk mixture. Pour into greased 1-quart baking dish. Bake in a moderate oven (350°F) about 40 minutes. Chill. Serve plain or with whipped topping. Makes 4 servings.

BROWN BETTY

4 slices bread, toasted and cubed
¼ cup melted butter or margarine
3 cups sliced apples
½ cup sugar
½ teaspoon cinnamon
¼ teaspoon nutmeg
½ cup chopped nuts (optional)
¾ cup orange juice

Toss bread cubes with melted butter. Fill buttered 6-cup baking dish with alternate layers of bread cubes and fruit sprinkled with sugar, spices and nuts, if used, beginning and ending with bread. Sprinkle with orange juice. Bake in a moderate oven (350°F) about 45 minutes, until fruit is tender. If necessary to cook longer, cover top with foil to prevent burning. Makes 6 servings.

Variations: Sliced peaches, stoned cherries, blueberries or raspberries may be substituted for the apples in this recipe; adjust spices and sugar to taste.

BANANA-CORNFLAKE BETTY

3 cups cornflakes
3 cups banana slices
½ cup raisins
½ cup brown sugar
½ teaspoon cinnamon
2 teaspoons lemon juice
¼ cup butter or margarine

Fill greased 6-cup baking dish with layers of one-third the cornflakes, half the bananas, raisins, sugar, cinnamon, lemon juice and butter. Repeat, ending with flakes. Bake in a moderately hot oven (375°F) 20 minutes, until crisp. Makes 6 servings.

APPLE CRISP

5 cooking apples
2 tablespoons butter or margarine
½ cup raisins
½ cup brown sugar
¾ cup flour (or half flour, half oatmeal)
½ teaspoon cinnamon
½ teaspoon nutmeg
⅓ cup butter

Peel and slice apples. Spread shallow 2-quart baking dish with 2 tablespoons butter, add apples. Sprinkle with raisins. Mix sugar, flour and spices. Blend in ⅓ cup butter with fork or fingers to make crumbly mixture. Sprinkle evenly over apples and raisins. Press down lightly. Bake in a moderate oven (375°F) 45 minutes, until crisp and golden. Makes 4 to 6 servings.

BLUEBERRY GRUNT

2 cups blueberries
2 cups water
1 cup sugar
1½ cups flour
1½ teaspoons double-acting baking powder
½ teaspoon salt
2 tablespoons shortening
½ cup milk (approximately)

Combine blueberries, water and sugar in a greased 2-quart casserole fitted with a lid. Stir. Toss flour, baking powder and salt to mix. Cut in shortening with a pastry blender. Add enough milk to make a soft dough. Bake berries in a hot oven (400°F) for 5 minutes, stir. Drop walnut-size balls of dough onto the berries. Cover the casserole, bake about 25 minutes, until the dumplings are puffed and cooked through. Makes 8 servings.

PEAR COBBLER

3 pounds winter pears
2 cups water
1 cup sugar
3 cloves
1½ teaspoons cornstarch
2 tablespoons lemon juice
½ recipe for Shortcake dough (page 200)
Sugar and cinnamon for garnish

Peel and core pears, cut into wedges. Simmer in water with sugar and cloves until tender. With a slotted spoon transfer fruit to a buttered 6-cup baking dish that can be brought to the table. Discard cloves, reserve liquid. Stir cornstarch with lemon juice, add to hot pear liquid, cook until clear. Pour over fruit

Extravagant, complicated, difficult to prepare? Not at all. This masterpiece Strawberry Cheese Cake is made with cottage cheese and topped with Ann Page Strawberry Preserves. There is no cooking; the cheese is thickened with gelatin. The ladyfingers are bakery fresh, a fail-proof crust. (See page 229.)

This spectacular dessert begins with a supermarket-fresh Angel Food Cake; the colorful "gems" that stud the crown are fashioned of brightly colored fruit gelatins; the frosting is fluffy whipped cream. How's that for a royal treat, the easy-does-it way? (See page 228.)

in baking dish. Pat shortcake biscuit dough to fit dish, cover fruit. Sprinkle with sugar and cinnamon. Bake in a very hot oven (450°F) about 15 minutes, until the crust is richly browned. Serve warm, with ice cream, whipped cream or whipped topping. Makes 6 or more servings.

APPLE PANDOWDY

  6 apples
½ cup brown sugar
¼ teaspoon cinnamon
¼ teaspoon nutmeg
  3 tablespoons butter or margarine
¼ cup water
½ recipe for Shortcake dough (page 200)

Pare, core and slice apples. Arrange apple slices in layers in greased 6-cup baking dish. Sprinkle layers with sugar, cinnamon and nutmeg. Add butter melted in water. Roll shortcake dough thin and place over apples. Sprinkle lightly with more brown sugar. Bake in a very hot oven (450°F) 10 minutes, reduce heat to moderate 350°F and bake 30 minutes, until apples are tender. Serve warm. Makes 6 servings.

UPSIDE-DOWN COTTAGE PUDDING

¼ cup butter or margarine
¾ cup sugar
  1 egg
  2 cups flour
  2 teaspoons double-acting baking powder
½ teaspoon salt
  1 cup milk
  1 teaspoon vanilla or lemon extract
    Fresh plum halves (or peaches, apple
      slices, pineapple rings)

Cream butter, add sugar and egg, beat well. Toss flour, baking powder and salt to mix. Add to butter mixture alternately with milk. Add vanilla. Grease a 9-inch square baking pan. Arrange fruit in bottom. Cover with batter. Bake in a moderate oven (350°F) about 30 minutes, until cake is browned and tests done. Cool on a rack for 5 minutes. Turn out, fruit side up. Serve warm. Makes 6 servings.

Right-Side-Up Cottage Pudding: Prepare batter, pour into greased and floured baking pan. Cover batter with pitted plums, peach halves or other fruit. Sprinkle fruit with sugar and cinnamon. Bake as directed; serve warm.

CHOCOLATE PUDDING CAKE

  1 cup flour
¾ cup sugar
⅓ cup cocoa
  1 teaspoon double-acting baking powder
½ teaspoon salt
½ cup milk
  2 tablespoons melted butter or margarine
  1 teaspoon vanilla
  1 cup brown sugar
1¾ cups boiling water

Toss flour, sugar, 2 tablespoons cocoa, baking powder and salt to mix. Add milk, melted butter and vanilla. Mix just until smooth. Fill a greased and floured 9-inch square baking pan. Sprinkle with brown sugar mixed with remaining cocoa. Pour boiling water gently over batter. Bake in a moderate oven (350°F) about 45 minutes. The cake will rise to the top of the pan, and the chocolate sauce will be in the bottom. Serve warm or cold, with whipped topping or ice cream, if desired. Makes 6 servings.

Mocha Pudding Cake: Add 1 teaspoon instant coffee to the boiling water before pouring it over the cake batter.

Caramel Pudding Cake: Omit cocoa from batter and from topping.

INDIAN PUDDING

½ cup corn meal
  4 cups milk
½ teaspoon salt
½ teaspoon cinnamon
¼ teaspoon ginger
¼ teaspoon nutmeg
½ cup molasses

Stir corn meal with ½ cup milk. Bring remaining milk to a boil, add salt. Gradually add corn meal. Cook, stirring, until thickened, about 15 minutes. Add remaining ingredients, to taste. Bake in a buttered 2-quart baking dish in a moderate oven (350°F) for 2½ hours. Serve warm or chilled, with cream or ice cream. Makes 6 servings.

BREAD PUDDING

  2 eggs
⅓ cup sugar
    Dash salt
  3 cups milk
  1 cup bread cubes
  1 teaspoon vanilla
    Cinnamon

Beat eggs with sugar and salt. Heat milk, add to bread cubes, stir, add vanilla. Blend with eggs. Pour into a buttered 6-cup baking dish. Sprinkle with cinnamon. Bake in a moderate oven (350°F) about 45 minutes, until the pudding is browned and a knife inserted near the center comes out clean and dry. Makes 6 servings.

Variations: Add ½ cup raisins, chopped prunes, figs, dates or candied fruit.

CHOCOLATE BREAD PUDDING

In Bread Pudding recipe (above), cut 2 squares (1 ounce each) unsweetened chocolate into small pieces. Add to milk, stir until chocolate is melted and milk is hot. Proceed as directed.

NOODLE PUDDING

½ pound broad egg noodles
2 tablespoons butter or margarine
1 pound cottage cheese
½ cup sour cream
3 eggs, separated
½ cup sugar
½ teaspoon salt
½ cup raisins

Cook noodles in boiling water until just tender. Drain, toss with butter. Blend cottage cheese and sour cream, beat well. Beat egg yolks, add to cheese with sugar and salt. Combine with noodles and raisins. Beat egg whites until stiff, fold in. Bake in a buttered baking dish in a moderate oven (350°F) about 45 minutes, until pudding is browned and set. Makes 6 servings.

OLD-FASHIONED RICE PUDDING

¼ cup long-grain rice
¼ teaspoon salt
¼ cup sugar
1 quart milk
1 teaspoon vanilla
⅓ cup raisins (optional)
    Cinnamon

Combine rice, salt, sugar and milk in a 5-cup baking dish. Bake in a moderately slow oven (325°F) about 2½ hours. Stir frequently during the first hour. Stir in crust two or three times during the second hour. Add vanilla and raisins, sprinkle with cinnamon, and finish baking without stirring. Good hot or cold, plain or with cream or fruit. Makes 6 servings.

QUICK RICE PUDDING

Prepare 1 package (3¼ ounces) vanilla pudding and pie filling mix as directed. Add 1½ cups freshly cooked rice (any type) to hot pudding. Add ⅓ cup raisins and ½ teaspoon nutmeg or cinnamon. Makes 6 servings.

Ice Cream

Old-fashioned ice creams are best frozen in a churn freezer. Constant stirring during the freezing process prevents the formation of coarse ice crystals. To vary the basic ice creams, add flavorings before freezing begins; add fruits, nuts or chocolate chips just before the ice cream freezes hard.

Store all frozen desserts in the freezer compartment at normal temperature; use as soon as possible for best texture and flavor.

PHILADELPHIA ICE CREAM

4 cups heavy cream
1 cup sugar
1 teaspoon vanilla

Heat 1 cup cream, add sugar, stir to dissolve. Cool. Add remaining cream and vanilla. Freeze in a churn ice-cream freezer, following manufacturer's directions. Makes 2 quarts.

CUSTARD ICE CREAM

4 cups light cream
8 egg yolks
1 cup sugar
2 teaspoons vanilla

Heat 2 cups cream in the top of a double boiler. Beat 8 yolks with sugar until very light. Beat egg yolks into cream. Cook over hot water, stirring constantly, until the custard is smooth and thick enough to coat the spoon. Cool, add remaining cream and vanilla. Freeze in a churn ice-cream freezer, following manufacturer's directions. Makes 2 quarts.

RUM-RAISIN ICE CREAM

Make Philadelphia Ice Cream or Custard Ice Cream. Soak 1 cup seedless raisins in ⅓ cup dark rum. Just before ice cream becomes solid, add rum and raisins, finish freezing.

OLD-FASHIONED CHOCOLATE ICE CREAM

1 cup sugar
2 tablespoons flour
    Dash salt

2 cups milk
2 squares (2 ounces) unsweetened
   chocolate
2 eggs
2 cups light cream
1 teaspoon vanilla

Combine sugar, flour, salt and milk in a saucepan. Cook over medium heat, stirring constantly, until sauce is thickened and smooth. Cut chocolate into sauce, stir until melted. Beat eggs until light, warm with a little hot sauce, add to pan. Cook for a minute without boiling. Cool thoroughly. Stir in cream and flavoring. Freeze in an ice-cream freezer, following manufacturer's directions. Makes 2 quarts.

Refrigerator Ice Cream

Very satisfactory ice creams can be made in the freezing compartment of a modern refrigerator. Set the temperature control at the lowest possible point before you begin to mix the ice cream. Notice that refrigerator ice creams all include an ingredient (gelatin, condensed or evaporated milk or starch) that helps prevent the formation of coarse crystals.

When ice cream is frozen solid, return freezer control to normal temperature for storage.

Remove freezer trays from the freezer compartment 5 minutes before serving.

BUTTER ALMOND ICE CREAM

 2 eggs
⅓ cup brown sugar
⅔ cup corn syrup
 1 cup heavy cream
 1 cup milk
½ teaspoon almond extract
 2 tablespoons butter or margarine
½ cup slivered almonds
  Dash salt

Set freezer control at lowest possible temperature. Beat eggs, add sugar, beat until fluffy. Beat in corn syrup, cream, milk and almond extract. Freeze until mushy. Meanwhile, melt butter in a small baking dish, add nuts and salt. Toast in a moderate oven (350°F) about 10 minutes, until nuts are crisp. Turn mushy ice cream into a mixing bowl, beat until smooth but not melted. Stir in nuts, return to freezer. Makes about 1 quart.

CHOCOLATE-CHIP ICE CREAM

1 can (15 ounces) sweetened condensed milk
1 cup water
3 teaspoons vanilla extract
2 cups heavy cream
1 cup chocolate chips

Stir milk, water and vanilla together, chill. Whip cream until thick but not stiff. Fold into chilled milk. Pour into 2 ice-cube trays; freeze at coldest setting of freezer compartment for 1 hour, until mushy. Turn into a mixing bowl, beat until fluffy but not melted. Stir in chocolate chips. Return to trays, cover with waxed paper, freeze until firm. Makes 1½ quarts.

PEACH ICE CREAM

⅔ cup evaporated milk
1 package (10 ounces) frozen peaches
  in syrup, thawed
¼ cup sugar
½ teaspoon almond extract
  Dash salt
1 tablespoon lemon juice

Set temperature control at lowest possible temperature. Chill evaporated milk thoroughly. Mash peaches with sugar, almond extract and salt. Whip chilled milk until fluffy, add lemon juice, continue to beat until stiff. Beat in peaches. Fill ice-cube tray, cover with waxed paper and freeze until firm. Makes 1 quart.

PEANUT-BRITTLE ICE CREAM

1 envelope unflavored gelatin
½ cup cold water
1 can (13 ounces) evaporated milk
½ cup sugar
2 teaspoons vanilla
1½ cups heavy cream, whipped stiff
1 cup crushed peanut brittle

Set freezer at lowest possible temperature. Sprinkle gelatin on cold water to soften. Heat milk, dissolve gelatin and sugar in milk. Cool, add vanilla and whipped cream. Pour into freezer tray, freeze until mushy. Turn into a mixing bowl, beat until smooth but not melted. Stir in crushed peanut brittle, return to freezer until solid. Makes about 1½ quarts.

BUTTERSCOTCH QUICK-MIX
ICE CREAM

1 package (4 ounces) butterscotch pudding
  and pie filling mix
2 cups milk
¼ cup sugar

Dash salt
1 cup heavy cream, whipped

Set freezer control at lowest possible temperature. Prepare pudding mix with milk and sugar, following package directions. Add salt. Cool. Fold in cream. Freeze in tray until mushy, about 1 hour. Remove to a mixing bowl and beat with a rotary beater until smooth but not melted. Return to freezer, cover with waxed paper, freeze solid. Makes about 1 quart.

Variations: Chocolate, vanilla, cherry-vanilla, coconut cream or banana cream pudding may be used in this recipe.

LEMON-PINEAPPLE ICE CREAM

**1 package (3⅜ ounces) lemon pudding
    and pie filling**
1 cup sugar
5 tablespoons water
2½ cups unsweetened pineapple juice
1 cup milk
¾ cup heavy cream, whipped

In saucepan, combine lemon pudding, sugar, water and pineapple juice. Stir over medium heat until thickened. Cool, stir in milk. Pour into refrigerator trays and freeze to a thick mush. Remove frozen mixture to chilled bowl and beat until smooth, fold in whipped cream. Return to trays, freeze solid. Makes about 1½ quarts.

ORANGE MILK SHERBET

1 can (13 ounces) evaporated milk
1 cup superfine sugar
⅛ teaspoon salt
1½ tablespoons lemon juice
½ cup orange juice

Combine milk, sugar and salt, add lemon and orange juice, stir to dissolve sugar. Pour into a refrigerator tray, freeze until firm. Remove to a chilled mixing bowl and beat until smooth and fluffy. Return to tray, cover with waxed paper, freeze solid. Makes about 1 quart.

GRAPE ICE

1 envelope unflavored gelatin
1 cup sugar
Pinch salt
1¾ cups boiling water
1 cup grape juice
¼ cup lemon juice

Set freezer control at lowest possible temperature. Combine gelatin, sugar and salt, add boiling water, stir until dissolved. Add fruit juices. Freeze in ice-cube trays until mushy, beat in a mixing bowl until smooth, return to trays, cover with waxed paper, freeze solid. Makes about 1 quart.

Variations: Use pineapple juice or prune juice or orange juice.

MELON ICE

4 cups mashed watermelon or cantaloupe
¾ cup superfine sugar
Dash salt

Blend melon, free of seeds and fibers, with sugar and salt. Freeze in a refrigerator tray until mushy. Beat in a chilled bowl until smooth but not melted. Return to freezer tray, cover with waxed paper, freeze until solid. Makes about 1½ quarts.

ORANGE-CRANBERRY ICE

1 can (1 pound) whole-berry cranberry sauce
**1 can (6 ounces) frozen orange-juice
    concentrate**

Set freezer control at lowest possible temperature. Combine ingredients, whip with a rotary beater to break up berries. Freeze in a freezer tray until mushy, beat again until smooth but not melted, return to freezer tray until solid. Makes about 3 cups.

Frozen Desserts

Great for many reasons; perhaps the most appreciated factor is that these can be prepared ahead and held in the freezer until shortly before serving time.

BOMBES

Bombes are molded ice-cream desserts, usually shaped of more than one flavor of ice cream, or of a combination of ice cream and a sherbet or mousse mixture.

To shape a bombe: Line a bombe mold, or an ordinary bowl, with a ½-inch layer of ice cream, homemade or purchased. Cover, freeze solid. Fill the center with another flavor of ice cream, or the same flavor mixed with nuts, chopped fruits, candied fruits, crushed peppermint or peanut brittle. Or fill it with a frozen mousse preparation (see page 243) or with purchased or homemade sherbet. Cover carefully, return to freezer to freeze solid. At serving time, dip mold into hot water, turn bombe out onto chilled serving dish. Garnish to taste with whipped cream or fresh fruit. Cut with a knife dipped into hot water for easy slicing.

SPANISH BOMBE

Line a bombe mold with chocolate ice cream and fill the center with Frozen Apricot Mousse (page 243).

NEW ENGLAND BOMBE

Line a bombe with Butter Almond Ice Cream (page 241), fill with Orange-Cranberry Ice (page 242).

VINEYARD BOMBE

Line a bombe mold with vanilla ice cream, fill with Grape Ice (page 242).

HEAVENLY HASH

  1 package (3 ounces) cream cheese
  2 tablespoons milk
1½ cups sour cream
  1 cup miniature marshmallows
  1 cup diced pineapple, fresh or canned
  1 cup seedless grapes
  1 cup sliced peaches, fresh or canned
  1 cup pitted sweet cherries, fresh or canned
½ cup nuts
  Sugar, salt

Mix cheese with milk until smooth. Add sour cream, marshmallows, fruits and nuts. Adjust seasoning with sugar and a pinch of salt to taste. Freeze until solid in refrigerator tray. Makes 6 or more servings.

FROZEN BANANA WHIP

¼ cup butter or margarine
¾ cup sugar
  2 eggs
  1 banana, mashed
½ cup ice-cold water
½ cup non-fat dry milk solids
1½ teaspoons vanilla
  2 tablespoons lemon juice

Set freezer control at lowest possible temperature. Cream butter with sugar until light, add eggs, beat until very light and fluffy. Blend in mashed banana. In a chilled bowl, combine cold water and dry milk, whip until thick, add vanilla and lemon juice, whip until stiff peaks form. Fold whipped milk into banana mixture. Freeze in refrigerator tray until

mushy, turn into chilled mixing bowl, whip until smooth but not melted. Return to freezer, cover with waxed paper, freeze solid. Makes 1 quart.

Frozen Peach Whip: Substitute 4 medium peaches, 2 mashed and 2 forced through a sieve, for bananas.

Frozen Blueberry Whip: Substitute 1 cup blueberries, forced through a sieve, for bananas.

Frozen Strawberry Whip: Substitute ¾ cup mashed strawberries for bananas.

FROZEN APRICOT MOUSSE

  1 cup dried apricots
1¼ cups water
⅔ cup sugar
  1 pint heavy cream, or 1 quart whipped topping
¼ cup chopped almonds
  1 teaspoon grated orange rind

Simmer apricots in water gently about 25 minutes, until fruit is tender. Add sugar, cook 5 minutes longer. Press fruit through food mill or whirl in an electric blender. Cool. Whip cream, fold in apricot pulp, almonds and orange rind. Spoon into refrigerator tray or mold, freeze firm. Makes about 1 quart.

FROZEN LEMON MOUSSE

3 eggs, separated
1 tablespoon sugar
1 lemon, juice and grated rind
2 tablespoons sherry
  Pinch salt
½ cup sugar
1 cup heavy cream, whipped, or 2 cups whipped topping

Combine egg yolks, sugar, lemon juice and rind in saucepan. Cook over low heat, stirring constantly, until smooth. Set pan in basin of water and ice and stir until cool. Add sherry. Beat egg whites until foamy, beat in salt and sugar, beat until stiff. Fold into lemon custard, fold in cream. Fill serving dish, cover, freeze. At serving time, garnish with more whipped cream, if desired. Makes 6 to 8 servings.

FROZEN CHERRY CHARLOTTE

12 ladyfingers, split in half
  1 package (3¼ ounces) cherry-vanilla pudding and pie filling mix
  2 eggs, separated

1½ cups milk
Pinch salt
¼ cup sugar

Line sides of a 6-cup glass dish with split lady-fingers. Combine pudding mix with egg yolks. Add milk, stir over medium heat until mixture boils. Cool. Beat egg whites with pinch of salt until foamy. Add sugar, beat until stiff. Fold into pudding and fill lined dish. Freeze. Unmold to serve. Garnish with whipped topping and cherries, if desired. Makes 6 to 8 servings.

Crêpes

Delicate, thin pancakes, useful for every course of the meal, are at their best when it's time for dessert. You can make crêpes well in advance, freeze them with pieces of waxed paper separating them, and have the makings of an elegant dessert always on hand.

DESSERT CRÊPES

1 cup flour
1½ cups milk
½ teaspoon salt
2 eggs, well beaten
2 tablespoons butter or margarine

Blend flour with milk and salt. Add eggs, beat well. Chill for ½ hour before cooking. Melt butter in small skillet, tip and roll pan to coat bottom. Pour excess butter into the crêpe batter. Pour 2 tablespoons batter into the pan, turn and tilt the pan to spread the batter evenly. Cook until bottom is brown, turn, brown other side. Serve folded or rolled with jam or preserves, or with lemon juice and powdered sugar. Makes 12 or more crêpes.

Apple Crêpes: Mix 1 cup chopped fresh apples with ¼ cup raisins. Cook in 2 table-spoons butter or margarine until apples are just tender. Add ¼ cup brown sugar, ¼ tea-spoon cinnamon, a dash of salt. Season with lemon juice to taste. Divide apple mixture onto hot crêpes, roll, serve with powdered sugar and lemon juice.

Apricot Crêpes: Stir over low heat 1 jar (12 ounces) apricot preserves, 2 tablespoons each lemon juice and water, 1 tablespoon butter or margarine. Add crêpes to hot sauce, one by one, heat gently, fold into quarters. Enough for 6 servings.

DESSERT OMELET

4 eggs, separated
¼ teaspoon salt
2 tablespoons milk
2 tablespoons flour
1 tablespoon butter or margarine
¼ cup marmalade
Confectioners' sugar
4 lemon wedges for garnish

Preheat oven to slow (300°F). Beat egg whites until they hold soft peaks, add salt, beat until stiff. Beat yolks with milk, add flour, beat until very light. Fold into stiffly beaten egg whites. Heat butter in an oven-proof 9-inch skillet. Add egg mixture. Cook over low heat until omelet rises and is browned on bottom. Transfer the skillet to the oven, cook about 8 minutes, until the omelet is delicately browned. Spread with marmalade (or preserves or jelly), fold. Sprinkle with confectioners' sugar, garnish with lemon wedges. Makes 4 servings.

Variations: Dessert omelets may be filled with drained stewed fruits, whole-berry cranberry sauce or applesauce. Cinnamon may be mixed with the sprinkling sugar. The folded omelet may be quickly glazed under the broiler before serving, if desired.

Dessert Sauces and Toppings

Don't underestimate the power of a dessert sauce or topping. A dab of whipped cream, a spoonful of chocolate sauce—even these simple additions can transform an everyday dessert into something special, a special dessert into a triumph!

CHOCOLATE MINT SAUCE

1 package (4 ounces) chocolate pudding
and pie filling mix
3¼ cups milk
¼ cup crushed peppermint candy, or
½ teaspoon mint flavoring

Add pudding mix to ½ cup milk in saucepan, stir until smooth. Add remaining 2¾ cups milk. Stir over medium heat, just until boiling. Add candy or flavoring. Serve as a hot dip for cake cubes or fruit chunks; or serve hot or cold as a sauce for ice cream. Makes about 3½ cups.

QUICK CUSTARD SAUCE

Prepare 1 package (3 ounces) home-style custard mix as directed on package, but use 3 cups milk plus 1 egg yolk, beaten. Serve cold. Makes about 3 cups.

Variations: Flavor custard sauce to taste with cinnamon, nutmeg or grated lemon rind.

QUICK ORANGE CUSTARD SAUCE

Combine 1 package (3 ounces) home-style custard mix with ½ cup frozen orange-juice concentrate. Add 1¾ cups milk, cook, stirring, until mixture boils. Serve cold. Makes about 2 cups.

QUICK BUTTERSCOTCH-NUT SAUCE

Prepare 1 package (4 ounces) butterscotch pudding as directed, but use 3¼ cups milk. Stir in ½ cup walnuts, 1 tablespoon brown sugar and ¼ teaspoon vanilla. Serve warm or chilled. Makes about 3¾ cups.

Variation: Add ½ cup applesauce instead of nuts.

QUICK CHOCOLATE MARSHMALLOW SAUCE

Prepare 1 package (4 ounces) chocolate pudding as directed, but use 3¼ cups milk. Cool. Stir in ½ cup miniature marshmallows. Makes about 3½ cups.

Variations: Add ¼ to ½ cup finely crushed peppermint candy, or chopped nuts, or shredded coconut, with or instead of marshmallows.

QUICK LEMON SAUCE

Prepare 1 package (3⅜ ounces) lemon pudding as directed, but add ½ cup sugar to package contents and increase water to 3 cups. To hot pudding add 2 tablespoons butter or margarine, a dash of vanilla. Makes about 3 cups.

BROWN SUGAR SAUCE

Stir 2 tablespoons cornstarch into 1 cup cold water. Add 1 cup dark brown sugar and ¼ cup butter or margarine. Stir over low heat until the sauce is thick and smooth and reaches the boiling point. Add 1 to 2 teaspoons vanilla or a little almond extract to taste. Serve warm or reheated. If the sauce seems too thick, add hot water to thin. Makes about 2 cups.

CHOCOLATE SYRUP

Combine ½ cup sugar, 1 square (1 ounce) unsweetened baking chocolate, grated, and 1 cup boiling water. Stir over low heat until sugar and chocolate are dissolved and syrup is smooth. Simmer for a few minutes to thicken. Add a pinch of salt and ½ teaspoon vanilla. Makes about 1 cup.

MAPLE-WALNUT SAUCE

Simmer 1 cup maple syrup (or favorite pancake syrup) for 5 minutes. Add ¼ cup walnut halves. Use warm as an ice-cream sundae sauce. Makes about 1 cup.

HOT FUDGE SAUCE

Combine 1 ounce (1 square) baking chocolate with 1 cup sugar, 2 tablespoons corn syrup, pinch salt, ⅓ cup water. Heat slowly, stirring, until chocolate melts. Bring to a boil, still stirring, and boil until the mixture will form a soft ball in cold water. (A candy thermometer will read 232°F.) Add 1 tablespoon butter or margarine and 1 teaspoon vanilla. Serve hot or reheated. Makes about 1 cup.

MOCHA FUDGE SAUCE

Add with the water in Hot Fudge Sauce (above) 1 teaspoon instant coffee powder. Makes about 1 cup.

CARAMEL SAUCE

1 cup sugar
1 cup water
1 teaspoon lemon juice

Dissolve sugar in ¼ cup water over gentle heat. Boil without stirring until sugar is a rich brown color. Remove at once from heat and hold bottom of pan in cold water for a moment to check boiling. Stir in ¾ cup water, return to heat, bring to a boil, stirring constantly. Add lemon juice. Sauce should be thick and syrupy. Makes about 1 cup.

LEMON SAUCE

3 egg yolks
½ cup sugar
⅓ cup melted butter or margarine
3 tablespoons lemon juice
1 tablespoon grated lemon rind
⅔ cup whipped cream or whipped topping

Beat egg yolks until thick and lemon-colored. Stir in sugar, melted butter, lemon juice and grated rind. Fold cream into lemon mixture. Makes about 1 cup.

VANILLA SAUCE

2 cups milk
1 cup sugar
1 tablespoon cornstarch
¼ cup butter or margarine
2 teaspoons vanilla

Mix milk with sugar and cornstarch, bring to a boil, stirring. Add butter and vanilla. Makes about 2 cups.

HARD SAUCE

½ cup butter or margarine
1 cup confectioners' sugar
1 teaspoon vanilla or 2 teaspoons or more brandy

Cream butter until fluffy. Gradually beat in sugar until creamy and smooth. Flavor with vanilla or brandy. Makes about 1 cup.

VELVET TOPPING

⅔ cup evaporated milk
3 tablespoons sugar
1 tablespoon lemon juice
½ teaspoon vanilla

Chill milk in refrigerator tray until crystals begin to form around the edges. Combine sugar and lemon juice in a chilled mixing bowl, stir to dissolve. Add milk, beat with chilled beater until topping is stiff. Fold in vanilla. Makes 2 cups.

WHIPPED CREAM

Put 1 cup chilled heavy cream (35 percent butterfat content) into a chilled small bowl. Beat with a rotary beater or a whisk until cream is thick and fluffy and will just hold its shape. Serve as is, or sweeten with 2 to 4 tablespoons sifted confectioners' sugar and ¼ teaspoon vanilla, to taste. Makes 2 cups.

WHIPPED DESSERT TOPPING

½ cup instant non-fat dry milk
½ cup ice water
3 tablespoons sugar
½ teaspoon vanilla

Combine dry milk and ice water in a mixing bowl. Beat with a rotary beater until stiff. Add sugar and vanilla, beat until sugar dissolves. Serve at once as a dessert topping. Makes 1½ cups.

Lemon Topping: Add 2 tablespoons lemon juice with the water, increase sugar to 4 tablespoons.

Chocolate Topping: Beat 2 tablespoons cocoa into the whipped topping along with the sugar.

Fruit Topping: Substitute ice-cold fruit juice —orange, apricot, grape or cranberry—for the water. Omit vanilla.

BEVERAGES

What'll you have to drink? Choose beverages for refreshment, satisfaction and more—fruit juices and milk drinks join with coffee and comforting tea to offer drinks of varied flavors that satisfy your nutritional requirements as well as your thirst.

How to Make a Good Cup of Coffee

Really good coffee begins with a fine blend of coffee beans, vacuum-packed, or better, freshly roasted and freshly ground. Or you may prefer quick coffee—instant or freeze-dried.

The coffee grinder is a living tradition at the A&P, and is your assurance of really fresh flavor. Three distinctive A&P blends of coffee beans give you a choice of coffee flavors from mild to robust. In addition, choose from a range of brands, anything from regular breakfast coffee to the more deeply flavored dark roast suggested for after-dinner coffee.

You can have the fresh-roasted beans ground to your order in seven different ways, from *extra-fine* for a vacuum pot, through *drip* grind for a drip pot, *medium fine* for an electric percolator, *medium* or *medium coarse* for a top-range percolator, to *coarse* or *very coarse* for boiling, campfire style.

Ready-ground, vacuum-packed coffees, in extra-fine, drip and perk grinds, are sold under the A&P label. There is also a 100 percent Colombian coffee, for those who prefer this blend, in drip and perk grinds. Larger sizes of most of these packs are offered at a savings.

Follow the utensil manufacturer's sug-gestions about the proper grind, at first. You may find that this makes coffee too weak for your taste, so choose a finer grind the next time you buy. Or you may find the coffee too strong, and decide on a coarser grind.

Buy only enough ground coffee for your immediate needs—a supply for two weeks or less. Ground coffee that is not vacuum-packed loses flavor rapidly, even under proper storage conditions, that is, in an airtight container in the refrigerator. Vacuum-packed cans of coffee should be used within a year, as should whole coffee beans. Both lose flavor, very slowly and gradually, with age.

Be scrupulous about cleaning your coffee maker. Coffee oils tend to cling to the surface and affect the flavor of the brew.

Measure coffee and water carefully, the same way each time, once you find a proportion that pleases you. Begin with the suggested standard 2 level tablespoons of coffee (1 coffee measure) for each 6 ounces (not 8 ounces) of water and revise to your taste.

Rinse your coffee maker with fresh water before you use it, and make the coffee with freshly drawn cold water.

Serve coffee immediately, if possible, since it tastes best then. If necessary, keep it warm over low heat—it should not be allowed to boil.

Instant and freeze-dried coffees, regular and 97 percent caffein-free, are a great convenience, since they dissolve instantly in hot liquid. All these begin with a coffee brew. Instant coffee is dried by spraying the liquid brew in a temperature/humidity-controlled chamber; freeze-dried coffee results from freezing, then drying the brew.

Coffee Specialties

Add to your repertoire of international coffee specialties. From French *café au lait* for breakfast to Italian *caffè espresso* after dinner, these add interest and variety to family meals or to parties. Add whipped cream or ice cream for coffee and dessert in one cup.

CAFÉ AU LAIT

Simultaneously pour equal parts of coffee and hot milk into a coffee cup. Serve with sugar.

CAFFÈ ESPRESSO (ITALIAN COFFEE)

The essential flavor difference in espresso comes from the use of dark-roast, Italian-style coffee, very finely ground. If you have an espresso pot, use 2 tablespoons very finely ground dark-roast coffee for every ¾ cup water, and follow the manufacturer's directions. If you have no espresso pot, use a drip pot, or even an ordinary percolator. In the latter case, line the percolator basket with a paper filter to keep the sediment from seeping through. Serve espresso in a small cup, or demitasse, with sugar and a lemon twist, if you like.

Minted Coffee: Place an after-dinner mint in each demitasse, add espresso coffee.

Cappuccino: Fill cup with equal parts very hot, but not boiled, milk and espresso coffee. Stir to foam. Sprinkle with cinnamon.

VIENNESE COFFEE

Top black coffee with swirls of sweetened whipped cream.

HOT AND COLD SIPPER

Top hot coffee with ice cream (vanilla or coffee flavor).

ITALIAN COFFEE

Add a sliver of lemon rind to black coffee in a glass.

CAFÉ ROYALE

Fill cup with Caffè Espresso (above). Put a small sugar cube in a teaspoon, lay the teaspoon across the top of the cup, soak it with brandy. Ignite the sugar, lower it into the coffee and stir until the flames die. The alcohol burns off, leaving only the flavor of the brandy and the fun of flaming.

IRISH COFFEE

Put a spoon and a sugar cube in a stemmed glass, pour a jigger of Irish or other whiskey over it. Add hot strong coffee almost to fill the glass and top with swirls of unsweetened whipped cream. Sip the coffee through the cream.

How to Make a Good Glass of Iced Coffee

To make perfect iced coffee, brew the beverage by your favorite method but use twice the usual amount of coffee. Pour this double-strength brew over ice cubes. Serve with superfine sugar, which dissolves readily even in cold liquid, and a pitcher of cream or milk.

Economical tricks: Freeze leftover coffee in ice-cube trays; use to cool freshly brewed regular-strength coffee. Or pour cold leftover coffee over the coffee cubes, for iced coffee without dilution.

LEMON ICED COFFEE

Cut peel from lemon in long spiral, place in tall glass. Fill with ice cubes, add double-strength hot coffee.

COFFEE SHAKES

Coffee Hawaiian: Combine in a blender or 1-quart measure, 1 cup black coffee, ½ cup pineapple juice, 1 cup coffee ice cream. Whirl or beat until smooth and frothy. Makes 2 servings.

Plantation Coffee: Combine in a blender or 1-quart measure, 1 cup cold black coffee, 1 small ripe banana, sliced, 1 scoop chocolate ice cream. Whirl or beat with a rotary beater until smooth and frothy. Makes 2 servings.

COFFEE TROPICANA

2 cups strong coffee brew
2 tablespoons sugar
½ teaspoon rum flavoring
Club soda, chilled

Combine coffee, sugar and rum flavoring, chill thoroughly. Divide into 3 tall glasses over ice cubes, add club soda to fill. Makes 3 drinks.

Tea

A&P, The Great Atlantic & Pacific Tea Company, began with tea expertise—and A&P's own teas are tops today. The most popular black teas, pekoe and orange pekoe, are available in tea bags and in cartons under the Our Own and Ann Page labels. A fairly recent addition to the tea party is Our Own Instant Tea, available in jars, plain and with lemon. Iced Tea Mix, convenient, in premeasured envelopes to make 1 glass or 1 quart, and in jars, is flavored with lemon and sugar. A low-calorie version of Iced Tea Mix, artificially sweetened, serves dieters' needs.

How to Make a Good Cup of Tea

Tea bags are a great convenience, and they make excellent tea—but for best results, don't take them to the table! The tag on the tea bag suggests that 3 to 5 minutes' steeping is required to get the full flavor of the tea, a difficult feat in the cup. Make tea in a pot, for best flavor, whether you use tea bags or loose tea leaves. The standard formula is 1 tea bag or 1 teaspoon tea leaves to each 6 ounces freshly boiling water. If you use loose tea, pour the brew through a strainer into the cups or into a second, heated, teapot. If, like many Americans, you prefer a milder tea brew, use less tea, not less steeping time, for best flavor and maximum economy. Dilute the strong brew with more boiling water, to taste.

HOT APPLE TEA

1 quart apple juice or cider
6 cloves
2-inch piece cinnamon stick
4 tea bags, or 4 teaspoons tea leaves

Combine juice and spices in a saucepan, bring to a boil, simmer over low heat 10 minutes. Add tea, steep 3 minutes. Strain into teapot. Serve in mugs, garnish with apple slices, if desired. Makes 4 servings.

SPICED FRUIT TEA

2 quarts boiling water
1 piece stick cinnamon
4 cloves
6 tea bags, or 6 teaspoons tea leaves
½ cup sugar
¼ cup honey

½ cup orange juice
⅓ cup lemon juice

Bring water and spices to a boil, simmer 2 minutes. Add tea bags or tea, steep 5 minutes. Add sugar and honey, stir. Strain into a teapot, add fruit juices. Serve hot. Makes about 15 servings.

How to Make a Good Glass of Iced Tea

Make tea half again as strong as you would for a hot drink, to allow for melting ice cubes. Cool at room temperature, pour over ice cubes. Serve with lemon and sugar, if desired.

Tip: Store a pitcher of tea in the refrigerator, if you like, for instant summer refreshment. The tea may turn cloudy, but this does not affect its taste or quality.

LEMON ICED TEA

Combine 4 cups water and 3 tablespoons lemon juice, freeze in ice-cube trays to make lemon cubes. Pour iced tea over 4 lemon cubes in a tall glass, add superfine sugar to taste.

ICED ORANGE TEA

Pour 1 quart boiling water over 4 tea bags or 4 teaspoons tea leaves. Steep 5 minutes. Remove tea bags or strain. Add 1 cup orange juice. Pour over ice cubes. Makes 5 tall drinks.

HOLIDAY TEA PUNCH

2 quarts water
8 tea bags or 8 teaspoons tea leaves
2 cups cranberry juice
1 can (1 pound 4 ounces) crushed pineapple
1 quart ginger ale

Boil water, add tea, steep 5 minutes. Remove tea bags or strain. Add cranberry juice and crushed pineapple, chill. Pour over ice cubes in a punch bowl, add ginger ale. Makes about 28 punch-cup servings.

BEACH PUNCH

Steep 5 tea bags or 5 teaspoons tea leaves in 5 cups boiling water for 5 minutes. Add 1 can (6 ounces) lemonade concentrate and 3 cans water or fruit juice—orange, pineapple or cranberry. Stir to dissolve. Chill thoroughly, pour into a half-gallon insulated picnic jug.

OPEN-HOUSE TEA PUNCH

Combine 4 cans (6 ounces each) frozen fruitade concentrate with 6 cups strong brewed tea and 2 quarts cold water. Chill, serve over ice cubes. Makes 35 punch-cup servings.

Chocolate Drinks

Great as occasional treats for all members of the family!

MEXICAN CHOCOLATE

  4 tablespoons cocoa
¼ cup sugar
  Dash salt
  3 cups water
  2 teaspoons instant coffee
  1 cup half-and-half, or milk
½ teaspoon cinnamon

Combine cocoa, sugar, salt and water. Stir over low heat until smooth. Add coffee and half-and-half, stir until frothy and hot. Add cinnamon. Makes 4 servings.

HOT COCOA

  1 tablespoon cocoa
  1 tablespoon sugar
  Pinch salt
⅓ cup water
⅔ cup milk

Mix cocoa, sugar and salt in a saucepan. Stir in ⅓ cup water, stir until smooth. Add ⅔ cup milk, cook over low heat, whisking constantly, until cocoa is hot and frothy. Do not boil. Makes 1 cup.

Rich Cocoa at a Price: Use ⅔ cup water, ⅓ cup evaporated milk, prepare as directed.

Low-Calorie Cocoa: Use 1 cup water, ½ cup non-fat dry milk solids. Omit sugar, or use artificial sweetener. Prepare as directed.

IN-STANT CHOCOLATE FLAVORED DRINK

IN-STANT chocolate-flavored drink is a mix with a dozen uses. Stir it into cold milk or hot, for a quick drink, or use it as the base for a shake or soda.

IN-STANT CHOCOLATE BANANA SHAKE

Combine in a blender container or a mixing bowl 2 heaping teaspoons IN-STANT chocolate-flavored drink powder, 1 cup cold milk and ½ ripe banana, sliced. Blend or beat until smooth and frothy.

IN-STANT CHOCOLATE ICE-CREAM SODA

Stir 3 heaping teaspoons IN-STANT with 2 tablespoons milk in a tall glass. Add a scoop of ice cream and chilled plain soda to fill. Serve with straws and a long-handled spoon.

Milk Shakes and Eggnogs

Refreshing and nutritious, these drinks may be the answer for children who don't like milk—or think they don't.

BANANA MILK COOLER

1½ cups chilled milk or buttermilk
  1 banana, sliced
  1 tablespoon molasses
¼ teaspoon cinnamon

Combine ingredients in blender and whirl until smooth; or combine in bowl and beat with a rotary beater. Makes 2 servings.

CHOCOLATE SHAKE

  2 cups milk
  2 tablespoons chocolate syrup
  2 scoops chocolate ice cream

Whirl ingredients in blender; or combine in bowl, beat with rotary beater until smooth and fluffy. Makes 2 shakes.

CHOCOLATE MALT

Add to Chocolate Shake (above) 4 tablespoons malted-milk powder, mix as directed. Makes 2 shakes.

APRICOT SMOOTHIE

  1 cup yogurt
  1 cup milk
  1 cup drained canned apricots or peaches
  2 tablespoons honey

Whirl ingredients in blender. Or mash fruit well, combine in bowl with remaining ingredients, beat with rotary beater until smooth. Makes 2 drinks.

QUICK EGGNOG

2 cups milk, or half-and-half
2 eggs
2 teaspoons sugar
 Dash vanilla
 Nutmeg

Combine milk, eggs and sugar in a blender or mixing bowl, whirl or beat until very frothy. Flavor with vanilla, sprinkle with nutmeg. Makes 3 to 4 servings.

Tip: Canned eggnog needs only to be chilled and poured; instant eggnog, in dry form, can be prepared in seconds.

CHOCOLATE EGGNOG

Flavor prepared eggnog with chocolate syrup to taste, serve with a spoonful of ice cream in each cup.

FRUIT EGGNOG

To 1 cup prepared eggnog, add ½ cup orange-pineapple or orange-apricot fruit juice drink. Blend well.

Fruit Juice Drinks

Keep fruit juices in the refrigerator, ready for instant refreshment. Drink as is, or pour over ice cubes; garnish with lemon or orange slices, maraschino cherries.

APPLE SPARKLE

1 jar (1 quart) apple juice
1 pint ginger ale
1 apple, cored and cut in wedges

Chill all ingredients thoroughly, Combine apple juice and ginger ale in pitcher, garnish with apple wedges. Makes 6 tall drinks.

ORANGE-APRICOT SOUR

1 can (46 ounces) orange-apricot fruit drink
1 cup lemon juice
3 bottles (16 ounces each) club soda
 Orange slices and maraschino cherries
 for garnish

Chill ingredients well. Combine fruit drink and lemon juice, pour over ice in tall glasses. Add soda to fill. Add garnishes. Makes 20 tall drinks.

SPARKLING SPRING PUNCH

½ gallon orange sherbet or vanilla
 ice cream
1 quart apple juice, chilled
1 can (46 ounces) tropical fruit punch,
 chilled
2 quarts lemon-lime soda, chilled

Put sherbet or ice cream into a 2-gallon punch bowl. Or use two 1-gallon bowls, or make half the punch at a time. Add juices and soda, stir lightly. Makes 40 or more tall drinks.

Tomato-Plus Drinks

Dress up tomato juice and use it as an appetizer, or as a beverage with a light lunch or after-school snack.

TOMATO JULEP

Mix 1 can (1 pint 2 ounces) tomato juice with the juice of 1 lemon. Pour into 4 tall glasses filled with crushed ice, garnish with fresh mint. Makes 4 servings.

TOMATO JUICE COCKTAIL

Chill 1 can (1 pint 2 ounces) tomato juice. Season with ⅓ teaspoon Worcestershire sauce, 2 dashes hot pepper sauce. Serve over ice cubes. Makes 3 or 4 servings.

CLAM-TOMATO JUICE

Combine 1 cup each clam juice and tomato juice, add ¼ teaspoon minced onion and dashes of salt, pepper and hot pepper sauce. Chill. Makes 2 tall glasses.

TOMATO-SAUERKRAUT JUICE

Combine 1 cup each tomato juice and sauerkraut juice, add ½ teaspoon lemon juice and a dash each of Worcestershire sauce and paprika. Chill thoroughly. Makes 2 tall glasses.

TANGY TOMATO DRINK

Blend together 2 cups chilled tomato juice and 1 cup chilled buttermilk. Makes 3 to 4 servings.

ENTERTAINING

Entertaining should be a pleasure, to you as well as to guests, from the coffee and cake you share with a neighbor who drops in without notice to the elaborate meal you hope will favorably impress a VIP or the elegant buffet you plan for an occasion as splendid and as important as a wedding.

The foresight shown by a well-organized pantry shelf (see page 18) will painlessly take care of the coffee-and-cake kind of entertaining. You will always be able to welcome callers hospitably, or to provide an emergency meal for unexpected guests.

When you plan a party, large or small, the best way to avoid party panic is to use your head, as well as your hands and feet.

Decide on the menu first—it should include dishes that add to the mood of the occasion, and that you can prepare without strain. Make a time schedule for shopping and cooking. Make lists of everything you need and everything you must do, and post the lists where you can't avoid seeing them.

The more items you can cook ahead, partly or completely, and freeze or store until the big day, the better. Decide which linens, dishes, glasses and tableware you want to use, and be sure that all are laundered, washed, or polished and ready to go!

If you plan a large party, you will find the quantity-buying guide below helpful in determining how much food and drink you will need. Foods for which recipes are supplied present only an arithmetical problem. Most recipes can safely be made in double batches, to serve twice as many people as originally indicated.

Quantity-Buying Guide for 50

Bread: A 1-pound loaf makes about 18 slices ⅜ inch thick. For 50 sandwiches, allow 6 loaves. Allow 2 slices per serving, unless yours is a do-it-yourself sandwich party, in which case allow more.

Crackers (for cheese, spreads): 3 pounds serve 50 people.

Rolls: Allow 2 per serving for men, 1½ per serving for women.

Butter: 1 pound will spread 50 sandwiches; 1½ pounds, each ¼-pound stick cut into 16 pats, will serve 50 people, 2 pats to a serving.

Jam: 3 jars, 1 pound each, will spread 50 sandwiches.

Sandwich Fillings: 2 quarts of filling will spread 50 sandwiches.

Peanut Butter: 3 jars, 1 pound each, will spread 50 sandwiches.

Mayonnaise: ½-pint jar will spread 50 sandwiches.

Lettuce: 3 medium heads will garnish 50 sandwiches.

Cookies: Allow 1 large or 2 small cookies per serving; double for children.

Pies: A 9-inch pie makes 7 servings; allow 8 pies for 50 people.

Cakes: A 9-inch-by-13-inch sheet cake makes 30 servings. Four 8-inch round 2-layer cakes make 48 servings. Four 9-inch round 2-layer cakes make 48 servings, slightly larger.

Heavy Cream: Whip 1 quart heavy cream to top 50 desserts; or make 2 quarts of any whipped topping.

Ice Cream: Allow ⅓ pint per serving, 2

gallons for 50 people; as topping for pie or cake, allow 5 quarts, ⅕ pint per serving.

Coffee: 1 pound coffee makes 40 cups brew, ¾ cup each; 6¼ cups make 50 cups brew.

Tea: 1 cup tea leaves, 2 gallons boiling water make 40 cups.

Cream: Allow 1½ tablespoons per cup of coffee or tea; 1¼ quarts for 50 people.

Sugar: Allow 2 teaspoons sugar or 2 sugar lumps per cup of coffee or tea; 1⅛ pounds sugar for 50 cups.

Punch: 2 gallons, 50 servings, about ⅔ cup each; or 64 servings, 4 ounces each.

Liquor: One fifth makes 17 drinks, 1 quart makes 21 drinks; allow 1½ ounces per drink.

Party Menus

TEEN-AGE MIDNIGHT SUPPER

Antipasto
Pizza Loaf
Apple Sparkle

SUNDAY BRUNCH

California Fruit Salad
Brunch Casserole
Honey Snails
Café au Lait

WINTER BUFFET

Swedish Meatballs with Buttered Noodles
Hearty Spinach Salad
Sugar-Glazed Carrots
Hot Rolls
Butter Cake with Broiled Topping
Spiced Fruit Tea

SPRING DINNER PARTY

Avocado Halves with Grapefruit Sections
Fish Fillets Bonne Femme
Tossed Salad with Green Goddess Dressing
Minted Carrots with Peas
New Potatoes
Strawberry Shortcake

SUMMER LUNCHEON

Chilled Gazpacho
Chinese Chicken Walnut Salad
Hot Corn Muffins
Strawberry Cheese Cake
Iced Tea—Iced Coffee

AUTUMN DINNER FOR 25

Pepper-Mill Cheese Balls—Assorted Crackers
Jambalaya
Coleslaw
Fresh Corn on the Cob
Lemon Cake with Lemon Glaze
Open-House Tea Punch

ALL RECIPES ARE IN THIS BOOK—SEE INDEX.

Party Recipes

For special occasions where a dozen to a hundred people gather. The recipes that follow are designed to make it a pleasure to entertain a crowd.

WEDDING CAKE

Six featherlight pecan layers add up to a wedding cake that boasts the personal touch and rich flavor you add at home. Make it well ahead of time, then freeze, to finish with frosting just before the wedding day.

The six tiers should be made in two batches. Make the single recipe and use the batter to fill 3-, 6-, 7½- and 9-inch layer pans. Next, make a double batch, to fill 10½-inch and 12-inch pans.

Single	Double
3¼ cups flour	6½ cups
1 tablespoon baking powder	2 tablespoons
1 teaspoon salt	2 teaspoons
¾ cup butter or margarine	1½ cups
1½ cups sugar	3 cups
1 teaspoon vanilla	2 teaspoons
4 eggs, separated	8 eggs
1 cup milk	2 cups
1½ cups finely chopped pecans	3 cups

Grease and flour cake pans needed for batch you are making. Toss together flour, baking powder and salt to mix. Cream butter, gradually add sugar and vanilla. Beat in egg yolks. Add flour mixture alternately with milk, stir in pecans. Beat egg whites until stiff but not dry, fold into cake batter. Turn batter into prepared pans and bake in a moderate oven (350°F) 20 to 35 minutes, depending on the size of the cake pan. Test for doneness with a toothpick or cake tester. Remove from cake pans and cool completely on racks before storing or freezing.

CREAMY WHITE FROSTING

3 egg whites
8 cups sifted confectioners' sugar
1 teaspoon almond or vanilla flavoring
2 tablespoons lemon juice
¼ cup white shortening
¼ cup sour cream

Beat egg whites, adding sugar a cup at a time; beat until stiff and fluffy. When 4 cups sugar have been added, beat in flavoring, lemon juice, shortening and sour cream, then remaining 4 cups sugar. Frosting should be smooth and firm. Makes about 4 cups. Make this recipe twice for the wedding cake. Assemble cake, spreading a little frosting between the layers. Warm ½ cup corn syrup. Brush loose crumbs from cake, brush cake with warm syrup. Spread frosting on cake with a spatula. Frost without stopping, as icing quickly forms a crisp crust. Keep bowl of icing covered with a damp cloth while working, to keep it from hardening. Color remaining icing as desired and use to decorate cake. This cake will serve 75 to 100 reception guests.

COFFEE FOR FORTY

Tie 1 pound of coffee loosely in a cloth bag. Put in a pot with 7½ quarts cold water. Bring to a boil, remove from heat. Repeat twice.

RECEPTION PUNCH

2 cups sugar
1 quart water
1 pint pineapple juice
1 pint orange juice
1 pint lemon or lime juice
1 pint fruit sherbet
2½ quarts ginger ale

Dissolve sugar in water, add fruit juices. Pour over fruit sherbet in punch bowl. Add ginger ale just before serving. Makes about 1½ gallons; 40 to 50 punch-cup servings.

Spirited Reception Punch: Substitute 1 quart white wine for water and add 1 cup light rum with fruit juices.

PARTY EGGNOG

4 eggs, separated
½ cup sugar
¼ teaspoon salt
2 cups light cream
1 cup milk
1 teaspoon vanilla
1 cup heavy cream
Nutmeg

Beat egg yolks with ¼ cup sugar until very light. Add salt, light cream, milk and vanilla, stir. Whip cream until very thick but not stiff, fold into yolk mixture. Beat egg whites until foamy, gradually beat in remaining sugar, beat until stiff. Fold into nog. Sprinkle with nutmeg. Makes 16 servings.

CLASSIC EGGNOG

6 eggs, separated
1 cup sugar
2 cups heavy cream
2 cups milk
1 pint bourbon or other whiskey
¼ cup brandy or dark rum
Nutmeg

Beat egg yolks until light and fluffy, gradually beat in half the sugar. Beat egg whites until foamy, gradually beat in remaining sugar, beat until stiff. Fold whites into yolks. Stir in cream, milk and liquor. Sprinkle with nutmeg. Makes about 20 punch-cup servings, 4 ounces each.

CHICKEN CURRY FOR TWENTY-FIVE

4 whole chickens, poached (see page 111)
½ cup oil
6 onions, chopped
4 tart apples, chopped
6 cups chicken broth
3 tablespoons curry powder
Salt, pepper
1 teaspoon cinnamon
1 can (8 ounces) mushrooms

Bone and dice chickens. Heat oil in large pan. Add onions and apples and cook until apples are soft. Stir in broth, curry powder, salt, pepper and cinnamon. If necessary, reduce sauce by rapid boiling to thicken. Add mushrooms and diced chicken, cover and cook 10 minutes. Serve over hot rice with several of the curry accompaniments listed below. Makes about 25 servings.

Curry Accompaniments:

Raisins	Chopped Eggs
Peanuts	Pickled Kumquats
Chutney	Sliced Radishes
Coconut	Sliced Cucumbers
Grapes	Chopped Apples

PARTY GLAZED HAMS

2 boneless canned hams (4 to 5 pounds each)
1 can (8¼ ounces) crushed pineapple
1 cup light brown sugar
¼ teaspoon ginger

Have the butcher cut the hams into thin slices and tie a cord around them to reshape. Combine pineapple with its juices and the remaining ingredients in a saucepan. Heat until sugar is dissolved. Spoon glaze over hams and bake in a moderately slow oven (325°F) 45 minutes, basting occasionally, until golden brown. Makes 30 to 40 servings.

JAMBALAYA

¼ cup oil
3 green peppers, diced
3 onions, chopped
2 cloves garlic, minced
2 pounds Italian or Spanish sausage, sliced
3 cups cubed cooked ham
4 cups raw rice
3 cans (1 pound 13 ounces each) tomatoes
6 cups chicken broth
1 tablespoon salt
¼ teaspoon pepper
½ teaspoon hot pepper sauce
1 teaspoon basil
½ teaspoon thyme
3 pounds shrimp, shelled and deveined

Heat oil in a large Dutch oven. Add green peppers, onions, and garlic, and cook until wilted. Add sausage slices and ham cubes and brown lightly. Add rice and cook, stirring often, until pale gold. Add tomatoes, broth and seasonings. Bring to a boil, cover and reduce heat. Simmer 20 minutes. Add shrimp, stir, cover and cook 5 minutes longer, until shrimp is pink, rice is tender and liquid is almost absorbed. Makes about 25 servings.

COUSCOUS

¼ cup oil
1 cup finely chopped onion
2 cloves garlic, minced
2 quarts beef broth
4 cups couscous
2 pieces stick cinnamon
1 teaspoon turmeric
2 quarts diced cooked beef or lamb
2 cups raisins
Salt, pepper, sugar
1 cup toasted slivered almonds

Heat oil in a large pot, cook onion and garlic until transparent. Add beef broth, bring to a boil. Add couscous, cinnamon and turmeric. Simmer until liquid is absorbed. Stir in meat and raisins, season to taste with salt, pepper and sugar. Remove from heat. Cover pot, allow to stand 15 to 20 minutes. Remove cinnamon. Serve sprinkled with toasted almonds. Makes 20 to 25 servings.

Variation: Use 4 cups long-grain white rice instead of couscous.

POTATO SALAD FOR TWENTY

5 pounds potatoes
⅓ cup vinegar
⅔ cup oil
2 teaspoons salt
Pepper
½ teaspoon mixed Italian herbs
1 cup mayonnaise
2 cups chopped celery
¾ cup chopped scallions, with green
¼ cup chopped stuffed olives
4 hard-cooked eggs, chopped
Green pepper and tomato for garnish

Cook potatoes in their jackets, in boiling salted water, until tender. Cool potatoes slightly, peel, slice thinly. Mix vinegar, oil, salt, pepper and herbs. Pour dressing over warm potatoes; cool. Mix mayonnaise with celery, scallions, olives and eggs. Combine with potatoes. Arrange on serving platter, garnish with strips of green pepper and tomato slices. Makes 20 servings.

COLESLAW

2 medium heads cabbage, shredded
4 large carrots, finely shredded
1 green pepper, slivered
2 cups mayonnaise
1 tablespoon salt
1 teaspoon sugar
½ teaspoon dried mustard
½ teaspoon pepper
⅓ cup vinegar or lemon juice
1 tablespoon celery seed

Toss cabbage, carrots and green pepper together. Mix remaining ingredients to make dressing. Pour dressing over cabbage mixture and chill until serving time. Makes about 25 servings.

CHINESE CHICKEN WALNUT SALAD

2 poached chickens (see page 111), boned
5 hard-cooked eggs, chopped

¼ **cup minced scallions**
1½ **cups chopped celery**
¼ **cup mayonnaise**
¼ **cup wine vinegar**
½ **cup chicken broth**
   Salt and pepper
 1 **cup coarsely chopped walnuts**
 2 **tablespoons butter or margarine**
   Shredded lettuce or Chinese cabbage
   Watercress

Dice chicken, toss with eggs, scallions and celery. Blend mayonnaise, vinegar, broth, salt and a dash of freshly ground pepper. Add to chicken, blend well. Fry walnuts in butter until crisp and golden, drain on absorbent toweling, add to chicken mixture. Chill until serving time. Arrange on a bed of shredded lettuce or Chinese cabbage and garnish with watercress. Makes 12 servings.

CARROTS À L'ORANGE

 6 **pounds carrots, peeled and cut in**
   ½ **-inch slices**
 3 **cups orange juice**
 3 **tablespoons sugar**
   Salt
   Ginger
¼ **cup butter or margarine**

 2 **tablespoons cornstarch**
¼ **cup water**

Simmer carrots in orange juice with seasonings and butter until tender, about 15 to 20 minutes. Remove carrots to serving dish and keep warm. Add cornstarch mixed with water to hot sauce, stir until thickened; cook 3 minutes longer. Pour sauce over carrots. Garnish with orange slices, if desired. Makes about 25 servings.

PEPPERMINT CHARLOTTE

 6 **envelopes unflavored gelatin**
 3 **cups cold water**
 2 **cups hot milk**
½ **pound peppermint candy, crushed**
½ **teaspoon salt**
 1 **quart whipping cream, chilled**
 1 **tablespoon vanilla**
 2 **dozen ladyfingers, split**

Sprinkle gelatin on cold water to soften. Add hot milk, stir to dissolve. Add crushed peppermint candy and salt. Stir until candy dissolves. Chill mixture until syrupy. Whip cream with vanilla, fold in. Line two 6-cup molds or one 3-quart mold with split ladyfingers. Fill with peppermint mixture. Chill until firm. Unmold to serve. Garnish with more whipped cream, if desired. Makes about 25 servings.

HEALTH AND BEAUTY

A&P's own health and beauty aids are equal in quality to the major national brands, but they sell at substantially lower prices. For example, compare A&P Aspirin for price and effectiveness with national-brand aspirin.

And remember that our guarantee of satisfaction or your money back applies to health and beauty aids as it does to everything you buy at A&P. No wonder A&P's own health and beauty aids outsell the national brands in many of our stores!

Shopper's Checklist for A&P Health and Beauty Aids—Moneysaving Values

Mouthwash—three flavor choices:
Antiseptic (amber).
Oral Hygienic (green)—peppermint flavor.
Astringent (red)—cinnamon flavor.
Toothpaste—two types:
Fluoride helps fight decay.
Mint-flavored, for those who like mint flavor and do not want fluoride.
Check the tube size that offers the best value for your needs.
Toothbrushes—all with nylon bristles:
A dual-textured adult brush, with soft outer bristles and firm inner bristles.
A child's toothbrush.
A preventive dentistry toothbrush, with very fine soft nylon bristles whose blunted or gently rounded tips allow you to brush right down into gum margins without irritation to the gum.
Denture Cleanser—in easy-to-use tablet form.
Shampoos—A&P; Amber; Green Shampoo.

Hair Spray—regular and unscented.
Vitamins—several choices:
Adult's Multiple 100's; Vitamins with Iron 100's.
Children's Vitamins 60's; Children's with Iron 60's.
Vitamin C.
Vitamin E.
Aspirin—100's; 250's; Buffered Aspirin 100's.
Shave Cream—regular; menthol; lemon-lime.
Razor Blades—double-edge and injector.
Deodorant—anti-perspirant and deodorant.
Cosmetic Puffs
Cotton
Cotton Swabs
Nail Polish Remover
Adhesive Strips—single size and assorted.
Adhesive Tape
Petroleum Jelly—three practical sizes.
Cold Cream
Extra-Care Skin Lotion
Baby Oil
Baby Powder
Baby Shampoo
Liquid Antacid
In addition, many conventional food products may serve as health and beauty aids. Cornstarch helps keep baby's skin smooth; bicarbonate of soda is soothing to rashes. Oatmeal can be used as a face mask and lemon juice as a hair rinse.

Natural Foods

While many foods sold in the supermarket rightly qualify as health foods, and are entirely natural in their production, a special selection of foods will appeal to those who want the assurance of natural quality with minimum processing. Official USDA shoppers compared prices of such foods at a chain supermarket and at a "natural" food store on the same day. The processed foods in the "natural" food store averaged 190 percent of the cost of the same items in the supermarket, almost twice as much. Cost of unprocessed "natural" foods averaged 164 percent of their cost in the supermarket, or two-thirds more. This comparison is reported in the *Shopper's Guide, USDA 1974 Yearbook of Agriculture.*

You can save even more by preparing some of the specialty "health food" products on your own. For example, you can make your own granola (page 23).

If unprocessed soybeans are available in the Health Foods Section, try them in this tasty casserole.

SOYBEAN CASSEROLE

1 package (16 ounces) soybeans
2 tablespoons oil
1 medium onion, chopped
1 medium green pepper, chopped
1 clove garlic, chopped
1 can (16 ounces) tomatoes
1 can (6 ounces) tomato paste
1 cup water
1 teaspoon honey
1 bay leaf
½ teaspoon basil
  Salt and pepper
½ pound sharp Cheddar cheese, shredded
½ cup dry bread crumbs

Cook soybeans as package directs. Heat oil, cook onion, green pepper and garlic until golden. Add tomatoes, tomato paste, water, honey and seasonings. Cook until slightly thickened. Layer cooked soybeans, tomato sauce and cheese in a greased 3-quart casserole. Sprinkle with bread crumbs. Bake in a moderate oven (350°F) about 20 minutes, until bubbling and browned. Makes 10 servings.

HEALTHFUL SNACKS

You may choose to buy health food nibbles. Or you can prepare your own, using natural raisins and other dried fruits, nutmeats and sesame seeds from the regular shelves, at lower prices.

Whole-grain cookies are another health food shelf specialty you may enjoy preparing for yourself—at a saving.

OATMEAL CHEWS

1 can (15 ounces) sweetened condensed milk
¼ cup non-fat dry milk solids
¼ cup unsweetened wheat germ
½ teaspoon salt
1 teaspoon vanilla
1 cup old-fashioned oatmeal
½ cup grated coconut
½ cup raisins

Combine all the ingredients in a bowl and mix well. Set aside for 30 minutes and stir occasionally. Drop teaspoonfuls of mixture onto a baking sheet lined with oiled brown paper. Bake in a moderately slow oven (325°F) 15 minutes. Remove cookies from paper to rack. Makes 3 dozen.

CEREAL SPECIAL

Wheat germ is a favorite health food product that you will find on the cereal shelves. Use it as a topping for cereal, for fruits, for ice cream, as a flavorful and nutritious coating for fried chicken, or to make bread.

WHEAT-GERM BREAD

1 envelope active dry yeast
¼ cup very warm water
2 cups hot water
⅔ cup non-fat dry milk
2 tablespoons shortening
2 tablespoons sugar
2 teaspoons salt
4 cups sifted all-purpose flour (approximately)
2½ cups wheat germ
  Butter or margarine

Dissolve yeast in very warm water. Pour hot water into large bowl. Add dry milk and whisk until dissolved. Beat in shortening, sugar and salt, cool to lukewarm. Add half the flour, to make a batter. Add yeast to batter, beat well. Add wheat germ and enough flour to make a soft dough. Let rest 10 minutes. Knead on a floured board until smooth and elastic. Let rise in greased bowl, covered, until double in bulk, about 1½ hours. Punch down, knead again. Divide dough in half, let rest 10 minutes. Shape loaves, arrange in 2 greased 9-inch loaf pans. Brush tops with butter or margarine, cover with cloth, let rise until doubled in bulk, about 1 hour. Bake in a moderate oven (350°F) about 50 to 55 minutes, until the loaves are richly browned and test done. Makes 2 loaves.

HOW TO SAVE COST AND TIME IN HOUSECLEANING

From cleaning up the kitchen to cleaning the house, you can save time and money, to say nothing of your own energy, with aware selection of cleaning materials and supplies, from paper goods to washing soda!

On some items, such as paper towels, unit prices are a good guide to the actual cost of various sizes and brands available.

For cleaning and laundry supplies, it is important to check off the types of materials that need to be cleaned, the types of soil that need to be removed. Match the cleaning problems you must solve with the selection of materials in the market. Try new products, but be guided by your real needs rather than by superpromises for new products.

Water and Suds Go Far

Use water and soap or detergent to clean porcelain, painted woodwork and other washable surfaces. If your water is hard and soap forms curds, use a water softener.

Don't waste detergent. Make up a bowlful of water and detergent, with just enough detergent to form sturdy suds, to clean grease and cooking stains from walls, woodwork and non-wood floors. For an inexpensive shampoo for rugs or upholstery, whip ¼ cup mild detergent with 1 pint warm water until it makes a stiff foam.

You may prefer to buy a prepared solution for rug and upholstery cleaning. These are premeasured and have high sudsing quality. Or you may prefer a dry, powdered cleaner that absorbs stains and dirt, then is vacuumed up. Explore the market shelves for specific cleaning aids that save money both by their low price and by eliminating costly special services.

Heavy-duty detergent is very alkaline and is excellent for such heavy jobs of dirt removal as soaking burner parts of the gas range, cleaning broiler pans and other greasy and oily surfaces, or for bathroom bowls. It is not recommended for cleaning linoleum or painted surfaces.

Many liquid all-purpose cleaners combine soap or detergent in selected strengths with water and ammonia, or with pine-oil disinfectant, or acid, or other cleaning agents.

Liquid cleaners often come in spray or aerosol containers. When you buy a convenient spray bottle, check whether refills are available. Choose aerosol cans only for special jobs. Simpler packaging saves both money and ecological waste.

Caustics—Use Care

Oven and drain cleaning are the two least popular household chores, so it pays to find effective products for these needs. Line the oven bottom and burner pans, where possible, with foil, so that you can lift out and dispose of the lining along with some of the dirt.

The main ingredient of many oven cleaners and drain openers is lye. This is highly toxic, but it does a good job of removing burned-on or built-up grease or soil. It is a good idea to remove simpler soils first with a liquid cleaner or detergent solution.

When you use a lye-based oven cleaner, avoid breathing the fumes or getting the lye on chromium or aluminum parts, or on your hands. Some oven cleaners contain ammonia, which also loosens burned-on grease and dirt. Avoid breathing ammonia, too. You can make your own oven cleaner with ammonia and detergent, but most homemakers are happy to discover a prepared product that will make this job as painless as possible!

Your choice of drain cleaner should depend on what caused the clog, and the location of the drain.

For clogged kitchen drains, try a non-caustic liquid cleaner first, since this may serve as a grease solvent. If it is not effective, try a caustic granular type. Follow manufacturer's directions for electric garbage disposers; most caustic cleaners should not be used in disposers.

For the bathroom drain, where hair may have caused the clog, use a caustic liquid. If this fails, try caustic granules. Follow directions carefully when using these products and avoid splashing—on yourself most of all. For a sluggish drain, try using ½ pound washing soda to 2 cups boiling water.

Toilet-bowl cleaners often have an acid base for removing discoloration. These are toxic—use with caution. And try scrubbing the bowl with ¼ cup detergent and a little laundry bleach (more about versatile bleach later). Hate the job? Invest in an attractive brush (or disposable scrubber) and canister for tidy storage. Circular brushes made of stiff bristles are effective and do not drip after the water is shaken out.

More's the Shine

Window and glass cleaners that contain ammonia are good for cleaning greasy fumes that collect on glass surfaces. You will find such cleaners in liquid form (some colored for easy visibility) and in spray or powdered form. Or you can make an effective cleaner with 4 tablespoons of ammonia to 1 quart of warm water.

Here's the Rub

Abrasives clean by friction—they help you rub off the dirt. Scouring powders and pads, sandpaper, meshes of metal, plastic or nylon, and steel wool are common abrasives.

Use the mildest or finest abrasive possible, to avoid marring the surface to be cleaned. Harsh abrasives, such as scouring powder,

will gradually cause damage by scratching the glossy finish on painted surfaces, porcelain, enamel or plastics. Once the surface is dull, it will soil faster and stain. Where possible, use cleaners in waxy compounds to remove soil without damage to surfaces.

Use chlorine bleach only in dilution; it can damage surfaces if used full strength. Used according to directions, chlorine bleach, like pine-oil, phenolic and other disinfectants, will kill harmful bacteria. But use with care. Chlorine bleach reacts with ammonia, and with acid cleaners, such as toilet-bowl cleaners, to form a dangerous and irritating gas. Never mix chlorine bleach with other cleaners.

Wax Is as Wax Does

Clean a floor before you wax it—with water and detergent for composition floors, with turpentine and wax (or a solvent wax) for wood or cork floors.

Use water-based wax on rubber and asphalt-tile floors.

For vinyl floors that require wax, linoleum, terrazzo and concrete floors, use a water-based or solvent cleaning wax.

Clean wood and cork floors with solvent cleaning and polishing wax; use paste wax where heavy protection is needed.

Rub heel marks and streaks with the appropriate wax on a nylon scrub pad or very fine steel wool.

For furniture, spray bottles are a handy way to deposit just enough wax to polish to a shine. Liquid cleaning wax used periodically protects some furniture. For antique or very fine furniture, use paste wax or lemon oil. Heavily soiled surfaces may be cleaned with oil soap.

A creamy cleaning wax is handy for painted furniture where a shine is desired, or for counter tops, ceramic tile, cabinets and appliances.

Tools Save Toil

Scan the handy rack of tools in the supermarket for low-cost and efficient cleaning power.

When choosing tools for cleaning, remember that you need two basic types, one to loosen and remove dust and dirt, the other to soften and remove moist soil.

You will want an old-fashioned, long-bristled broom for dense, scattered dirt and a wide, short-bristled push broom with angled edges for getting into the corners. A soft, long-stranded mop to pick up and hold dust, with lint-free fibers and angled corners, is useful for wooden floors.

For washable surfaces, check off a wet mop, sponges or cloths, containers for water and a brush for the toilet bowl.

Choose wet mops of string or of sponge; in either case, check for a wringing arrangement and easy replacement.

Laundry Tips

Think of laundry in two parts: small personal items, which are best hand-washed by individual family members and bathroom-dried for quick and efficient reuse, and larger items, which are collected and laundered in a full load, for savings of money, time and electrical energy.

Modern washers and dryers have largely taken the effort and the weather-permit out of doing the laundry. What remains is your own challenge to shop for the proper soaps or detergents and to use them sparingly, just enough to get the job done.

You can choose from detergents that wash in cold water (efficient for woolens) and those used with hot water, to clean very soiled clothes especially effectively. You may want to check for detergents with no phosphates, for the additional cleaning power of washing soda and bleaches, and for aids to smoother results—water softeners and conditioners. Include mild soap flakes or powder for fine hand laundry. Moisten and rub very soiled spots with soap or detergent before washing.

Compare prices of soaps and detergents for both cost per ounce *and* quantity recommended for a load.

For efficiency in planning, sort and group clothes according to type and color, then wash and dry on the proper cycle for the fabrics you are doing. Wherever possible, wash a full load, or set the machine for a partial load if that is all you have. Check water-temperature adjustments.

Set a table or ironing board near the dryer and place a broad, flat-based container on this, to avoid bending as you fill it (a modern plastic wash basket does well). Sort and fold dry clothes, grouping according to destination, tote in the basket for easy replacement in closets and dressers. Sprinkle clothes that require ironing; if it is necessary to hold moist clothes, store in the freezer to prevent molding, or redry.

Dishwashing Made Easy

Since this is the most frequently repeated washing chore, it pays to make it as efficient as possible. Keep the following tools and supplies at the sink center; replace them as needed, checking specials and unit prices for best values:

Paper towels
Rubber gloves
Cellulose sponge
Heavy-duty sponge with dirt release
Bottle brush and sink brush
Drain tray
Dish drainer
Dishwashing detergent
Dishwasher detergent (if used)
Silver polish
Metal polish
Ammonia
Scouring pads
Scouring powder
Dish towels
Hand lotion

Housecleaning Specials Pay

Since most housecleaning aids are non-perishable products, it pays to watch for sales and specials and to buy the largest-sized units that you can conveniently store. Watch store ads and displays for specials, particularly of products you use regularly. The best buy, however, is not worth stocking if you have no real need for it.

In planning your shopping budget, remember that housecleaning and other non-food products are real moneysavers in the supermarket. They do add to your total bill, however, so plan for major housecleaning purchases, such as a large-sized package of detergent, in a week when your food purchases are relatively low.

Good shopping can make your housekeeping easier on the budget and easier on you!

SPICE COOKING CHART

Spice	Appetizers	Soups	Meats	Eggs	Fish	Poultry	Sauces	Vegetables	Salads	Desserts
Allspice	Meatballs Cheeses	Fruit Sweet-Sour	Pork		Fish Stews	Duck	Barbecue Creole	Eggplant Squash	Fruit	Fruits Puddings
Basil	Cheeses Tomato Cocktail	Seafood Poultry Vegetable	Any Meat	Omelets Soufflés	Any Fish	Any Poultry	Creole Tomato	Tomatoes Summer Squash	Poultry Vegetable Seafood	
Bay Leaves	Pickles	Bean Fish Vegetable	Stews Pot Roasts		Poached Fish Stews	Stewed Chicken	Spaghetti	Potatoes Tomatoes	Dressings	
Caraway Seeds	Crackers Cheeses	Cabbage Cheese	Pork Variety Meats	Deviled		Chicken	Cheese	Cabbage Carrots Potatoes	Slaw Cucumber	
Cayenne	Dips Tomato Cocktail	Vegetable	Any Meat	Omelets Deviled	Any Fish	Any Poultry	Cream Hollandaise	Potatoes Onions	French Dressing	
Celery Salt and Seed	Dips	Potato Vegetable	Any Meat	Omelets Scrambled	Any Fish	Any Poultry	Cream Fish	Any Vegetable	Slaw Tossed	
Chili Powder	Cocktail Sauce Dips	Bean Vegetable	Pot Roasts Chili	Omelets		Stews Casseroles	Barbecue Mexican	Corn Beans Onions	Bean Salad French Dressing	
Chives	Dips Cheeses	Cream Potato	Stews	Deviled Omelets	Any Fish	Any Poultry	Cream Butter	Carrots Potatoes	Vegetable	
Cinnamon	Fruits Pickles	Fruit	Stuffed Pork Fruit Stews		Sweet-Sour	Stuffings	Ketchup Sweet-Sour	Winter Squash Yams	Fruit	Puddings Fruits Pies
Cloves	Pickles	Fruit	Marinades	Creamed	Broiled Fish	Baked Chicken	Chili Barbecue	Beets Carrots	Fruit Dressings	Cakes Cookies
Cumin	Dips Cheeses	Bean Tomato	Kebabs Chili	Omelets	Broiled Fish	Curried Chicken	Chili Tomato	Corn Dried Beans	Potato	
Curry Powder	Dips	Curried Soups	Any Meat	Deviled Creamed	Any Fish	Any Poultry	Curry Cream	Beans Onions	Vegetable	

Dill Seed or Weed	Dips Pickles	Seafood Pea	Roasts Stews	Omelets	Broiled Fish	Chicken	Cream Sour	Green Beans	Vegetable	
Garlic	Dips	Vegetable	Any Meat	Omelets	Any Fish	Any Poultry	Butter Tomato	Potatoes Tomatoes	Vegetable Meat	
Ginger	Fruits	Bean Fruit	Sauerbraten Pot Roasts		Broiled Fish	Roast Chicken	Sweet-Sour Dessert	Beets Sweet Potatoes	Fruit	Cookies Fruits Pies
Mace	Dips Spreads	Chicken	Pot Roasts		Stews	Stews	Creole	Corn	Fruit Meat	Pies Puddings
Marjoram	Dips Mushrooms	Meat Seafood Vegetable	Any Meat	Omelets Soufflés	Any Fish	Any Poultry	Brown Cream	Any Vegetable	Vegetable Meat	
Mint	Fruits	Fruit Pea	Lamb Veal		Garnish	Any Poultry	Mint Fruit	Peas Carrots	Fruit Vegetable	Fruits Chocolate
Mustard	Any Appetizer	Potato Pea	Cured Meats Pork	Deviled	Marinades	Glazes	Mustard Sweet-Sour	Baked Beans	Slaw Vegetable	
Nutmeg	Fruits	Cream	Pot Roasts	French Toast	Any Fish	Any Poultry	Cream	Any Vegetable	Fruit	Any Dessert
Onion	Vegetables Meats Cheeses	Vegetable Consommé	Ground Meat Any Meat	Omelets Salad	Any Fish	Any Poultry	Tomato Cream	Any Vegetable	Meat Vegetable	
Oregano	Pizzas Dips Cheeses	Vegetable Bean	Stews Any Meat	Omelets Soufflés	Any Fish	Any Poultry	Italian Barbecue	Any Vegetable	Vegetable	
Paprika	Any Appetizer	Cream	Any Meat	Any Eggs	Any Fish	Any Poultry	Cream Spicy	Any Vegetable	Any Salad	
Parsley Flakes	Any Appetizer	Any Soup	Any Meat	Any Eggs	Any Fish	Any Poultry	Any Sauce	Any Vegetable	Any Salad	
Red Pepper, Crushed	Dips Cheeses	Vegetable	Chili Stews	Omelets	Stews	Stews	Hot	Corn Beans Tomatoes	Vinaigrette	

Spice	Appetizers	Soups	Meats	Eggs	Fish	Poultry	Sauces	Vegetables	Salads	Desserts
Rosemary	Fruits	Chicken Fish	Lamb Pork Stews	Scrambled Deviled	Poached Fish	Baked Chicken	Butter Cream	Mushrooms Cauliflower	Fruit Meat	
Sage	Cheeses	Consommé Vegetable	Any Meat	Creamed	Any Fish	Any Poultry	Cheese Duck	Any Vegetable		
Savory	Cheeses Pâtés	Chicken Bean	Any Meat	Deviled Omelets	Any Fish	Any Poultry	Butter Fish	Beets Beans Sauerkraut	Vegetable	
Tarragon	Cheeses Seafoods	Chicken Vegetable Seafood	Lamb Stews Roasts	Deviled Omelets	Any Fish	Any Poultry	Mustard Tartar	Broccoli	Any Salad	
Thyme	Seafoods Vegetables	Fish Mushroom	Any Meat	Soufflés	Stuffings Any Fish	Any Poultry	Curry Creole	Any Vegetable	Any Salad	
Turmeric	Vegetable Dips	Curry Cream	Marinades Curries	Creamed Deviled	Curries	Curries	Cream Basting	Pickles	Seafood Slaw	

WEIGHTS AND EQUIVALENT MEASURES OF COMMON FOODS

Food Item	Weight and Units	Volume
Beans, dried	1 pound	2½ cups uncooked 6 cups cooked
Butter or Margarine	1 pound 4 sticks	2 cups
Cheese, grated	1 pound	4 cups grated
Chicken	3½ pounds (ready-to-cook)	2 cups diced cooked
Chocolate	1 ounce 1 square 1 envelope melted	
Cocoa	1 pound	4 cups
Coconut, finely grated	3½ ounces	1 cup
Coffee	1 pound	5 cups 40 cups brewed
Corn Meal	1 pound	3 cups
Cottage Cheese	1 pound	2 cups
Dates	1 pound	2½ cups pitted, cut
Flour, all-purpose	4 ounces	1 cup
Flour, cake	4 ounces	1 cup plus 2 tablespoons
Flour, whole wheat	7 ounces	1 cup
Macaroni	8 ounces	2 cups uncooked 4 to 5 cups cooked
Meat, beef	1 pound (uncooked)	2 cups ground
Mushrooms	1 pound raw	4 cups sliced 8-ounce can
Noodles	½ pound	3 cups uncooked 3 cups cooked
Oats, quick-cooking	1 pound	6 cups uncooked 8 cups cooked
Oil	1 pound	2 cups
Peanuts	1 pound (in shell)	2 cups nutmeats
Peanuts	1 pound (shelled)	3¼ cups nutmeats
Peas, split	1 pound	2 cups uncooked 5 cups cooked
Pecans	1 pound (shelled)	4¼ cups nutmeats
Potatoes	1 pound 3 medium	2 cups cooked, mashed
Raisins, whole seedless	1 pound	2¾ cups
Rice	1 pound	2½ cups uncooked 8 cups cooked
Spaghetti	½ pound	2½ cups uncooked 4 to 5 cups cooked
Sugar, brown, packed	1 pound	2¼ cups
Sugar, confectioners'	1 pound	3½ cups
Sugar, granulated	1 pound	2¼ cups
Tea Leaves	1 pound	6¼ cups
Walnuts	1 pound (in shell)	2 cups nutmeats
Walnuts	1 pound (shelled)	4½ cups
Yeast, active dry	1 package ¼ ounce	2 teaspoons

CONTENTS OF CANS AND PACKAGES

HOW MUCH DO CANS CONTAIN?

Size	Usual Weight	Contents in Cups
6 ounces	6 ounces	¾ cup
8 ounces	8 ounces	1 cup
Picnic or No. 1	10½ to 12 ounces	1¼ cups
No. 300	14 ounces to 1 pound	1¾ cups
No. 303	1 pound to 17 ounces	2 cups
No. 2	1 pound 4 ounces or 1 pint 2 fluid ounces	2½ cups
No. 2½	1 pound 13 ounces	3½ cups
No. 3 cylinder or 46 ounces	3 pounds 3 ounces or 1 quart 14 ounces	5¾ cups
No. 10	6½ pounds to 7 pounds 5 ounces	12 to 13 cups

FROZEN-FOOD PACKAGES

Vegetables	9 to 16 ounces
Fruits	10 to 16 ounces
Canned Frozen Fruits	13½ to 16 ounces
Frozen Juice Concentrates	6 and 12 ounces
Soups	10 ounces

OVEN TEMPERATURES

Fahrenheit		Celsius or Centigrade
250°F	(very slow)	= 121°C
300°F	(slow)	= 149°C
325°F	(moderately slow)	= 163°C
350°F	(moderate)	= 176°C
375°F	(moderately hot)	= 191°C
400°F	(hot)	= 205°C
450°F	(very hot)	= 232°C

METRIC SYSTEM

Weight
1 ounce = 28.4 grams
16 ounces = 454 grams or .454 kilograms
2.2 pounds = 1 kilogram

Volume
1 tablespoon = 1.5 deciliters
1 teaspoon = .5 deciliter
1 fluid ounce = 3 deciliters
1 quart = .95 liter
1 gallon = 3.8 liters
1.06 quarts = 1 liter
1 cup = 237 milliliters

CHART OF SUBSTITUTIONS

For	*Substitute*	*For*	*Substitute*
1 cup cake flour	1 cup minus 2 tablespoons all-purpose flour	2 egg yolks (in sauces and custards)	1 whole egg
1 tablespoon corn-starch (for thickening)	2 tablespoons flour or 4 teaspoons quick-cooking tapioca	1 square (1 ounce) unsweetened chocolate	3 tablespoons cocoa plus 1 tablespoon butter or margarine, or 1 envelope melted chocolate
1 cup brown sugar, packed	1⅓ cups granulated brown sugar		
1 cup honey	1¼ cups sugar plus ¼ cup liquid used in recipe	1 tablespoon fresh chopped herbs	1 teaspoon dry herbs
1 teaspoon baking powder	¼ teaspoon baking soda plus ½ cup buttermilk or sour milk (replacing ½ cup liquid used in recipe)	1 small fresh onion	1 tablespoon instant minced onion, soaked
		1 teaspoon dry mustard	1 tablespoon prepared mustard
1 cake compressed yeast	1 envelope, or 2 teaspoons, active dry yeast dis-solved in ¼ cup very warm water, *not milk*	1 clove garlic	⅛ teaspoon garlic powder
		1 cup tomato sauce	1 cup condensed tomato soup
1 cup sour milk or buttermilk	1 tablespoon lemon juice or vinegar plus sweet milk to make 1 cup	1½ cups medium white sauce	1 can condensed cream soup or thick soup plus ⅓ cup liquid
1 cup heavy cream	¾ cup milk plus ⅓ cup butter	1 cup bouillon or consommé	½ cup condensed bouillon or consommé plus ½ cup water or other liquid, or 1 cup water plus 1 bouillon cube
1 cup whole fresh milk	½ cup evaporated milk plus ½ cup water, or 1 cup reconstituted non-fat dry milk and 2 teaspoons butter or margarine		
		½ cup strong dark coffee	1 teaspoon instant coffee in ½ cup water

INDEX

A&P
  and Butchers' Pledge, 8, 57
  Consumer Affairs Depart-
    ment of, consumerism,
    7–8
  Creative Food Service, 8
  function of purchasing
    agent in, 9
  health and beauty aids at,
    257
  history of, 7
  and Jane Parker Bakeries,
    224
  nutrition labeling at, 8
  and Operation Aware, 8
  private brands, 11, 247, 249
  and rain-check policy, 8
  Super Right quality meat, 57
  total guarantee at, 8
  Universal Product Code of,
    16
  use of open dating by, 8,
    13–16
  unit pricing at, 8
  See also Ann Page
Allemande Sauce, 174
Almond
  Butter Ice Cream, 241
  Butter Sauce, 174
  Chicken, Chinese, 108
  Frosting, 207
  Iced Cream Cheese, 34
  Wafers, 223
Ambrosia, 166
  Festive, 166
Anadama Bread, 191
Anchovy(ies)
  Butter, 80, 174
  on Cheese Toast, 43
  and Potato Casserole, Scan-
    dinavian, 130
  Roast Chicken, 104
  Sauce, 79
Angel Pie, 214
Ann Page
  as A&P brand, 11, 249
  history of, 7–8

Ann Page (cont.)
  Marmalade Glaze, 68
  Mayonnaise (brand name),
    173
Antipasto, 39
Appetizers, see Snacks and
    Appetizers
Apple(s)
  general notes, 160
  in Applesauce Cake, 203
  Applesauce Hermits, 220
  in Brown Betty, 235
  Cake, 203
  Casserole, Sausage-Sweet-
    Potato-, 130
  Crêpes, 244
  Crisp, 236
  in Easy Applesauce, 161
  Folds, 35
  Grapefruit with, 164
  Green Cabbage with Cara-
    way and, 142
  Pandowdy, 239
  Pie, see Pies
  -Potato Scallop, 161
  Slices, Fried, 161
  Sparkle, 251
  Stuffing
    Roast Duckling with, 106
    Roast Goose with Onion-
      and-, 106
  Tart
    French, 212
    Strawberry-, 212
  Tea, Hot, 249
  Waffles, 24
Applesauce, Easy, 161
  See also Apples
Apricot(s)
  general notes, 161
  Crêpes, 244
  Glaze and Sauce, 68
  Hats, 222
  Mousse, Frozen, 243
  -Orange Bars, 218
  Smoothie, 250
  Sour, Orange-, 251

Artichoke(s), 139
  Hearts, Marinated, 39
Asparagus, Steamed, 139
Aspic, Jellied Turkey in, 113
Avocado(s)
  general notes, 161
  Filling, 226
  and Fillings, 39
  Guacamole, 37

Babka, 192
Bacon, 25
  in Brunch Puff, 25
  Cabbage with Cheese and,
    142
  -Cheddar Dip, 37
  Chick-peas and, 129
  -Egg Dip, 37
  -Flavored Onion Dip, 37
  Green Beans and, 140
  Grill, 226
  Peas and, 149
  Scramble, 29
  Skillet Sprouts with, 141
  -Tomato Dip, 37
  Waffles, 24
  See also Canadian Bacon
Baked
  Alaska, 235
  Apples, 161
  Bananas, 162
  Barley with Mushrooms, 134
  Bluefish Creole, 116
  Chicken, see Chicken
  Eggplant, 146
  Glazed Ham, 68
  Halibut Steaks, 118
  Lasagne with Meat Sauce,
    134
  Potatoes, 151
  Ravioli Marinara, 182
  Rhubarb, 169
  Stuffed Mushrooms, 41
  Stuffed Red Snapper, 16
  Summer Squash, 152
  Sweet Potatoes or Yams, 153

Baked (*cont.*)
Whiting Creole, 116
Winter Squash, 153
Banana(s)
general notes, 161–62
Baked, 162
Bread, Pantry, 198
Cake, 203
-Cornflake Betty, 236
Dessert, Quick, 162
Fritters, 162
Milk Cooler, 250
Pan-Browned, 162
in Salad, 162
shake, IN-STANT Choco-
late, 250
Spread, 226
Upside-Down Cake, 200
Versatility—and Style, 162
Whip, Frozen, 243
Barbecue(d)
Beef Short Ribs, 66
Corn, Grilled, 145
Ham Steak, 82
Lamb Rib, Curried, 82
Pig Feet, 91
Sauce, *see* Sauces
Turkey, 109
Barley with Mushrooms, Baked,
134
Basic
Biscuits, 199
Burgers, 83
Green Salad, 170
Pot Roast, 70
Sweet Yeast Dough, 192
Batter-Fried Chicken, 96
Batter-Fried Fish, 119
Bavarian Cream, 231
Bayou Chicken Bowl, 55
Beach Punch, 249
Bean(s)
as meat extender, 61
as source of protein, 20, 128
suggested servings of, 20
Baked, New England, 128
in Beany Fish Bake, 183
and Beefburgers, 180
Black, with Quick Rice, 185
Black-Bean Soup, 48
Chili-Cheese, 180
Dip, 179
-and-Frank Stew, 182
Hawaiian, 180
Kidney, in Three-Bean Salad,
172
Lima, in Succotash, 140
Loaf, 129
Refried, 129
Salad, Hot, 129
Southwestern Cowpoke, 128
Three-Bean Salad, 172
See also Green Beans; Wax
Beans
Beany Fish Bake, 183
Béarnaise Sauce, 173
Beef
broiling chart for, 80
cost per serving, 58–59
leftovers, meals from, 73
Birds, 87

Beef (*cont.*)
Boeuf Bourguignonne, 74
Boeuf à la Mode, 70
Bones, Deviled, 73
Chuck Roast
meals from, 61
Marinated, 62
Tenderized, 62
Corned
and Cabbage, 92
in Hash Florentine with
Poached Eggs, 186
in Red-Flannel Hash, 141
in Stuffed Peppers, 150
in Couscous, 255
Creamed Chipped, 25
Filet Mignon, 80
Fillet of
meals from, 67
in Fondue Bourguignonne,
41
Roast, 67
Ground
in Chili Pie, 86
in Deviled Meatballs, 41
in Frikadellen, 85
in The Great American
Meat Loaf, 84
in Lillie's Chili, 86
in Meat Loaf Viennese, 85
in Salisbury Patties and
Red-Eye Gravy, 182
in Seven-Layer Dinner,
158
in Skillet Meat-Loaf Din-
ner, 85
in Spaghetti with Meat-
balls, 131
in Swedish Meatballs, 85
See also Hamburgers
in Hungarian Goulash, 77
Kebabs, Turkish, 82
Kidney Pie, Beefsteak-and-,
90
in Linden Rouladen, 87
Liver
cost per serving, 58–59
Broiled, 89
and Onions, 89
Pan-Browned, 89
London Broil, 80
-and-Macaroni Casserole,
132
Oxtail Ragout, 77
Pot, 180
in Pot-au-Feu, 46
Pot Roast
Basic, 70
French Style, 70
Jellied, 70
Oven Onion, 62
Yankee, 70
Rib Roast(s)
meals from, 66
of, Browned Potatoes, 66
Roast(s)
boneless, meals from,
65–66
Hash, Wonderful, 73
Marinated Rolled, 66
Sauerbraten, 70

Beef (*cont.*)
in Shepherd's Pie, 130
Short Ribs, Barbecued, 66
Sirloin-Tip Grill, 81
Steak(s)
grilled, general notes, 81
Diane, 62
Flambé, 80
Flank, 80
French Pepper, 81
Garlic, 80
-and-Kidney Pie, 90
Minute, Pan-Broiled, 81
Oriental, 81
Peppercorn, 80
Salt-Mine, 81
Swiss, Skillet, 78
Stock, 45
Stew, *see* Stews
Stroganoff, 78
in Sukiyaki, 87
Tongue with Raisin Sauce,
90
Tripe Creole, 91
Wellington, 67
Mock, 67
Beets, 140
in Borscht, 54
Harvard, 140
with Orange Sauce, 141
Pickled, 140
in Red-Flannel Hash, 141
Berry(ies)
general notes, 162
Preserves, Perfect, 162
See also names of berries
Beverages
Apple Sparkle, 251
Apricot Smoothie, 250
Banana Milk Cooler, 250
Chocolate
Eggnog, 251
Flavored Drink, IN-
STANT, 250
IN-STANT, Banana
Shake, 250
IN-STANT, Ice Cream
Soda, 250
Malt, 250
Mexican, 250
Shake, 250
Clam-Tomato Juice, 251
Cocoa
Hot, 250
Low-Calorie, 250
Rich, at a Price, 250
Coffee
A&P brands of, 247
general notes, 247
how to make, 247
Café au Lait, 248
Café Royale, 248
Caffè Espresso, 248
Cappuccino, 248
for Forty, 254
Hawaiian, 248
Hot and Cold Sipper, 248
Iced, 248
Iced, Lemon, 248
Irish, 248
Italian, 248

Beverages (*cont.*)
  Minted, 248
  Plantation, 248
  Shakes, 248
  Tropicana, 248
  Eggnog
    Chocolate, 251
    Classic, 254
    Fruit, 251
    Party, 254
    Quick, 251
  Lemonade
    Fresh, 165
    Pink, 166
  Malt, Chocolate, 250
  Punch(es)
    Beach, 249
    Reception, 254
    Reception, Spirited, 254
    Sparkling Spring, 251
    Tea, Holiday, 249
    Tea, Open-House, 250
  Sauerkraut-Tomato Juice, 251
  Shake(s)
    Chocolate, 250
    Coffee, 248
  Tea
    A&P brands, 249
    general notes, 249
    how to make, 249
    Apple, Hot, 249
    in Beach Punch, 249
    Fruit, Spiced, 249
    Iced, 249
    Iced, Lemon, 249
    Iced, Orange, 249
    Punch, Holiday, 249
    Punch, Open-House, 250
  Tomato
    Drink, Tangy, 251
    Juice, Clam-, 251
    Juice Cocktail, 251
    Julep, 251
    -Sauerkraut Juice, 251
Biscuits, *see* Breads Quick
Bisques, *see* Soups, Cream
Black-Bean Soup, 48
Black-eyed Peas
  Ham Hocks with, 91
  in Hoppin' John, 129
Blanquette de Veau, 64
Blender Mayonnaise, 176
Blintzes, 34
Blueberry
  Grunt, 236
  Muffins, Rich, 199
  Pie, Fresh, 210
  Whip, Frozen, 243
Blue Cheese
  Burgers, 84
  Dip, Green-Onion, 37
  Dressing, 176
Bluefish Creole, Baked, 116
Blushing Bunny, 32
Boeuf Bourguignonne, 74
Boeuf à la Mode, 70
Boiled
  Carrots, 144
  New Potatoes, 150
  Onions, 148

Boiled (*cont.*)
  Shrimp, 126
  Summer Squash, 152
Bombes, *see* Frozen Desserts
Boned Pork Shoulder Roast, 66
Borscht, 54
Boston Lemon Pie, 234
Bouillabaisse, American Style, 52
Bowl of Cherries, A, 163
Box O'Chicken, as A&P brand, 11, 93
Braised Lamb Shanks, 73
Bran Muffins, 23
Brandied Prune Compote, 168
Bread(s)
  breakfast, 23–24
  day-old, values in, 224
  home storage of, 224
  money-saving tips on, 21
  nutritional value of, 224
  as source of protein, 21
  stale, value of, 224
  suggested servings of, 21
  into Cake, 227
  Croutons, Tasty, 225
  Crumbs, Dry, 225
  in Easy Fruit Tarts, 228
  in Eleanor Roosevelt's Huckleberry Pudding, 227
  in Huckleberry Refrigerator Pudding, 227
  in Mock Angel Food Cake, 227
  Pudding, *see* Puddings, Dessert
  Stuffing, 103
  Toast, *see* Toast
  See also Breads, Quick; Breads, Yeast
Breads(s), Quick
  general notes, 197
  Apple Folds, 35
  Banana, Pantry, 198
  Biscuit(s)
    refrigerator, uses for, 35
    Baked Chicken and, 103
    Basic, 199
    Buttermilk, 199
    Cheese, 199
    Cinnamon, 199
    Drop, 199
    Herb, 199
    Onion, 35
    Orange, 199
    Pantry, 197
    Prune-Walnut, 35
    Ring, 35
    Snack, 35
    Sticks, Cheesy, 179
    Sticks, Spicy, 180
    Sticky, 35
  Buns, Caramel Pecan, 199
  Corn, Northern-Style, 198
  Cornsticks, Buttermilk, 198
  Cranberry-Orange Tea, 198
  Fried, Indian, 198
  Garlic French, 224
  Herb, 224
  Hot-Bread Mix, Pantry, 197

Bread(s), Quick (*cont.*)
  Muffins, Toasted English
    in Bacon Grill, 226
    in Pizza Grill, 226
    in Tuna Pimiento, 226
  Popovers, 24
  Puri, 198
  Spoon, 135
  Wafflers, 35
  See also Breads, Yeast; Pancakes; Waffles
Bread(s), Yeast
  general notes, 189
  Anadama, 191
  Babka, 192
  Batter
    White, 191
    Whole-Wheat, 191
  Buns, Hot Cross, 197
  Cinnamon Pinwheels, 194
  Coffee Braid, 194
  Doughnuts
    Jelly, 197
    Yeast, 197
  Egg Twist, 190
  French, 189
  Fruit Ring, Winter, 192
  Honey Snails, 194
  Hungarian Bubble Loaf, 194
  Kolacky, 197
  Muffins, English, 191
  Oatmeal, 190
  Pita, 191
  Pizza, *see* Snacks and Appetizers
  Pumpernickel, 190
  Rolls
    Cloverleaf, 194
    Crescent, 192
    Fantans, 194
    Pan, 194
    Parker House, 192
  Stollen, 194
  Swedish Limpa, 190
  Sweet Yeast Dough, Basic, 192
  Wheat-Germ, 258
  White, 189
  White Batter, 191
  Whole-Wheat Batter, 191
  See also Breads, Quick
Breakfast
  breads, 23–24
  eggs, 24–25
  general notes, 22, 23
  meats, 25–26
  Vermont, 26
Breasts of Chicken Parmesan, 107
Broccoli
  with Lemon Butter, 141
  Puff, 141
  Steamed, 141
Broiled
  Chicken, *see* Chicken
  Duck, 98
  Grapefruit, 164
  Ham Steak with Peaches, 68
  Lamb Steak, **65**
  Liver, 89

Broiled (*cont.*)
  Pork Chops with Orange
      Glaze, 81
  Rock Cornish Hens, 99
  Shrimp, 127
  Swordfish Steaks, 120
  Topping, 208
  Turkey, 98
Broth(s)
  Scotch, 48
  Turkey, 105
  See also Consommé; Soups
Brown Betty, 235
Brown Butter, *see* Butter
Brown Stock, 45
Brown Sugar, *see* Sugar
Brownies, *see* Cookies
Brunch Puff, 25
Brunch Waffles, 24
Brussels Sprouts
  Skillet, 141
  Skillet, with Bacon, 141
  Steamed, 141
Buckwheat Groats, 134
Bulgur, in Wheat Pilaf, 135
Buns, *see* Breads, Quick;
      Breads, Yeast
Burgers, *see* Hamburgers
Butchers' Pledge (A&P), 8, 57
Butter(s)
  Anchovy, 80, 174
  Basting Sauce, 98
  Brown(ed)
    Calf Brains with, 91
    Sauce, 174
    Trout with, 120
  Cake, 201
  Cream Frosting, 207
  -Crust Roast Chicken, 104
  Frosting, Cooked, 207
  Garlic, 224
  Lemon, Broccoli with, 141
  Maître d'Hôtel, 80
  Mushrooms Braised in, 148
  Pecan Bars, 220
Butter Almond Ice Cream, 241
Buttered Corn, 146
Butterflied Lamb Leg, Grilled,
      82
Buttermilk
  general notes, 27
  Biscuits, 200
  Cornsticks, 199
  Salad Dressing, 176
  Soup, 54
Butterscotch
  -Nut Sauce, Quick, 245
  Quick-Mix Ice Cream, 242

Cabbage
  general notes, 142
  with Cheese and Bacon, 142
  Chinese-Cabbage Dish, 144
  Coleslaw, 255
  Coleslaw, Old-fashioned, 171
  Corned Beef and, 92
  Green
    with Caraway and Apple,
        142
    Red-and- Salad, 171

Cabbage (*cont.*)
  Red
    -and-Green Salad, 171
  and Pineapple, 142
  Salad, Red-and-Green, 171
  Soup with Pork, 64
  Stuffed, 142
  Sweet-and-Sour, 142
Caesar Salad, 171
Café, Caffè, *see* Beverages,
      Coffee
Cake(s)
  baking pans for, 201
  how to bake, 200–01
  how to frost, 206
  mixes, 199
  Angel Food, Mock, 227
  Apple, 203
  Applesauce, 203
  Banana, 203
  Banana Upside-Down, 200
  Bread into, 227
  Butter, 201
  Caramel, 202
  Caramel Pudding, 239
  Cheese, Strawberry, 229
  Chiffon, 205
  Chocolate, 202
    -Ginger Refrigerator, 234
    Icebox, 228
    Roll, Meringue, 205
    Pudding, 239
  Cocoa Marble, 202
  Coffee
    Date-Nut, 205
    Devil's Food, 202
    Streusel, 205
  Cookie Refrigerator, 229
  Crumb, Velvet, 200
  Cupcakes, 203
  Devil's Food, Coffee, 202
  Doughnuts, 229
  Filling(s), 208
    Easy, 209
  Fruitcake
    Molasses, 204
    Sarah's California, 204
  Fruit Kuchen, 204
  Gold, 202
  Irish Tipsy, in a Hurry, 228
  Lemon, Double, 200
  Mocha Pudding, 239
  Marble, 202
    Cocoa, 202
  Orange
    -Coconut, 199
    Quick, 200
  Pavlova, 206
  Pineapple Upside-Down, 200
  Plantation, 202
  Pumpkin, 204
  Shortcake, 200
  Snacking, 203
  Sparkle Crown, 228
  Spice, 202
  Sponge Roll, 206
  Torte, Linzer, 205
  Wedding, 253
  White, 202
Calf Brains with Browned
      Butter, 91

Calf Liver
  Broiled, 89
  and Onions, 89
  Pan-Browned, 89
  See also Liver
California Fruit Salad, 172
Canadian Bacon, canned, gen-
      eral notes, 91
Candied Sweet Potatoes, 154
Canned Ham, 91
Cans, contents of (table), 266
Cantaloupe(s)
  general notes, 162–63
  in Melon Ice, 242
Caper
  Cream Sauce, 175
  French Dressing, 176
  Sauce, Mayonnaise, 174
Capon, *see* Chicken
Cappuccino, 248
Caramel
  Cake, 202
  Pecan Buns, 199
  Pudding Cake, 239
  Sauce, 245
Caraway and Apple, Green
      Cabbage with, 142
Carbonara Sauce for Spaghetti,
      131
Catfish Stew, 123
Carrot(s)
  Boiled, 144
  Celery and, 145
  Curls, 144
  Fried, 144
  Minted, with Peas, 144
  à l'Orange, 256
  Pickled, 144
  Puff, 151
  Salad, 172
  Sticks, 144
    Dilled, 39
Casabas, general notes, 163
Casserole(s)
  Bake, Garden, 187
  Beef-and-Macaroni, 132
  Brunswick Stew, 102
  Cassoulet, 63
    Easy, 130
  Country, 158
  Ham-and-Potato Scallop,
      186
  Jansson's Temptation, 130
  Lamb-and-Eggplant, Turk-
      ish, 74
  Lentil, 129
  Lima Bean-and-Cheese, 129
  Lima Bean-and-Corn, 129
  Onion-Tomato, 149
  Pineapple Chicken, 102
  Soybean, 258
  Scandinavian Potato-and-
      Anchovy, 130
  Shepherd's Pie, 130
  Summer Squash, 153
  Tamale, 135
  Turkey-and-Stuffing, 113
  See also Pasta Dishes; Stews
Cassoulet, 63
  Easy, 130

Cauliflower
  with Cheese, 144
  Pickled, 145
Caviar
  Red-, Filling for Appetizer
    Puffs, 42
  and Sour Cream, Omelet
    with, 29
Celery
  and Carrots, 145
  with Corn, 145
  Stuffed, 39
Cereal
  cold, general notes, 23
  hot
    cooking chart for, 22
    general notes, 22, 23
  money-saving tips on, 21
  as source of protein, 21
  suggested servings of, 21
  Granola, 23
  Nibbles, Spicy, 36
Cervelat, in Sausage Dump-
    lings, 88
Charlottes, *See* Gelatin Des-
    serts; Frozen Desserts
Cheddar Cheese
  in Blushing Bunny, 32
  in Cheesy Biscuit Sticks, 179
  Dip, Bacon-, 37
  Soup, 52
  in Welsh Rabbit, 32
Cheese
  how to buy, 31
  natural, general notes, 31
  process, general notes, 31
  and Bacon, Cabbage with,
    142
  -Baked Potatoes, 151
  Ball(s)
    Crusty, 39
    Pepper-mill, 39
  Biscuits, 199
  Board(s)
    Appetizer, 31
    Salad, 31
    Dessert, 31
  Cake, Strawberry, 229
  Casserole, Lima-Bean-and,
    129
  Cauliflower with, 144
  Chili-Cheese Beans, 180
  -Filled Burgers, 84
  Filling(s)
    Chocolate-, 209
    Cress-and-, 226
  Fondue, Swiss, 32
  Horns, 221
  Lasagne, 134
  Lemon, 165
  Macaroni and, 132
  in Onion Quiche, 32
  Pineapple Wedges with, 168
  Puffs, 42
    Mayonnaise, 179
  in Quiche Lorraine, 32
  Sauce, *see* Sauces
  Scramble, 29
  in Shortcut Main-Dish
    Soufflé, 30
  Soufflé, 30

Cheese (*cont.*)
  Toast, Anchovies on, 43
  Waffles, 24
  See also names of cheeses
Cheesy Biscuit Sticks, 179
Cherry(ies)
  general notes, 163
  A Bowl of, 163
  Bread Pudding, 227
  Charlotte, Frozen, 243
  -Cheese Pie, 34
  Jubilee, 234
  Pie, 211
  Sour, Stewed, 163
Cherry Tomatoes, Stuffed, 39
Chestnut(s)
  general notes, 145
  Purée, 145
  Stuffing, Roast Turkey, 105
Chewy Raisin Bars, 218
Chicken
  cost per serving, 60–61
  Box O', as A&P brand, 11,
    93
  broiler-fryers, general notes,
    93
  cooked, uses for, 111–113
  fowl, general notes, 93
  general notes, 93
  parts, general notes, 93, 109
  roasters, general notes, 93
  in Arroz con Pollo, Quick,
    185
  Baked
    and Biscuits, 103
    Florentine, 102
    and Mushrooms, 102
    Bercy, 99
  Bowl, Bayou, 55
  Breasts of, Parmesan, 107
  Broiled, 96
    out of doors, 96
    Lemon-, 98
    Marinated Broilers, 98
  Cacciatore, Quick, 100
  Capon
    general notes, 93
    Roast, 104
  en Casserole
    general notes, 101
    Casserole Brunswick Stew,
      102
    Orange-Ginger, 102
    Pineapple, 102
  Chinese, 101
  Chinese Almond, 108
  and clams, 108
  Consommé or Broth, 46
  Coq au Vin, 101
  in Country Captain, 100
  Cranberry, 100
  Creamed, 180
  Curry for Twenty-Five, 254
  Devil-Crusted, 98
  Deviled, Spread, 111
  Drumsticks, Marinated, 109
  in Easy Cassoulet, 130
  Fat
    uses for, 93
    Rendered, 110
  Filling, 226

Chicken (*cont.*)
  Fried
    how to fry, 95
    Batter, 96
    Crisp, 95
    Corn-Meal Crust, 96
    Crusty, 95
    Maryland, 96
  Fritters, 112
  Giblet Stew, 111
  Gizzards and Hearts, 111
  Gumbo, 48
  à la King, 112
  Legs
    Deviled, 109
    Grilled, 109
  Liver, *see* Chicken Livers
  Loaf, Jellied, 112
  in Macaroni Supper, Quick,
    183
  -Mushroom Chowder, 55
  with Mushrooms, 99
  Noodle Soup, Tomato-, 54
  à l'Orange, 99
  Orange-Ginger, 102
  Oven-Fried
    Chili, 96
    Garlic-Butter, 96
    Herb, 96
  Pan-Browned, 99
  Pie, 111
    Oyster-, New England, 111
  Pineapple, en Casserole, 102
  Poached, 111
  in Quick Chop Suey, 185
  in Red Wine, 101
  with Rice and Peas, 100
  Roast
    in foil, timetable for, 101
    Butter-Crust, 104
    Ginger, 104
    Glazed, 105
    Gravy for, 105
    Sherry-Basted, 105
  Rotisseried, 107
    Basting Sauces for, 107
  Salad, *see* Salads
  Sherry-Basted, 105
  Soup, *see* Soups
  Spanish Rice and, 185
  Spread, Deviled, 111
  Stock, 45
  -Vegetable Soup
    Italiano, 55
    Old-Fashioned, 55
  Walnut Salad, Chinese, 255
Chicken Liver(s)
  cost per serving, 58–59
  general notes, 110
  uses for, 93
  en Brochette, 110
  Chopped, 110
  Egg Bows with, 133
  Pâté, 110
  Risotto with, 110
  in Spaghetti Caruso, 110
Chick-Peas and Bacon, 129
Chiffon Cake, 206
Chili
  -Cheese Beans, 180
  Chicken, Oven-Fried, 96

Chili (*cont.*)
Dogs, 89
Lillie's, 86
Pie, 86
Chilled Orange Delight, 166
Chinese
Almond Chicken, 108
-Cabbage Dish, 144
Chicken, 101
Chicken Walnut Salad, 255
Egg-Drop Soup, 47
Fruit Sauce, 174
Glaze, 79
Omelets, 29
Pork and Peppers, 86
Chitterlings, 91
Chocolate
Bread Pudding, 240
Cake, 202
-Cheese Filling, 209
-Chip Cookies, 220
-Chip Ice Cream, 241
Cream
Charlotte, 231
Filling, 208
Frosting, 207, 208
Drops, 218
Fancy, Quick, 228
-Ginger Refrigerator Cake, 234
Glaze, 207
Icebox Cake, 228
Ice Cream, Old-Fashioned, 241
Marshmallow Sauce, Quick, 245
Meringue, 208
Cake Roll, 205
Mint Sauce, 244
Mousse, 231
-Peanut Butter Drops, 223
Pie, Double, 234
Pudding Cake, 239
Soufflé, 30
Cold, 232
Syrup, 245
Tapioca Soufflé, 235
Topping, 246
Velvet Frosting, 207
See also Beverages
Chopped Chicken Livers, 110
Chopped-Liver Filling, for Appetizer Puffs, 42
Chop Suey, Quick, 185
Choucroute Garni, 63
Chowder, *see* Soups
Chow Mein, 114
Chuck Roast, *see* Beef
Chutney,
Apple, Fresh, 161
Dressing, 175
Cinnamon
Biscuits, 199
Pinwheels, 194
Toast, 23
Clam(s)
Bisque, 53
Chicken and, 108
Chowder, *see* Soups
Dip, 37
Fritters, 124

Clam(s) (*cont.*)
Rafts, 43
Sauce for Spaghetti,
Red, 131
White, 131
Steamed, 124
-Tomato Juice, 251
Classic Eggnog, 254
Classic French Dressing, 176
Cloverleaf Rolls, 194
Cobbler, Pear, 236
Cocktail Folds, 35
Cocoa
Brownies, 217
Marble Cake, 202
See also Beverages
Coconut
Butterfly Shrimp, Hawaiian, 127
Cake, Orange-, 199
Macaroons, 220
Toasted, Melba, 233
Cod, Codfish
Balls, 119
in Fish Teriyaki, 121
Kedgeree, 123
Coffee
Braid, 194
Cream Frosting, 207
Cake, *see* Cakes
See also Beverages
Cold
Chocolate Soufflé, 232
Glazed Ham, 91
Lemon Soufflé, 232
Salmon, Mayonnaise, 122
Strawberry Soufflé, 232
Coleslaw, 255
Old-fashioned, 171
Collard Greens
in Greens and Salt Pork, 147
in Pig Knuckles and Greens, 90
Confectioners' Sugar Glaze, 207
Consommé(s)
Bellevue, 46
Garnishes for, 47
Madrilène, 47
in Petite Marmite, 46
in Pot-au-Feu, 46
Stracciatella, 46
See also Broths; Soups; Stocks
Consumerism, and A&P, 7–8
Convenience foods, *see* Foods
Cooked Butter Frosting, 207
Cookie(s)
molded, general notes, 221
unbaked, general notes, 222
Almond Wafers, 222
Applesauce Hermits, 220
Apricot Hats, 222
Apricot-Orange Bars, 218
Bar(s)
general notes, 217
Apricot-Orange, 218
Butter Pecan, 218
Chewy Raisin, 218
Brownies
Cocoa, 217
Treasure, 164
Butter Pecan Bars, 218

Cookie(s) (*cont.*)
Cheese Horns, 221
Chocolate
Drops, 218
-Chip, 220
-Chip Oatmeal, 220
-Peanut Butter Drops, 223
Coconut Macaroons, 220
Cutout(s)
general notes, 221
Sugar-Cookie, 221
-Crumb Shell, 210
-Dough Pie Crust, 210
Drop(s)
general notes, 218
Chocolate, 218
Chocolate-Peanut Butter, 223
Gingerbread Men, 222
Hermits, Applesauce, 220
Macaroons, Coconut, 220
Marble Refrigerator, 220
Marshmallow Squares, 223
Oatmeal Brittle, 218
Oatmeal Chews, 258
Peanut-Butter, 218
Raisin Bars, Chewy, 218
Refrigerator
general notes, 220
Cake, 229
Marble, 220
Rum Balls, 222
Russian Balls, 221
Shortbread, 222
Snickerdoodles, 221
Spritz, 221
Sugar-Cookie Cutouts, 221
Thimbles, 221
Wafers, Almond, 222
Coq au Vin, 101
Coquilles Saint-Jacques, 125
Curried, 125
with Mushrooms, 125
Corn
Barbecued Grilled, 145
Bread, Northern-Style, 198
Buttered, 146
Celery with, 145
on the Cob, 145
Lima Bean-and, Casserole, 129
Meal, *see* Corn Meal
Mexican, 146
"Oysters," 146
Pudding, 146
in Succotash, 140
Corn Bread, Northern-Style, 198
Corned Beef, *see* Beef
Cornflake Betty, Banana, 236
Corn Meal
as source of protein, 128
in Buttermilk Cornsticks, 198
in Corn Bread, Northern-Style, 198
Crust, 96
Mush, 135
in Spoon Bread, 135
Cornstarch Pudding, 234
Cornsticks, Buttermilk, 198

Cottage Cheese
   general notes, 31, 32
   in Blintzes, 34
   in Manicotti, 32
   Mold, 34
Country Captain, 100
Country Casserole, 158
Country Ham, 68
Couscous, 255
Crab, Crab Meat
   Deviled, 126
   Louis, 126
   Sauce for Spaghetti, 131
Cranberry(ies)
   general notes, 163
   Chicken, 100
   -Orange
      Ice, 242
      Relish, 163
      Tea Bread, 198
   Sauce, Jellied, 163
   Stuffing, Crown Roast of
      Lamb with, 67
Cream
   half-and-half, general notes,
      28
   heavy whipping, general
      notes, 28
   light, general notes, 28
   Mushrooms Braised in, 148
   Pie, Peaches-and-, 211
   Puffs, *see* Pastries
   Salmon Steaks with To-
      matoes and, 118
   Sauce, *see* Sauces
   Soups, *see* Soups, Cream
   Tarts, 212
   Topping, for Fruit Kuchen,
      204
   See also Cream Desserts;
      Sour Cream
Cream Cheese
   Almond Iced, 34
   in Heart of Cream, 234
   in Cherry-Cheese Pie, 34
   Pie, 34
Cream Desserts
   Chocolate Fancy, Quick, 228
   Danish Cream, 233
   Heart of Cream, 235
   See also Gelatin Desserts
Creamed
   Chicken, 180
   Chipped Beef, 25
   Kohlrabi, 147
   Onions, 148
   Potatoes, 151
   Spinach, 147
Creamy White Frosting, 253
Creative Food Service
      (A&P), 8
Crème Brulée, 235
Crenshaws, general notes, 163
Creole
   Franks, 186
   Omelet, 29
   Sauce, 175
Crêpes, Dessert
   general notes, 244
   Apple, 244
   Apricot, 244

Crescent Rolls, 192
Cress-and-Cheese Filling, 226
Crisp Fried Chicken, 95
Croutons, Tasty, 225
Crown Roast, *see* Lamb; Pork;
      Veal
Crumb-Topped Mince Pie, 211
Crust, Pie, *see* Pastry, Pie
Crusty
   Cheese Balls, 39
   Fried Chicken, 95
   Sardines in Tomato Sauce,
      185
Crystallized Grapes, 164
Cucumber(s)
   how to pickle, 145
   Mayonnaise, 174
Cumberland
   Franks, 41
   Glaze and Sauce, 68
Cumin Dip, 37
Cupcakes, 203
Currant Glaze, Pork Loin
      Roast, 62
Curry(ied)
   Chicken, for Twenty-Five,
      254
   Coquilles Saint-Jacques, 125
   Dressing, 174
   Lamb, 74
      Rib Barbecue, 82
   Nuts, 36
   Rice, 136
   Scallop, 125
   Scalloped Potatoes, 152
Custard(s), Dessert
   Baked Alaska, 235
   Crème Brulée, 235
   Custard, 235
   Flan, 235
   Floating Island, 233
   Wine, 233
   Zabaglione, 233

Dairy Foods
   general notes, 27–28
   money-saving tips, 20
   suggested servings, 20
   See also names of dairy
      foods
Danish Cream, 233
Date-Nut Coffee Cake, 205
Deep-Dish Pizza, 43
Deep-Dish Turkey Pie, 187
Deep-Fried Fish Fillets, 119
Desserts
   baked, 235–241
   general notes, 230
   top-of-the-counter, 234–35
   top-of-the-range, 232–34
   Cheese Board, 31
   Sauces, *see* Sauces, Desserts
   See also Cakes; Cookies;
         Cream Desserts; Crêpes,
         Dessert; Custards, Des-
         sert; Frozen Desserts;
         Fruit; Gelatin Desserts;
         Omelets, Dessert; Pies;
         Tarts

Deviled
   Chicken Legs, 109
   Chicken Spread, 111
   Crab, 126
   Meatballs, 41
   Oysters, 124
   Turkey Wings, 109
Devils on Horseback, 124
Dilled Carrot Sticks, 39
Dilled Potatoes, 151
Dips, *see* Sauces; Snacks and
      Appetizers
Dishwashing, materials for,
      checklist of, 261
Double Chocolate Pie, 234
Double Lemon Cake, 200
Dough, Sweet Yeast, Basic, 192
Doughnuts, *see* Breads, Yeast
Dressing(s)
   Corn-Bread-and-Sausage,
      Southern, 103
   Curry, 174
   Fruited-Rice, 103
   Salad, *see* Salad Dressings
   See also Stuffings
Drop Biscuits, 199
Drop Cookies, *see* Cookies
Dry Bread Crumbs, 225
Duchesse Potatoes, 151
Duck, Duckling
   fat, uses for, 95
   general notes, 95
   how to skin, 98
   livers, uses for, 95
   Broiled, 98
   à l'Orange, 106
   in Red Wine, 101
   Roast, Apple Stuffing, 106
Dumplings, Sausage, 88

Easy
   Cake Filling, 209
   Cassoulet, 130
   Fruit Tarts, 228
   Lemon Chiffon Pie, 216
Egg(s)
   breakfast, 24–25
   general notes, 28
   as source of protein, 20
   suggested servings of, 20
   A&P brands, 24, 28
   in Bacon Scramble, 29
   Benedict, 25
   Bows with Chicken Livers,
      133
   in Brunch Puff, 25
   in Cheese Scramble, 29
   Crescent Pizza, Ham-and-,
      180
   Dip
      Bacon-, 37
      Green-Onion, 37
   -Drop Soup, Chinese, 47
   Foo Yong, 29
   Fried, 25
   Goldenrod, 30
   Grits and, 25
   in Ham Scramble, 28
   Hard-Cooked, 28

Egg(s) (*cont.*)
  Poached, 24
    Florentine, 30
    Hash Florentine with, 186
    in Milk, 25
    In Potato Scramble, 28
  Sauce, 175
  Scrambled, 28
  Shirred, 28
  Soft-Cooked, 28
  Twist, 190
  See also Omelets; Soufflés
Eggnog, *see* Beverages
Eggplant
  Baked, 146
  Casserole, Turkish Lamb-
    and-, 74
  Fried, 146
  in Moussaka, 86
  Parmigiana, 146
  in Ratatouille, 147
  Stuffed, 147
Elbow-Macaroni Supper Salad,
  134
Elbow-Spaghetti-and-Ham
  Skillet, 134
Eleanor Roosevelt's Huckle-
  berry Pudding, 227
Elegant Green Salad, 170
English Muffins, *see* Breads,
  Quick; Breads, Yeast
English Pork Pie, 74
Entertaining
  general notes, 252
  menus for, 253
  quantity-buying guide for
    50, 252
  recipes for, *see* Quantity
    Cooking

Fantans, 194
Farina, in Gnocchi, 135
Festive Ambrosia, 166
Figaro Sauce, 173
Figs, general notes, 163–64
Filet Mignon, 80
Fillet of Flounder Marguery,
  122
Filling(s), Appetizer
  Chopped-Liver, for Appe-
    tizer Puffs, 42
  Seafood, for Appetizer Puffs,
    42
  See also Sandwiches
Filling(s), Dessert
  general notes, 208
  Chocolate-Cheese, 209
  Chocolate Cream, 208
  Easy Cake, 209
  Lemon, 209
  Pastry Cream, 208
Fish
  to bake, 115, 116–19
  to broil, 116, 120–21
  cooked dishes from, 123–
    124
  to cook in liquid, 121–23
  cooking guide for, 115–16
  cost per serving, 58–59
  to deep-fry, 116, 119

Fish (*cont.*)
  money-saving tips on, 20
  to pan-fry, 116, 120–21
  as source of protein, 20
  to steam, 116
  whole stuffed, to bake,
    115
  Bake, Beany, 183
  Batter-Fried, 119
  and Chips, 119
  Fillets
    Bonne Femme, 122
    Deep-Fried, 119
    Lemon-Broiled, 120
    "Oven-Fried," 119
  Pudding, Norwegian, 119
  Salad, Jellied, 123
  Soufflé with Shrimp Sauce,
    123
  Steamed, 121
    Chinese Style, 121
  Sticks
    Cacciatore, 183
    Sweet-and-Pungent, 183
  Stock, 46
  Teriyaki, 121
  in Tomato Sauce, 123
  See also names of fish,
    shellfish
Flaming Cherries Jubilee, 234
Flan, 235
Flank Steak, *see* Beef
Floating Island, 233
Flounder
  Fillet of, Marguery, 122
  in Fish Fillets Bonne
    Femme, 122
Fondue Bourguignonne, 41
Food(s)
  basic
    guide to, 20–21
    shopping for, 18–19
  cans, contents of, 266
  common, weights and equiv-
    alent measures of, 265
  convenience, meals from,
    179–88
  homemade, savings in, 11
  natural, general notes, 257–
    258
  packages, contents of, 266
  prepared, savings in, 9–11
  processing of, 9
  shopping
    alternate choices in, 13–16
    for basics, 20–21
    budgeting for, 18
    comparison in, 11–13
    hints for, 8, 18, 19
    and nutrition labeling, 13
    and open dating, 13–16
    saving in, 16, 17, 20–21
    and unit pricing, 11–13
  spoiled, dealing with, 18
  storage, 18
Foo Yong Sauce, 29
Frankfurters, Franks
  general notes, 88
  with Canned Yams and
    Tomatoes, 188
  Chili Dogs, 89

Frankfurters (*cont.*)
  Creole, 186
  Cumberland, 41
  Frank-Mac Meal, 133
  Mexican, 89
  Pigs in Blankets, 35
  Simmered in Barbecue
    Sauce, 89
  Speared Dogs, 89
  Stew, Beans-and-, 182
  Stuffed Dogs, 88
  in Wraps, 89
    Hawaiian, 188
French
  Apple Tart, 212
  Bread, 189
  -Fried Potatoes, 151
  Onion Soup, 47
  Peas, 150
  Pepper Steak, 81
  -Style Beef Stew, 74
  Toast, 23
  -Toasted Sausages, 41
  Veal Stew, 64
Fresh
  Apple Chutney, 161
  Blueberry Pie, 210
  Cranberry Sauce, 163
  Cream of Tomato Soup, 50
  Lemonade, 165
  Prunes, *see* Prunes
  Mint Sauce for Lamb, 65
  Vegetables with Onion Dip,
    179
Fried
  Apple Slices, 161
  Carrots, 144
  Eggplant, 146
  Eggs, 25
  Green Beans, 140
  Green Tomatoes, 156
  Onion Rings, 149
  Pies, 216
Frikadellen, 85
Frittata, 29
Fritters
  Banana, 162
  Chicken, 112
  Clam, 124
Frosting(s)
  general notes, 206
  mixes, general notes, 208
  Almond, 207
  Brown-Sugar Icing, 208
  Butter
    Cooked, 207
    Cream, 207
  Chocolate
    Cream, 208
    Meringue, 208
    Velvet, 207
  Coffee Cream, 207
  Creamy White, 253
  Italian Meringue, 207
  Lemon Cream, 207
  Orange Cream, 207
  Sea Foam, 207
  Seven-Minute, 207
  Snowy, 207
  See also Fillings; Glazes;
    Toppings

Frozen Cream Chicken Salad, 112
Frozen Desserts
  Almond Iced Cream Cheese, 34
  Bombes
    general notes, 242–43
    New England, 243
    Spanish, 243
    Vineyard, 243
  Butterscotch Quick-Mix, 242
  Charlotte, Frozen Cherry, 243
  Heavenly Hash, 243
  Ice(s)
    Grape, 242
    Melon, 242
    Orange-Cranberry, 242
  Ice Cream
    general notes, 240
    refrigerator, general notes, 241
    Butter Almond, 241
    Chocolate-Chip, 241
    Chocolate, Old-Fashioned, 240
    Custard, 240
    Lemon-Pineapple, 242
    Mousse, Quick, 231
    Peach, 241
    Peanut-Brittle, 241
    Philadelphia, 240
    Rum-Raisin, 240
    Soda, IN-STANT Chocolate, 250
    in Strawberries Romanoff, 234
  Mousse(s), Frozen
    Apricot, 243
    Lemon, 243
  Pineapple Slices, Frozen, 168
  Sherbet, Orange Milk, 242
  Whip(s), Frozen
    Banana, 243
    Blueberry, 243
    Peach, 243
    Strawberry, 243
Fruit(s)
  as "convenience" food, 159
  general notes, 159–60
  money-saving tips on, 20, 159
  as source of vitamins, 20, 21
  suggested servings of, 20
  in Ambrosia, 166
  Cocktail, 164
  Eggnog, 251
  in Festive Ambrosia, 166
  Gelatin with, 230
  Kuchen, 204
  Pie, Quick Jellied, 216
  Ring, Winter, 192
  Salad, California, 172
  Sauce, Chinese, 174
  Tarts, Easy, 228
  Tea, Spiced, 249
  Topping, 246
  See also names of fruits
Fruitcake, *see* Cakes
Fruited
  Gelatin, 230

Fruited (*cont.*)
  Pancakes, 24
  -Rice Dressing, 103
Fudge, *see* Sauces, Dessert

Garlic
  Basting Sauce, 98
  Butter, 224
  Butter Chicken, Oven Fried, 96
  French Bread, 224
  Olives, 36
  Steak, 80
Garnishes
  for Consommé, 47
  Crystallized Grapes, 164
  Matzoh Balls for Soup, 47
  Spaetzle, 47
Gazpacho, 53
Gelatin, *see* Gelatin Desserts
Gelatin Desserts
  Charlotte, Peppermint, 256
  Cream(s)
    Bavarian, 231
    Charlotte, Chocolate, 231
    Spanish, 231
  Gelatin(s)
    with Fruit, 231
    Fruit, Quick, 230
    Fruited, 230
    Snow, 230
    Whipped, 230
  Mousse(s)
    Chocolate, 231
    Ice Cream, Quick, 231
  Soufflé(s)
    Chocolate, Cold, 232
    Lemon, Cold, 232
  Sparkle Crown Cake, 228
Giblet Stew, 111
Ginger
  Chicken, Orange-, 102
  Refrigerator Cake, Chocolate, 234
  Roast Chicken, 104
Gingerbread Men, 223
Glaze(s)
  Apricot, 68
  Brown Sugar, 68
  Chinese, 79
  Chocolate, 207
  Confectioners' Sugar, 207
  Cumberland, 68
  Currant, Pork Loin Roast, 62
  Honey-Mustard, 65
  Madeira, 68
  Marmalade, Ann Page, 68
  Mint, 65
  Orange, 200
    Broiled Pork Chops with, 81
  Peach, 68
  See also Frostings; Toppings
Glazed
  Ham Squares, 41
  Kumquats, 165
  Parsnips, 149
  Roast Chicken, 105
Gnocchi, 135
Gold Cake, 202

Goose
  fat, uses for, 95
  general notes, 95
  liver, uses for, 95
  Roast, with Onion-and-Apple Stuffing, 106
Grains
  as source of protein, 21
  suggested servings of, 21
  See also names of grains
Granola, 23
Grape(s)
  general notes, 164
  Crystallized, 164
  Ice, 242
  Seedless, Sole with, 122
Grapefruit
  general notes, 164
  Broiled, 164
  with Orange or Apple, 164
Gravy
  Red Eye, Salisbury Patties and, 182
  for Roast Chicken, 105
  Turkey, 105
Great American Meat Loaf, The, 84
Great Ribs on the Grill, 82
Greek Salad, 171
Green Beans, 139
  how to pickle, 145
  Amandine, 139
  and Bacon, 140
  Fried, 140
  Marinated, 140
  and Mushrooms, 140
  with Mustard Sauce, 139
  in Three-Bean Salad, 172
Green Cabbage with Caraway and Apple, 142
Green Onion
  Blue-Cheese Dip, 37
  Egg Dip, 37
  Party Dip, 37
  Shrimp Dip, 37
  Pig Knuckles and, 90
  and Salt Pork, 147
Green Tomatoes, Fried, 156
Grilled Chicken Legs, 109
Grilled Garden Special, 43
Grits and Eggs, 25
Groats and Corn, 135
Groats and Noodles, 135
Guacamole, 37

Haddock
  Fillets, Rolled Stuffed, 116
  in Fish Teriyaki, 121
  in Fish in Tomato Sauce, 123
  Kebabs, 121
Hake
  in Fish Fillets Bonne Femme, 122
  in Fish Soufflé with Shrimp Sauce, 123
Half Grapefruit, 164
Halibut
  in Jellied Fish Salad, 123
  in Norwegian Fish Pudding, 119

Halibut (*cont.*)
  Steaks
    Baked, 118
    Broiled, 120
Ham
  meals from, 67–68
  picnic, canned, general notes, 91
  Baked Glazed, 68
  Canned, 91
  Cold Glazed, 91
  Country, 68
  Cumberland, Quick, 186
  -and-Eggs Crescent Pizza, 180
  Filling, 226
  Glazed, Party, 255
  Glazes for
    Ann Page Marmalade, 68
    Apricot, 68
    Brown-Sugar, 68
    Cumberland, 68
    Madeira, 68
    Peach, 68
  Hocks with Black-Eyed Peas, 91
  in Jambalaya, 255
  Kebabs, 83
  Pea Soup with, 68
  -and-Potato Scallop, 186
  in Quick Chop Suey, 185
  in Salamagundi, 171
  Sauces for
    Apricot, 68
    Cumberland, 68
    Madeira, 68
  Sauerkraut and, 186
  Scramble, 28
  Skillet, Elbow-Spaghetti-and-, 134
  in Speedy Jambalaya, 185
  Squares, Glazed, 41
  Steak
    Barbecued, 82
    Broiled, with Peaches, 68
    with Orange Slices, 68
  Strips and Macaroni Bake, 186
Hamburgers, Burgers
  breads for, 83
  garnishes for, 83
  grilling, general notes, 83
  Basic, 83
  Beefburgers, Beans and, 180
  Blue-Cheese, 84
  Cheese-Filled, 84
  Extra-Moist, 83
  Oriental, 84
  Pizzaburgers, 83
  Provençale, 83
  Soyburger au Jus, 182
  Spinach Sauce for, 84
  Tomato-Stuffed, 84
  Tuna, 185
  Wineburger Steaks, 84
Hard-Cooked Eggs, 28
Hard Sauce, 246
Harvard Beets, 140
Hash
  Florentine with Poached Eggs, 186

Hash (*cont.*)
  Heavenly, 243
  Spanish, 186
Hawaiian
  Coconut Butterfly Shrimp, 127
  Franks in Wraps, 188
Health and beauty aids, checklist for, 257
Heart(s)
  general notes, 89
  Pie, 90
Heart of Cream, 235
Hearty Pancakes, 24
Hearty Spinach Salad, 171
Heavenly Hash, 243
Herb(ed)
  Biscuits, 200
  Bread, 224
  Butter, 174
  Chicken, Oven-Fried, 96
  Scalloped Potatoes, 152
Herring, in Quick Smorgasbord, 41
Hollandaise Sauce, 173
Homemade Potato Chips, 37
Honey
  -Mustard Glaze, 65
  Snails, 197
  Toast, 23
Honeydews, general notes, 165
Hoppin' John, 129
Horseradish Cream Sauce, 175
Hot
  Anchovy Cream Sauce, 175
  Apple Tea, 249
  Bean Salad, 129
  Cocoa, 250
  and Cold Sipper, 248
  Cross Buns, 197
  Dogs, *see* Frankfurters
  Fudge Sauce, 245
Housecleaning
  abrasives, use in, 260
  caustics, use in, 259–260
  detergents, use in, 259
  glass cleaners, use in, 260
  materials, shopping for, 259, 261
  tools, use in, 260–61
  waxes, use in, 260
Huckleberries, *see* Puddings, Dessert
Hungarian
  Bubble Loaf, 194
  Poppy-Seed Noodles, 132
  Pork and Sauerkraut, 77

Ice Cream, *see* Frozen Desserts
Icing, *see* Frostings
Indian Fried Bread, 199
Indian Pudding, 239
IN-STANT, *see* Beverages, Chocolate
Irish
  Coffee, 248
  Lamb Stew, 77
  Tipsy Cake in a Hurry, 228
Italian
  Coffee, 248

Italian (*cont.*)
  Meringue, 208
  Omelet, 29
  -Style Dressing, 176

Jambalaya, 255
  Speedy, 185
Jam, Fresh Prune, 168
Jane Parker
  as A&P brand, 11
  Bakeries, 224
Jansson's Temptation, 130
Japanese Soy-Sauce Dip, 175
Jellied
  Chicken Loaf, 112
  Cranberry Sauce, 163
  Fish Salad, 123
  Turkey in Aspic, 113
Jelly Doughnuts, 197

Kebab(s)
  general notes, 82
  Haddock, 121
  Ham, 83
  Pork, Oriental, 82
  Scallop, 125
  Shish Kebab, 83
  Turkish, 82
Ketchup French Dressing, 176
Kidney(s)
  general notes, 89
  Lamb, in Wine Sauce, 90
  Pie, Beefsteak-and-, 90
Kiwis, general notes, 165
Kohlrabi, Creamed, 147
Kolacky, 197
Kumquats
  general notes, 165
  Glazed, 165

Lamb
  broiling chart for, 80
  cost per serving, 58–59
  leftover, meals from, 73
  roasts, meals from, 66
  in Couscous, 255
  Crown Roast of, with Cranberry Stuffing, 67
  Curry, 74
  -and-Eggplant Casserole, Turkish, 74
  Ground
    in Lamburgers, 80
    in Moussaka, 86
  Kidneys in Wine Sauce, 90
  Leg of
    meals from, 65
    Butterflied, Grilled, 82
    Roast, 65
  Liver
    Pan-Browned, 89
    Broiled, 89
  Loin Chops, Minted, 80
  Rib, Barbecue, Curried, 82
  Scaloppine, 65, 79
    alla Marsala, 79
  Shanks, Braised, 73
  in Shepherd's Pie, 130

Lamb *(cont.)*
in Shish Kebab, 83
Shoulder, Rolled, 66
Shoulder Chops in Wine, 78
Steak(s)
Broiled, 83
Minute, Pan-Broiled, 81
Stew
Irish, 77
Russian, 78
in Turkish Kebabs, 82
Lamburgers, 80
Langostina Marinara, 126
Lasagne, *see* Pasta dishes
Lattice Top (pastry), 209
Laundry, tips for doing, 261
Leek(s)
and Potato Soup, Cream of, 50
Lemon(s)
general notes, 165
-Broiled
Chicken, 98
Fish Fillets, 120
Trout, 120
Butter
Broccoli with, 141
Sauce, 174
Cake, Double, 200
Cheese, 165
Chiffon Pie, 216
Easy, 216
Cream Frosting, 207
Filling, 209
Iced Coffee, 248
Iced Tea, 249
Meringue Pie, 214
Mousse, Frozen, 243
Pie, *see* Pies
-Pineapple Ice Cream, 242
Pudding Sponge, 236
Sauce, *see* Sauces, Dessert
Soufflé, Cold, 232
Topping, 246
Lemonade, *see* Beverages
Lentil Casserole, 129
Lillie's Chili, 86
Linzer Torte, 205
Lima Bean(s)
-and-Cheese Casserole, 129
-and-Corn Casserole, 129
in Succotash, 140
Limes, general notes, 166
Linden Rouladen, 87
Linguine Alfredo, 132
Liver
cost per serving, 58–59
general notes, 89
Broiled, 89
Chopped-, Filling for Appetizer Puffs, 42
and Onions, 89
Pan-Browned, 89
See also Chicken Livers
Lobster
Rock, Thermidor, 125
Salad, 126
Sauce, Fish Soufflé with, 123
Steamed, 125
Stew, 53
London Broil, 80

Look-Fit milk, as A&P brand, 27
Low-Calorie Cocoa, 250
Luncheon Meat
canned, general notes, 91
Potato-Topped, 187
in Spanish Hash, 186

Macaroni, *see* Pasta Dishes
Macaroons, Coconut, 220
Mac Homeburgers, 44
Mackerel
Spanish, 118
Spanish Style, 185
Mac Sausage, 183
Madeira Glaze and Sauce, 68
Magnificent Meatballs, 85
Maître d'Hôtel Butter, 80
Mangoes, general notes, 166
Manhattan Clam Chowder, 52
Quick, 54
Manicotti, 32
Maple Candied Sweet Potatoes, 154
Maple-Walnut Sauce, 245
Marinade, Tarragon, 79
Marinated
Artichoke Hearts, 39
Broilers, 98
Chicken Drumsticks, 109
Chuck Roast, 62
Green Beans, 140
Rolled Beef Roast, 66
Marble Cake, 202
Marble Refrigerator Cookies, 220
Marmalade
Glaze, Ann Page, 68
Spareribs, 82
Top-Range Soufflé, 233
Marshmallow
Sauce, Quick Chocolate, 245
Squares, 223
Sweets, 154
Maryland Fried Chicken, 96
Mashed
Potatoes, 151
Pumpkin, 152
Sweet Potatoes, 154
Turnips, 156
Matzoh Balls for Soup, 47
Mayonnaise, *see* Salad Dressings
Mayonnaise-Cheese Puffs, 179
Mayonnaise-Onion Puffs, 179
Meals, styles of, 18
Meat(s)
breakfast, 25–26
broiling, general notes, 79
canned, general notes, 91
chopped, general notes, 84
estimating portions per pound, 56-57
home freezing, tips on, 58
pan-broiling, general notes, 81
roasting, timetable for, 60
shopping for, tips on, 20, 56
as source of protein, 20
storage timetable, 57

Meat(s) *(cont.)*
suggested servings for, 20
Super Right (A&P), 56, 57
use of extenders with, 57, 58
Loaf
general notes, 84
Dinner, Skillet, 85
The Great American, 84
Viennese, 85
Luncheon, *see* Luncheon Meat
Sauce, Baked Lasagne with, 134
See also Meatballs; names of meats
Meatballs
Deviled, 41
Frikadellen, 85
Magnificent, 85
Spaghetti with, 131
Stew, 182
Swedish, 85
Meat Sauce, Baked Lasagne with, 134
Melon(s)
general notes, 166
Ice, 242
and Prosciutto, 39
See also names of melons
Meringue(s)
Chocolate, 208
Italian, 207
Pie, Lemon, 214
Topping for Pie, 214
Metric system, table, 266
Mexican Chocolate, 250
Mexican Corn, 146
Mezzani with Creamy Cheese Sauce, 133
Milk
evaporated, general notes, 27
A&P brands of, 27
non-fat dry, general notes, 27
skim, general notes, 27
sweetened condensed, general notes, 27
whole, general notes, 27
Buttermilk, *see* Buttermilk
Cooler, Banana, 250
Eggs Poached in, 25
Sherbet, Orange, 242
Minestrone, 48
Mint(ed)
Carrots with Peas, 144
Coffee, 248
Glaze, 65
Loin Lamb Chops, 80
Peas, 149
Sauce
Chocolate, 244
Fresh, for Lamb, 65
Mocha
Fudge Sauce, 245
Pudding Cake, 239
Soufflé, 31
Mock Angel Food Cake, 227
Molasses Fruitcake, 204
Mostaccioli with Sausage-Tomato Sauce, 132
Moules Marinière, 124

Moussaka, 86
Mousse(s)
  Turkey, 113
  See also Frozen Desserts;
    Gelatin Desserts
Mousseline Sauce, 173
Muffins, see Breads, Quick;
  Breads, Yeast
Mulligatawny Soup, 54
Mushroom(s)
  general notes, 148
  Baked Chicken and, 102
  Baked Stuffed, 41
  Barley with, Baked, 134
  Braised in Butter, 148
  Braised in Cream, 148
  Chicken with, 99
  Chowder, Chicken-, 55
  Coquilles Saint-Jacques
    with, 125
  Filling, 226
  Green Beans and, 140
  Sauce, 175
  Stuffed, 39
Mussels
  Moules Marinière, 124
  Wine-Steamed, 124
Muskmelons, general notes,
  162–63
Mustard
  Glaze, Honey-, 65
  Mayonnaise, 176
  Sauce, *see* Sauces
Mustard Greens, in Greens and
  Salt Pork, 147

Natural foods, *see* Foods
Nectarines, general notes, 166
Nesselrode Pie, 214
Nesselrode Pudding Pie, 214
New England
  Baked Beans, 128
  Bombe, 243
  Clam Chowder, 52
  Oyster-Chicken Pie, 111
  Poached Salmon, 121
  Pumpkin Soup, 50
Noodles, *see* Pasta Dishes
Northern-Style Corn Bread,
  199
Norwegian Fish Pudding, 119
Nut(s)
  as source of protein, 20
  Coffee Cake, Date-, 205
  Curried, 36
  Sauce, Quick Butterscotch-,
    245
Nutrition
  and food processing, 9
  labeling, general notes, 8, 11
  purchasing agent and, 9
  and value of breads to, 224
  See also Foods, basic
Nutted Sweet Potatoes, 154
Nutty Pancakes, 24

Oatmeal
  Bread, 190
  Brittle, 218
  Chews, 258

Oatmeal (*cont.*)
  Chocolate-Chip Cookies, 220
  Muffins, 23
Oil Pie Pastry, 210
Okra with Tomatoes and Rice,
  148
Old-Fashioned
  Beef Stew, 62
  Chicken-Vegetable Soup, 54
  Chocolate Ice Cream, 240
  Coleslaw, 171
  Rice Pudding, 240
Olives, Garlic, 36
Omelet(s), 28
  with Caviar and Sour Cream,
    29
  Chinese, 29
  Creole, 29
  Dessert, 244
  Italian, 29
  Quick Spanish, 29
  Soufflé, 29
  Western, 29
Onion(s)
  small white, to pickle, 145
  -and-Apple Stuffing, Roast
    Goose with, 106
  Biscuits, 35
  Boiled, 148
  Creamed, 148
  Dip, Bacon-Flavored, 37
  Liver and, 89
  Pot Roast, Oven, 62
  Puffs, Mayonnaise-, 179
  Quiche, 32
  Rings, Fried, 149
  Sausage-Stuffed, 149
  Soup
    French, 47
    Quick, 54
  Steamed, 148
  -Tomato Casserole, 149
Open dating, 8, 13–16
Open-House Tea Punch, 250
Operation Aware (A&P), 8
Orange(s)
  general notes, 166
  in Ambrosia, 166
  Apricot Sour, 251
  Bars, Apricot-, 218
  Basting Sauce, 96
  Biscuits, 199
  Blossom Filling, 226
  Carrots à l', 256
  Chicken à l', 99
  Chiffon Pie, 216
  -Coconut Cake, 200
  -Cranberry Ice, 242
  Cranberry Tea Bread, 198
  Cream Frosting, 207
  Delight, Chilled, 166
  Duck à l', 106
  -Ginger Chicken, 102
  Glaze, 200
    Broiled Pork Chops with,
      81
  Grapefruit with, 164
  Milk Sherbet, 242
  Relish, Cranberry-, 163
  Sauce, *see* Sauces; Sauces,
    Dessert

Orange(s) (*cont.*)
  Slices, Ham Steak with, 68
  Soufflé, 31
  Tea, Iced, 249
Oriental Hamburgers, 84
Oriental Steak, 81
Our Own tea, as A&P brand,
  249
Oven
  Temperatures, table of, 266
  -Browned Potatoes, 151
  -Fried
    Chicken, *see* Chicken
    Fillets, 119
  Onion Pot Roast, 62
  -Poached Turkey Breast, 108
Oxtail Ragout, 77
Oyster(s)
  Bisque, 53
  Casino, 125
  -Chicken Pie, New England,
    111
  Corn, 146
  Deviled, 124
  in Devils on Horseback, 124
  Sauce, 175
  Stew, 53
  Stuffing, 104

Pacific Sole Hawaiian, 120
Page, Ann, *see* Ann Page
Pan-Browned
  Bananas, 162
  Chicken, 99
  Liver, 89
Pancakes
  general notes, 24
  Fruited, 24
  Hearty, 24
  Nutty, 24
  Pantry, 197
  Plain Jane, 24
Pan Rolls, 194
Pantry
  Banana Bread, 198
  Biscuits, 197
  Hot-Bread Mix, 197
  Muffins, 197
  Pancakes, 197
  Shelf Pie Crust Mix, 209
  Waffles, 197
Papayas, general notes, 167
Paprika
  Butter Sauce, 174
  Veal Chops, 78
Parmesan
  Breasts of Chicken, 107
  Salad Dressing, 176
Parker House Rolls, 192
Parker, Jane, *see* Jane Parker
Parsnips, 149
  Glazed, 149
  Puff, 151
Parties, *see* Entertaining
Party Eggnog, 254
Party Glazed Hams, 254
Pasta
  as meat extender, 57
  as source of protein, 128
  suggested servings of, 21

Pasta (*cont.*)
　Homemade, 34
　See also Pasta Dishes
Pasta Dishes
　Egg Bows with Chicken
　　Livers, 133
　Frank-Mac Meal, 133
　Lasagne with Meat Sauce,
　　Baked, 134
　Linguini Alfredo, 132
　Macaroni
　　Bake, Tuna-, 183
　　Bake, Ham Strips and, 186
　　Casserole, Beef-and-, 132
　　and Cheese, 132
　　Elbow, Supper Salad, 134
　　in Frank-Mac Meal, 133
　　in Mac Sausage, 183
　　Salad, 172
　　Supper, Quick, 182
　Manicotti, 32
　Mezzani with Creamy Cheese
　　Sauce, 133
　Mostaccioli with Sausage-
　　Tomato Sauce, 132
　Noodle(s)
　　Hungarian, Poppy-Seed,
　　　132
　　Pudding, 240
　　Soup, Tomato-Chicken, 54
　　and Turkey, 133
　Perciatelli and Zucchini, 133
　Ravioli Marinara, Baked,
　　182
　Rigatoni Sausage Bowl, 133
　Sea Shells
　　Florentine, 133
　　with Quick Tuna Sauce,
　　　132
　Spaghetti
　　sauces for, at A&P, 130
　　Caruso, 110
　　Elbow, and Ham Skillet,
　　　134
　　with Meatballs, 131
　　in Pepper Shells, 182
　　and Salami, 182
　　-Spinach Bake, 183
　　in Tuna Tetrazzini, 183
Pastry(ies)
　Cream Puff(s), 217
　　to fill, 217
　　Paste, 217
　Fried Pies, 216
　Pie
　　Cookie-Crumb Shell, 210
　　Cookie-Dough Crust, 210
　　Lattice Top, 209
　　Oil, 210
　　for 1-Crust Pie, 209
　　for 2-Crust Pie, 209
　　Pantry Shelf Mix, 209
　　Tart Shells, 210
　Profiteroles, 217
　Prunes in Blankets, 35
　Turnovers, Apple, 217
Pâté, Chicken-Liver, 110
Pavlova Cake, 206
Pea(s)
　general notes, 149
　and Bacon, 149

Pea(s) (*cont.*)
　Chicken with Rice and, 100
　French, 150
　Green, Soup, Cream of, 50
　Minted, 149
　　Carrots with, 144
　in Risi Bisi, 135
　Soup with Ham, 68
Peach(es)
　general notes, 167
　Broiled Ham Steak with, 68
　Candied Sweet Potatoes,
　　154
　-and-Cream Pie, 211
　Glaze, 68
　Ice Cream, 241
　Quick-Brandied, 167
　Stewed, 167
　Whip, Frozen, 243
Peanut(s)
　as source of protein, 20
　suggested servings of, 20
　Soup, 50
Peanut-Brittle Ice Cream, 241
Peanut Butter-Chocolate
　　Drops, 223
Peanut Butter Cookies, 218
Pear(s)
　general notes, 167
　Cobbler, 236
　Stewed, 167
Pecan
　Bars, Butter, 218
　Buns, Caramel, 199
　Pie, 214
Pepper(s) (vegetable)
　general notes, 150
　Chinese Pork and, 86
　Roasted, 150
　Stuffed, 150
　Sausage-Stuffed, 88
　Shells, Spaghetti in, 182
　with Tomatoes, 150
Peppercorn(s)
　French Pepper Steak, 81
　Pepper-Mill Cheese Ball, 39
　-Steak, 80
Peppermint Charlotte, 256
Pepperoni
　Pizza, 42
　in Sausage Dumplings, 88
Perciatelli and Zucchini, 133
Perfect Berry Preserves, 162
Persian melons, general notes,
　　167
Persimmons, general notes,
　　167–68
Petite Marmite, 46
Philadelphia Ice Cream, 240
Pickled
　Beets, 140
　Carrots, 144
　Cauliflower, 145
Pie(s)
　Angel, 214
　Apple
　　Sour-Cream, 210
　　Vermont, 210
　Blueberry, Fresh, 210
　"Cheese," Instant, 235
　Cherry, 211

Pie(s) (*cont.*)
　-Cheese, 34
　Chocolate, Double, 234
　Cream-Cheese, 34
　Fried, 216
　Fruit, Quick Jellied, 216
　Lemon
　　Boston, 234
　　Chiffon, 216
　　Chiffon, Easy, 216
　　Meringue, 214
　Meringue Topping for, 214
　Mince, Crumb-Topped, 211
　Nesselrode, 214
　　Pudding, 214
　Orange Chiffon, 216
　Pastry, *see* Pastry, Pie
　Peaches-and-Cream, 211
　Pecan, 214
　Plus, 229
　Prune, 211
　Pumpkin, 212
　Raisin, 211
　Rhubarb, 211
　Shoofly, 212
　Sweet Potato, 212
　See also Pies and Tarts,
　　Main-Course; Tarts
Pies and Tarts, Main-Course
　Beefsteak-and-Kidney Pie,
　　90
　Beef-Stew Pie, 187
　Chicken Pie, 111
　Chili Pie, 86
　Heart Pie, 90
　Onion Quiche, 32
　Oyster-Chicken Pie, New
　　England, 111
　Pork Pie, English, 74
　Quiche Lorraine, 32
　Turkey Pie, Deep-Dish,
　　187
Pig(s)
　in Blankets, 35
　Feet, Barbecued, 91
　Knuckles and Greens, 90
Pimiento Tuna, 226
Pineapple(s)
　general notes, 168
　Basting Sauce, 96
　Chicken en Casserole, 102
　Ice Cream, Lemon-, 242
　Ninon, 168
　Red Cabbage and, 142
　Slices, Frozen, 168
　Upside-Down Cake, 200
　Wedges with Cheese, 168
Pink Lemonade, 166
Pita, 191
Pizza, *see* Sandwiches; Snacks
　　and Appetizers
Pizzaburgers, 83
Plain Jane Pancakes, 24
Plantation Cake, 202
Plantation Coffee, 248
Plum(s)
　general notes, 168
　Pudding, 233
Poached Chicken, 111
Poached Eggs, *see* Eggs
Pompano Tropicale, 122

Popcorn, 37
Popovers, 24
Poppy-Seed Noodles, Hungarian, 132
Pork
  cost per serving, 58–59
  leftover, meals from, 73
  roasts, meals from, 66
  Cabbage Soup, 64
  in Cassoulet, 63
  Chops
    Broiled, with Orange Glaze, 81
    Charcutière, 78
    Stuffed, 63
  Crown Roast of, 67
  -Fried Rice, 73
  Ground
    in Frikadellen, 85
    in The Great American Meat Loaf, 84
    in Meat Loaf Viennese, 85
  Heart Pie, 90
  Kebabs, Oriental, 82
  Liver, Pan-Browned, 89
  Loin
    meals from, 62
    in Choucroute Garni, 63
    Roast, Currant Glaze, 62
    and Peppers, Chinese, 86
    Pie, English, 74
    in Quick Chop Suey, 185
    Salt, Greens and, 147
    and Sauerkraut, Hungarian, 77
  Sausage, *see* Sausage
  Scaloppine, 79
    alla Marsala, 79
  in Scrapple, 25
  Shoulder
    fresh, meals from, 63
    Picnic, Stuffed, 63
    Pot Roast, 73
    Roast, Boned, 66
  Spareribs, Ribs
    Great, on the Grill, 82
    Marmalade, 82
  Sweet-and-Pungent, 87
  in Szekelys Gulyas, 77
  See also Pig
Potage St. Germain, 50
Potato(es)
  general notes, 151
  -and-Anchovy Casserole, Scandinavian, 130
  Baked, 151
  Browned, Rib Roast of Beef, 66
  Cheese-Baked, 151
  Chips, Homemade, 37
  Creamed, 151
  Curried Scalloped, 152
  Dilled, 151
  Duchesse, 151
  French-Fried, 151
  Herbed Scalloped, 152
  Mashed, 151
  New Boiled, 150
  Oven-Browned, 151
  Roesti, 152

Potato(es) (*cont.*)
  Salad, 172
    for Twenty, 255
  Scallop(ed), 152
    Apple-, 161
    Curried, 152
    Ham-and-, 186
    Herbed, 152
  Scramble, 28
  Soup, Cream of Leek and, 50
  -Spinach Puff, 151
  Sweet, *see* Sweet Potatoes
  Swiss Fried, 152
  -Topped Luncheon Meat, 187
  in Vichyssoise, 54
Pot Cheese, general notes, 31
Pot-au-Feu, 46
Pot Roast, *see* Beef; Pork
Poultry
  money-saving tips on, 20
  roasting in bags or foil, 107
  as source of protein, 20
  storage, timetable for, 57
  stuffing for, 103
  suggested servings, 20
  timetable for, 104
  trussing, 104
  See also names of poultry
Preserves, Berry, Perfect, 162
Private brands, *see* A&P
Profiteroles, 217
Prosciutto, Melon and, 39
Protein
  needs, chart for, 13
  sources of, 20
Prune(s)
  in Blankets, 35
  Fresh
    general notes, 168
    Jam, 168
  Grunt, 234
  Pie, 211
  Stuffed, 39
  -Walnut Biscuits, 35
Pudding(s)
  Corn, 146
  Norwegian Fish, 119
  See also Puddings, Dessert
Pudding(s), Dessert
  Bread, 239
    Cherry, 227
    Chocolate, 240
    Raisin, 227
  Brown Betty, 235
  Caramel, Cake, 239
  Chocolate
    Bread, 240
    Cake, 239
  Coconut Melba, Toasted, 233
  Cornstarch, 234
  Cottage
    Right-Side-Up, 239
    Upside-Down, 239
  Huckleberry
    Eleanor Roosevelt's, 227
    Refrigerator, 227
  Indian, 239
  Lemon, Sponge, 236
  Marmalade Top-Range Soufflé, 233

Pudding(s) (*cont.*)
  Mocha, Cake, 239
  Noodle, 240
  Plum, 233
  Prune Grunt, 234
  Rice
    Old-Fashioned, 240
    Quick, 240
  Tapioca, 232
    Triflette, 232
Pumpernickel Bread, 190
Pumpkin, 152
  Cake, 204
  Chiffon Pie, 216
  Mashed, 152
  Pie, 212
  Puff, 151
  Puréed, 152
  Soup, New England, 50
Punch, *see* Beverages
Purée(d)
  Mongol, 55
  Pumpkin, 152
Puri, 198

Quantity-buying guide for, 50, 252
Quantity Cooking
  Cake, Wedding, 253
  Carrots à l'Orange, 256
  Chicken
    Curry for Twenty-five, 254
    Walnut Salad, 255
  Coffee for Forty, 254
  Coleslaw, 255
  Couscous, 255
  Eggnog
    Classic, 254
    Party, 254
  Frosting, Creamy White, 253
  Hams, Party Glazed, 255
  Jambalaya, 255
  Peppermint Charlotte, 256
  Potato Salad for Twenty, 255
  Punch
    Reception, 254
    Reception, Spirited, 254
Quiche(s)
  Lorraine, 32
  Onion, 32
Quick
  Arroz con Pollo, 185
  -Brandied Peaches, 167
  Breads, *see* Breads, Quick
  Butterscotch-Nut Sauce, 245
  Chicken Cacciatore, 100
  Chocolate
    Fancy, 228
    Marshmallow Sauce, 245
  Chop Suey, 185
  Custard Sauce, 244
  Eggnog, 251
  Fruit Gelatin, 230
  Ham Cumberland, 186
  Jellied Fruit Pie, 216
  Lemon Sauce, 245
  Macaroni Supper, 182

Quick (*cont.*)
  Manhattan Clam Chowder, 54
  Muffins, 23
  Onion Soup, 54
  Orange Cake, 201
  Orange Custard Sauce, 245
  Rice and Black Beans, 185
  Rice Pudding, 240
  Shrimp Creole, 185
  Smorgasbord, 41
  Spanish Omelet, 29

Rain-check policy (A&P), 8
Raisin
  Bread Pudding, 227
  Ice Cream, Rum-, 240
  Pie, 212
  Sauce for Tongue, 90
Ratatouille, 147
Ravioli Marinara, Baked, 182
Reception Punch, 254
  Spirited, 254
Red
  Cabbage and Pineapple, 142
  -Caviar Filling, for Appetizer Puffs, 42
  Clam Sauce for Spaghetti, 131
  -Flannel Hash, 41
  -and-Green-Cabbage Salad, 171
Red Snapper, Baked Stuffed, 116
Refried Beans, 129
Relish(es)
  Cranberry-Orange, 163
  Sauerkraut, for Franks, 89
Rhubarb
  general notes, 169
  Baked, 169
  Pie, 211
  Stewed, 169
Ribbon Sandwich Loaf, 225
Rib Roast of Beef, Browned Potatoes, 66
Rice
  as meat extender, 67
  as source of protein, 128
  and Black Beans, Quick, 185
  Curried, 136
  Fried
    Pork-, 73
    Shrimp, 127
  in Hoppin' John, 129
  in Jambalaya, 254
  and Peas
    Chicken with, 100
    Italian Style, 135
  Okra with Tomatoes and, 148
  Pilaf, 136
  Pudding
    Old-Fashioned, 240
    Quick, 240
  in Quick Arroz con Pollo, 185
  in Risotto with Chicken Livers, 110
  in Risi Bisi, 135

Rice (*cont.*)
  Salad, 172
  Spanish, 136
    and Chicken, 185
  in Speedy Jambalaya, 185
  Wild or Brown, Stuffing, 104
Rich Blueberry Muffins, 199
Rich Cocoa at a Price, 250
Ricotta cheese, in Manicotti, 32
Rigatoni Sausage Bowl, 133
Right-Side-Up Cottage Pudding, 239
Risi Bisi, 135
Risotto with Chicken Livers, 110
Roast(s)
  Capon, 104
  Chicken, *see* Chicken
  Duckling, Apple Stuffing, 106
  Goose with Onion-and-Apple Stuffing, 106
  Turkey, *see* Turkey
  See also Beef; Lamb; Pork
Roasted
  Peppers, 150
  Rock Cornish Hens, 106
  Rolled Veal Marinara, 64
Rock Cornish Hen
  general notes, 95
  Broiled, 99
  Roasted, 106
  Skillet, 101
Rock Lobster Thermidor, 125
Roesti, 152
Rolled
  Lamb Shoulder, 66
  Sandwiches, 225
  Stuffed Haddock Fillets, 116
Rolls, *see* Breads, Yeast
Rotisseried Chicken, 107
Rum Balls, 222
Rum-Raisin Ice Cream, 240
Russian
  Balls, 221
  Dressing, 175
  Lamb Stew, 78
Rutabaga(s)
  general notes, 156
  Puff, 151
  See also Turnips

Salad(s)
  Bananas in, 162
  Bean
    Hot, 129
    Three-, 172
  Cabbage, Red-and-Green, 171
  Caesar, 171
  Carrot, 172
  Cheese Board, 31
  Chicken
    Frozen Cream, 112
    Texas, 112
    Walnut, Chinese, 255
  Coleslaw, 255
    Old-Fashioned, 171

Salad(s) (*cont.*)
  Elbow-Macaroni Supper, 134
  Fruit, California, 172
  Greek, 171
  Green(s)
    general notes, 170
    Basic, 170
    Elegant, 170
  Lobster, 126
  Macaroni, 172
  Peppers, Roasted, 150
  Potato, 172
    for Twenty, 255
  Rice, 172
  Salamagundi, 171
  Spinach, Hearty, 171
  Spring, 170
  Tongue, Vinaigrette, 187
  Waldorf, 172
Salad Dressing(s)
  Blue-Cheese, 176
  Buttermilk, 176
  Chutney, 175
  French
    Caper, 176
    Classic, 176
    Ketchup, 176
  Italian-Style, 176
  Mayonnaise, 175
    Blender, 175
    Mustard, 176
    Parmesan, 176
  Russian, 175
  Sour Cream, 176
  Tomato-Soup, 176
  Thousand Island, 175
Salt-Mine Steak, 81
Salt Pork and Greens, 147
Salamagundi, 171
Salami
  in Sausage Dumplings, 88
  Sausage-Stuffed Peppers, 88
  Spaghetti and, 182
Salisbury Patties and Red Eye Gravy, 182
Salmon
  Chowder, 52
  Cold, Mayonnaise, 122
  Poached, New England, 121
  Steaks
    Broiled, 120
    with Tomatoes and Cream, 118
Salsa Borracho, 79
Sarah's California Fruitcake, 204
Sardine(s)
  Crusty, in Tomato Sauce, 185
  Grill, 43
  in Quick Smorgasbord, 41
Sandwich(es)
  Bacon Grill, 226
  Filling(s)
    Avocado, 226
    Banana Spread, 226
    Chicken, 226
    Cress-and-Cheese, 226
    Ham, 226

Sandwich(es) (*cont.*)
  Lemon Cheese, 165
  Mushroom, 226
  Orange Blossom, 226
  Grill(ed)
    Bacon, 226
    Garden Special, 43
    Pizza, 224
    Sardine, 43
    Skillet-, 43
  Loaf, Ribbon, 225
  Mac Homeburgers, 44
  Pizza Grill, 226
  Rolled, 225
  Sardine Grill, 43
  Tea, 225
  Tuna Pimiento, 226
  See also Toasts
Sauce(s)
  Allemande, 174
  Almond Butter, 174
  Anchovy, 79
    Cream, Hot, 175
  Apricot, 68
  Barbecue
    Anchovy, 79
    Chinese Glaze, 79
    Franks Simmered in, 79
    Salsa Borracho, 79
    Sherry, 79
    Tarragon Marinade, 79
    Vinaigrette, 79
  Basting
    Butter, 98
    Garlic, 98
    Orange, 96
    Pineapple, 96
    for Rotisseried Chicken, 107
    Tarragon, 98
  Béarnaise, 173
  Butter
    Almond, 174
    Basting, 98
    Browned, 174
    Lemon, 174
    Paprika, 174
    See also Butters
  Caper
    Cream, 175
    Mayonnaise, 174
  Carbonara, for Spaghetti, 131
  Cheese, 175
    Creamy, Mezzani with, 133
    Scallops in, 125
    Vegetables with, 156
    Whitefish Fillets with, 118
  Clam, for Spaghetti
    Red, 131
    White, 131
  Cocktail, Spicy, 173
  Cranberry
    Fresh, 163
    Jellied, 163
  Cream, 174
    Anchovy, Hot, 175
    Caper, 175
    Horseradish, 175
  Creole, 175

Sauce(s) (*cont.*)
  Cucumber Mayonnaise, 174
  Cumberland, 68
  Curry Dressing, 174
  Egg, 175
  Figaro, 173
  Foo Yong, 29
  Fruit, Chinese, 174
  Garlic Basting, 98
  Hollandaise, 173
  Horseradish Cream, 175
  Lemon Butter, 174
  Lobster, Fish Soufflé with, 123
  Madeira, 68
  Mayonnaise Caper, 174
  Meat, Baked Lasagne with, 134
  Mint, Fresh, for Lamb, 65
  Mousseline, 173
  Mushroom, 175
  Mustard, 174
    Green Beans with, 139
    Tongue in, 187
  Orange
    Basting, 96
    Beets with, 141
  Oyster, 175
  Paprika Butter, 174
  Pineapple Basting, 96
  Raisin, for Tongue, 90
  Sausage-Tomato, Mostaccioli with, 132
  Shrimp, Fish Soufflé with, 123
  Salsa Borracho, 79
  Sherry, 79
  for Spaghetti
    Carbonara, 131
    Crab, 131
    Red Clam, 131
    Tomato, 130
    White Clam, 131
  Tomato
    Crusty Sardines in, 185
    Fish in, 123
    Mostaccioli with, Sausage, 132
    for Spaghetti, 130
  Tarragon Basting, 98
  Tartar, 174
  Tuna, Quick, Sea Shells with, 132
  Vinaigrette, 79
  White, 174
  Wine, Lamb Kidneys in, 90
Sauce(s), Dessert
  Brown Sugar, 245
  Butterscotch-Nut, Quick, 245
  Caramel, 245
  Chocolate
    Marshmallow, Quick, 245
    Mint, 244
    Syrup, 245
  Custard, Quick, 244
  Fudge
    Hot, 245
    Mocha, 245
  Hard, 246
  Lemon, 245
    Quick, 245

Sauce(s), Dessert (*cont.*)
  Maple-Walnut, 245
  Mocha Fudge, 245
  Orange, 202
    Custard, Quick, 245
  Vanilla, 246
  See also Toppings, Dessert
Sauerbraten, 70
Sauerkraut
  in Choucroute Garni, 63
  and Ham, 186
  Hungarian Pork and, 77
  Juice, Tomato-, 251
  Relish for Franks, 89
  and Sausage, 186
Sausage(s)
  general notes, 88
  Bowl, Rigatoni, 133
  in Cassoulet, 63
  Dumplings, 88
  in Easy Cassoulet, 130
  French-Toasted, 41
  in Jambalaya, 255
  Mac, 183
  Sauerkraut and, 186
  -Stuffed Onions, 149
  -Stuffed Peppers, 88
  -Sweet-Potato-Apple-Casserole, 130
  -Tomato Sauce, Mostaccioli with, 132
  Vienna, canned, general notes, 91
  Wheel Snacks, 41
Scallop(s)
  in Cheese Sauce, 125
  Coquilles Saint-Jacques, 125
  Curry, 125
  Kebabs, 125
  Newburg, 125
Scalloped
  Potatoes, 152
  Sole, 118
  Tomatoes, 154
  Vegetables, 156
Scaloppine, *see* Lamb; Pork; Turkey; Veal
Scandinavian Potato-and-Anchovy Casserole, 130
Schur, Sylvia, 8
Scotch Broth, 48
Scrambled Eggs, 28
Scrapple, 25
Scrod
  in Fish Teriyaki, 121
  in Jellied Fish Salad, 123
Sea Bass, in Steamed Fish Chinese Style, 121
Sea Foam Frosting, 208
Seafood Filling, for Appetizer Puffs, 42
Sea Shells, *see* Pasta Dishes
Senate Bean Soup, 48
Seven-Layer Dinner, 158
Seven-Minute Frosting, 208
Shad and Shad Roe in Foil Packets Steamed, 121
Shad Roe
  on Toast, 120
  in Foil Packets, Steamed Shad and, 121

Shellfish
  general notes, 124
  See also names of shellfish;
    Fish
Shepherd's Pie, 130
Sherry-Basted Chicken, 105
Sherry Sauce, 79
Shirred Eggs, 28
Shish Kebab, *see* Kebabs
Shoofly Pie, 212
*Shopper's Guide, USDA Year-
    book of Agriculture,*
    258
Shopping for household ma-
    terials, 259
  See also Food, shopping
Shortbread, 222
Shortcake, 200
Shortcut Dessert Soufflé, 31
Shortcut Main-Dish Soufflé, 30
Shrimp
  general notes, 126
  Boiled, 126
  Broiled, 127
  Butterfly, Hawaiian Coco-
    nut, 127
  Creole, 127
    Quick, 185
  Dip, Green-Onion, 37
  -Fried Rice, 127
  in Jambalaya, 255
  Marinara, 126
  Sauce, Fish Soufflé with, 123
  in Speedy Jambalaya, 185
  Tempura, 127
Sirloin-Tip Grill, 81
Skillet
  Brussels Sprouts, 141
    with Bacon, 141
  Meat-Loaf Dinner, 85
  Summer Squash, 152
  Swiss Steak, 78
Snacks and Appetizers
  general notes, 36
  healthful, general notes, 258
  money-saving tips on, 21
  Anchovies on Cheese Toast,
    43
  Antipasto, 39
  Appetizer Puffs, 42
  Apple, Grapefruit, with, 164
  Artichoke Hearts, Marinated,
    39
  Avocado and Fillings, 39
  Biscuits, Snack, 35
  Biscuit Sticks
    Cheesy, 179
    Spicy, 180
  Carrot Sticks, Dilled, 39
  Celery, Stuffed, 39
  Cereal Nibbles, Spicy, 36
  Cheese
    Ball, Pepper-Mill, 39
    Balls, Crusty, 39
    Board, 31
    Puffs, 42
    Puffs Mayonnaise, 179
    Toast, Anchovies on, 43
  Cherry Tomatoes, Stuffed, 39
  Clam Rafts, 43
  Cocktail Folds, 35

Snacks and Appetizers (*cont.*)
  Dip(s)
    Bacon-Cheddar, 37
    Bacon-Egg, 37
    Bacon-Flavored Onion, 37
    Bacon-Tomato, 37
    Bean, 179
    Clam, 37
    Cumin, 37
    Green-Onion Blue-Cheese,
      37
    Green-Onion Egg, 37
    Green-Onion Party, 37
    Green-Onion Shrimp, 37
    Onion, Fresh Vegetables
      with, 179
  Fondue Bourguignonne, 41
  Franks, Cumberland, 41
  Fruit Cocktail, 164
  Garlic Olives, 36
  Grapefruit Half, 164
  Grapefruit with Orange or
    Apple, 164
  Guacamole, 37
  Ham Squares, Glazed, 41
  Mayonnaise-Cheese Puffs,
    179
  Mayonnaise-Onion Puffs,
    179
  Meatballs, Deviled, 41
  Melon and Prosciutto, 39
  Mushrooms
    Baked Stuffed, 41
    Stuffed, 39
  Nuts, Curried, 36
  Olives, Garlic, 36
  Onion Puffs, Mayonnaise-,
    179
  Orange, Grapefruit with, 164
  Peppers, Roasted, 141
  Pizza, 42
    Deep-Dish, 43
    Ham-and-Eggs Crescent,
      180
    Loaf, 42
    Pepperoni, 42
    Tuna-and-Mushroom, 42
  Popcorn, 37
  Potato Chips, Homemade,
    37
  Prosciutto, Melon and, 39
  Prunes, Stuffed, 39
  Sausage(s)
    French-Toasted, 41
    Wheel Snacks, 41
  Smorgasbord, Quick, 41
  See also Sandwiches
Snacking Cake, 203
Snickerdoodles, 221
Snowy Frosting, 207
Soft-Cooked Eggs, 28
Sole
  in Fish Fillets Bonne Femme,
    122
  Pacific, Hawaiian, 120
  Scalloped, 118
  with Seedless Grapes, 122
  Veronique, 122
Soufflé(s), Main-Course
  Cheese, 30
  Fish, with Shrimp Sauce, 123

Soufflé(s), Main-Course (*cont.*)
  Omelet, 29
  Shortcut Main-Dish, 30
  See also Soufflés, Dessert
Soufflé(s), Dessert
  Chocolate, 30
  Chocolate Tapioca, 235
  Mocha, 31
  Orange, 31
  Shortcut, 31
  Surprise, 31
  See also Gelatin Desserts
Soup(s)
  Bayou Chicken Bowl, 55
  Bean
    Black-, 48
    Senate, 48
  Bouillabaisse, American
    Style, 52
  Cheddar-Cheese, 52
  Clam Chowder, *see*
    Chowders
  Chicken
    -Mushroom Chowder, 55
    Noodle, Tomato-, 54
    Bowl, Bayou, 55
    Gumbo, 48
    Vegetable, Italiano, 55
    Vegetable, Old-Fashioned,
      55
  Chinese Egg-Drop, 47
  Chowder(s)
    Chicken-Mushroom, 55
    Clam, Manhattan, 52
    Clam, New England, 52
    Clam, Quick Manhattan,
      54
    Salmon, 52
    Tomato, 55
  Franks 'N Tomato, 55
  Lobster Stew, 53
  Matzoh Balls for, 47
  Minestrone, 48
  Mulligatawny, 54
  Onion
    French, 47
    Quick, 54
  Oyster Stew, 53
  Pea, with Ham, 68
  Pork Cabbage, 64
  Pot Supreme, 54
  Purée Mongol, 55
  Salmon Chowder, 52
  Tomato
    -Chicken Noodle, 54
    Chowder, 55
    Franks 'N, 55
  Turkey, 110
  See also Broths; Consommés;
    Soups, Cold; Soups,
    Cream; Stocks
Soup(s), Cold
  Borscht, 54
  Buttermilk, 54
  Cream of Chicken, Curried,
    53
  Gazpacho, 53
  Vichyssoise, 54
Soup(s), Cream
  of Chicken, Curried, 53
  Clam Bisque, 53

Soup(s), Cream (*cont.*)
  of Green Pea, 50
  of Leek and Potato, 50
  Oyster Bisque, 53
  Peanut, 50
  Potage St. Germain, 50
  Spinach Velvet, 50
  Pumpkin, New England,
    50
  of Tomato, Fresh, 50
Sour Cherries, Stewed, 163
Sour Cream
  general notes, 28
  Apple Pie, 211
  Dressing, 176
  Omelet with Caviar and,
    29
  Spinach with, 147
Southern Corn-Bread-and-
    Sausage Dressing, 103
Southwestern Cowpoke Beans,
    128
Soy, Soybeans
  protein, as meat extender, 57
  Casserole, 258
  in Soyburger au Jus, 182
  Dip, Japanese, 175
Soyburger au Jus, 182
Spaghetti, *see* Pasta Dishes
Spanish
  Bombe, 243
  Cream, 231
  Hash, 186
  Mackerel, 118
  Rice, 136
  Rice and Chicken, 185
Spareribs, *see* Pork
Sparkle Crown Cake, 228
Sparkling Spring Punch, 251
Speared Dogs, 89
Speedy Jambalaya, 185
Spice(s)
  cooking chart for, 262–64
  Cake, 202
Spiced Fruit Tea, 249
Spiced Peaches, 167
Spicy
  Biscuit Sticks, 180
  Cereal Nibbles, 36
  Cocktail Sauce, 173
Spinach, 147
  Bake, Spaghetti, 183
  in Baked Chicken Floren-
    tine, 102
  Creamed, 147
  in Hash Florentine with
    Poached Eggs, 186
  in Poached Eggs Florentine,
    30
  Puff, Potato-, 151
  Salad, Hearty, 171
  Sauce for Hamburgers, 84
  in Sea Shells Florentine, 133
  with Sour Cream or Yogurt,
    147
  Velvet Soup, 50
Sponge Roll, 206
Spread, Deviled Chicken, 111
Spring Salad, 170
Spritz, 221
Spoon Bread, 135

Squash
  Acorn, Stuffed, 153
  Puff, 151
  Summer
    general notes, 152
    Baked, 152
    Boiled, 152
    Casserole, 153
    Skillet, 152
    Stuffed, 152
  Winter, Baked, 53
  See also Zucchini
Steak, *see* Beef; Ham; Lamb
Steamed
  Asparagus, 139
  Broccoli, 141
  Brussels Sprouts, 141
  Clams, 124
  Fish Chinese Style, 121
  Lobster, 125
  Onions, 148
  Shad and Shad Roe in Foil
    Packets, 121
  Turkey Breast, 108
Stew(s)
  general notes, 74
  Beans-and-Frank, 182
  Beef
    Old-Fashioned, 62
    Pie, 187
    French Style, 74
    Blanquette de Veau, 64
  Casserole Brunswick, 102
  Catfish, 123
  Giblet, 111
  Hungarian Goulash, 77
  Lamb
    Irish, 77
    Russian, 78
  Lobster, 53
  Meatball, 182
  Oxtail Ragout, 77
  Oyster, 53
  Pork and Sauerkraut, Hun-
    garian, 77
  Veal, French, 64
Stewed
  Peaches, 167
  Pears, 167
  Rhubarb, 169
  Sour Cherries, 163
  Tomatoes, 154
Sticky Biscuits, 35
Stir-Fried Vegetables, 156
Stollen, 194
Strawberry(ies)
  -Apple Tart, 212
  Cheese Cake, 229
  Romanoff, 235
  Soufflé, Cold, 232
  Whip, Frozen, 243
Stretchers, *see* Casseroles
Streusel Coffee Cake, 205
Stuffed
  Acorn Squash, 153
  Breast of Veal, 67
  Cabbage, 142
  Eggplant, 147
  Peppers, 150
  Pork Chops, 63
  Pork Shoulder Picnic, 63

Stuffed (*cont.*)
  Prunes, 39
  Summer Squash, 152
  Tomatoes, 154
Stuffing(s)
  poultry for roasting, 103
  Apple, Roast Duckling, 106
  Bread, 103
  Chestnut, Roast Turkey, 105
  Cranberry, Crown Roast of
    Lamb with, 67
  Onion-and-Apple, Roast
    Goose with, 106
  Oyster, 104
  -and-Turkey Casserole, 113
  Wild or Brown Rice, 104
  See also Dressings
Stock(s)
  general notes, 45
  Beef, 45
  Brown, 45
  Chicken, 45
  Fish, 46
  Vegetable, 46
  See also Soups
Substitutions, chart of, 267
Succotash, 140
Sugar
  Brown
    Sauce, 245
    Icing, 208
  Confectioners', Glaze, 207
  -Cookie Cutouts, 221
Sukiyaki, 87
Summer Squash, *see* Squash
Sunnybrook eggs, as A&P
    brand, 24, 28
Supermarket, *see* A&P
Super Right quality meat
    (A&P), 56, 57
Surprise Soufflé, 31
Swedish Meatballs, 85
Swedish Limpa Bread, 190
Sweet Potato(es)
  general notes, 153
  -Apple Casserole, Sausage-,
    130
  Baked, 153
  Candied, 154
    Maple, 154
    Peach, 154
  Marshmallow Sweets, 154
  Mashed, 154
  Nutted, 154
  Pie, 212
  Puff, 151
Sweet-and-Sour Cabbage, 142
Sweet-and-Pungent Fish Sticks,
    183
Sweet-and-Pungent Pork, 87
Swiss cheese, in Swiss Fondue,
    32
Swiss Fondue, 32
Swiss Fried Potatoes, 152
Swordfish Steaks, Broiled, 120
Syrup, Chocolate, 245

Tamale Casserole, 135
Tangelos, general notes, 169
Tangerines, general notes, 169

Tangy Tomato Drink, 251
Tapioca Pudding, 232
Tapioca Triflette, 232
Tarragon Basting Sauce, 98
Tarragon Marinade, 79
Tart(s)
　Apple, French, 212
　Cream, 212
　Fruit, Easy, 228
　Shells, 210
　Strawberry-Apple, 212
　See also Pies; Pies and Tarts,
　　Main-Course
Tartar Sauce, 174
Tea, *see* Beverages
Tea Bread, Cranberry-Orange,
　198
Tea Sandwiches, 225
Tenderized Chuck Roast, 62
Texas Chicken Salad, 112
Thimbles, 221
Thousand Island Dressing, 175
Three-Bean Salad, 172
Toad in the Hole, 88
Toast(s)
　Basket, 225
　Burger, 43
　Cheese, Anchovies on, 43
　Cinnamon, 23
　Cups, 225
　French, 23
　Honey, 23
　Shad Roe on, 120
　See also Sandwiches
Toasted Coconut Melba, 233
Tomato(es)
　as fruit, 169
　general notes, 154
　to peel, 154
　Casserole, Onion-, 149
　-Chicken Noodle Soup, 54
　Chowder, 55
　and Cream, Salmon Steaks
　　with, 118
　Dip, Bacon-, 37
　Franks with Canned Yams
　　and, 188
　Green, Fried, 156
　Peppers with, 150
　and Rice, Okra with, 148
　Sauce, *see* Sauces
　Scalloped, 154
　Skillet, Zucchini-, 153
　Soup, *see* Soups
　Stewed, 154
　Stuffed, 154
　-Stuffed Burgers, 84
　See also Beverages
Tongue
　canned, general notes, 91
　in Mustard Sauce, 187
　with Raisin Sauce, 90
　Salad Vinaigrette, 187
Topping, for Moussaka, 86
　See also Toppings, Dessert
Topping(s), Dessert
　Broiled, 208
　Cream, for Fruit Kuchen,
　　204
　Chocolate, 246
　Fruit, 246

Topping(s), Dessert (*cont.*)
　Lemon, 246
　Meringue, for Pie, 214
　Whipped, 246
　Whipped Cream, 246
　See also Sauces, Dessert
Torte, Linzer, 205
Treasure Brownies, 164
Tripe Creole, 91
Trout
　with Brown Butter, 120
　Lemon-Broiled, 120
Tuna
　Burgers, 185
　-Macaroni Bake, 183
　Pimiento, 226
　in Quick Macaroni Supper,
　　183
　Sauce, Sea Shells with Quick,
　　132
　Tetrazzini, 183
Turkey
　cooked, dishes from, 113–14
　cost per serving, 60–61
　general notes, 93–95
　suggested servings for, 93
　Barbecued, 109
　Breast of
　　Oven-Poached, 108
　　Roast, 105
　　Steamed, 108
　Broiled, 98
　Brown, 105
　in Chow Mein, 114
　Gravy, 105
　Half, Roast, 105
　Jellied, in Aspic, 113
　Mousse, 113
　and Noodles, 113
　Parts
　　general notes, 95
　　Roast, 105
　Pie, Deep-Dish, 187
　Quarters, Roast, 106
　in Quick Arroz con Pollo,
　　185
　Roast
　　in foil, timetable for, 107
　　with Chestnut Stuffing, 105
　Scaloppine, 79
　　alla Marsala, 79
　　Parmigiana, 108
　Soup, 110
　Stuffed Drumstick, Roast,
　　106
　-and-Stuffing Casserole, 113
　Terrapin, 114
　Virginia, 108
　Wings, Deviled, 109
Turkish Lamb-and-Eggplant
　　Casserole, 74
Turnip(s)
　general notes, 156
　Mashed, 156
　Puff, 151
　See also Rutabagas
Turnip Greens
　in Greens and Salt Pork, 147
　in Pig Knuckles and Greens,
　　90
Turnovers, Apple, 217

Unit pricing, 8, 11–13
Universal Product Code
　　(A&P), general notes,
　　16
Upside-Down Cottage Pudding,
　　239
U.S. Recommended Daily
　　Allowances (USRDA),
　　13

Vanilla Sauce, 246
Veal
　cost per serving, 60–61
　shoulder, meals from, 64
　in Blanquette de Veau, 64
　Breast of, Stuffed, 67
　Cacciatore, 87
　Chops Paprika, 78
　Crown Roast of, 67
　Ground
　　in Frikadellen, 85
　　in The Great American
　　　Meat Loaf, 84
　　in Meat Loaf Viennese, 85
　　in Swedish Meatballs, 85
　Heart Pie, 90
　in Hungarian Goulash, 77
　Roasted Rolled, Marinara,
　　64
　Scalloppine alla Marsala, 79,
　　99
　Scalloppine Neapolitan, 64
　Stew, French, 64
　See also Calf
Vegetable(s)
　buying guide for, 138
　cooking methods, basic,
　　137–39
　general notes, 137
　as meat extender, 57, 58
　money-saving tips on, 20
　to pickle, 145
　as source of vitamins, 20,
　　21
　suggested servings for, 20
　with Cheese Sauce, 156
　Fresh, with Onion Dip, 179
　Platters, 139
　Scalloped, 156
　Soup, *see* Soups
　Stir-Fried, 156
　Stock, 46
　See also names of vegetables
Velvet Crumb Cake, 200
Velvet Topping, 246
Vermont Apple Pie, 210
Vermont Breakfast, 26
Vichyssoise, 54
Vienna sausages, canned,
　　general notes, 91
Viennese Coffee, 248
Vinaigrette Sauce, 79
Vineyard Bombe, 243
Vitamins, sources of, 21

Wafers, Almond, 222
Wafflers, 35
Waffles
　Apple, 24

Waffles (*cont.*)
  Bacon, 24
  Brunch, 24
  Cheese, 24
  Pantry, 19
Waldorff Salad, 172
Walnut
  Biscuits, Prune-, 35
  Salad, Chinese Chicken,
    255
  Sauce Maple, 245
  Watercress, *see* Cress
Watermelon(s)
  general notes, 169
  in Melon Ice, 242
Wax Beans, in Three-Bean
    Salad, 172
  See also Green Beans
Wedding Cake, 253
Weights and equivalent
    measures of common
    foods, 265
Welsh Rabbit, 32
Western Omelet, 29
Wheat Pilaf, 135
Wheat Germ
  general notes, 258

Wheat Germ (*cont.*)
  Muffins, 23
Whipped
  Cream, 246
  Dessert Topping, 246
  Gelatin, 230
White
  Batter Bread, 191
  Bread, 189
  Cake, 202
  Sauce, 174
Whitefish Fillets with Cheese
    Sauce, 118
Whiting
  Baked, Creole, 116
  in Jellied Fish Salad, 123
  Whole-Wheat Batter Bread,
    191
Wild or Brown Rice Stuffing,
    104
Wildmere eggs, as A&P brand,
    28
Wine
  Lamb Shoulder Chops in, 78
  Red
    Chicken in, 101
    Duckling in, 101

Wine (*cont.*)
  Sauce, Lamb Kidneys in, 90
  -Steamed Mussels, 124
Wineburger Steaks, 84
Winter Fruit Ring, 192
Winter Squash, *see* Squash
Wonderful Roast Beef Hash,
    73

Yam(s)
  general notes, 153
  Baked, 153
  Canned, and Tomatoes,
    Franks with, 188
  Puff, 151
  See also Sweet Potatoes
Yankee Pot Roast, 70
Yeast Breads, *see* Breads, Yeast
Yogurt
  general notes, 27–28
  Spinach with, 147

Zabaglione, 233
Zucchini
  Perciatelli and, 133
  -Tomato Skillet, 153